P9-CRO-036

Mini-Mickey

THE POCKET-SIZED *unofficial* GUIDE®

TO Walt Disney World®

11TH EDITION

COME CHECK US OUT!

Supplement your valuable guidebook with tips, news, and deals by visiting our website:

theunofficialguides.com

Also, while there, sign up for our Unofficial Guide newsletter for even more travel tips and special offers.

Join the conversation on social media:

 @theUGSeries

 theUnofficialGuides

theUGSeries

 theUGSeries

#theUGseries

Other *Unofficial Guides*

Beyond Disney: The Unofficial Guide to SeaWorld, Universal Orlando, & the Best of Central Florida

The Disneyland Story: The Unofficial Guide to the Evolution of Walt Disney's Dream

Mini-Mickey: The Pocket-Sized Unofficial Guide to Walt Disney World

Universal vs. Disney: The Unofficial Guide to American Theme Parks' Greatest Rivalry

The Unofficial Guide Color Companion to Walt Disney World

The Unofficial Guide to Disney Cruise Line

The Unofficial Guide to Disneyland

The Unofficial Guide to Las Vegas

The Unofficial Guide to Universal Orlando

The Unofficial Guide to Walt Disney World

The Unofficial Guide to Walt Disney World with Kids

The Unofficial Guide to Washington, D.C.

Mini-Mickey

THE POCKET-SIZED *unofficial* GUIDE® TO Walt Disney World®*

11TH EDITION

RITCHEY HALPHEN *with*
BOB SEHLINGER *and* **LEN TESTA**

*Walt Disney World is officially known as the Walt Disney World Resort.

keen
communications

Please note that prices fluctuate in the course of time and that travel information changes under the impact of many factors that influence the travel industry. We therefore suggest that you write or call ahead for confirmation when making your travel plans. Every effort has been made to ensure the accuracy of information throughout this book, and the contents of this publication are believed to be correct at the time of printing. Nevertheless, the publishers cannot accept responsibility for errors or omissions, for changes in details given in this guide, or for the consequences of any reliance on the information provided by the same. Assessments of attractions and so forth are based upon the authors' own experiences; therefore, descriptions given in this guide necessarily contain an element of subjective opinion, which may not reflect the publisher's opinion or dictate a reader's own experience on another occasion. Readers are invited to write the publisher with ideas, comments, and suggestions for future editions.

The Unofficial Guides
An imprint of Keen Communications, LLC
2204 1st Ave. S., Suite 102
Birmingham, AL 35233
theunofficialguides.com, facebook.com/theunofficialguides, twitter.com/theugseries

Copyright © 2016 by Robert W. Sehlinger. All rights reserved. No part of this publication may be reproduced, stored in a retrieval system, or transmitted in any form or by any means, electronic, mechanical, photocopying, recording, scanning, or otherwise, except as permitted under Section 107 or 108 of the 1976 United States Copyright Act, without either the prior written permission of the Publisher or authorization through payment of the appropriate per-copy fee to the Copyright Clearance Center, 222 Rosewood Dr., Danvers, MA 01923; 978-750-8400; fax 978-646-8600; or on the web at copyright.com. Requests to the publisher for permission should be addressed to Keen Communications, LLC, 2204 1st Ave. S., Suite 102, Birmingham, AL 35233, 205-322-0439, fax 205-326-1012.

Unofficial Guide is a registered trademark of Google Inc. in the United States and other countries and may not be used without written permission. Used under license. All other trademarks are the property of their respective owners. Google Inc. is not associated with any product or vendor mentioned in this book.

Cover design by Scott McGrew

Text design by Vertigo Design and Annie Long

For information on our other products and services or to obtain technical support, please contact us from within the United States at 888-604-4537 or by fax at 205-326-1012.

Keen Communications, LLC, also publishes its books in a variety of electronic formats. Some content that appears in print may not be available electronically.

ISBN: 978-1-62809-046-8; eISBN: 978-1-62809-047-5

Distributed by Publishers Group West

Manufactured in the United States of America

5 4 3 2 1

CONTENTS

LIST *of* MAPS

SPECIAL THANKS

A BIG SALUTE TO OUR WHOLE *UNOFFICIAL* TEAM, who time and time again render a Herculean effort in what must seem like a fantasy version of Sartre's *No Exit* to the tune of "It's a Small World." We hope you all recover to tour another day.

Kudos to cartoonist Tami Knight; *Unofficial Guide* statistician Fred Hazleton; child psychologist Karen Turnbow, PhD; and a horde of contributors and friends too numerous to list here.

Much appreciation also to editors Holly Cross and Amber Kaye Henderson; typesetter Annie Long; cartographers Steve Jones, Scott McGrew, and Cassandra Poertner; and indexer Frances Lennie.

—*Ritchey, Bob, and Len*

ABOUT *the* AUTHORS

RITCHEY HALPHEN is a project editor at Keen Communications in Birmingham, Alabama. He started his publishing career as a copy editor at *Cooking Light* magazine, later serving as senior copy editor at *Southern Living* and copy chief at *Health*.

BOB SEHLINGER, a Lowell Thomas Award–winning journalist, is the creator and producer of the *Unofficial Guides*. Three titles in the series—*The Unofficial Guide to Walt Disney World, The Unofficial Guide to Disneyland,* and *The Unofficial Guide to Las Vegas*— are the best-selling travel guidebooks in the world on their respective subjects. Bob is also the founder and co-owner of Keen Communications, which publishes the *Unofficial Guides* as well as outdoors and trade-nonfiction books under the Clerisy Press, Menasha Ridge Press, Nature Study Guild Press, and Wilderness Press imprints.

LEN TESTA is the coauthor of *The Unofficial Guide to Walt Disney World, The Unofficial Guide to Disneyland, The Unofficial Guide to Walt Disney World with Kids, The Unofficial Guide Color Companion to Walt Disney World,* and *The Unofficial Guide to Disney Cruise Line.* A computer scientist, Len created both the *Unofficial Guides* touring plan software and the **touringplans.com** website.

Mini-Mickey

THE POCKET-SIZED *unofficial* **GUIDE**®
TO Walt Disney World®

11TH EDITION

INTRODUCTION

▌▐ WHY *this* POCKET GUIDE?

THE OPTIMUM STAY AT WALT DISNEY WORLD is seven days, but many visitors don't have nearly that long to devote to all that this massive destination affords. Some folks are in town on business, with only a day or two available for Disney's enticements; others are en route elsewhere, or they want to sample additional attractions in Orlando and Central Florida. For these visitors, efficient, time-effective touring is a must. They can't afford long waits in line for rides, shows, or meals. It's imperative that they determine as far in advance as possible what they really want to see.

This "lite" guide distills essential information from our comprehensive *Unofficial Guide to Walt Disney World* to help short-stay or last-minute visitors decide quickly how best to spend their limited hours. It aids these guests in answering questions vital to their enjoyment: "What are the rides and attractions that appeal to me most? Which additional rides and attractions would I like to experience if I have time? What am I willing to skip?"

DECLARATION OF INDEPENDENCE

THE AUTHORS AND RESEARCHERS OF THIS GUIDE are totally independent of Walt Disney Co., Inc.; Disneyland, Inc.; Walt Disney World, Inc.; and all other members of the Disney corporate family. The material in this guide originated with the authors and researchers and has been neither reviewed nor edited by The Walt Disney Company, Disneyland, or Walt Disney World.

Ours is the first comprehensive *critical* appraisal of Walt Disney World. It aims to provide the information necessary to tour Walt Disney World with the greatest efficiency and economy.

WALT DISNEY WORLD:
An Overview

WALT DISNEY WORLD COMPRISES 43 square miles, an area twice as large as Manhattan. Situated strategically in this vast expanse are the **Magic Kingdom, Epcot, Disney's Hollywood Studios,** and **Disney's Animal Kingdom** theme parks; 2 swimming theme parks; a sports complex; 5 golf courses; 41 hotels and a campground; more than 100 restaurants; 4 interconnected lakes; 2 shopping complexes; 8 convention venues; a nature preserve; and a transportation system consisting of four-lane highways, elevated monorails, and a network of canals.

The World employs around 62,000 people, or "cast members," making it the largest single-site employer in the United States. Keeping the costumes of those cast members clean requires the equivalent of 16,000 loads of laundry a day and the dry cleaning of 30,000 garments daily. (Mickey Mouse alone has 290 different sets of duds, ranging from a scuba wet suit to a tux; Minnie boasts more than 200 outfits.) Each year, Disney restaurants serve 10 million burgers, 6 million hot dogs, 75 million Cokes, 9 million pounds of French fries, and 150 tons of popcorn. In the state of Florida, only the cities of Miami and Jacksonville have bus systems larger than Disney World's. The Disney monorail trains have logged mileage equal to more than 30 round-trips to the moon.

THE THEME PARKS
The Magic Kingdom

When people think of Walt Disney World, most think of the Magic Kingdom, the World's first theme park, opened in 1971. It consists of the adventures, rides, and shows that feature the Disney cartoon characters, along with the iconic **Cinderella Castle.** The Magic Kingdom is just one element of Disney World, but it remains the heart.

The park is divided into six "lands," with five arranged spokelike around a hub called the **Central Plaza.** First you come to **Main Street, U.S.A.,** which connects the Magic Kingdom entrance with the hub. Clockwise around the hub are **Adventureland, Frontierland, Liberty Square, Fantasyland,** and **Tomorrowland.** Five hotels (**Bay Lake Tower;** the **Contemporary, Polynesian Village,** and **Grand Floridian Resorts;** and **The Villas at the Grand Floridian**) are connected to the Magic Kingdom by monorail and boat. Three other hotels, **Shades of Green, Wilderness Lodge & Villas,** and **Four Seasons Resort Orlando at Walt Disney World Resort,** are nearby but aren't served by the monorail.

Epcot

Opened in October 1982, Epcot is twice as large as the Magic Kingdom but comparable in scope. It has two major areas: **Future World** consists of pavilions concerning human creativity and technological advancement; **World Showcase,** arranged around a 40-acre lagoon, presents the architectural, social, and cultural heritages of almost a dozen nations, each country represented by replicas of famous landmarks and settings familiar to world travelers.

The Epcot resort hotels—the **BoardWalk Inn & Villas, Caribbean Beach Resort, Dolphin, Swan,** and **Yacht & Beach Club Resorts and Beach Club Villas**—are within a 5- to 15-minute walk of the International Gateway, the World Showcase entrance to the theme park. The hotels are also linked to Epcot and Disney's Hollywood Studios by canal and walkway. Epcot is connected to the Magic Kingdom and its hotels by monorail.

Disney's Animal Kingdom

About five times the size of the Magic Kingdom, Disney's Animal Kingdom combines zoological exhibits with rides, shows, and live entertainment. The park is arranged in a hub-and-spoke configuration somewhat like that of the Magic Kingdom. A lush tropical rainforest funnels visitors to **Discovery Island,** the park's hub. Dominated by the 14-story-tall, hand-carved **Tree of Life,** Discovery Island offers services, shopping, and dining. From there, guests can access the themed areas: **Africa, Asia,** and **DinoLand U.S.A.** Africa, the largest themed area, at 100 acres, features free-roaming herds in a re-creation of the Serengeti Plain. Camp Minnie-Mickey, the park's character-greeting area, closed in 2014 to make way for a new "land" based on James Cameron's *Avatar* films, with construction ongoing until 2017.

Animal Kingdom has its own parking lot and is connected to other Walt Disney World destinations by the Disney bus system. Although no hotels lie within the park proper, the **All-Star Resorts, Animal Kingdom Lodge & Villas,** and **Coronado Springs Resort** are all nearby.

Disney's Hollywood Studios

Opened in 1989 as Disney-MGM Studios and a little larger than the Magic Kingdom, Disney's Hollywood Studios has two areas. One area, occupying about 75% of the Studios, is a theme park focused on the motion picture, music, and television industries. Highlights include re-creations of Hollywood and Sunset Boulevards from Hollywood's Golden Age, four high-tech rides, several musical shows, and a movie stunt show. The second area encompasses soundstages, a backlot of streets and sets, and an outdoor theater for an automobile stunt show. Until 2014, the public could access the soundstages on a behind-the-scenes tour.

In August 2015, Disney announced that not only is a long-rumored *Star Wars*–themed land coming to both DHS and Disneyland, but a *Toy Story*–themed land is on its way to Orlando as well. No opening dates had been announced at press time; check **touringplans.com** for updates, and may The Force be with you . . . to infinity and beyond!

Disney's Hollywood Studios is connected to other Walt Disney World areas by highway and canal but not by monorail. Guests can park in the Studios' pay parking lot or commute by bus. Guests at Epcot resort hotels can reach the Studios by boat or on foot.

THE WATER PARKS

DISNEY WORLD HAS TWO WATER THEME PARKS: **Typhoon Lagoon** and **Blizzard Beach.** Typhoon Lagoon has a wave pool capable of producing 6-foot waves; Blizzard Beach features more slides. Typhoon Lagoon and Blizzard Beach have their own parking lots and can be reached by bus.

OTHER DISNEY WORLD VENUES
Disney Springs

Redevelopment of the sprawling shopping, dining, and entertainment complex formerly known as Downtown Disney began in 2013 and is scheduled to be completed in 2016. Themed to evoke a Florida waterfront town, Disney Springs currently comprises the **Marketplace** on the east, the **West Side** on the west, and **The Landing** on the waterfront. Redevelopment of the old Pleasure Island nightlife district began in late 2014; the reimagined area, called **Town Center,** will feature shops and restaurants and Florida–meets–Spanish Colonial architecture. Two desperately needed multistory parking garages opened in 2015.

The Marketplace contains the world's largest store selling Disney-character merchandise; upscale resort-wear and specialty shops; and numerous restaurants, including **Rainforest Cafe** and **T-REX.** The West Side is a diverse mix of nightlife, shopping, dining, and entertainment, most notably featuring a Disney outpost of **House of Blues** and a permanent showplace for the extraordinary **Cirque du Soleil *La Nouba*.** The Landing, partially open at press time, offers additional shopping and dining options; **The Boathouse,** an upscale waterfront seafood eatery, opened here in spring 2015. Disney Springs is accessed via Disney transportation from Disney resort hotels.

Disney's BoardWalk

Near Epcot, the BoardWalk is an idealized replication of an East Coast 1930s waterfront resort. Open all day, the BoardWalk features upscale restaurants, shops and galleries, a brewpub, and an ESPN sports bar. In the evening, a nightclub with dueling pianos and a DJ dance club join the lineup. This area is anchored by the BoardWalk Inn & Villas and its adjacent convention center.

The BoardWalk is within walking distance of the Epcot resorts, Epcot's International Gateway, and Disney's Hollywood Studios. Boat transportation is available to and from Epcot and Disney's Hollywood Studios; buses serve other Disney World locations.

ESPN Wide World of Sports Complex

The 220-acre Wide World of Sports is a state-of-the-art competition and training facility consisting of a 9,500-seat ballpark, two field houses, and venues for baseball, softball, tennis, track and field, beach volleyball, and 27 other sports. The spring-training home of the Atlanta Braves, the complex also plays host to a mind-boggling calendar of professional and amateur competitions. Walt Disney World guests not participating in events may pay admission to watch any of the scheduled competitions.

HOW TO CONTACT
the AUTHORS

YOU CAN WRITE OR E-MAIL US at the following addresses:

Ritchey, Bob, and Len
*Mini-Mickey: The Pocket-Sized Unofficial Guide to
   Walt Disney World*
2204 1st Ave. S., Suite 102
Birmingham, AL 35233
unofficialguides@menasharidge.com

You can also find the *Unofficial* gang on social media at **face book.com/theunofficialguides, twitter.com/theugseries, instagram .com/theugseries,** and **pinterest.com/theugseries.**

READER SURVEY

Our website hosts a questionnaire you can use to express opinions about your Walt Disney World visit. Access it here: **touringplans .com/walt-disney-world/survey.** The questionnaire lets every member of your party, regardless of age, tell us what he or she thinks about attractions, hotels, restaurants, and more.

Walt Disney World

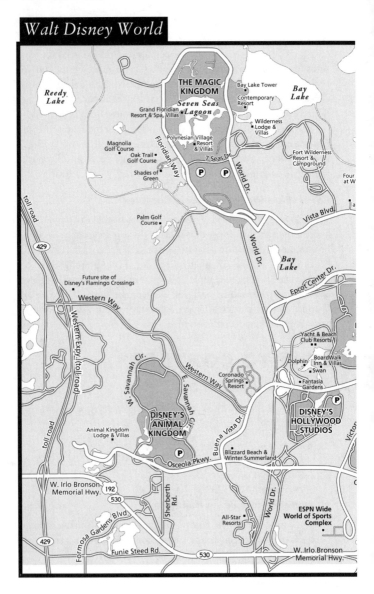

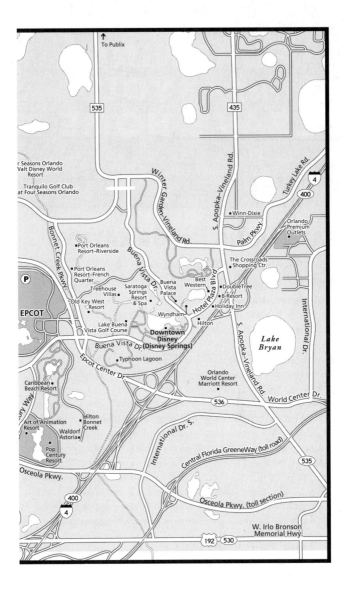

PART ONE

PLANNING *before* YOU LEAVE HOME

GATHERING INFORMATION

IN ADDITION TO THIS GUIDE, we recommend the following resources:

1. TOURINGPLANS.COM Our website offers touring plans for the Walt Disney World theme and water parks, along with Disney news and updates, details on ticket discounts, a 365-day Crowd Calendar to help you find out which theme parks will be least crowded when you visit, photos and videos of Disney hotel rooms, FastPass+ information, complete menus for every dining venue in the World, and much more.

Our most popular feature for site subscribers is **Lines,** a mobile app that provides continuous real-time updates on wait times at Walt Disney World and Disneyland, plus touring plans that you can update while you're in the parks. Lines is free to subscribers for the Apple iPhone and iPad at the iTunes Store (search for "Touring Plans"; requires iOS 4.3 or later) and for Android-based devices at the Google Play Store (requires Android 2.1 Eclair or later). Owners of BlackBerries, Windows Phones, and other Internet-capable phones can use the web-based version at **m.touringplans.com.**

Our Online Trip-Planning Library

Because this (relatively) tiny tome doesn't have room to discuss trip planning at the same level of detail as *The Unofficial Guide to Walt Disney World* (a.k.a. the "Big Book"), we highly recommend these **touringplans.com** links as starting points for further reading.

- For general *CliffsNotes*-style advice, see **touringplans.com /walt-disney-world/trip-planning.**

- If it's feasible to schedule your visit to the World a year ahead, see our **Disney Trip-Planning Timeline** at **tinyurl.com/wdw planningtimeline.**
- For in-depth discussions of travel topics such as budgeting, packing, and transportation, check out our **Trip Planning 101** blog series. Go to **blog.touringplans.com** and enter "Trip Planning 101" in the search box.

2. THE WALT DISNEY TRAVEL COMPANY FLORIDA VACATIONS BROCHURE AND DVD These cover Walt Disney World in its entirety, list rates for all Disney resort hotels and campgrounds, and describe Disney World package vacations. They're available from most travel agents, by calling the Walt Disney Travel Company at ☎ 407-828-8101 or 407-934-7639, or by visiting **disneyworld .com.** Be prepared to hold if you inquire by phone; when you reach a representative, ask for the DVD vacation planner.

3. DISNEY CRUISE LINE (DCL) BROCHURE AND DVD This brochure provides details on vacation packages that combine a Disney cruise with a stay at Disney World. DCL also offers a free DVD that tells all you need to know about Disney cruises and then some. To obtain a copy, call ☎ 800-951-3532 or order at **disneycruise.com,** where you can also view the entire DVD online.

4. ORLANDO MAGICARD If you're considering lodging, dining, or visiting other attractions outside of Walt Disney World, it's worthwhile to obtain an Orlando Magicard, a Vacation Planner, and the *Orlando Official Visitors Guide* (all free) from the Visit Orlando Official Visitors Center. The card can be conveniently downloaded from **orlandoinfo.com/magicard.** To order the accommodations guide, call ☎ 800-643-9492. For more information and materials, call ☎ 407-363-5872 or go to **visitorlando.com.** Phones are staffed during weekday business hours and 9 a.m.–3 p.m. EST weekends.

5. *HOTELCOUPONS.COM FLORIDA GUIDE* Sign up at **hotelcoupons .com** to have a free monthly guide sent to you by e-mail; you can also view the guide online. To request a hard copy, call ☎ 800-222-3948 Monday–Friday, 8 a.m.–5 p.m. EST. The guide is free, but you pay $4 for handling ($6 if you need it mailed to Canada).

6. *KISSIMMEE VISITOR'S GUIDE* This full-color guide is one of the most complete available and is of particular interest to those who intend to book lodging outside of Disney World. It features ads for rental houses, time-shares, and condominiums, as well as a directory of attractions, restaurants, and other useful info. To order a copy, call ☎ 800-327-9159 or 407-742-8200, or view it online at **floridakiss.com.**

IMPORTANT WALT DISNEY WORLD ADDRESSES

General Information
Walt Disney World Guest Communications
PO Box 10040, Lake Buena Vista, FL 32830-1000
wdw.guest.communications@disneyworld.com
General online help: **disneyworld.disney.go.com/help/email**

Merchandise Mail Order (Guest Service Mail Order)
PO Box 10070, Lake Buena Vista, FL 32830-0070
☎ 877-560-6477, **merchandise.guest.services@disneyparks.com**

Walt Disney World Central Reservations
PO Box 10100, Lake Buena Vista, FL 32830-0100
☎ 407-W-DISNEY (407-934-7639), 407-939-7670 (TTY)

Walt Disney World Ticket Mail Order
PO Box 10140, Lake Buena Vista, FL 32830-0140
☎ 407-566-4985, **ticket.inquiries@disneyworld.com**

IMPORTANT WALT DISNEY WORLD PHONE NUMBERS

General Information ☎ 407-824-4321 or 2222, 407-939-5141 (TTY)	
Advance Dining Reservations	☎ 407-939-3463
Disabled-Guest Special Room Requests	☎ 407-939-7807
Lost and Found	
Today at Disney's Animal Kingdom	☎ 407-938-2784
Today at Disney's Hollywood Studios	☎ 407-560-4668
Today at Epcot	☎ 407-560-7500
Today at the Magic Kingdom	☎ 407-824-4521
Yesterday or before (all Disney parks)	☎ 407-824-4245
Security ☎ 407-560-7959 (routine), 407-560-1990 (urgent)	

7. GUIDEBOOK FOR GUESTS WITH DISABILITIES This handout is available at Guest Relations when you enter the theme and water parks, at Disney-resort front desks, and wheelchair-rental areas (listed in each theme park chapter). A printable PDF version for each park can be downloaded at **tinyurl.com/wdwguestswithdisabilities.**

DISNEY ONLINE: OFFICIAL AND OTHERWISE

THE WALT DISNEY WORLD WEBSITE (**disneyworld.com**) is the glue that binds the components of a high-tech reservation system called **MyMagic+,** rolled out in early 2014. Its linchpin is the **MagicBand,** a rubber wristband with an embedded computer chip that functions as an admission ticket and hotel key. MyMagic+ also encompasses Disney World's **FastPass+** ride-booking system; Disney dining reservations; food, beverage, and merchandise payment for on-site resort guests; and the **Memory Maker** online photo service.

The downside? Whether you're planning a weekend jaunt or a weeklong family vacation, you have to make detailed decisions about every day of your trip—up to two months in advance—if you want any chance of avoiding long waits in line.

To use of some of the website's features, you'll need to register by providing your e-mail address and choosing a password. You'll also need to have reserved a room at a Disney-owned hotel or have in your possession a valid theme park ticket.

GETTING STARTED   In the upper-right corner of the home page, click "My Disney Experience" to access a welcome page with links to any existing hotel and dining reservations. Click the "My Family & Friends" link, then enter the names and ages of everyone traveling with you. You'll need this information when you make your FastPass+ and dining reservations.

Back on the "My Disney Experience" page, click "My Itinerary" in the top right corner of the page. A calendar will then appear—if you've got a Disney-hotel reservation, the calendar should display those dates of travel. If not, you'll need to manually enter your reservation number, then select your travel dates using the calendar.

For each day of your trip, the website will display operating hours for the theme and water parks. Select the theme park you'll be visiting on a particular day; if you're visiting more than one, select the one at which you want to make reservations now.

MAKING FASTPASS+ RESERVATIONS   Click the "FastPass+" link from the menu on the right side of your screen. Next, select one of your displayed travel dates, then indicate which members of your group will be with you and which park you'll be visiting on that date. At press time, you could use FastPass+ at just one park per day.

Now you'll see a list of your chosen park's FastPass+ attractions. Select the ones you'd like to reserve; if an attraction isn't selectable, all of its available FastPass+ reservations are gone.

The website will then give you a "Best Match" set of Fast-Pass+ reservations and return times for your attractions, plus three optional sets of return times. Select the set that most closely fits the rest of your plans for the day, or, if you're using our touring plans, select the set that most closely matches the suggested FastPass+ return times on the plans. After confirming your selections, you can check for alternative return-time windows for each attraction.

You'll need to repeat these steps for every day for which you want to use FastPass+ in the theme parks. Having fun yet?

If you're unsure of the attractions or times of day for which you should use FastPass+, our touring plan software can make recommendations that will minimize your time in line.

MAKING DINING RESERVATIONS From the "My Itinerary" page, click the "Reserve Dining" link. (You may have to reenter your travel dates.) A list of every Disney World eatery will be displayed. Use the filtering criteria at the top of the page to narrow the list.

Once you've settled on a restaurant, click the restaurant's name to check availability for your dining time and the number of people in your party. If space is available and you want to make a reservation, you'll need to indicate which members of your party will be joining you. If you want to make other dining reservations, you'll need to repeat this process for every reservation.

Once you've made your initial set of FastPass+ and dining reservations, you'll be able to view and edit them (along with your hotel reservation) in "My Reservation."

Our Recommended Websites

Searching online for Disney information is like navigating an immense maze for a very small piece of cheese: There's a lot of stuff out there, but you may find a lot of dead-ends before getting what you want. Our picks follow.

BEST Q&A SITE Who knew? Walt Disney World has a **Mom's Panel** all chosen from among 10,000-plus applicants. The panelists have a website, **disneyworldmoms.com,** where they offer tips and discuss how to plan a Disney World vacation. The parents are unpaid and are free to speak their minds.

BEST GENERAL UNOFFICIAL WALT DISNEY WORLD WEBSITE
Besides **touringplans.com,** Deb Wills's **allears.net** is the first website we recommend to friends who want to make a trip to Disney World. Updated several times a week, the site includes breaking news, tons of photos, Disney restaurant menus, resort and ticket information, tips for guests with special needs, and more. We also check **wdw magic.com** for news and happenings around Walt Disney World.

BEST MONEY-SAVING SITE MouseSavers (**mousesavers.com**) keeps an updated list of discounts and reservation codes for use at Disney resorts. Anyone who calls or books online can use a current code and get the discounted rate. Savings can be considerable—up to 40% in many cases. MouseSavers also has discount codes for rental cars and non-Disney hotels in the area, along with a calendar showing when Disney sales typically launch.

BEST WALT DISNEY WORLD PREVIEW SITE If you want to see what a particular attraction is like, **touringplans.com** offers free videos or photos of every attraction. Videos of indoor ("dark") rides are sometimes inferior to those of outdoor rides due to poor lighting, but even the videos and photos of indoor rides generally provide a good sense of what the attraction is about. **YouTube** is also an excellent place to find Disney World videos.

SOCIAL MEDIA Facebook, Twitter, and **Instagram** are popular places for Disney fans to gather online and share comments, tips, and photos.

BEST INTERNET RADIO STATION MouseWorld Radio (mouse worldradio.com) plays everything from attraction themes and hotel background music to sound clips from old TV ads for Disney resorts. The tracks match what the Disney parks are playing at the time of day you're listening. Or catch the **Walt Disney World Today Podcast,** cohosted by our own Len Testa, on iTunes and at **wdwtoday.com.**

BEST THEME-PARK-INSIDER SITE Jim Hill of **jimhillmedia.com** has insider accounts of the politics, frantic project management, and pipe dreams that combine into the attractions that Disney creates.

BEST DISNEY DISCUSSION BOARDS There are tons of these; among the most active are **disboards.com, forums.wdwmagic.com,** our own **forum.touringplans.com,** and, for Brits, **thedibb.co.uk** (*DIBB* stands for "Disney Information Bulletin Board").

BEST SITE FOR GUESTS WITH FOOD ALLERGIES At **allergyeats .com/disney,** you put in your allergies and your park, and it shows you where and what you can eat.

BEST SITES FOR TRAFFIC, ROADWORK, CONSTRUCTION, AND SAFETY INFORMATION Visit **expresswayauthority.com** for the latest information on roadwork in the Orlando and Orange County areas. The site also contains detailed maps, directions, and toll-rate information for the most popular tourist destinations.

A seven-year construction project to improve I-4 was launched in 2015. Information on the northern section, near Universal and downtown Orlando, can be found at **i4ultimate.com.** Construction updates on the southern section in Polk County are available at **i4express.com.**

Check **flhsmv.gov/fhp/cps** to learn about state child-restraint requirements. Finally, we like **Google Maps** for driving directions.

WHEN *to* GO *to* WALT DISNEY WORLD

SELECTING THE TIME OF YEAR FOR YOUR VISIT

WALT DISNEY WORLD IS BUSIEST Christmas Day through the first few days of January. Next busiest is the spring-break period from mid-March through the week of Easter, then Thanksgiving week. Following those are the first few weeks of June, when summer vacation starts, and the week of Presidents Day.

The least-busy time is from Labor Day in September through the beginning of October. Next slowest are the weeks in mid-January after the Martin Luther King Jr. holiday weekend up to Presidents Day in February (except when the Walt Disney World Marathon runs after MLK Day). The weeks after Thanksgiving and before Christmas are less crowded than average, as is mid-April–mid-May, after spring break and before Memorial Day.

Late February, March, and early April are dicey. Crowds ebb and flow according to spring-break schedules and the timing of Presidents Day weekend. Besides being asphalt-melting hot, July brings throngs of South American tourists on their winter holiday. Though crowds have grown somewhat during September and October as a result of promotions aimed at locals and the international market, these months continue to be good for touring.

THE PROS AND CONS OF OFF-SEASON TOURING Though we strongly recommend going to Disney World in the fall, winter, or spring, there are a few trade-offs. The parks often close early during the off-season, either because of low crowds or special events such as the Halloween and Christmas parties at the Magic Kingdom. This drastically reduces touring hours. Even when crowds are small, it's difficult to see big parks such as the Magic Kingdom between 9 a.m. and 7 p.m. Early closing also usually means no evening parades or fireworks. And because these are slow times, some rides and attractions may be closed. Finally, Central Florida temperatures fluctuate wildly during late fall, winter, and early spring; daytime highs in the 40s and 50s aren't uncommon. Given the choice, however, smaller crowds, bargain prices, and stress-free touring are worth risking cold weather or closed attractions.

unofficial **TIP**
Touring in fall and other "off" periods is so much easier that our research team, at the risk of being blasphemous, advises taking kids out of school for a Disney World visit.

CROWD CONDITIONS AND THE BEST AND WORST PARKS TO VISIT FOR EACH DAY OF THE YEAR We receive thousands of e-mails and letters inquiring about crowd conditions on specific dates throughout the year. Readers also want to know which park is best to visit on each day of their stay. To make things easier for you (and us!), we provide at **touringplans.com** a calendar covering the next year (click "Crowd Calendar" on the home page). For each date, we offer a crowd-level index based on a scale of 1–10, with 1 being least crowded and 10 being most crowded. Our calendar takes into account all holidays, special events, and more The same calendar lists the best and worst park(s) to visit in terms of crowd conditions on any given day.

Collecting data for the Crowd Calendar requires us to have researchers in the parks year-round. To keep the calendar current on a daily basis, we charge a modest subscription fee, which also provides access to additional touring plans and other features. Owners of the current edition of *The Unofficial Guide to Walt Disney World,* as well as owners of the previous year's Big Book, are eligible for a substantial subscription discount.

EXTRA MAGIC HOURS

EXTRA MAGIC HOURS (EMHs) are a perk for families staying at a Walt Disney World resort, including the Swan, Dolphin, and Shades of Green. On selected days of the week, Disney resort guests will be able to enter a Disney theme park 1 hour earlier or stay in a selected theme park about 2 hours later than the official park-operating hours. Theme park visitors not staying at a Disney resort may stay in the park for Extra Magic Hour evenings, but they can't experience any rides, attractions, or shows. In other words, they can shop and eat. The swimming theme parks, Typhoon Lagoon and Blizzard Beach, rarely offer EMHs. If they do, it's usually during the summer.

WHAT'S REQUIRED? A valid admission ticket or MagicBand wristband is required to enter the park, and you must show your Disney resort ID or have your MagicBand scanned when entering. For evening EMHs, you may be asked to show your Disney resort ID or MagicBand to experience rides or attractions.

WHEN ARE EMHs OFFERED? Check the Crowd Calendar at **touringplans.com** for the dates of your visit, check the parks calendar at **disneyworld.com,** or call Disney at ☎ 407-824-4321 or 407-939-6244 (press *0* for a live representative).

Morning Extra Magic Hours (a.k.a. Early Entry)

Morning Extra Magic Hours are offered at all four theme parks throughout the year, and rarely (during summer) at Blizzard Beach and Typhoon Lagoon water parks. Several days of the week, Disney resort guests are invited to enter a designated theme park 1 hour before the general public. During this hour, guests can enjoy selected attractions opened early just for them.

Morning EMHs strongly affect attendance at Disney's Hollywood Studios and Epcot, especially during busier times of the year. Magic Kingdom crowds are about average when it has morning EMHs (usually Thursday). Because Disney's Animal Kingdom typically has two morning EMHs but none at night, crowds are spread out, resulting in lower-than-average waits on both days.

During holiday periods and summer, when Disney hotels are full, getting in early makes a tremendous difference in crowds at the designated park. The EMH program funnels so many people into that park that it fills by about 10 a.m. and is practically gridlocked by noon.

Evening Extra Magic Hours

The evening EMH program lets Disney resort guests enjoy a different theme park on specified nights for about 2 hours after it closes to the general public. Guests pay no additional charge to participate but must scan their MagicBands at each ride or attraction they wish to experience. You can also show up at the turnstiles at any point after evening Extra Magic Hours have started. Note that if you've been in another park that day, you'll need the Park Hopper feature on your admission ticket to enter (see Part Two).

unofficial **TIP**
Evening Extra Magic Hours are offered at the Magic Kingdom, Epcot, and Disney's Hollywood Studios but not at Disney's Animal Kingdom.

Evening sessions are usually more crowded at the Magic Kingdom and the Studios than at Epcot. Those evening EMH crowds can be just as large as those throughout the day. During summer, when the Magic Kingdom's evening EMH session runs until 1 a.m., lines at headliner attractions can still be long at midnight.

SUMMER AND HOLIDAYS

IF YOU VISIT ON A NONHOLIDAY MIDSUMMER DAY, arrive at the turnstile 40–60 minutes before the stated opening on a non-morning-EMH day. If you visit during a major holiday period, arrive 1 hour before. To save time in the morning, buy your admission in advance. Also, consider bringing your own stroller or wheelchair instead of renting one of Disney's.

Hit your favorite rides early using one of our touring plans, then go back to your hotel for lunch, a swim, and perhaps a nap. If you're interested in the special parades and shows, return to the park in late afternoon or early evening. Assume that unless you use FastPass+, early morning will be the only time you can experience the attractions without long waits. Finally, don't wait until the last minute in the evening to leave the park—the exodus at closing is truly mind-boggling. Above all, bring your sense of humor, and pay attention to your group's morale.

PART TWO

MAKING *the* MOST *of* YOUR TIME *and* MONEY

ALLOCATING MONEY

HOW MUCH YOU SPEND AT DISNEY WORLD depends on how long you stay. But even if you visit for just an afternoon, be prepared to drop a bundle. The following chapter will give you some sense of what you can expect to pay for admission, as well as which admission options will best meet your needs.

CAN YOU AFFORD A DISNEY VACATION? WE CRUNCH THE NUMBERS

EVERY YEAR, WE GET E-MAILS from tens of thousands of families who are either planning or just back from a Walt Disney World vacation, and we talk with travel agents who hear from thousands more. And the thing that surprises these families the most—the number-one thing they're unprepared for—is how expensive their trip turned out to be.

Those families are surprised for a good reason: Excluding transportation, a two-day, one-night night visit to Disney World for four costs more than what 80% of American families spend on vacations *in an entire year.* And that assumes the family stays at a no-frills budget motel in Kissimmee and eats fast food for two days.

So that you know what you're dealing with up front, we've put together a spreadsheet that shows how much Disney vacation you get for $500, $1,000, $1,500, and $2,000, for groups of various sizes. The whole thing takes up three pages in the Big Book, but this being *Mini-Mickey* and brevity being of the essence, we've boiled it down a bit—turn the page to see how things shake out at each price point for a family of two adults and two kids.

WHAT YOU GET AND WHAT YOU PAY AT WDW

2 ADULTS, 2 KIDS: $500

Nothing

2 ADULTS, 2 KIDS: $1,000

• 1 day theme park admission
• 1 counter-service breakfast and lunch, 1 sit-down dinner, and one of the
  following lodging options:
    • 1 night at a budget off-site motel ($659)
    • 1 night at a Disney Value resort ($739)
    • 1 night at a Disney Moderate resort ($779)
    • 1 night at a Disney Deluxe resort ($939)

2 ADULTS, 2 KIDS: $1,500

BUDGET OPTION ($1,273):
• 2 days theme park admission
• 2 counter-service breakfasts and lunches, 2 sit-down dinners
• 2 nights at a budget off-site motel

VALUE OPTION ($1,433):
• 2 days theme park admission
• 2 counter-service breakfasts and lunches, 2 sit-down dinners
• 2 nights at a Disney Value resort

MODERATE OPTION ($1,513):
Same as Value with 2 nights at a Disney Moderate resort

DELUXE OPTION ($1,503):
Same as Value with 1 night at a Disney Deluxe resort

2 ADULTS, 2 KIDS: $2,000

BUDGET OPTION ($2,010):
• 4 days theme park admission
• 4 counter-service breakfasts, lunches, and dinners
• 4 nights at a budget off-site motel

VALUE OPTION ($1,967):
• 3 days theme park admission
• 3 counter-service breakfasts, lunches, and dinners
• 3 nights at a Disney Value resort

MODERATE OPTION ($2,087):
• 3 days theme park admission
• 3 counter-service breakfasts, lunches, and dinners
• 3 nights at a Disney Moderate resort

DELUXE OPTION ($1,833):
• 2 days theme park admission
• 2 counter-service breakfasts and lunches, 2 sit-down dinners
• 2 nights at a Disney Deluxe resort

If you'd like to plug in your own numbers, you can down-load the entire spreadsheet in Excel format at **tinyurl.com/wdw youget.** All hotel prices quoted are for mid-June nights in 2015 and include sales tax.

In most cases, theme park admission ranges from 30% to 60% of the cost of a trip, regardless of family size. If you're not staying at a Deluxe resort, it's safe to assume that ticket costs will take half of your budget (again, excluding transportation).

MAGIC YOUR WAY 2015-16 TICKET PRICES

TICKET TYPE

7-Day	6-Day	5-Day	4-Day	3-Day	2-Day	1-Day
Base Ticket (ages 3–9)						
$335	$325	$314	$304	$273	$191	$105/$97*
$48/day	$54/day	$63/day	$76/day	$91/day	$95/day	—
Base Ticket (ages 10+)						
$357	$346	$335	$325	$293	$204	$112/$103*
$51/day	$58/day	$67/day	$81/day	$98/day	$102/day	—
Park Hopper Add-On (1-day prices include admission)						
$68	$68	$68	$68	$68	$68	$159/$165**
$10/day	$11/day	$14/day	$17/day	$23/day	$34/day	—
Water Park Fun & More Add-On (1-day prices include admission)						
$64 for 7 visits	$64 for 6 visits	$64 for 5 visits	$64 for 4 visits	$64 for 3 visits	$64 for 2 visits	$174/$180** for 2 visits

* 1-Day Base Tickets cost more for the Magic Kingdom than for the other three parks.
** 1-Day Park Hopper and WPFAM cost more for guests age 10 and up.
All prices include tax and are rounded to the nearest dollar.

WALT DISNEY WORLD ADMISSION OPTIONS

DISNEY OFFERS A NUMBER OF different admission options in order to accommodate various vacation needs. These range from the humble **1-Day Base Ticket,** good for a single day's entry into one Disney theme park, to the blinged-out **Premium Annual Pass,** good for 365 days of admission into every Disney theme or water park, plus DisneyQuest, Disney's Oak Trail Golf Course, and more. See the chart above for a summary of the most common options.

Problem is, the number of ticket choices available can make your head spin. Many families, we suspect, become so overwhelmed trying to sort them all out that they simply buy an expensive ticket with far more features than they'll actually use.

THIS IS A JOB FOR . . . A COMPUTER!

IT'S COMPLICATED ENOUGH that we wrote a computer program to solve it. Visit **touringplans.com** and try our **Park Ticket Calculator,** on the home page. It aggregates ticket prices from Disney and a number of online ticket vendors. Answer a few questions relating to the size of your party and the parks you intend to visit, and the calculator will identify your four cheapest ticket options. It'll also show you how much you'll save.

The program will also make recommendations for considerations other than price. For example, an Annual Passes might cost you more, but it gets you substantial resort discounts and other deals that can more than offset the price of the pass.

MAGIC YOUR WAY

WALT DISNEY WORLD OFFERS AN ARRAY of theme park ticket options, grouped into a program called Magic Your Way. The simplest option—visiting one theme park for one day—is called a **1-Day Base Ticket.** Other features, such as the ability to visit more than one park per day ("park-hopping"), or the inclusion of admission to Disney's minor venues (Typhoon Lagoon, Blizzard Beach, Disney-Quest, mini-golf, and the like), are available as individual add-ons to the Base Ticket.

In 2013 Disney introduced separate pricing for a single day's admission to the Magic Kingdom versus the World's other theme parks. For 2015–16, an adult 1-Day Base Ticket for the Magic Kingdom costs $111.83, while one day's admission to any other theme park is $103.31 (including tax)—not exactly a good value if you have just a day to spend in the World.

Multiday pricing is still uniform across the parks: The more days of admission you buy, the lower the cost per day. For example, if you buy an adult 5-Day Base Ticket for $335.48 (tax included), each day costs $67.10, compared with $103.31 a day for a one-day pass to Epcot, the Studios, or Animal Kingdom and $111.83 for the Magic Kingdom. Tickets can be purchased from 1 up to 10 days and admit you to exactly one theme park per day; you can reenter your chosen park as many times as you like on that day.

Disney says its tickets expire within 14 days of the first day of use. In practice, they really mean 13 days after the first day of use. If, say, you purchase a 4-Day Base Ticket on June 1 and use it that day for admission to the Magic Kingdom, you'll be able to visit a single Disney theme park on any of your three remaining days from June 2 through June 14. After that, the ticket expires and you lose any unused days.

BASE TICKET ADD-ON OPTIONS

THREE ADD-ON OPTIONS ARE OFFERED with the Base Ticket, each at an additional cost:

PARK HOPPER This add-on you lets you visit more than one Disney World theme park per day. The cost is about $37–$46 (including tax) on top of the price of an adult 1-Day Base Ticket and a flat $68.16 tacked on to adult or child 2- and 3-Day Base Tickets—exorbitant for one or two days, but more affordable the longer your stay. As an add-on to a 7-Day Base Ticket, the flat fee works out to $9.74 per day for park-hopping privileges. If, for instance, you want to visit the Magic Kingdom in the morning and eat at Epcot in the evening, this is the feature to request.

WATER PARK FUN AND MORE (WPFAM) This option gives you a single admission to one of Disney's water parks (Blizzard Beach and Typhoon Lagoon), DisneyQuest, Oak Trail Golf Course, Fantasia Gardens or Winter Summerland mini-golf, or the ESPN Wide World of Sports Complex. The cost is a flat $63.90, including tax. Except for the single-day WPFAM ticket, which gives you two admissions, the number of admissions equals the number of days on your ticket. If you buy an 8-Day Base Ticket, for example, and add the WPFAM option, you get eight WPFAM admissions. What you *can't* do is, say, buy a 10-Day Base Ticket with only three WPFAM admissions or a 3-Day Base Ticket with four WPFAM admissions. You can, however, skip WPFAM entirely and buy an individual admission to any of these minor parks—that's frequently the best deal if you want to visit only one of the venues above.

Disney Annual Passes

An **Annual Pass** provides unlimited use of the major theme parks for one year; a **Premium Annual Pass** also provides unlimited use of the minor parks. Annual Pass holders also get perks, including free parking and seasonal offers such as room-rate discounts at Disney resorts; however, the Annual Pass is not valid for special events, such as admission to Mickey's Very Merry Christmas Party. Tax included, Annual Passes run $696.51 for both adults and kids age 3 and up. A Premium Annual Pass, at $829.64 for adults and kids age 3 and up, provides unlimited admission to Blizzard Beach, Typhoon Lagoon, DisneyQuest, and Oak Trail Golf Course, in addition to the four major theme parks, plus mini-golf discounts.

HOW TO GET THE MOST FROM MAGIC YOUR WAY

FIRST, BE REALISTIC about what you want out of your vacation. A seven-day theme park ticket with seven WPFAM admissions might seem like a wonderful idea when you're snowbound in February and planning your trip. But actually trying to visit all those parks in a week in July might end up feeling more like Navy SEAL training. If you're going to visit only one water park, DisneyQuest, or the ESPN Wide World of Sports Complex, you're almost always better off purchasing that admission separately rather than in the WPFAM option.

WHERE TO PURCHASE MAGIC YOUR WAY TICKETS

YOU CAN BUY YOUR ADMISSION PASSES on arrival at Walt Disney World or purchase them in advance. Admission passes are available at Walt Disney World resorts and theme parks. Passes are also available at some non-Disney hotels and certain Walt Disney World–area grocery stores, and from independent ticket brokers.

Offers of free or heavily discounted tickets abound, but there's nearly always a catch: You have to sit through a high-pressure time-share sales pitch, or the seller is offering partially used passes that may or may not be expired.

unofficial **TIP**
Never buy tickets from an unauthorized reseller—chances are good they'll be worthless if you try to use them. Likewise, don't buy tickets off of eBay or Craigslist.

Magic Your Way tickets are available at Disney Stores and at **disneyworld.com** for the same prices listed on page 19.

If you're trying to keep costs to an absolute minimum, consider an online ticket wholesaler, such as **mapleleaftickets.com** or **undercovertourist.com,** especially for trips with five or more days in the theme parks. All tickets sold are brand-new, and the savings can range from $4 to more than $65, depending on the tickets and options you choose.

The Official Ticket Center, Maple Leaf Tickets, and Undercover Tourist offer discounts on tickets for almost all Central Florida attractions, including Disney World, Universal Orlando, SeaWorld, and Cirque du Soleil. Discounts for the major theme parks are about 6–12%. Tickets for other attractions are more deeply discounted.

Finally, if all this is too confusing, our website will help you navigate all of the choices and find you the least-expensive ticket options for your vacation. Visit **touringplans.com** for more details.

For Additional Information on Passes

Call **Disney Ticket Inquiries** at ☎ 407-566-4985, or e-mail **ticket.inquiries@disneyworld.com.** If you need current prices or routine information, check **disneyworld.disney.go.com/tickets.**

Special Passes

Walt Disney World offers a number of special and situational passes that are not known to the general public and are not sold at any Disney World ticket booth. The best information we've found on these passes is available at **tinyurl.com/wdwdiscounttix.**

ALLOCATING TIME

WHICH PARK TO SEE FIRST?

FIRST-TIME VISITORS should see Epcot first; you'll be able to enjoy it fully without having been preconditioned to think of Disney entertainment as solely fantasy or adventure.

See Disney's Animal Kingdom second. Like Epcot, it's educational, but its live animals provide a change of pace.

Next, see Disney's Hollywood Studios, which helps all ages make a fluid transition from the educational Epcot and Animal Kingdom to the fanciful Magic Kingdom. Also, because Disney's Hollywood Studios is smaller, you won't walk as much or stay as long. Save the Magic Kingdom for last.

OPERATING HOURS

THE DISNEY WORLD WEBSITE publishes preliminary park hours 180 days in advance, but schedule adjustments can happen at any time, including the day of your visit. Check **disneyworld.com** or call ☎ 407-824-4321 for exact hours before you arrive. Off-season, parks may be open as few as 8 hours (9 a.m.–5 p.m.). At busy times (particularly holidays), they may operate 8 a.m.–2 a.m.

THE CARDINAL RULES
FOR SUCCESSFUL TOURING

EVEN THE MOST EFFICIENT TOURING PLAN won't allow you to cover two or more major theme parks in one day. Plan to allocate at least an entire day to each park. (An exception to this rule is when the parks close at different times, allowing you to tour one park until closing and then proceed to another.)

One-Day Touring

A comprehensive one-day tour of the Magic Kingdom, Disney's Animal Kingdom, Epcot, or Disney's Hollywood Studios is possible, but it requires knowledge of the park, good planning, and plenty of energy and endurance. One-day touring can be fun and rewarding, but allocating two days per park, especially for the Magic Kingdom and Epcot, is always preferable.

unofficial **TIP**
If your schedule allows only one day of touring, concentrate on one park and save the rest for another visit.

Successful touring of the Magic Kingdom, Animal Kingdom, Epcot, or Disney's Hollywood Studios hinges on *three rules:*

1. Determine in Advance What You Really Want to See

To help you set your touring priorities, we describe the theme parks and their attractions in detail. We include the authors' evaluation of the attraction and the opinions of Walt Disney World guests expressed as star ratings. Five stars is the best possible rating.

Finally, because attractions range from midway-type rides and horse-drawn trolleys to colossal, high-tech extravaganzas, we've developed a hierarchy of categories to pinpoint an attraction's magnitude:

SUPER-HEADLINERS The best attractions that the theme park has to offer. Mind-boggling in size, scope, and imagination, they represent the cutting edge of modern attraction technology and design.

HEADLINERS Full-blown multimillion-dollar themed adventures and theater presentations. They are modern in technology and design and employ a full range of special effects.

MAJOR ATTRACTIONS Themed adventures on a more modest scale but which incorporate state-of-the-art technologies, or larger-scale attractions of older design.

MINOR ATTRACTIONS Midway-type rides, small "dark" rides (cars on a track, zigzagging through the dark), small theater presentations, transportation rides, and walk-through attractions.

DIVERSIONS Exhibits, both passive and interactive, such as playgrounds, video arcades, and street theater.

2. Arrive Early! Arrive Early! Arrive Early!

Have breakfast before you arrive so you won't waste prime touring time sitting in a restaurant. The earlier a park opens, the greater your potential advantage. This is because most vacationers won't make the sacrifice to rise early and get to a theme park before it opens. Fewer people are willing to be on hand for an 8 a.m. opening than for a 9 a.m. opening. On those rare occasions when a park opens at 10 a.m., almost everyone arrives at the same time, so it's almost impossible to get a jump on the crowd. If you're visiting during midsummer, arrive at the turnstile 30–40 minutes before official opening time. During holiday periods, get to the parks 45–60 minutes before official opening.

3. Avoid Bottlenecks

Our touring plans for the Disney World theme parks help you do just that. Plans for the Magic Kingdom begin on page 159; Epcot, on page 197; Disney's Animal Kingdom, on page 224; and Disney's Hollywood Studios, on page 247.

TOURING PLANS EXPLAINED

OUR TOURING PLANS ARE STEP-BY-STEP guides for seeing as much as possible with a minimum of standing in line. They're designed to help you avoid crowds and bottlenecks on days of moderate-to-heavy attendance.

What You Can Expect from the Touring Plans

Though we present one-day touring plans for each theme park, be aware that the Magic Kingdom and Epcot have more attractions than you can reasonably expect to see in one day. Because the two-day plans for the Magic Kingdom and Epcot are the most comprehensive, efficient, and relaxing, we strongly recommend them over the one-day plans. However, if you must cram your visit into a single day, the one-day plans will allow you to see as much as is humanly possible. Because construction at Disney's Hollywood Studios has closed many attractions, seeing the attractions that remain open in one day is doable; likewise, Disney's Animal Kingdom is a one-day outing.

Customize Your Touring Plans

The attractions included in our touring plans are the most popular as determined by almost 57,000 reader surveys. Even so, your favorite attractions may be different. In that case, you can create personalized versions at **touringplans.com**. Tell the software the date, time, and park you've chosen to visit, along with the attractions you want to see. The plan will tell you, for your specific travel date and time, the exact order in which to visit the attractions to minimize your waits in line. Our Lines app also supports "switching off" (see page 93) on thrill rides. Besides attractions, you can schedule meals, breaks, character greetings, and more. Plus, Lines can handle any FastPass+ reservations you've already got and tell you which attractions would benefit most from your using them.

Alternatively, some changes are simple enough to make on your own. If a plan calls for an attraction you're not interested in, simply skip it. You can also substitute similar attractions in the same area of the park. If a plan calls for, say, riding Dumbo and you'd rather not, but you would enjoy the Mad Tea Party (which is not on the plan), then go ahead and substitute that for Dumbo.

Variables That Affect the Success of the Touring Plans

How quickly you move from one ride to another; when and how many refreshment and restroom breaks you take; when, where, and how you eat meals; and your ability to find your way around will all have an impact on the success of the plans. Smaller groups almost always move faster than larger groups, and parties of adults generally can cover more ground than families with young children.

If your kids collect character autographs, you need to anticipate these interruptions by including character greetings when creating your online touring plans, or else negotiate some understanding with your children about when you'll collect autographs. Note that queues for autographs, especially in the Magic Kingdom and Disney's Animal Kingdom, are sometimes as long as or longer than the queues for major attractions. The only time-efficient ways to collect autographs are to use FastPass+ where available (such as for Mickey Mouse and the Disney princesses at the Magic Kingdom) or to line up at the character-greeting areas first thing in the morning. Early morning is also the best time to experience popular attractions, so you may have some tough choices to make.

While we realize that following the plans isn't always easy, we nevertheless recommend continuous, expeditious touring until around noon. After that, breaks and diversions won't affect the plans significantly.

FASTPASS+

IN EARLY 2014, a new version of Disney World's ride-reservation system replaced the one that had been in use since 1999. Whereas the old system printed your reservation times on small slips of paper dispensed from ATM-like kiosks next to each attraction, the current FastPass+ system is (with one exception described later) entirely electronic: You must use a computer, mobile device, or in-park terminal to make and modify FastPass+ reservations, and you must use your MagicBand (see page 10) to redeem the reservation. As before, FastPass+ is free of charge to all Walt Disney World guests.

Somewhat like making a dinner reservation at a restaurant, FastPass+ allows you to reserve a ride on an attraction at a Disney theme park. You can request a specific time, such as 7:30 p.m., or you can let the system give you its "first available" reservation.

unofficial **TIP**
Disney offers FastPass+ only for select attractions—around 70 in all—and only during busy times of year for some. Specific FastPass+ information for each Disney theme park is provided in its respective chapter.

FastPass+ does *not* eliminate the need to arrive early at a theme park. Because each park offers a limited number of FastPass+ attractions, and because an attraction's FastPass+ availability is limited by its hourly rider capacity, you still have to make an early start if you want to avoid long lines at non-FastPass+ attractions. Those who book last-minute trips or buy admission at the gate may find that reservations are no longer available at their favorite attractions.

Making a FastPass+ Reservation

Anyone with an upcoming stay at a Walt Disney World hotel can make FastPass+ reservations up to 60 days in advance at **mydisney experience.com** or through the My Disney Experience (MDE) mobile app; Annual Pass holders staying off-property may reserve up to 30 days in advance, as may day guests with a valid ticket. At press time, you could use FastPass+ at just one park per day.

If you buy your admission the day you arrive at the park or you want to change your previous FastPass+ selections once you're inside, you can do so using the mobile app or in-park computer terminals.

You should set aside *at least* 30 minutes to complete the advance-booking process. Before you begin, make sure that you have the following items on hand:

- A valid admission ticket or purchase-confirmation number for everyone in your group
- Your hotel reservation number, if you're staying on-site
- A computer, or mobile device connected to the Internet
- An e-mail account that you can access easily while traveling
- An MDE account
- A schedule of the parks you'll be visiting each day, including arrival and departure times as well as midday breaks
- The dates, times, and confirmation numbers of any dining or recreation reservations you've already made

We think it's easier to use **mydisneyexperience.com** than the MDE app, so here's how to make reservations using the website:

1. MY DISNEY EXPERIENCE ACCESS Now go to the MDE site and click "Sign In or Create Account" in the upper right corner; then click "Create Account" on the screen that follows. You'll be asked for your e-mail address, along with your name, home address, and birthdate. (Disney uses your home address to send your MagicBands and, if applicable, hotel reservation information.) You'll also be asked to choose two security questions and answers. If you forget your login information, Disney will ask you these questions to verify your identity, so write them down or save them as a text file.

2. DISNEY HOTEL INFORMATION Next, MDE asks whether you'll be staying at a Disney hotel. If you are, enter your reservation number. This associates your MDE account with your hotel stay in Disney's computer systems. If you've booked a travel package that includes theme park admission, Disney computers will automatically link the admission to your MDE account, allowing you to skip Step 4 below.

3. REGISTER FRIENDS AND FAMILY You'll now be asked for the names, ages, and e-mail addresses of everyone traveling with you. This is so you can make dining and FastPass+ reservations for your entire group at the same time later in the process.

4. REGISTER TICKETS If you've bought your admission from a third-party ticket reseller or you have tickets or MagicBands left over from a previous trip, you'll be asked to register those next. On each ticket is printed a unique ID code, usually a string of 12–20 numbers, located in one corner on the back; on MagicBands, look for a 12-digit number printed inside the band. Enter the ID code for each ticket you have.

You can make FastPass+ reservations for as many days as there are on your ticket. If you decide later to extend your stay, you'll be able to make reservations for additional days. If you have a voucher that needs to be converted to a ticket at the parks, you can register it by calling Disney tech support at ☎ 407-939-7765.

5. SELECT A DATE Click on the My Disney Experience logo in the upper right corner of your screen. A menu should appear, with "FastPass+" as one of the choices. Click on "FastPass+."

The next screen should display a rolling seven-day calendar, beginning around the start of your trip's dates. Select one of these dates and click "Next."

6. SELECT TRAVEL PARTY On the screen that follows, you'll choose which of your friends and family will use the FastPass+ reservations you're making. Note that everyone you select during this step will get the same set of FastPass+ attractions and times; you can tweak everyone's selections in Step 9, so for now, choose all the members of your group and click "Next."

7. SELECT ATTRACTIONS On this screen you choose your Fast-Pass+ experiences from a list of eligible attractions. Because Disney has rules governing the combinations of FastPasses you can get at Epcot and Disney's Hollywood Studios (see page 30), the attractions will be grouped into the correct tiers for those parks, and you'll see how many opportunities you have in each tier. If all FastPasses for an attraction have been distributed, the message "Standby Available" will appear next to its name. If you don't choose an attraction for every opportunity MDE gives you, you'll be automatically assigned random attractions for all remaining opportunities.

8. CHOOSE INITIAL RETURN TIMES Next, MDE will give you four different sets of FastPass+ return times, grouped as Options A, B, and C, plus Best Match. Each option contains one return time for each attraction that you selected in Step 7. Choose the set of return times that's closest to what you want, and you'll be able to modify them in the next step.

9. MODIFY RETURN TIMES OR ATTRACTIONS If the initial set of FastPass+ return times conflicts with your plans, you can check whether alternate times are available that better fit your schedule. The good news is that you can change each attraction's return times separately. Plus, if none of the return times for a particular attraction work for you, you can pick another attraction at this stage without having to start over.

OK, you've booked one set of FastPasses for one park visit— now you'll need to repeat Steps 6–10 for every park you plan to visit, on every day of your trip . . . thus proving that FastPass+ is a milestone in Disney's never-ending quest to create something more complicated than the US tax code or the Affordable Care Act.

Buying Tickets and Making FastPass+ Reservations On Arrival

If (1) you buy your admission the day you arrive at the parks or (2) you have to delay making your FastPass+ selections until you're inside, Disney has placed new computer terminals throughout the parks where you can make on-the-spot reservations; we've listed the specific locations in each theme park's chapter. Each set of terminals—look for the FP+ KIOSK signs—is staffed by a group of cast members who can walk you through the reservation process.

If you're tech-challenged, not to worry: You can use a paper FastPass+ form, sort of like a cafeteria menu, that lets you tick off checkboxes next to the rides you want to experience. A cast member will take your form and enter your selections into the kiosk for you. You'll still need to provide your MDE username and password, however.

RETURNING TO RIDE Each FastPass+ reservation lasts for an hour, and, just like a restaurant reservation, your FastPass+ may be canceled if you don't show up on time. In practice, however, we've found that you can usually be up to 5 minutes early or 15 minutes late to use your reservation.

When you return to Space Mountain at the designated time, you'll be directed to a FASTPASS+ RETURN line. Before you get in line, you'll have to validate your reservation by touching your MagicBand or RFID ticket to a reader at the FastPass+ Return entrance. Then you'll proceed with minimal waiting to the attraction's preshow or boarding area.

If technical problems cause an attraction to be closed during your return time, Disney will automatically adjust your FastPass+ reservation in one of three ways:

1. If it's early in the day, Disney will offer you the chance to return to the attraction at any point in the day after it reopens.
2. Alternatively, Disney may let you choose another FastPass+ attraction in the same park, on the same day.
3. If it's late in the day, Disney will automatically give you another selection good for any FastPass+ attraction at any park the next day.

At the FastPass+ attractions on tbe next page, the time gap between getting your pass and returning to ride can range from 3 to 7 hours. To ensure that you have enough time to ride on the day of your visit, either book FastPass+ in advance for these attractions or reserve them in the parks as early in the day as possible.

MAGIC KINGDOM Buzz Lightyear's Space Ranger Spin,
Evening Parade, Frozen Meet and Greet, Seven Dwarfs Mine Train,
Space Mountain, Splash Mountain

EPCOT Frozen Ever After, IllumiNations, Mission: Space (Orange),
Soarin' Test Track

ANIMAL KINGDOM Expedition Everest, Kilimanjaro Safaris,
Meet Mickey and Minnie at Adventurers Outpost

DHS Rock 'n' Roller Coaster, The Twilight Zone Tower of Terror,
Toy Story Midway Mania!

FastPass+ Rules

Disney has rules in place to prevent you from obtaining certain combinations of FastPass+ reservations before you get to the parks:

Rule #1: You can obtain only one advance FastPass+ reservation per attraction, per day, but you can get more once you're in the park and you've used your first set of three.

Rule #2: FastPass+ reservation times can't overlap—Disney's computer system doesn't allow it. If you have a FastPass+ reservation for 2–3 p.m., for instance, you can't make another reservation later than 1 p.m. or earlier than 3 p.m. in the same park.

FASTPASS+ TIERS Disney also prohibits guests from using Fast-Pass+ on all of a park's headliner attractions—they must choose one attraction from one group and two more from another group. The practice, known informally as "FastPass+ tiers," was in effect only at Epcot and Disney's Hollywood Studios at press time but will probably be extended to all four parks eventually (see pages 170 and 232 for specifics). Again, though, the tiers don't apply beyond your first three advance FastPass+ reservations—any reservations you make beyond the first three when you're in the parks are totally up to you.

How FastPass+ Affects Your Touring Plans

We think most *Unofficial Guide* readers probably spend fewer minutes per day walking around the parks with the introduction of FastPass+, because they no longer need to walk to an attraction's FastPass machines. The time saved by walking is slightly more than the overall increases in standby waits at secondary attractions, so FastPass+—when it works—is roughly a break-even proposition for folks using our touring plans.

We say "when it works" because on a recent trip to the Magic Kingdom, we (Bob and Len) spent the better part of a day observing just how wrong things can go at a FastPass+ return point. The most common snafu we saw was a family arriving too early or too late for their reservation. That's understandable, because MagicBands don't display reservation times, and they're cumbersome to find on My Disney Experience.

The next most frequent issue we saw was from families, particularly those who don't speak English as their first language, who simply didn't get how FastPass+ works. For example, many families seemed to think that simply wearing the MagicBand allowed them access to the FastPass+ line, without their having to make a reservation.

When a MagicBand doesn't work at a FastPass+ return point, a cast member can usually resolve the problem fairly quickly. When the problem is more complex, the line stops while the issue is sorted.

On the upside, Disney has made great progress in streamlining these "recovery" processes, and we expect them to continue to pour resources into further speed-ups.

Your FastPass+ Priorities at Each Park

Including the touring plans in this book and on our website, we've updated almost 200 touring plans to use FastPass+ exclusively. Each plan now lists the suggested FastPass+ start times for the attractions that will save you the most time in line, like this:

SUGGESTED START TIMES FOR FASTPASS+ RESERVATIONS

- Peter Pan's Flight: 10 a.m.
- Buzz Lightyear's Space Ranger Spin: 5 p.m.
- *Enchanted Tales with Belle:* 7 p.m.

When we updated the plans, we kept count of how many times each attraction was identified as needing FastPass+. It turns out that this is a prioritized list of the attractions for which you should use FastPass+ to avoid long waits in line. We've added this information to the FastPass+ section in each theme park's chapter.

PART THREE

ACCOMMODATIONS

▌*The* BASIC CONSIDERATIONS

BENEFITS OF STAYING IN THE WORLD

WALT DISNEY WORLD RESORT HOTEL and campground guests have privileges and amenities unavailable to those staying outside the World. Though some of these perks are only advertising gimmicks, others are real and potentially valuable:

1. CONVENIENCE If you don't have a car, the commute to the theme parks is short via the Disney Transportation System. This is especially advantageous if you stay in one of the hotels connected by the monorail or boat service. If you have a car, however, there are dozens of hotels outside Disney World that are within 5–10 minutes of theme-park parking lots.

2. EXTRA MAGIC HOURS AT THE THEME PARKS Disney World lodging guests (excluding guests at the independent hotels of the Downtown Disney Resort Area) are invited to enter a designated park an hour earlier than the general public each day or to enjoy a designated theme park for up to 2 hours after it closes to the general public in the evening. Extra Magic Hours can be valuable if you know how to use them. They can also land you in gridlock. (See our detailed discussion starting on page 15.)

3. BABYSITTING AND CHILD-CARE OPTIONS Disney hotel and campground guests have several options for babysitting, child care, and children's programs. The **Polynesian Village & Villas** and **Animal Kingdom Lodge,** along with several other Disney hotels, offer "clubs"— themed child-care centers where potty-trained children ages 3–12 can stay while the adults go out.

4. PRIORITY THEME PARK ADMISSIONS On days of unusually heavy attendance, Disney may restrict admission into the theme parks for all customers. When deciding whom to admit into the parks, priority is given to guests staying at Disney resorts. In practice, no guest is turned away until a park's parking lot is full. When this happens, that park will be packed to gridlock. Under such conditions, you would exhibit the common sense of an amoeba to exercise your priority-admission privilege.

5. CHILDREN SHARING A ROOM WITH THEIR PARENTS There is no extra charge per night for children younger than age 18 sharing a room with their parents. Many hotels outside Disney World also offer this benefit.

6. FREE PARKING Disney resort guests with cars pay nothing to park in theme park lots or hotels. This saves $17 per day at the parks and up to $20 per day at the hotel.

7. RECREATIONAL PRIVILEGES Disney resort guests get preferential treatment for tee times at the golf courses.

STAYING IN OR OUT OF THE WORLD: WEIGHING THE PROS AND CONS

1. COST If this is a primary consideration, you'll lodge much less expensively outside Disney World. Our ratings of hotel quality and cost (see pages 64–69) compare specific hotels both in and out of the World.

2. EASE OF ACCESS Even if you stay in Walt Disney World, you're dependent on some mode of transportation. It may be less stressful to use the Disney transportation system, but with the single exception of commuting to the Magic Kingdom, the fastest, most efficient, and most flexible way to get around is usually a car. Walt Disney World is so large that some destinations within the World can be reached more quickly from off-property hotels than from Disney hotels. For example, guests at hotels and motels on US 192 (near the so-called Walt Disney World Maingate) are closer to Disney's Hollywood Studios, Disney's Animal Kingdom, and Blizzard Beach water park than guests at many hotels inside Disney World.

3. YOUNG CHILDREN Although the hassle of commuting to most non-World hotels is only slightly (if at all) greater than that of commuting to Disney hotels, a definite peace of mind results from staying in Walt Disney World. The salient point, regardless of where you stay, is to make sure you get your young children back to the hotel for a nap each day.

4. SPLITTING UP If you're in a party that probably will split up to tour (as frequently happens in families with children of varying ages), staying in the World offers more transportation options and, thus, more independence. Mom and Dad can take the car and return to the hotel for a relaxed dinner and early bedtime while the teens remain in the park for evening parades and fireworks.

5. FEEDING THE ARMY OF THE POTOMAC If you have a large crew that chows down like cattle on a finishing lot, you may do better staying outside the World, where food is far less expensive.

6. VISITING OTHER ORLANDO-AREA ATTRACTIONS If you'll be visiting SeaWorld, Kennedy Space Center Visitor Complex, Universal Orlando, or other area attractions, it may be more convenient to stay outside the World.

HOW TO GET DISCOUNTS ON LODGING AT WALT DISNEY WORLD

THERE ARE SO MANY GUEST ROOMS in and around Disney World that competition is brisk, and everyone, including Disney, wheels and deals to fill them. Disney, however, has its own atypical way of managing its room inventory. To uphold the brand integrity of its hotels, Disney prefers to use "sweeteners" rather than discounts per se. (For example, Disney might include free dining if you reserve a certain number of nights at rack rate, or offer special deals only by e-mail to returning guests.) Consequently, many of the strategies for obtaining discounted rates in most cities and destinations don't work well for Disney hotels. Nonetheless, there are good deals to be found—check out our tips below.

1. SEASONAL SAVINGS You can save 15–35% per night or more on a Disney hotel room by visiting during slower times of year. However, Disney uses so many adjectives ("Regular," "Holiday," "Peak," "Value," and the like) to describe its seasonal calendar that it's hard to keep up. Plus, the dates for each "season" vary among resorts. If you're set on staying at a Disney resort, order a copy of the **Walt Disney Travel Company Florida Vacations Brochure and DVD** (see page 9).

2. ASK ABOUT SPECIALS When you talk to Disney reservationists, inquire specifically about special deals. Ask, for example, "What special rates or discounts are available at Disney hotels during the time of our visit?"

3. TRADE-UP OR UPSELL RATES If you request a room at a Disney Value resort and none are available, you may be offered a discounted room in the next category up (Moderate resorts, in this example). Similarly, if you ask for a room in a Moderate resort and none is available, Disney will usually offer a deal for Disney Deluxe Villa rooms or a Deluxe resort. You can angle for a trade-up rate by asking for a resort category that's more likely to be sold out.

4. KNOW THE SECRET CODE The folks at **MouseSavers** (**mouse savers.com**) maintain an updated list of discounts and reservation codes for Disney resorts. The codes are separated into categories such as "for anyone," "for residents of certain states," and "for Annual Pass holders." Anyone who calls the Disney Reservation Center at ☎ 407-W-DISNEY can use a current code and get the discounted rate.

unofficial **TIP** Dozens of discounts are usually listed at the MouseSavers site, covering almost all Disney resort hotels.

MouseSavers maintains a great historical list of when hotel discounts were released and what they encompassed at **mousesavers .com/historicalwdwdiscounts.html.** The MouseSavers newsletter features discount announcements, Disney news, and exclusive offers not available to the general public.

5. INTERNET SELLERS Online travel sellers **Expedia** (**expedia .com**), **One Travel** (**onetravel.com**), **Priceline** (**priceline.com**), and **Travelocity** (**travelocity.com**) offer discounted rooms at Disney hotels, but usually at a price approximating the going rate obtainable from the Walt Disney Travel Company or Walt Disney World Central Reservations. Most breaks are in the 7–25% range, but they can go as deep as 40%. Always check these websites' prices against Disney's—while updating this guide, we noticed that for the same dates during summer 2015, Priceline was charging $30 more per night than Disney for the same standard-view room at the Beach Club.

6. WALT DISNEY WORLD WEBSITE Disney still offers deals when it sees lower-than-usual future demand. Go to **disneyworld.com** and look for "Explore Our Special Offers" on the home page. In the same place, also look for seasonal discounts, usually listed as "Summertime Savings" or "Fall Savings" or something similar. You can also go to "Places to Stay" at the top of the home page, where you'll find a link to Special Offers. You must click on the particular special to get the discounts: If you fill out the information on "Price Your Vacation," you'll be charged the full rack rate. Reservations booked online are subject to a penalty if canceled fewer than 45 days before you arrive. Before booking rooms on Disney's or any website, click "Terms and Conditions" and read the fine print.

7. RENTING DISNEY VACATION CLUB POINTS The Disney Vacation Club (DVC) is Disney's time-share-condominium program. DVC resorts at Walt Disney World are **Animal Kingdom Villas, Bay Lake Tower** at the Contemporary Resort, the **Beach Club Villas,**

BoardWalk Villas, Grand Floridian Villas, Old Key West Resort, Polynesian Villas & Bungalows, Saratoga Springs Resort & Spa, Treehouse Villas at Saratoga Springs, and **Wilderness Lodge Villas.** Each resort offers studios and one- and two-bedroom villas. (Some resorts also have three-bedroom villas, while the new Polynesian Village DVC resort is limited to studios and two-bedroom bungalows.)

DVC members receive a number of "points" annually that they use to pay for their accommodations. Sometimes members elect to "rent" (sell) their points to others instead of using them in a given year. Though Disney is not involved in the transaction, it permits DVC members to make these points available to the general public. The going rental rate is usually about $14 per point.

You have two options when renting points: go through a company that specializes in DVC points rental, or locate and deal directly with the selling DVC member. For a fixed rate of around $14 per point, the folks at **David's Disney Vacation Club Rentals** (**dvcrequest.com**) will act as a points broker in your behalf, matching your request for a specific resort and dates to their available supply.

The DVC discussion site **MouseOwners** (**mouseowners.com**) has a specific forum for matching DVC sellers and renters.

8. TRAVEL AGENTS In our opinion, a Disney-savvy travel agent is the best friend a traveler can have. The best of the best include **Sue Pisaturo** of **Small World Vacations,** whom we've used many times (**sue@smallworldvacations.com**); **Minnie Babb** (**minnie@smallworld vacations.com**); **Caroline Baggerly** (**caroline@mei-travel.com**); **Holly Biss** (**holly@magicalvacationstravel.com**); **Coleen Bolton** (**coleen@ mei-travel.com**); **Belle Meyers** (**belle@smallworldvacations.com**); and **Darren Wittko** (**darren@magicalvacationstravel.com**).

9. ORGANIZATIONS AND AUTO CLUBS Disney has developed time-limited programs with some auto clubs and organizations. AAA, for example, can often offer discounts on hotels and packages comparable to those Disney offers its Annual Pass holders. Such deals come and go, but the market suggests there will be more. If you're a member of AARP, AAA, or any travel or auto club, ask whether the group has a program before shopping elsewhere.

10. ROOM UPGRADES Sometimes a room upgrade is as good as a discount. If you're visiting Disney World during a slower time, book the least expensive room your discounts will allow. Checking in, ask very politely about being upgraded to a "water view" or "pool view" room. A fair percentage of the time, you'll get one at no additional charge. Hotels are under no obligation to upgrade you, so if your request is not met, accept the decision graciously. Also, note that suites are exempt from discount offers.

11. MILITARY DISCOUNTS The **Shades of Green Armed Forces Recreation Center,** near the Grand Floridian Resort & Spa, offers luxury accommodations at rates based on a serviceman's rank as well as attraction tickets to the theme parks. Call ☎ 888-593-2242 or see **shadesofgreen.org.**

12. YEAR-ROUND DISCOUNTS AT THE SWAN AND DOLPHIN RESORTS Government workers, teachers, nurses, military, and AAA and *Entertainment Coupon Book* members can save on their rooms at the Dolphin or the Swan resort (when space is available, of course). Call ☎ 800-227-1500.

CHOOSING A WALT DISNEY WORLD HOTEL

IF YOU WANT TO STAY IN WALT DISNEY WORLD but don't know which hotel to choose, consider the following:

1. COST Consider your budget. Rooms start at about $100 a night at the **All-Star** and **Pop Century Resorts** during Value season and top out near $1,600 at the **Grand Floridian Resort & Spa** during Holiday season. Suites, of course, are more expensive than standard rooms.

Disney's Animal Kingdom Villas, Bay Lake Tower, Beach Club Villas, BoardWalk Villas, Grand Floridian Villas, Old Key West Resort, Saratoga Springs Resort & Spa and **Wilderness Lodge Villas** offer condo-type accommodations with one-, two-, and (at Saratoga Springs, BoardWalk Villas, Old Key West, Animal Kingdom Villas, Grand Floridian Villas, and Bay Lake Tower) three-bedroom units with kitchens, living rooms, DVD players, and washers and dryers. The new **Polynesian Villas & Bungalows** consist solely of studios and two-bedroom freestanding units.

Studios have a kitchenette (with microwave, mini-fridge, and sink) but no washer or dryer. Prices range from $358 per night for a studio suite at Animal Kingdom Villas to more than $3,400 per night for a two-bedroom bungalow at Polynesian Village Villas. Fully equipped cabins (minus a washer and dryer) at **Fort Wilderness Resort & Campground** cost $336–$562 per night. The **Family Suites** at All-Star Music and Art of Animation have kitchenettes, separate bedrooms, and two bathrooms. A few suites without kitchens are available at the more expensive Disney resorts.

For any extra adults in a room (more than two), the nightly surcharge for each extra adult is $10 at Value resorts, $15 at Moderates, and $25 at Deluxes, plus tax. *DDV resorts levy no surcharge.*

COSTS PER NIGHT OF DISNEY RESORT HOTEL ROOMS (late-2015 rack rate)	
All-Star Resorts	$104–$199
All-Star Music Resort Family Suites	$244–$443
Animal Kingdom Lodge	$320–$556
Animal Kingdom Villas (studio, Jambo/Kidani)	$358–$674
Art of Animation Family Suites	$304–$514
Art of Animation Resort	$129–$224
Bay Lake Tower (studio)	$500–$740
Beach Club Resort	$400–$672
Beach Club Villas (studio)	$415–$687
BoardWalk Inn	$429–$683
BoardWalk Villas (studio)	$415–$687
Caribbean Beach Resort	$191–$285
Contemporary Resort	$400–$630
Coronado Springs Resort	$197–$290
Dolphin (Sheraton)	$189–$430
Fort Wilderness Resort & Campground (cabins)	$336–$562
Grand Floridian Resort & Spa	$582–$856
Grand Floridian Villas (studio)	$570–$890
Old Key West Resort (studio)	$368–$531
Polynesian Village Resort	$483–$760
Polynesian Villas & Bungalows (studio)	$494–$772
Pop Century Resort	$115–$209
Port Orleans Resort (French Quarter, Riverside)	$191–$285
Saratoga Springs Resort & Spa (studio)	$368–$531
Swan (Westin)	$189–$430
Treehouse Villas	$818–$1,377
Wilderness Lodge	$325–$561
Wilderness Lodge Villas (studio)	$421–$621
Yacht Club Resort	$400–$672

Also at Disney World are the seven hotels of the **Downtown Disney Resort Area (DDRA).** Accommodations range from fairly luxurious to motel-like. While the DDRA is technically part of Disney World, staying there is like visiting a colony rather than the motherland. Free parking at theme parks isn't offered—nor is early entry—and hotels operate their own buses rather than use Disney transportation. See our profiles of **B Resort,** the **Buena**

WHAT IT COSTS TO STAY IN THE DOWNTOWN DISNEY RESORT AREA	
Best Western Lake Buena Vista Resort Hotel	S80-$170
B Resort	$119-$237
Buena Vista Palace Hotel & Spa	$139-$169
DoubleTree Guest Suites	$119-$229
Hilton Orlando Lake Buena Vista	$139-$289
Holiday Inn in the WDW Resort	$104-$190
Wyndham Lake Buena Vista Resort	$104-$300

Vista Palace, and the **Hilton Orlando Lake Buena Vista** in the section beginning on page 49.

2. LOCATION If you intend to use your own car, the location of your Disney hotel isn't especially important unless you plan to spend most of your time at the Magic Kingdom. (Disney transportation is always more efficient than your car in this case because it bypasses the Transportation and Ticket Center and deposits you at the theme park entrance.)

Most convenient to the Magic Kingdom are the three resort complexes linked by monorail: the **Grand Floridian** and its **Villas,** the **Contemporary** and **Bay Lake Tower,** and the **Polynesian Village, Villas, & Bungalows.** Commuting to the Magic Kingdom by monorail is quick and simple.

Contemporary Resort and Bay Lake Tower, in addition to being on the monorail, are only a 10- to 15-minute walk to the Magic Kingdom. Guests reach Epcot by monorail but must transfer at the Transportation and Ticket Center. Buses connect the resorts to Disney's Hollywood Studios, Disney's Animal Kingdom, the water parks, and Disney Springs. No transfer is required, but the bus makes several stops before reaching either destination.

The Polynesian Village, Villas, & Bungalows is served by the monorail and is an easy walk from the transportation center, where you can catch an express monorail to Epcot. This makes the Polynesian Village the only Disney resort with direct monorail access to both Epcot and the Magic Kingdom. To minimize your walk to the transportation center, request a standard room in Tokelau or a DVC studio in Pago Pago or Moorea.

Wilderness Lodge & Villas, along with **Fort Wilderness Resort & Campground,** are linked to the Magic Kingdom by boat and to everywhere else in the World by somewhat-convoluted bus service. The **Four Seasons Resort Orlando at Walt Disney World,**

behind the former Osprey Ridge Golf Course, has its own bus service to the Magic Kingdom.

The most centrally located resorts in Walt Disney World are the Epcot hotels: the **BoardWalk Inn, BoardWalk Villas, Yacht & Beach Club Resorts, Beach Club Villas, Swan,** and **Dolphin**—and **Coronado Springs,** near Disney's Animal Kingdom. The Epcot hotels are within easy walking distance of Disney's Hollywood Studios and Epcot's International Gateway. Except at Coronado Springs, boat service is also available at these resorts, with vessels connecting to DHS. Epcot hotels are best for guests planning to spend most of their time at Epcot or DHS.

Caribbean Beach Resort, Pop Century Resort, and **Art of Animation Resort** are just south and east of Epcot and DHS. Along Bonnet Creek, **Disney's Old Key West** and **Port Orleans Resorts** also offer quick access to those parks.

Though not centrally located, the **All-Star Resorts** and **Animal Kingdom Lodge & Villas** have very good bus service to all Disney World destinations and are closest to Animal Kingdom.

3. ROOM QUALITY Few Disney guests spend much time in their hotel rooms, though these rooms are among the best designed and most well appointed anywhere. Plus, they're meticulously maintained. At the top of the line are the luxurious rooms of the **Contemporary, Grand Floridian,** and **Polynesian Village Resorts.** Bringing up the rear are the small rooms of the **All-Star Resorts,** but even these economy rooms are sparkling-clean and quite livable. Check our "How the Hotels Compare" tables on pages 64–69 for ratings of all Disney and non-Disney hotels.

4. THE SIZE OF YOUR GROUP Larger families and groups may be interested in how many persons a Disney resort room can accommodate, but only Lilliputians would be comfortable in a room filled to capacity. Groups requiring two or more guest rooms should consider condo or villa accommodations in or out of the World. The most cost-efficient Disney resorts for groups of five are the **Alligator Bayou** section of **Port Orleans Riverside** and **Caribbean Beach Resort.** The cheapest digs for six are the **All-Star Music Family Suites.** For detailed room schematics that show the maximum number of persons per room as well as the rooms' relative size and configuration, see *The Unofficial Guide to Walt Disney World.*

unofficial **TIP**
If there are more than six in your party, you will need either two hotel rooms, a suite, or a condo.

5. THEME All Disney hotels are themed. Each is designed to make you feel you're in a special place or period of history.

Some resorts carry off their themes better than others, and some themes are more exciting. **Wilderness Lodge & Villas,** for example, is extraordinary, reminiscent of a grand national-park lodge from the early 20th century. The lobby opens eight stories to a timbered ceiling supported by giant columns of bundled logs. One look eases you into the Northwest-wilderness theme. The lodge is a great choice for couples and seniors and is heaven for children.

Animal Kingdom Lodge & Villas replicates grand safari lodges of Kenya and Tanzania and overlooks its own African game preserve. By far the most exotic Disney resort, it's made to order for couples on romantic getaways and for families with children. The **Polynesian Village,** likewise dramatic, conveys the feeling of the Pacific Islands. It's great for romantics and families. Many waterfront rooms offer a perfect view of Cinderella Castle and the Magic Kingdom fireworks across Seven Seas Lagoon.

Grandeur, nostalgia, and privilege are central to the **Grand Floridian Resort & Spa, Grand Floridian Villas, Yacht & Beach Club Resorts, BoardWalk Inn,** and **BoardWalk Villas.** Although modeled after Eastern-seaboard seaside hotels of different eras, the resorts are similar. **Saratoga Springs Resort & Spa,** supposedly representative of an upstate New York country retreat, looks like what you'd get if you crossed the Beach Club with the Wilderness Lodge. For all the resorts inspired by northeastern resorts, thematic distinctions are subtle and lost on many guests.

Port Orleans French Quarter Resort lacks the mystery and sultriness of the real New Orleans French Quarter but captures enough of its architectural essence to carry off the theme. **Port Orleans Riverside Resort** likewise succeeds with its plantation and bayou setting. **Old Key West Resort** gets the architecture right, but cloning its inspiration on such a large scale totally glosses over the real Key West's idiosyncratic patchwork personality. The **Caribbean Beach Resort**'s theme is much more effective at night, thanks to creative lighting. By day, it looks like a Miami condo development.

The **All-Star Resorts** comprise 30 three-story, T-shaped buildings with almost 6,000 guest rooms. There are 15 themed areas: 5 celebrate sports (surfing, basketball, tennis, football, and baseball), 5 recall Hollywood movies, and 5 have musical motifs. The resort's design, with entrances shaped like giant Dalmatians, Coke cups, footballs, and the like, is pretty adolescent, sacrificing grace and beauty for energy and novelty. Guest rooms are small, with decor reminiscent of a teenage boy's bedroom. Despite the theme, there is no sports, music, or movies at All-Star Resorts. **Pop Century Resort** is pretty much a clone of All-Star Resorts, only this time the giant icons symbolize decades of the 20th century (Big Wheels, 45-rpm records, silhouettes of people doing period dances, and such), and period memorabilia decorate the rooms. Across the lake from Pop Century Resort is the **Art of Animation Resort,** with icons and decor based on four Disney animated features: *Cars, Finding Nemo, The Lion King,* and *The Little Mermaid.*

Pretense aside, the **Contemporary, Swan,** and **Dolphin** are essentially themeless though architecturally interesting. The original Contemporary Resort is a 15-story A-frame building with monorails running through the middle. Views from guest rooms here and in Bay Lake Tower are among the best at Disney World. Swan and Dolphin are massive yet whimsical. Designed by Michael Graves, they're excellent examples of "entertainment architecture."

6. DINING The best resorts for dining quality and selection are the Epcot resorts: the **Beach Club Villas, BoardWalk Inn & Villas, Dolphin, Swan,** and **Yacht & Beach Club Resorts.** Each has good restaurants and is within easy walking distance of the others and of the 14 restaurants in Epcot's World Showcase section. If you stay at an Epcot resort, you have a total of 31 restaurants within a 5- to 12-minute walk.

The only other place in Disney World where restaurants and hotels are similarly concentrated is in the **Downtown Disney Resort Area.** In addition to restaurants in the hotels themselves, the **Hilton, Holiday Inn at Walt Disney World, Wyndham Lake Buena Vista Resort,** and **Buena Vista Palace Hotel & Spa,** as well as **Saratoga Springs Resort & Spa,** are within walking distance of restaurants in Disney Springs.

Guests at the **Contemporary, Polynesian Village,** and **Grand Floridian** can eat in their hotels, or they can commute to restaurants in the Magic Kingdom (not recommended) or in other monorail-linked hotels. Riding the monorail to another hotel or to the Magic Kingdom takes about 10 minutes each way, plus waiting for the train.

All the other Disney resorts are somewhat isolated. This means you're stuck dining at your hotel unless (1) you have a car or (2) you're content to eat at the theme parks or Disney Springs.

7. AMENITIES AND RECREATION Disney resorts provide elaborate swimming pools, themed shops, restaurants or food courts, nightclubs or lounges, and access to five Disney golf courses. The more you pay for your lodging, the more amenities and opportunities are at your disposal. **Animal Kingdom Lodge & Villas, BoardWalk Inn, Wilderness Lodge,** and the **Contemporary, Grand Floridian, Polynesian Village,** and **Yacht & Beach Club Resorts,** for example, all offer concierge floors.

For swimming and sunning, the **Contemporary, Bay Lake Tower,** the **Polynesian Village & Villas, Wilderness Lodge & Villas,** and the **Grand Floridian & Villas** offer both pools and white-sand nonswimming beaches on Bay Lake or Seven Seas Lagoon. **Caribbean Beach Resort,** the **Dolphin,** and the **Yacht & Beach Club** also provide both pools and nonswimming beaches. Though lacking a lakefront beach, **Saratoga Springs Resort & Spa, Animal Kingdom Lodge & Villas, Port Orleans** and **Coronado Springs** resorts, and **BoardWalk Inn & Villas** have exceptionally creative pools.

Bay Lake and Seven Seas Lagoon are the best venues for boating. Resorts fronting these lakes are the **Contemporary** and **Bay Lake Tower, Polynesian Village & Villas, Wilderness Lodge & Villas, Grand Floridian & Villas,** and **Fort Wilderness Resort & Campground.** Though on smaller bodies of water, the **Dolphin** and the **Yacht & Beach Club** also rent watercraft.

Most convenient for golf are **Shades of Green, Saratoga Springs, Old Key West, Contemporary–Bay Lake Tower,** the **Polynesian,** the **Grand Floridian & Villas,** and **Port Orleans.**

While there are many places to bike or jog at Disney World (including golf-cart paths), the best biking and jogging are at **Fort Wilderness Resort & Campground** and the adjacent **Wilderness Lodge & Villas. Caribbean Beach Resort** offers a lovely hiking, biking, and jogging trail around the lake. Also good for biking and jogging is the area along Bonnet Creek extending through **Port Orleans** and **Old Key West** toward Disney Springs. Epcot resorts offer a lakefront promenade and bike path, as well as a roadside walkway suitable for jogging. Of the Value resorts, only **Art of Animation** and **Pop Century** have good jogging options.

On-site child-care programs are offered at **Animal Kingdom Lodge & Villas,** the **Dolphin,** the **Hilton Orlando Lake Buena Vista,** the **Polynesian Village & Villas,** the **Swan, Wilderness Lodge & Villas,** and the **Yacht & Beach Club Resorts.** All other resorts offer in-room babysitting (see pages 101 and 102 for details).

8. NIGHTLIFE The boardwalk at **BoardWalk Inn & Villas** has an upscale dance club (albeit one that has never lived up to its potential), a club featuring dueling pianos and sing-alongs, a brewpub, and a sports bar. The BoardWalk clubs are within easy walking distance of all Epcot resorts. Most non-Disney hotels in the **Downtown Disney Resort Area,** as well as **Saratoga Springs Resort & Spa,** are within walking distance of Disney Springs nightspots. Nightlife at other Disney resorts is limited to lounges that stay open late.

At the Contemporary Resort's **California Grill Lounge,** you can relax over dinner and watch the *Wishes* fireworks show at the nearby Magic Kingdom.

CAMPING AT WALT DISNEY WORLD

DISNEY'S **Fort Wilderness Resort & Campground** is a spacious area for tent and RV camping. Fully equipped, air-conditioned prefabricated log cabins are also available for rent.

Tent/Pop-Up campsites provide water, electricity, and cable TV and run $56–$120 a night depending on season. **Full Hook-Up** campsites have all the previous amenities, accommodate large RVs, and run $78–$145 per night. **Preferred Hook-Up** campsites for tents and RVs add sewer connections and run $89–$158 per night. **Premium** campsites add an extra-large concrete parking pad and run $96–$163 a night. All sites are level and provide picnic tables, waste containers, grills, and free Wi-Fi. Sites are arranged on loops accessible from one of three main roads. There are 28 loops, with Loops 100–2000 for tent and RV campers, and Loops 2100–2800 offering cabins at $336–$562 per night. RV sites are roomy by eastern-US standards, with the Premium and Full Hook-Up campsites able to accommodate RVs more than 45 feet long, but tent campers will probably feel a bit cramped.

The recreational facilities and activities, arguably the most available at any Disney resort, include two video arcades; nightly campfire programs; Disney movies; a dinner theater; two swimming pools; a beach; walking paths; bike, boat, canoe, golf-cart, and water-ski rentals; a petting zoo; horseback riding; hayrides; fishing; and tennis, basketball, and volleyball courts.

Access to the Magic Kingdom is by boat from Fort Wilderness Landing and to Epcot by bus, with a transfer at the Transportation and Ticket Center (TTC) to the Epcot monorail. Boat service may be suspended during thunderstorms, so if it's raining or looks like it's about to, Disney will provide buses. An alternate route to the Magic Kingdom is by internal bus to the TTC, then by monorail or ferry to the park. Transportation to all other Disney destinations is by bus. Motor traffic within the campground is permitted only when entering or exiting. Get around within the campground by bus, golf cart, or bike, the latter two available for rent.

HOTELS *outside* WALT DISNEY WORLD

SELECTING AND BOOKING A HOTEL OUTSIDE WALT DISNEY WORLD

LODGING COSTS OUTSIDE DISNEY WORLD vary incredibly. If you shop around, you can find a clean motel with a pool within 5–20 minutes of the World for as low as $40 a night.

There are four primary out-of-the-World areas to consider:

1. INTERNATIONAL DRIVE AREA This area, about 15–25 minutes northeast of the World, parallels I-4 on its eastern side and offers a

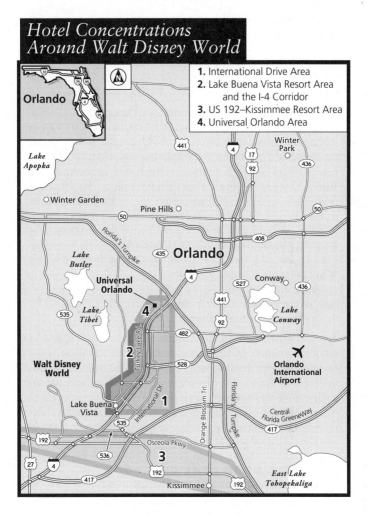

Hotel Concentrations Around Walt Disney World

Orlando

1. International Drive Area
2. Lake Buena Vista Resort Area and the I-4 Corridor
3. US 192–Kissimmee Resort Area
4. Universal Orlando Area

wide selection of hotels and restaurants. Prices range from $56 to $400 per night. The chief drawbacks of this area are its terribly congested roads, countless traffic signals, and inadequate access to westbound I-4. While International's biggest bottleneck is its intersection with Sand Lake Road, the mile between Kirkman and Sand Lake Roads is almost always gridlocked.

I-Drive hotels are listed in the **Orlando Official Visitors Guide,** published by Visit Orlando. To obtain a copy, call ☎ 800-972-3304 or 407-363-5872, or check **visitorlando.com.**

2. LAKE BUENA VISTA AND THE I-4 CORRIDOR A number of hotels are along FL 535 and west of I-4 between Disney World and I-4's intersection with Florida's Turnpike. They're easily reached from the interstate and are near many restaurants, including those on International Drive. The *Orlando Official Visitors Guide* (see previous page) lists most of them.

3. US 192 (IRLO BRONSON MEMORIAL HIGHWAY) This is the road to Kissimmee, to the south of Disney World. In addition to large, full-service hotels, there are many small, privately owned motels that are often a good value. Several dozen properties on US 192 are nearer Disney parks than are more expensive hotels inside the World. The number and variety of restaurants on US 192 have increased markedly, compensating for the area's primary short-coming. Locally, US 192 is called Irlo Bronson Memorial Highway. The section to the west of I-4 and the Disney World Maingate is designated Irlo Bronson Memorial Highway West, while the section from I-4 running southeast toward Kissimmee is Irlo Bronson Memorial Highway East.

Hotels along US 192 and in Kissimmee are listed in the ***Kissimmee Visitor's Guide.*** Order a copy by calling ☎ 800-327-9159, or view it online at **floridakiss.com.**

4. UNIVERSAL STUDIOS AREA In the triangular area bordered by I-4 on the southeast, Vineland Road on the north, and Turkey Lake Road on the west are Universal Orlando and the hotels most convenient to it. Running north–south through the middle of the triangle is Kirkman Road, which connects to I-4. On the east side of Kirkman are a number of independent hotels and restaurants. Traffic in this area isn't nearly as congested as on International Drive, and there are good interstate connections in both directions.

GETTING A GOOD DEAL ON A ROOM OUTSIDE WALT DISNEY WORLD

1. ORLANDO MAGICARD This discount program is sponsored by Visit Orlando. Cardholders are eligible for discounts of 12%–50% at about 50 hotels. The Magicard is also good for discounts at some area attractions, three dinner theaters, museums, performing-arts venues, restaurants, shops, and more. Valid for up to six persons, the card isn't available for larger groups or conventions.

To obtain a free Magicard and a list of participating hotels and attractions, call ☎ 800-643-9492 or 407-363-5872. On the web, go to **visitorlando.com/magicard;** the Magicard and accompanying brochure can be printed from a personal computer. If you miss getting one before you leave home, obtain one at the Visit Orlando Official Visitors Center at 8723 International Dr.

When you call for your Magicard, also request the *Orlando Official Visitors Guide.*

2. *HOTELCOUPONS.COM* FLORIDA GUIDE This book of coupons for lodging statewide is free in many restaurants and motels on main highways leading to Florida. Because most travelers make reservations before leaving home, picking up the book en route doesn't help much. To view it online or sign up for a free monthly guide sent by e-mail, visit **hotelcoupons.com.** For a hard copy ($4 for handling, $6 if it's shipped to Canada), call ☎ 800-222-3948 Monday–Friday, 8 a.m.–5 p.m. Eastern time.

3. HOTEL SHOPPING ON THE INTERNET The Internet has become the primary tool for travelers seeking to shop for and book their own air travel, hotels, rental cars, entertainment, and travel packages. It's the best direct-to-consumer distribution channel in history.

Our advice: Shop the web for the lowest room price available, then call your travel agent or the hotel itself to ask if they can beat it. Any savvy reservationist knows that selling you the room directly will both cut the hotel's cost and improve gross margin. If the reservationist can't help you, ask to speak to his or her supervisor. (We've actually had to explain hotel economics to more than a few clueless reservation agents.)

When it comes to travel agents, they have clout based on the volume of business they send to a particular hotel or chain and can usually negotiate a rate even lower than what you've found online. Even if the agent can't beat the price, he or she can often obtain upgrades, preferred views, free breakfasts, and other deal sweeteners.

When we're really hungry for a deal, there are a number of sites that we always check out:

OUR FAVORITE ONLINE HOTEL RESOURCES	
experiencekissimmee.com	Primarily US 192–Kissimmee hotels
hotelcoupons.com	Self-explanatory
mousesavers.com	Best for hotels inside Walt Disney World
orlandoinfo.com	Good info, though not user-friendly for booking
orlandovacation.com	Great rates for condos and home rentals

We scour these sites for unusually juicy hotel deals that meet our criteria: location, quality, price, and amenities. If we find a hotel that fills the bill, we check it out at other websites and comparative travel search engines such as **Kayak** (**kayak.com**) and **Mobissimo** (**mobissimo.com**) to see who has the best rate. Your initial shopping effort should take about 15–20 minutes, faster if you can zero in quickly on a particular hotel.

Now, armed with your insider knowledge of hotel economics, call the hotel or have your travel agent call. Start by asking about specials. If there are none, or if the hotel can't beat the best price you've found on the Internet, share your findings and ask if the hotel can do better. Sometimes you'll be asked for proof of the rate you've discovered online—to be prepared for this possibility, go to the site and enter the dates of your stay, plus the rate you've found to make sure it's available. If it is, print the page with this information and have it handy for your travel agent or for when you call the hotel.

unofficial **TIP**
Always call the hotel's local number, not its national toll-free number. Often, reservation agents at the toll-free number are unaware of local specials.

4. CONDOMINIUM AND VACATION-HOME DEALS The best deals in lodging in the Walt Disney World area are vacation homes and single-owner condos. Prices range from about $65 a night for two-bedroom condos and town homes to $200–$500 a night for three- to seven-bedroom vacation homes. Look for bargains, especially during off-peak periods. Reservations and information can be obtained from the following online resources:

All Star Vacation Homes	allstarvacationhomes.com
#1 Dream Homes	floridadreamhomes.com
Orlando's Finest Vacation Homes	orlandosfinest.com
Last Minute Villas	lastminutevillas.net
Vacation Rental by Owner	vrbo.com
Vacation Rentals 411	vacationrentals411.com
Visit Orlando	visitorlando.com

Disney's Flamingo Crossings

In 2007, right before the global financial meltdown, Disney announced ambitious plans for a new 450-acre, Value-oriented hotel and restaurant complex, just beyond the western edge of the main Disney World property. Plans were quietly dropped when the Great Recession came, but in 2015 construction finally begun on the first two hotels, scheduled to open in early 2016. Both are Marriott brands: **TownePlace Suites,** an extended-stay hotel, and **SpringHill Suites.** These two hotels will be adjacent and share parking, a pool, and a gym. Other planned amenities include batting cages, a basketball court, and a practice field capable of being configured for different sports. Assuming there's a market for these, the developer plans to build up to five more hotels in the same area.

THE BEST HOTELS FOR FAMILIES OUTSIDE WALT DISNEY WORLD

WHAT MAKES A SUPER FAMILY HOTEL? Roomy accommodations, in-room fridge, great pool, complimentary breakfast, child-care options, and programs for kids are a few of the things the *Unofficial Guide* hotel team researched in selecting the top hotels for families from among hundreds of properties in the Disney World area. Some of our picks are expensive, others are more reasonable, and some are a bargain. Regardless of price, be assured that these hotels understand a family's needs.

Though all of the following hotels offer some type of shuttle to the theme parks, some offer very limited service, so call the hotel before you book and ask what the shuttle schedule will be when you visit. Because families, like individuals, have different wants and needs, we haven't ranked the following properties here; they're listed by zone and alphabetically.

International Drive & Universal Areas

CoCo Key Hotel and Water Resort–Orlando ★★★½

7400 International Dr., Orlando; ☎ 407-351-2626 or 877-875-4681; cocokeywaterresort.com

Rate per night $75–$108. **Pools** ★★★★. **Fridge in room** Yes. **Shuttle to parks** Yes (Aquatica, SeaWorld, Universal, Wet 'n Wild). **Maximum number of occupants per room** 4. **Special comments** Daily $24 resort fee for use of the water park; day guests may use the water park for $24.95/person Monday–Friday ($26.95 on weekends and $21.95 for Florida residents).

DESCRIPTION AND COMMENTS CoCo Key is on International Drive, not far from the Universal Orlando theme parks. It combines a tropical-themed hotel with a canopied water park featuring 3 pools and 14 waterslides, as well as poolside food and arcade entertainment. A full-service restaurant serves breakfast and dinner; a food court offers family favorites such as burgers, chicken fingers, and pizza.

A unique feature of the resort is its cashless payment system, much like that on a cruise ship. At check-in, families receive bar-coded wristbands that allow purchased items to be easily charged to their room.

The unusually spacious guest rooms include 37-inch flat-panel TVs, free Wi-Fi, granite showers and countertops, and plenty of accessible outlets for guests' electronics.

DoubleTree by Hilton Orlando at SeaWorld ★★★★½

10100 International Dr., Orlando; ☎ 407-352-1100 or 800-327-0363; doubletreeorlandoidrive.com

Rate per night $129–$179. **Pools** ★★★½. **Fridge in room** Standard in some rooms; available in others for $10/day. **Shuttle to parks** Yes. **Maximum number of occupants per room** 4. **Special comments** Good option if you're visiting SeaWorld or Aquatica. Pets welcome (1 per room, 25-pound limit, $75).

DESCRIPTION AND COMMENTS On 28 lush, tropical acres with a Balinese feel, the DoubleTree is adjacent to SeaWorld and Aquatica water park. The 1,094 rooms and suites—classified as resort or tower—are equally suitable for business travelers or families. We recommend the tower rooms for good views and the resort rooms for maximum convenience. The Bamboo Grille serves steak and seafood along with breakfast; you can also get a quick bite at Bangli Lounge, the deli, or the pool bar. Relax and cool off at one of the three pools (there are three more just for kids), or indulge in a special spa treatment. A fitness center, minigolf course, children's day camp, and game area afford even more diversions. The resort is about a 15-minute drive to Walt Disney World, a 12-minute drive to Universal, or a short walk to SeaWorld.

Nickelodeon Suites Resort ★★★½

14500 Continental Gateway, Orlando; ☎ 407-387-5437 or 877-NICK-111; nickhotel.com

---

Rate per night $149–$209. **Pools ★★★★. Fridge in room** Yes. **Shuttle to parks** Yes. **Maximum number of occupants per room** 8. **Special comments** Daily character breakfast; resort fee of $35/night.

DESCRIPTION AND COMMENTS This resort is as kid-friendly as they come and is sure to please any fan of TV shows the likes of and Nickelodeon characters hang out in the resort's lobby and mall area, greeting kids while parents check in. Guests can choose from among 777 suites—one-bedroom Family Suites and two- and three-bedroom KidSuites—executed in a number of different themes—all very brightly and creatively decorated.

All suites include kitchenettes or full kitchens; also standard are a microwave, fridge, coffeemaker, TV, iron and board, hair dryer, and a safe. KidSuites feature a semiprivate kids' bedroom with bunk or twin beds, pull-out sleeper bed, 32-inch TV, CD player, and activity table. Additional amenities include a high-tech video arcade, Studio Nick—a game-show studio that hosts several game shows a night for the entertainment of a live studio audience, a buffet (kids 3 and younger eat free with a paying adult), a food court offering Subway and other choices, the full-service Nicktoons Cafe (offers character breakfasts), a convenience store, a lounge, a gift shop, a fitness center, a washer and dryer in each courtyard, and a guest-activities desk (buy Disney tickets and get recommendations on babysitting).

Not to be missed—don't worry, your kids won't let you—are the resort's two pools, Oasis and Lagoon. Oasis features a water park complete with water cannons, rope ladders, geysers, and dump buckets, as well as a hot tub for adults (with a view of the rest of the pool to keep an eye on little ones) and a smaller play area for younger kids. Kids will love the huge, zero-depth-entry Lagoon Pool, replete with 400-gallon dump bucket, plus nearby basketball court and nine-hole minigolf course.

Universal's Cabana Bay Beach Resort ★★★★

6550 Adventure Way, Orlando; ☎ 407-503-4000 or 888-464-3617; tinyurl.com/cabanabay

---

Rate per night $119–$210 standard rooms, $174–$294 suites. **Pools ★★★★. Fridge in room** Suites only. **Shuttle to parks** Yes (Universal, SeaWorld, Discovery Cove, Aquatica, and Wet 'n Wild). **Maximum number of occupants per room** 4 for standard rooms, 6 for suites.

DESCRIPTION AND COMMENTS Opened in spring 2014, Cabana Bay is Universal's first on-site hotel aimed at the value and moderate markets. The theme is midcentury modern, with lots of windows, bright colors, and period-appropriate lighting and furniture. We think the resort would be right at home in the deserts of Palm Springs or Las Vegas.

Whatever Cabana Bay reminds you of, we think you'll like it. Kids will love the two large and well-themed pools (one with a lazy river), the amount of space they have to run around in, the video arcade, and the vintage cars parked outside the hotel lobby. Adults will appreciate the sophisticated kitsch of the decor, the multiple lounges, the business center, and the on-site Starbucks. Cabana Bay is an excellent choice for price- and/or space-conscious families visiting Universal.

Like Disney's Art of Animation Resort (the resort's closest competitor), Cabana Bay has standard rooms and family suites. At 430 square feet per suite, Cabana Bay suites are about 135 square feet smaller than comparable suites at A of A and have only one bathroom. We found them well appointed for two to four people per room (though not for the six Loews claims as its capacity). Rack rates for the suites are about $140–$300 per night less than Art of Animation's.

Each family suite has a small bedroom with two queen beds, divided from the living area and kitchenette by a sliding screen; a foldout sofa in the living area offers additional sleeping space. (Standard rooms also have two queen beds.) The bath is divided into three sections: toilet, sink area, and shower room with additional sink. The kitchenette has a microwave, coffeemaker, and mini-fridge. A bar area allows extra seating for quick meals, and a large closet has enough space to store everyone's luggage. Built-in USB charging outlets for your devices are a thoughtful touch.

Recreational options include the 10-lane Galaxy Bowl (about $15 per person with shoe rental), poolside table tennis and billiards, and a large Jack LaLanne fitness center. (Fitness centers aren't found at any Disney Value or Moderate resort except Coronado Springs.) Outdoor movies are shown nightly near the pool. We're also told that Cabana Bay guests can use the pools at the other three Universal hotels.

In addition to the Starbucks, a food court with seating area shows 1950s TV clips. Swizzle Lounge in the lobby, two pool bars, in-room pizza delivery, and the Galaxy Bowl round out the on-site dining options. You'll find more restaurants and clubs nearby at the Royal Pacific Resort and Universal CityWalk.

Unlike the other Universal resorts, Cabana Bay offers no watercraft service to the parks—it's either take the bus or walk. In November 2014, a new pedestrian bridge opened connecting Cabana Bay to CityWalk and the rest of Universal Orlando, but we still recommend the bus service for most people. Cabana Bay guests are eligible for early entry at Universal but do not get a complimentary Universal Express pass.

Universal's Hard Rock Hotel   ★★★★½

5800 Universal Blvd., Orlando; ☎ 407-503-2000 or 888-464-3617; hardrockhotelorlando.com

Rate per night $259–$464. **Pool** ★★★★. **Fridge in room** Yes. **Shuttle to parks** Yes (Universal, SeaWorld, Discovery Cove, Aquatica, and Wet 'n Wild). **Maximum number of occupants per room** 5 (double-queen) or 3 (king). **Special comments** Microwaves available for $15/day. Character dinner on Saturday. Pets welcome ($50/night).

DESCRIPTION AND COMMENTS Opened in 2001, the Hard Rock is both Universal Orlando's least-expensive on-site resort and the closest resort to Universal's theme parks. The exterior has a California Mission theme, with white stucco walls, arched entryways, and rust-colored roof tiles. Inside, the lobby is a tribute to rock-and-roll style, all marble, chrome, and stage lighting. The eight floors hold 650 rooms and 29 suites, with the rooms categorized into standard, deluxe, and club-level tiers.

The Hard Rock Hotel completed a top-to-bottom "remastering" of its rooms in early 2015, giving the formerly masculine decor a major makeover, with light-gray walls and linens, pastel furniture, and colorful retro-inspired accents. We rate these renovated rooms at Hard Rock slightly ahead of the more-expensive Portofino Bay's (see next profile).

Standard rooms are 375 square feet and furnished with two queen beds, with plush linens and more pillows than you'll know what to do with. Amenities include a flat-panel LCD television, refrigerator, coffee-maker, and an alarm clock with a 30-pin iPhone docking port.

Deluxe rooms with king beds are around 500 square feet and can accommodate up to three people with an optional rollaway bed rental. These rooms feature a U-shaped sitting area in place of the second bed, and the rest of the amenities are the same as in standard rooms. Deluxe queen rooms can hold up to five people using a pullout sofa.

The pool is an attraction unto itself. Situated in the middle of the resort's C-shaped main building, the 12,000-square-foot pool includes a 250-foot waterslide, a sand beach, and underwater speakers so you can hear the music while you swim. Adjacent to the pool are a fountain play area for small children, a sand-volleyball court, hot tubs, and a poolside bar. The Hard Rock also has a fitness center, business center, and video arcade.

On-site dining includes The Kitchen, a casual full-service restaurant open for breakfast, lunch, and dinner, featuring American food such as burgers, steaks, and salads. The Palm Restaurant is an upscale steakhouse available for dinner only. And, of course, the Hard Rock Café is just a short distance away at Universal CityWalk.

Universal's Portofino Bay Hotel ★★★★½

5601 Universal Blvd., Orlando; ☎ 407-503-1000 or 888-464-3617; tinyurl.com/portofinobay

Rate per night $294–$479. **Pools** ★★★★. **Fridge in room** Minibar; fridge available for $15/day. **Shuttle to parks** Yes (Universal, SeaWorld, Discovery Cove, Aquatica, and Wet 'n Wild). **Maximum number of occupants per room** 5 (double-queen) or 3 (king). **Special comments** Character dinner on Friday. Pets welcome ($50/night).

DESCRIPTION AND COMMENTS Universal's top-of-the-line hotel evokes the Italian seaside city of Portofino, complete with a man-made Portofino Bay. Inside, the lobby is decorated with pink marble floors, whitewood columns, and arches.

Portofino Bay was refurbished in 2013. Most guest rooms are 450 square feet and have either one king bed or two queen beds. King rooms sleep up to three people with an optional rollaway bed; the same option allows queen rooms to sleep up to five. Two room-view options are available: "Garden" rooms look out over the landscaping and trees; "bay view" rooms face either west or south and overlook Portofino Bay, with a view of the piazza behind the lobby, too.

Rooms come furnished with a 32-inch LCD flat-panel TV, a refrigerator, a coffeemaker, and an alarm clock with a 30-pin iPhone docking port. Wi-Fi is $15 per day in guest rooms, free in the lobby. Beds are large and comfortable.

Guest bathrooms at Portofino Bay the best on Universal property. The shower has enough water pressure to strip paint from old furniture, not to mention an adjustable spray nozzle that varies the water pulses to simulate everything from monsoon season in the tropics to the rhythmic thumps of wildebeest hooves during migrating season. We love it.

Portofino Bay has three pools, the largest of which is the Beach Pool, on the west side of the resort. It has a zero-entry design and a waterslide themed after a Roman aqueduct, plus a children's play area, hot tubs, and a poolside bar and grill. The Villa Pool has private cabana rentals for that Italian Riviera feeling. Rounding out the luxuries are a full-service Mandara Spa and a complete fitness center with weight machines, treadmills, and more.

On-site dining includes three sit-down restaurants serving Italian cuisine; a deli; a pizzeria; and a café serving coffee and gelato. Perhaps because Universal figures that most guests have an expense account, some of the food prices go well beyond what we'd consider reasonable, even for a theme park hotel.

Universal's Royal Pacific Resort ★★★★½

6300 Hollywood Way, Orlando; ☎ 407-503-1000 or 888-464-3617; tinyurl.com/royal pacific

Rate per night $234–$404. **Pools ★★★★. Fridge in room** Yes. **Shuttle to parks** Yes (Universal, SeaWorld, Discovery Cove, Aquatica, and Wet 'n Wild). **Maximum number of occupants per room** 5 (double-queen) or 3 (king). **Special comments** Character breakfast on Sunday; character dinners on Monday, Wednesday, and Thursday. Pets welcome ($50/night).

DESCRIPTION AND COMMENTS The Royal Pacific's South Seas–inspired theming is both relaxing and structured. You enter the lobby from a walkway two stories above an artificial stream that surrounds the resort. Once you're inside, the lobby's dark teak-wood accents contrast nicely with the enormous amount of light coming in from the windows and three-story A-frame roof. Palms line the walkway through the lobby.

The 1,000 rooms are spread among three Y-shaped wings attached to the resort's main building. Standard rooms, at 335 square feet, have one king or two queen beds. King rooms sleep up to three people with an optional rollaway bed; queen rooms sleep five with that rollaway bed.

The rooms and hallways of Royal Pacific's first tower were refurbished in 2015, and the remainder will be done by early 2016, with modern monochrome wall treatments and carpets, accented with boldly colored floral graphics. Rooms include a 32-inch flat-panel LCD TV, a refrigerator, a coffeemaker, and an alarm clock with a 30-pin iPhone docking port. Other amenities include a small desk with two chairs, a comfortable reading chair, a chest of drawers, and a large closet. Wi-Fi is $15 per day in guest rooms, free in the lobby.

Guests in north- and west-facing rooms in Tower 1 are closest to attractions at Islands of Adventure. East-facing rooms in Towers 1 and 2 are exposed to traffic noise from Universal Boulevard and, more distantly, I-4. Quietest are south-facing pool-view rooms in Tower 1 and south-facing rooms in Tower 3.

As at the Hard Rock, the Royal Pacific's zero-entry pool includes a sand beach, volleyball court, play area for kids, hot tub, and cabanas for rent, plus a poolside bar and grill.

The Royal Pacific includes a 5,000-square-foot fitness facility, two full-service restaurants, three bars, and a luau. The Islands Dining Room is open for breakfast. Emeril Lagasse's Tchoup Chop, the other table-service option, serves Asian-inspired food; it's open for lunch and dinner (reservations recommended).

Universal's Sapphire Falls Resort *(opening 2016)*

6601 Adventure Way, Orlando; ☎ 407-503-5000 or 888-464-3617; loewshotels.com/sapphire-falls-hotel

DESCRIPTION AND COMMENTS Universal's fifth on-site Loews hotel, Sapphire Falls Resort, seeks to bring a sunny Caribbean island vibe to the moderate-price market when its 1,000 rooms open in summer 2016. Sandwiched between Royal Pacific and Cabana Bay—both physically and pricewise—Sapphire Falls will sport all of the amenities of Universal's three Deluxe hotels, including water taxi transportation to the parks, with the crucial exception of complimentary Express Passes.

Water figures heavily at Sapphire Falls, whose namesake waterfalls form the scenic centerpiece of the resort. The zero-entry main pool features a white-sand beach, waterslide, children's play areas, fire pit, and cabanas for rent. A fitness room holds a sauna and hot tub. For dinner, Amatista Cookhouse offers table-service Caribbean dining, with an open kitchen and waterfront views. Club Katine serves tapas-style small plates near the pool bar's fire pit. New Dutch Trading Co. is an island-inspired grab-and-go marketplace, and Strong Water Tavern in the lobby has rum tastings and tableside ceviche.

Sapphire Falls also contains 131,000 square feet of meeting space and a business center. Covered walkways connect to a parking structure, which in turn connects to the meeting facilities at Royal Pacific, making the new sister properties ideal for conventions.

The rooms range from 364 square feet in a standard queen or king to 529 square feet in the 36 Kids' Suites, up to 1,358 square feet in the 15 Hospitality Suites. All rooms have a 49-inch flat-panel HDTV, mini-fridge, and coffeemaker.

Universal will begin accepting reservations in the spring of 2016. At press time, no official pricing information was available, but we expect rack rates to be between those of Royal Pacific and Cabana Bay.

Lake Buena Vista and I-4 Corridor

B Resort ★★★½

1905 Hotel Plaza Blvd., Lake Buena Vista; ☎ 407-828-2828 or 800-66-BHOTELS; bresortlvb.com

Rate per night $135–$172. **Pools** ★★★½. **Fridge in room** Yes. **Shuttle to parks** Yes (Disney only). **Maximum number of occupants per room** 4 plus child in crib. **Special comments** $20/night resort fee.

DESCRIPTION AND COMMENTS B Resorts, a Florida hotel chain, relaunched the former Royal Plaza in the summer of 2014 after an extensive multiyear renovation. Located within walking distance of shops and restaurants and situated 5 miles or less from the Disney parks, the 394-room hotel targets couples, families, groups, and business travelers.

Decorated in cool blues, whites, and grays, guest rooms and suites afford views of downtown Orlando, area lakes, and theme parks. Along with B Resorts–exclusive Blissful Beds, each room is outfitted with sleek modern furnishings and a large interactive flat-screen TV. Additional touches include a mini-fridge and gaming consoles (available on request). Some rooms are also equipped with bunk beds, kitchenettes, or wet bars.

Our most recent stay at the B Resort was in early 2015, and we enjoyed it quite a bit. Our standard room was spotlessly clean, and the room decor is fun without being faddy. The bathroom is spacious, with plenty of storage. The glass shower is well-designed and has good water pressure. There's absolutely nothing wrong with this hotel at this price point, except for the terrible traffic you have to endure every night because of Disney Springs. And that's a shame because it's not the hotel's doing. But if the B were on the other side of Disney Springs, we'd gladly stay here again.

Amenities include free Wi-Fi, a spa, beauty salon, and fitness center. The main restaurant, American Q, serves a modern upscale take on classic barbecue in regional styles ranging from Carolina to Kansas City. Hungry guests can also choose from a poolside bar and grill; The Pickup, a grab-and-go shop just off the lobby that serves quick breakfasts, snacks, picnic lunches, and ice cream; and 24/7 in-room dining.

Other perks: a zero-entry pool with interactive water features; a kids' area; loaner iPads; Monscierge, a digital touchscreen concierge and destination guide in the lobby; and more than 25,000 square feet of meeting and multiuse space. Though not served by Disney transportation, B Resort provides bus service to the parks and other Disney World venues. A resort fee of $22.50 per day applies.

Buena Vista Palace Hotel & Spa ★★★½

1900 E. Buena Vista Dr., Lake Buena Vista; ☎ 407-827-2727 or 866-397-6516; buenavistapalace.com

Rate per night $121–$226. **Pools** ★★★½. **Fridge in room** Yes. **Shuttle to parks** Yes (Disney only). **Maximum number of occupants per room** 4. **Special comments** Sunday character brunch available; $22/night resort fee..

DESCRIPTION AND COMMENTS In the Downtown Disney Resort Area, the Buena Vista Palace is upscale and convenient. Surrounded by an artificial lake and plenty of palms, the spacious pool area contains three heated pools, the largest of which is partially covered (nice for when you need a little shade); a whirlpool and sauna; a basketball court; and a sand-volleyball court. Plus, a pool concierge will fetch your favorite magazine or fruity drink. On Sunday, the Watercress Café hosts a Disney-character brunch ($25 for adults and $12 for children).

The 897 guest rooms are posh and spacious; each comes with a desk, coffeemaker, hair dryer, satellite TV with pay-per-view movies, iron and board, and minifridge. There are also 117 suites. In-room babysitting is available through All About Kids. One lighted tennis court, the sumptuous Kay Casperson Lifestyle Spa, a fitness center, an arcade, and a playground round out the amenities. Two restaurants and a mini-market are on-site. And if you aren't wiped out after time in the parks, drop by the Lobby Lounge or the full-menu sports bar for a nightcap. Be aware that all these amenities and services come at a price—a $22-per-night resort fee is added to your bill.

Four Seasons Resort Orlando at
Walt Disney World Resort ★★★★★

10100 Dream Tree Blvd., Golden Oak; ☎ 407-313-7777 or 800-267-3046;
fourseasons.com/orlando

Rate per night $545–$845. **Pools** ★★★★★. **Fridge in room** Yes. **Shuttle to
parks** Yes (Disney only). **Maximum number of occupants per room** 4 (3 adults
or 2 adults and 2 children). **Special comments** The best pool complex in Walt
Disney World.

DESCRIPTION AND COMMENTS At 444 guest rooms, the Four Seasons
Resort Orlando is simultaneously the largest hotel in the Four Seasons
chain and the smallest on Disney property. Its comfort, amenities, and
personal service far surpass anything Disney's Deluxes offer..

Standard guest rooms average around 500 square feet and feature
either one king bed with a sleeper sofa or two double beds (a crib is
available in double rooms). Amenities include two flat-panel televisions, a
coffeemaker, a small refrigerator, a work desk with two chairs, a personal
digital video recorder (DVR) to record TV shows, and Bluetooth speakers
for your personal audio. In keeping with the room's gadget-friendly spirit,
each nightstand has four electrical outlets and two USB ports.

Bathrooms have glass-walled showers, a separate tub, marble vani-
ties with two sinks, mosaic-tile floors, hair dryers, lighted mirrors, and a
TV in the mirror above the sink.

Most rooms have an 80-square-foot balcony with table and chairs—
perfect for your morning coffee or evening nightcap. Standard-view rooms
look out onto the resort's lawns, gardens, and nearby homes in Golden
Oak. Lake-view rooms—which overlook the lake, the Tom Fazio–designed
Tranquilo Golf Club, or the pool—cost about $100 more per night than
standard-view rooms. Park-view rooms, on floors 6–16, cost about $200
more per night than standard-view rooms and offer views of the Magic
Kingdom's nightly fireworks. (Suites are available with views of Epcot, too.)

The resort's 5-acre pool area is the best on Walt Disney World property, and the least crowded. It features an adult pool, a family pool, an
11,000-square-foot lazy river, and a splash zone with two 242-foot waterslides. Private pool cabanas are available for rent (around $200/day).

Capa, a Spanish-themed rooftop restaurant, serves seafood and
steaks (open nightly, 6–10 p.m.; dress is resort casual, and reservations
are recommended). Ravello, on the first floor, serves American breakfasts (6:30–11 a.m.) and Italian dinners (5:30–10 p.m.; reservations are
recommended, and dress is smart casual). PB&G (Pool Bar and Grill)
serves barbecued meats and salads by the main pool (11 a.m.–6 p.m.).

The hotel has a full-service spa and fitness center, as well as a beautiful late-checkout lounge that allows use of the showers and bathrooms
in the spa. At the Disney Planning Center, Disney cast members can help
with reservations or other Disney needs. Disney will also deliver your
in-park purchases to the Four Seasons, but staying at the Four Seasons
does not qualify guests for Extra Magic Hours, 60-day FastPass+ reservations, or use of Disney's Magical Express from the airport.

Service is excellent at the Four Seasons. About 25% of the staff
transferred from other Four Seasons properties, bringing years of experience and knowledge to this resort. On one visit, the front desk recep-
tionist walked us to our room after check-in, and we were often greeted
by name as we walked through the resort.

Hilton Orlando Lake Buena Vista ★★★★

1751 Hotel Plaza Blvd.; ☎ 407-827-4000; hilton-wdwv.com

Rate per night $161–$241. **Pools** ★★★½. **Fridge in room** Minibar; mini-fridge available free on request. **Shuttle to parks** Yes (Disney theme and water parks only). **Maximum number of occupants per room** 4. **Special comments** Sunday character breakfast; $22/night resort fee.

DESCRIPTION AND COMMENTS Although the Hilton's fees are outrageous and its decor is dated, the rooms are comfortable and nicer than some others in the DDRA. On-site dining includes Covington Mill Restaurant, offering sandwiches and pasta (plus a Disney-character breakfast on Sundays), and Benihana, a Japanese steakhouse and sushi bar. The two pools are matched with a children's spray pool and a 24-hour fitness center. An exercise room and a game room are on-site, as is a 24-hour market. Babysitting is available, but there are no organized kid's programs.

Hilton Orlando Bonnet Creek ★★★★

14100 Bonnet Creek Resort Lane, Orlando; ☎ 407-597-3600; hiltonbonnetcreek.com

Rate per night $119–$249. **Pool** ★★★★½. **Fridge in room** Yes. **Shuttle to parks** Yes. **Maximum number of occupants per room** 4. **Special comments** $22/night resort fee.

DESCRIPTION AND COMMENTS The Hilton Bonnet Creek is one of our favorite non-Disney hotels in Lake Buena Vista, and the value for the money beats anything in Disney's Deluxe category. Behind Disney's Caribbean Beach and Pop Century Resorts, this Hilton is much nicer than the one in the Downtown Disney Resort Area.

Standard rooms measure around 414 square feet—comparable to Disney's Deluxe resorts—and have either one king bed or two queen beds. The beds' mattresses and linens are very comfortable. Other features include a 37-inch flat-panel TV, a spacious work desk, an armoire, a small reading chair with floor lamp, a nightstand, and a digital clock. A coffeemaker, small refrigerator, ironing board, and iron are all standard, along with free wired and wireless Internet.

Bathrooms include tile floors with glass showers and a hairdryer. Unfortunately, the layout isn't as up-to-date as other hotels'—where many upscale hotel bathrooms have two sinks (so two people can primp at once), the Hilton's has only one. And where modern bathroom configurations often include a dressing area separate from the bath and a separate water closet for the commode, everything is in the bathroom here. That makes it harder for four-person families to get ready in the morning.

The Hilton's public areas are stylish and spacious. Families will enjoy the huge zero-entry pool, complete with waterslide, as well as the 3-acre lazy river. Even better, the Hilton staff run arts-and-crafts activities poolside during the day, allowing parents to grab a quick swim and a cocktail. Pool-facing cabanas are also available for rent at around $300 per day or $150 per half-day. If you're trying to stay in swimsuit shape, a nice fitness center sits on the ground floor.

The Hilton participates in the Waldorf Astoria's Kids Club next door, for children ages 5–12. A daytime program is available 10:30 a.m.–2:30 p.m., and an evening program is available 6–10 p.m. on Friday and Saturday. Price is $75 for the first child, $25 for each additional child.

There are more than a dozen restaurants and lounges between the Hilton and the Waldorf Astoria, with cuisine including an upscale steakhouse, Italian, sushi, tapas, a coffee bar, an American bistro, and breakfast buffet choices. Breakfast hours usually run 7–11:30 a.m., lunch 11:30 a.m.–5 p.m., and dinner 5–10 p.m. Reservations are recommended for the fancy places.

Marriott Village at Lake Buena Vista ★★★

8623 Vineland Ave., Orlando; ☎ 407-938-9001 or 800-761-7829; marriottvillage.com

Rate per night $74–$189. **Pools** ★★★. **Fridge in room** Yes. **Shuttle to parks** Disney only, $7. **Maximum number of occupants per room** 4 (Courtyard and Fairfield) or 5 (SpringHill). **Special comments** Free Continental breakfast at Fairfield and SpringHill.

DESCRIPTION AND COMMENTS This gated hotel community includes a 388-room Fairfield Inn, a 400-suite SpringHill Suites, and a 312-room Courtyard. Amenities at all three properties include fridge, cable TV, iron and board, hair dryer, and microwave. Cribs and roll-away beds are available at no extra charge at all locations. Swimming pools at all three hotels are attractive and medium-sized, featuring children's interactive splash zones and whirlpools; in addition, each property has its own fitness center. The incredibly convenient Village Marketplace food court includes Pizza Hut, Village Grill, and Village Coffee House, along with a 24-hour convenience store. Other services and amenities include a Disney planning station and ticket sales, an arcade, and a Hertz car-rental desk. Shoppers will find the Orlando Premium Outlets adjacent.

Sheraton Vistana Resort Villas ★★★★½

8800 Vistana Centre Dr., Lake Buena Vista; ☎ 407-239-3100 or 866-208-0003; sheraton.com

Rate per night $127–$254. **Pools** ★★★½. **Fridge in room** Yes. **Shuttle to parks** Yes (Disney free; other parks for a fee). **Maximum number of occupants per room** 4–8. **Special comments** Though time-shares, the villas are also rented nightly.

DESCRIPTION AND COMMENTS The Vistana is one of Orlando's best off-Disney properties. The spacious villas come in one-bedroom, two-bedroom, and two-bedroom-with-lock-off models (which can be reconfigured as one studio room and a one-bedroom suite). All are decorated in beachy pastels, but the emphasis is on the profusion of amenities.

Each villa has a full kitchen (including fridge/freezer, microwave, oven/range, dishwasher, toaster, and coffeemaker, with an option to prestock with groceries and laundry products), clothes washer and dryer, TVs in the living room and each bedroom (one with DVD player), stereo with CD player in some villas, separate dining area, and private patio or balcony in most. Grounds offer seven swimming pools (three with bars), four playgrounds, two restaurants, game rooms, fitness centers, a minigolf course, sports equipment rental (including bikes), and courts for basketball, volleyball, tennis, and shuffleboard. A mind-boggling array of activities for kids (and adults) ranges from crafts to games and sports tournaments. Of special note: Vistana is highly secure, with locked gates bordering all guest areas, so children can have the run of the place without parents worrying about them wandering off.

Waldorf Astoria Orlando ★★★★½

14200 Bonnet Creek Resort Lane, Lake Buena Vista; ☎ 407-597-5500; waldorfastoriaorlando.com

Rate per night $234–$424. **Pool** ★★★★. **Fridge in room** Yes. **Shuttle to parks** Yes (Disney only) **Maximum number of occupants per room** 4, plus child in crib. **Special comments** Good alternative to Disney Deluxe resorts; $30/night resort fee.

DESCRIPTION AND COMMENTS The Waldorf Astoria is between I-4 and Disney's Pop Century Resort, near the Hilton Orlando at the back of the Bonnet Creek Resort property. Getting here requires a GPS or good directions, but once you arrive, however, you'll know the trip was worth it. Beautifully decorated and well manicured, the Waldorf is more elegant than any Disney resort. Service is excellent, and the staff-to-guest ratio is far lower than at Disney properties.

At just under 450 square feet, standard rooms feature either two queen beds or one king. A full-size desk allows you to get work done if it's absolutely necessary, and rooms also have flat-screen televisions, high-speed Internet, and Wi-Fi. The bathrooms are spacious and gorgeous, with cool marble floors, glass-walled showers, separate tubs, and enough counter space for a Broadway makeup artist. This space is so nice that when we stayed here in 2009, we debated whether we'd rather stay at Pop Century with three others or sleep in a Waldorf bathroom by ourselves.

Amenities include a fitness center, a spa, a golf course, six restaurants, and two pools (including one zero-entry for kids). Pool-size cabanas are available for rent. The resort offers shuttle service to the Disney parks about every half-hour, but check with the front desk for the exact schedule when you arrive.

Wyndham Bonnet Creek Resort ★★★★½

9560 Via Encinas, Lake Buena Vista; ☎ 407-238-3500 or 888-743-2687; wyndhambonnetcreek.com

Rate per night $229–$359. **Pool** ★★★★. **Fridge in room** Yes. **Shuttle to parks** Yes (Disney only). **Maximum number of occupants per room** 4–12 depending on room/suite. **Special comments** A non-Disney suite hotel within Disney World.

DESCRIPTION AND COMMENTS This condo hotel lies on the south side of Buena Vista Drive, about a quarter-mile east of Disney's Caribbean Beach Resort. It's part of the Bonnet Creek Resort, a hotel, golf, and convention complex that also includes a 500-room Waldorf Astoria (see above), a 400-room Wyndham Grand, and a 1,000-room Hilton. The development is surrounded on three sides by Disney property and on one side by I-4.

The Wyndham Bonnet Creek offers upscale, family-friendly accommodations: one- and two-bedroom condos with fully equipped kitchens, washer-dryers, jetted tubs, and balconies. Activities and amenities on-site include two outdoor swimming pools, a "lazy river" float stream, a children's activities program, a game room, a playground, and miniature golf. Free scheduled transportation serves all the Disney parks. One-bedroom units are equipped with a king bed in the bedroom and a sleeper sofa in the living area; two-bedroom condos have two double beds in the second bedroom, a sleeper sofa in the living area, and an additional bath.

US 192

Clarion Suites Maingate ★★★½

7888 W. Irlo Bronson Memorial Hwy., Kissimmee; ☎ 407-390-9888 or 888-390-9888; clarionsuiteskissimmee.com

Rate per night $99–$169. **Pool** ★★★. **Fridge in room** Yes. **Shuttle to parks** Yes (Disney, Universal, and SeaWorld). **Maximum number of occupants per room** 6 for most suites. **Special comments** Free Continental breakfast served daily for up to two guests; additional breakfast $5.99 advance, $6.99 day of.

DESCRIPTION AND COMMENTS This property has 150 spacious one-room suites, each with double sofa bed, microwave, fridge, coffeemaker, TV, hair dryer, and safe. The suites are clean and contemporary, with muted deep-purple and beige tones. The large, heated pool has plenty of lounge chairs and moderate landscaping. A kiddie pool, whirlpool, and poolside bar complete the courtyard. Other amenities include an arcade and a gift shop. But Maingate's big plus is its location next door to a shopping center with about everything a family could need. There, you'll find dining options that include Outback Steakhouse, Red Lobster, Subway, and T.G.I. Friday's; a Winn-Dixie Marketplace; a bank; a dry cleaner; and a tourist-information center with park passes for sale, among other services.

Gaylord Palms Resort & Convention Center ★★★★

6000 W. Osceola Pkwy., Kissimmee; ☎ 407-586-2000; gaylordpalms.com

Rate per night $257–$283. **Pool** ★★★★. **Fridge in room** Yes. **Shuttle to parks** Yes (Disney only). **Maximum number of occupants per room** 4. **Special comments** Probably the closest you'll get to Disney-level extravagance out of the World. Resort fee of $20/day.

DESCRIPTION AND COMMENTS This decidedly upscale resort has a colossal convention facility and caters strongly to business clientele, but it's still a nice (if pricey) family resort.

Hotel wings are defined by the three themed, glass-roofed atriums they overlook. Key West's design is reminiscent of island life in the Florida Keys; Everglades is an overgrown spectacle of shabby swamp chic, complete with piped-in cricket noise and a robotic alligator; and the immense, central St. Augustine harks back to Spanish Colonial Florida. Lagoons, streams, and waterfalls cut through and connect all three, and walkways and bridges abound.

Rooms reflect the colors of their respective areas, though there's no particular connection in decor. A fourth wing, Emerald Bay Tower, over-looks the Emerald Plaza shopping and dining area of the St. Augustine atrium. These rooms are the nicest and the most expensive, and they're mostly used by convention-goers.

Rooms have fridges and alarm clocks with CD players (as well as other perks such as high-speed Internet access). Children will enjoy wandering the themed areas and playing in the family pool (with water-squirting octopus). in-room child care is provided by Kid's Nite Out.

Orange Lake Resort ★★★★½

8505 W. Irlo Bronson Memorial Hwy., Kissimmee; ☎ 407-239-0000 or 800-877-6522; orangelake.com

Rate per night $107–$159. **Pools** ★★★★. **Fridge in room** Yes. **Shuttle to parks** Yes (fee varies depending on destination). **Maximum number of occupants per room** Varies. **Special comments** This is a time-share property, but if you rent directly through the resort as opposed to the sales office, you can avoid time-share sales pitches; $8/night resort fee.

DESCRIPTION AND COMMENTS You could spend your entire vacation never leaving this property, about 6–10 minutes from the Disney theme parks. From its 10 pools and 2 mini–water parks to its golfing opportunities (36 holes of championship greens plus two 9-hole executive courses), Orange Lake offers an extensive menu of amenities and recreational opportunities. If you tire of lazing by the pool, try waterskiing, wakeboarding, tubing, fishing, or other activities on the 80-acre lake. There's also a live alligator show, exercise programs, organized competitive sports and games, arts-and-crafts sessions, and miniature golf. Activities don't end when the sun goes down. Karaoke, live music, a Hawaiian luau, and movies at the resort cinema are some of the evening options.

The 2,412 units are tastefully decorated and comfortably furnished, ranging from suites and studios to three-bedroom villas, all containing fully equipped kitchens. Seven restaurants are scattered across the resort: two cafes, three grills, one pizzeria, and a fast-food eatery. If you need help with (or a break from) the kids, babysitters are available.

HOTELS *and* MOTELS:
Rated and Ranked

IN THIS SECTION, WE COMPARE HOTELS in four main areas outside Walt Disney World with those inside the World.

ROOM RATINGS

TO EVALUATE PROPERTIES FOR THEIR QUALITY, tastefulness, state of repair, cleanliness, and size of their standard rooms, we have grouped the hotels and motels into classifications denoted by stars—the overall star rating. Our ratings are tied to expected levels of quality established by specific American hotel corporations.

Overall star ratings apply only to room quality and describe the property's standard accommodations. For most hotels, a standard accommodation is a room with one king bed or two queen beds. In an all-suite property, the standard accommodation is either a studio or one-bedroom suite. Star ratings for rooms are assigned without regard to whether a property has restaurant(s), recreational facilities, entertainment, or other extras.

In addition to stars (which delineate broad categories), we use a numerical rating system—the room-quality rating. Our scale is 0–100, with 100 being the best possible rating and zero (0) the worst. Numerical ratings show the difference we perceive between one property and another. For instance, rooms at both the Stay Sky Suites I-Drive Orlando and the Clarion Suites Maingate are rated three and a half stars (★★★½). In the supplemental numerical ratings, the former is an 82 and the latter a 76. This means that within the ★★★½ category, Stay Sky Suites has slightly nicer rooms than Clarion Suites.

The location column identifies the area around Walt Disney World where you'll find a particular property. The designation **WDW** means the property is inside Walt Disney World. A **1** means it's on or near International Drive. Properties on or near US 192 (a.k.a. Irlo Bronson Memorial Highway) are indicated by a **3,** those in the vicinity of Universal Orlando as **4.** All others are marked with **2** and for the most part are along FL 535 and the I-4 corridor, though some are in nearby locations that don't meet any other criteria.

OVERALL STAR RATINGS		
★★★★★	Superior rooms	Tasteful and luxurious by any standard
★★★★	Extremely nice rooms	What you'd expect at a Hyatt Regency or Marriott
★★★	Nice rooms	Holiday Inn or comparable quality
★★	Adequate rooms	Clean, comfortable, and functional without frills—like a Motel 6
★	Super-budget	These exist but are not included in our coverage

Cost estimates are based on the hotel's published rack rates for standard rooms. Each **$** represents $50. Thus a cost symbol of **$$$** means that a room (or suite) at that hotel will be about $150 a night; for space, rates of $250+ are indicated by **$ x 5** and so on.

We've focused on room quality and excluded consideration of location, services, recreation, or amenities. In some instances, a one- or two-room suite is available for the same price or less than that of a single standard hotel room.

THE 30 BEST HOTEL VALUES

LET'S LOOK AT THE BEST COMBINATIONS of quality and value in a room. Listed opposite are our top 30 buys for the money regardless of location or star rating, based on average rack rates. These rankings were made without consideration for the availability of restaurant(s), recreational facilities, entertainment, and/or other amenities.

A reader recently wrote to complain that he had booked one of our top-ranked rooms for value and had been very disappointed in it. The room had a quality rating of ★★½, but remember that the list of top deals is intended to give you some sense of value received *for dollars spent*. Regardless of whether it's a good deal, a ★★½ room is still a ★★½ room.

THE TOP 30 BEST DEALS

HOTEL	LODGING AREA	OVERALL QUALITY	ROOM QUALITY	($ = $50)
1. Rodeway Inn Maingate	3	★★½	59	$-
2. Monumental Hotel	1	★★★★½	94	$$-
3. Shades of Green	WDW	★★★★½	91	$$-
4. Extended Stay America Orlando Lake Buena Vista	2	★★★★	83	$$-
5. Extended Stay America Convention Center/Westwood	1	★★★★	84	$$-
6. Holiday Inn Main Gate East	3	★★★★½	90	$$+
7. Monumental MovieLand Hotel	1	★★★	68	$+
8. Vacation Village at Parkway	3	★★★★½	91	$$+
9. Motel 6 Orlando–I-Drive	1	★★★	66	$+
10. Westgate Vacation Villas	2	★★★★½	90	$$+
11. Super 8 Kissimmee/Maingate	3	★★★	70	$+
12. Radisson Resort Orlando-Celebration	3	★★★★	86	$$
13. The Inn at Calypso	3	★★★½	82	$$-
14. Westgate Town Center	2	★★★★½	93	$$+
15. Hampton Inn & Suites Orlando–South Lake Buena Vista	3	★★★½	80	$$-
16. Super 8 Kissimmee	3	★★½	60	$-
17. Hilton Grand Vacations Club at SeaWorld	1	★★★★½	95	$$$-
18. Extended Stay America Deluxe Orlando Theme Parks	4	★★★½	75	$$-
19. Extended Stay America Orlando Theme Parks	4	★★★½	75	$$-
20. Hilton Orlando Bonnet Creek	1	★★★★	88	$$+
21. Four Points by Sheraton Orlando Studio City	1	★★★½	90	$$$-
22. Legacy Vacation Club Orlando	3	★★★½	80	$$$-
23. Knights Inn Maingate Kissimmee/Orlando	3	★★★	58	$-
24. Extended Stay America Orlando Convention Center	1	★★★	72	$+
25. Orange Lake Resort	3	★★★★½	94	$$$-
26. La Quinta Inn Orlando I-Drive	1	★★★	73	$$-
27. Barefoot'n Resort	3	★★★★	85	$$+
28. Ramada Convention Center I-Drive	1	★★★	65	$+
29. Celebration Suites	3	★★½	61	$+
30. Galleria Palms Kissimmee Hotel	3	★★★	74	$$-

How the Hotels Compare

HOTEL	LODGING AREA	OVERALL QUALITY	ROOM QUALITY	($ = $50)
Four Seasons Resort Orlando at Walt Disney World Resort	WDW	★★★★★	98	$ x 9
Omni Orlando Resort at ChampionsGate	2	★★★★★	96	$+ x 5
Hilton Grand Vacations Club at SeaWorld	1	★★★★½	95	$$$–
Rosen Centre Hotel	1	★★★★½	95	$$$+
Disney's Animal Kingdom Villas (Kidani Village)	WDW	★★★★½	95	$– x 10
Bay Lake Tower at Disney's Contemporary Resort	WDW	★★★★½	95	$– x 12
Monumental Hotel	1	★★★★½	94	$$–
Orange Lake Resort	3	★★★★½	94	$$$–
Gaylord Palms Hotel & Convention Center	3	★★★★½	94	$$$+
The Ritz-Carlton Orlando, Grande Lakes	1	★★★★½	94	$+ x 5
Westgate Town Center	2	★★★★½	93	$$+
Waldorf Astoria Orlando	2	★★★★½	93	$$$$+
JW Marriott Orlando Grande Lakes	1	★★★★½	93	$+ x 5
Universal's Hard Rock Hotel	4	★★★★½	93	$ x 8
Disney's Contemporary Resort	WDW	★★★★½	93	$+ x 9
The Villas at Disney's Grand Floridian Resort & Spa	WDW	★★★★½	93	$– x 13
Disney's Grand Floridian Resort & Spa	WDW	★★★★½	93	$– x 14
DoubleTree by Hilton Orlando at SeaWorld	1	★★★★½	92	$$$+
Marriott's Grande Vista	1	★★★★½	92	$$$+
Westgate Lakes Resort & Spa	2	★★★★½	92	$$$+
Villas of Grand Cypress	2	★★★★½	92	$– x 5
Hyatt Regency Grand Cypress	2	★★★★½	92	$– x 5
Marriott's Sabal Palms	2	★★★★½	92	$+ x 6
Universal's Portofino Bay Hotel	4	★★★★½	92	$+ x 8
Disney's Polynesian Village, Villas & Bungalows (studios)	WDW	★★★★½	92	$+ x 11
Disney's Polynesian Village Resort	WDW	★★★★½	92	$– x 12
Shades of Green	WDW	★★★★½	91	$$–
Vacation Village at Parkway	3	★★★★½	91	$$+
Disney's Animal Kingdom Villas (Jambo House)	WDW	★★★★½	91	$ x 8
Holiday Inn Main Gate East	3	★★★★½	90	$$+
Westgate Vacation Villas	2	★★★★½	90	$$+
Four Points by Sheraton Orlando Studio City	1	★★★★½	90	$$$–

How the Hotels Compare

HOTEL	LODGING AREA	OVERALL QUALITY	ROOM QUALITY	($ = $50)
Polynesian Isles Resort (Diamond Resorts)	3	★★★★½	90	$$$
Bohemian Celebration Hotel	2	★★★★½	90	$$$+
Renaissance Orlando at SeaWorld	1	★★★★½	90	$$$+
Marriott's Harbour Lake	2	★★★★½	90	$$$$-
Hyatt Regency Orlando	1	★★★★½	90	$$$$-
Lighthouse Key Resort & Spa	3	★★★★½	90	$$$$-
Liki Tiki Village	3	★★★★½	90	$$$$-
Grand Beach	1	★★★★½	90	$$$$-
Walt Disney World Dolphin	WDW	★★★★½	90	$$$$+
Walt Disney World Swan	WDW	★★★★½	90	$$$$+
Orlando World Center Marriott Resort	2	★★★★½	90	$$$$+
Wyndham Bonnet Creek Resort	2	★★★★½	90	$$$$+
Universal's Royal Pacific Resort	4	★★★★½	90	$+ x 6
Disney's Old Key West Resort	WDW	★★★★½	90	$+ x 8
Disney's Saratoga Springs Resort & Spa	WDW	★★★★½	90	$+ x 8
Disney's Beach Club Resort	WDW	★★★★½	90	$+ x 9
The Villas at Disney's Wilderness Lodge	WDW	★★★★½	90	$- x 10
Disney's Beach Club Villas	WDW	★★★★½	90	$- x 10
Disney's BoardWalk Villas	WDW	★★★★½	90	$- x 10
Treehouse Villas at Disney's Saratoga Springs Resort & Spa	WDW	★★★★½	90	$- x 20
DoubleTree Universal	4	★★★★	89	$$$-
Courtyard Orlando Lake Buena Vista at Vista Centre	2	★★★★	89	$$$-
Sheraton Vistana Resort Villas	2	★★★★	89	$$$$-
Disney's Animal Kingdom Lodge	WDW	★★★★	89	$ x 8
Disney's Yacht Club Resort	WDW	★★★★	89	$- x 10
Disney's BoardWalk Inn	WDW	★★★	89	$+ x 10
Hilton Orlando Bonnet Creek	1	★★★★	88	$$+
WorldQuest Orlando Resort	1	★★★★	88	$$$-
Caribe Royale All-Suite Hotel & Convention Center	1	★★★★	88	$$$+
Hilton Garden Inn Lake Buena Vista/ Orlando	2	★★★★	88	$$$+
Hilton Grand Vacations Club on I-Drive	1	★★★★	88	$$$+
Sheraton Lake Buena Vista Resort	2	★★★★	88	$$$+
Universal's Cabana Bay Beach Resort	4	★★★★	88	$$$$-

How the Hotels Compare (continued)

HOTEL	LODGING AREA	OVERALL QUALITY	ROOM QUALITY	($ = $50)
Hilton Orlando Lake Buena Vista	WDW	★★★★	87	$$$-
Mystic Dunes Resort & Golf Club	3	★★★★	87	$$$-
Wyndham Cypress Palms	3	★★★★	87	$$$
Westin Orlando Universal Boulevard	1	★★★★	87	$$$$+
Radisson Resort Orlando-Celebration	3	★★★★	86	$$
Embassy Suites Orlando–LBV Resort	2	★★★★	86	$$$+
Floridays Resort Orlando	1	★★★★	86	$$$$
Marriott's Cypress Harbour	1	★★★★	86	$ x 6
Disney's Fort Wilderness Resort (cabins)	WDW	★★★★	86	$- x 8
Disney's Wilderness Lodge	WDW	★★★★	86	$- x 9
Marriott's Imperial Palms	1	★★★★	86	$- x 9
Barefoot'n Resort	3	★★★★	85	$$+
Hawthorn Suites Lake Buena Vista	2	★★★★	85	$$+
Wyndham Orlando Resort I-Drive	1	★★★★	85	$$+
Residence Inn Orlando at SeaWorld	2	★★★★	85	$$$-
Legacy Vacation Club Lake Buena Vista	2	★★★★	85	$$$-
Homewood Suites by Hilton LBV-Orlando	2	★★★★	85	$$$$-
Marriott's Royal Palms	1	★★★★	85	$- x 6
Extended Stay America Convention Center/Westwood	1	★★★★	84	$$-
Star Island Resort & Club	3	★★★★	84	$$$+
Hyatt Place Orlando/Universal	4	★★★★	84	$$$+
Disney's Port Orleans Resort–French Quarter	WDW	★★★★	84	$- x 5
Extended Stay America Orlando LBV	2	★★★★	83	$$-
Buena Vista Suites	1	★★★★	83	$$$+
Disney's Coronado Springs Resort	WDW	★★★★	83	$- x 5
Disney's Port Orleans Resort-Riverside	WDW	★★★★	83	$- x 5
The Inn at Calypso	3	★★★½	82	$$-
Courtyard Orlando LBV in Marriott Village	2	★★★½	82	$$+
Stay Sky Suites I-Drive Orlando	1	★★★½	82	$$+
CoCo Key Water Resort-Orlando	1	★★★½	82	$$+
The Point Universal Orlando Resort	1	★★★½	82	$$+
Holiday Inn Resort Lake Buena Vista	2	★★★½	82	$$+
Castle Hotel	1	★★★½	82	$$$
Radisson Hotel Orlando Lake Buena Vista	2	★★★½	82	$$$-

How the Hotels Compare (continued)

HOTEL	LODGING AREA	OVERALL QUALITY	ROOM QUALITY	($ = $50)
B Resort	WDW	★★★½	82	$$$+
Nickelodeon Suites Resort	1	★★★½	82	$$$$
Parkway International Resort	3	★★★½	82	$- x 5
Westgate Towers	2	★★★½	81	$$+
Hampton Inn & Suites Orlando–South LBV	3	★★★½	80	$$-
Legacy Vacation Club Orlando	3	★★★½	80	$$$-
Comfort Inn Orlando–Lake Buena Vista	2	★★★½	80	$$
Hilton Garden Inn Orlando I-Drive North	1	★★★½	80	$$+
Hawthorn Suites Orlando Convention Center	1	★★★½	80	$$+
Fairfield Inn & Suites Near Universal Orlando Resort	4	★★★½	80	$$$-
Hilton Garden Inn Orlando at SeaWorld	1	★★★½	80	$$$-
Embassy Suites Orlando I-Drive/Jamaican Court	1	★★★½	80	$$$-
Residence Inn Orlando Convention Center	1	★★★½	80	$$$-
Buena Vista Palace Hotel & Spa	WDW	★★★½	80	$$$-
Disney's Art of Animation Resort	WDW	★★★½	80	$$$$-
SpringHill Suites Orlando Convention Center	1	★★★½	80	$$$$-
Orbit One Vacation Villas	3	★★★½	80	$$$$-
Disney's Caribbean Beach Resort	WDW	★★★½	80	$$$$+
Fairfield Inn & Suites Orlando Lake Buena Vista	2	★★★½	79	$$+
Holiday Inn in the Walt Disney World Resort	WDW	★★★½	79	$$$+
Courtyard Orlando I-Drive	1	★★★½	78	$$+
Park Inn by Radisson Resort and Conference Center	3	★★★½	78	$$$-
Clarion Suites Maingate	3	★★★½	76	$$
The Palms Hotel & Villas	3	★★★½	76	$$+
Grand Lake Resort	1	★★★½	76	$$+
Hampton Inn Orlando/Lake Buena Vista	2	★★★½	76	$$$-
Quality Suites Lake Buena Vista	2	★★★½	76	$$$-
Quality Suites Royale Parc Suites	3	★★★½	76	$$$+
Extended Stay America Deluxe Orlando Theme Parks	4	★★★½	75	$$-
Extended Stay America Orlando Theme Parks	4	★★★½	75	$$-
Best Western Plus Universal Inn	4	★★★½	75	$$-

How the Hotels Compare (continued)

HOTEL	LODGING AREA	OVERALL QUALITY	ROOM QUALITY	($ = $50)
Hawthorn Suites Orlando I-Drive	1	★★★½	75	$$+
Fairfield Inn & Suites Orlando LBV in Marriott Village	2	★★★½	75	$$+
Holiday Inn & Suites Orlando Universal	4	★★★½	75	$$$-
Wyndham Lake Buena Vista Resort	WDW	★★★½	75	$$+
DoubleTree Guest Suites	WDW	★★★½	75	$$$
Residence Inn Orlando Lake Buena Vista	2	★★★½	75	$$$+
Best Western Premier Saratoga Resort Villas	3	★★★½	75	$$$$-
Galleria Palms Kissimmee Hotel	3	★★★	74	$$-
Crown Club Inn	3	★★★	74	$$-
Best Western Lake Buena Vista Resort Hotel	WDW	★★★	74	$$$+
La Quinta Inn Orlando I-Drive	1	★★★	73	$$-
Disney's All-Star Movies Resort	WDW	★★★	73	$$$-
Disney's All-Star Music Resort	WDW	★★★	73	$$$-
Disney's All-Star Sports Resort	WDW	★★★	73	$$$-
Extended Stay America Orlando Convention Center	1	★★★	72	$+
Baymont Inn & Suites Celebration	3	★★★	72	$$
Staybridge Suites Lake Buena Vista	2	★★★	72	$$$+
SpringHill Suites Orlando LBV in Marriott Village	2	★★★	71	$$$+
Disney's Pop Century Resort	WDW	★★★	71	$$$+
Super 8 Kissimmee/Maingate	3	★★★	70	$+
Hampton Inn I-Drive/Convention Center	1	★★★	70	$$+
Comfort Suites Universal	4	★★★	70	$$+
Monumental MovieLand Hotel	1	★★★	68	$+

How the Hotels Compare (continued)

HOTEL	LODGING AREA	OVERALL QUALITY	ROOM QUALITY	($ = $50)
Westgate Palace	1	★★★	68	$$$$-
Maingate Lakeside Resort	3	★★★	67	$$-
The Enclave Hotel & Suites	1	★★★	67	$$$-
Hampton Inn Universal	4	★★★	67	$$$-
Motel 6 Orlando–I-Drive	1	★★★	66	$+
Comfort Inn I-Drive	1	★★★	66	$$-
Ramada Convention Center I-Drive	1	★★★	65	$+
Rosen Inn International Hotel	1	★★★	65	$$+
Best Western I-Drive	1	★★★	65	$$+
Magnuson Grand Hotel Maingate West	3	★★★	65	$$+
Clarion Inn & Suites at I-Drive	1	★★½	64	$+
Clarion Inn Lake Buena Vista	2	★★½	64	$$-
Hampton Inn South of Universal	1	★★½	64	$$$-
Silver Lake Resort	3	★★½	64	$$$
The Floridian Hotel & Suites	1	★★½	63	$$-
La Quinta Inn Orlando–Universal Studios	4	★★½	63	$$-
Country Inn & Suites Orlando Universal	1	★★½	63	$$
Comfort Inn Maingate	3	★★½	62	$$+
Celebration Suites	3	★★½	61	$+
Super 8 Kissimmee	3	★★½	60	$-
Destiny Palms Maingate West	3	★★½	60	$+
Royal Celebration Inn	3	★★½	60	$+
Rodeway Inn Maingate	3	★★½	59	$-
Knights Inn Maingate Kissimmee/Orlando	3	★★	58	$-
Red Roof Inn Orlando Convention Center	1	★★	58	$+

WALT DISNEY WORLD DINING

DINING *outside the* WORLD

LIKE ALL VISITORS TO WALT DISNEY WORLD, short-stay and last-minute visitors have an economic incentive to find dining options outside the parks: The food inside ain't cheap, in case you haven't heard. But these visitors have a logistical incentive as well—unless they book well ahead of time, their chances of getting a seat at a full-service restaurant on-property can be a crap shoot. Our recommendations for tasty, reasonably priced fare outside Walt Disney World are summarized on the next two pages.

MEAL DEALS You'll find discounts and two-for-one coupons for many area restaurants in freebie visitor guides available at hotels outside of Walt Disney World. The **Orlando–Orange County Official Visitors Center** (8723 International Dr.; ☎ 407-363-5872; open daily, 8:30 a.m.–6:30 p.m., except Christmas) offers a treasure trove of coupons and free visitor magazines. Online, check out **coupons alacarte.com** and **orlandocoupons.com** for printable coupons.

DISNEY DINING 101

MORE THAN 135 RESTAURANTS operate within Walt Disney World, including about 70 full-service establishments. The variety is exceptional: everything from Moroccan lamb to Texas barbecue. Most eateries are expensive, and many serve less-than-distinguished fare, but there are good choices in every area of the World.

ADVANCE RESERVATIONS

MOST DINING RESERVATIONS AT DISNEY WORLD don't guarantee you a table at a specific time as they would at your typical hometown restaurant. Instead of scheduling Advance Reservations

Where to Eat Outside Walt Disney World

AMERICAN

JOHNNIE'S HIDEAWAY 12551 FL 535, Orlando; ☎ 407-827-1111; **talkof thetownrestaurants.com/johnnies.html;** moderate–expensive. Seafood and steaks, with an emphasis on Florida cuisine.

THE RAVENOUS PIG* 1234 N. Orange Ave., Winter Park; ☎ 407-628-2333; **theravenouspig.com;** moderate–expensive. New American cuisine with an award-winning menu that changes frequently, with seasonal ingredients.

BARBECUE

BUBBALOU'S BODACIOUS BAR-B-QUE 5818 Conroy Rd., Orlando (near Universal Orlando); ☎ 407-295-1212; **bubbalous.com;** inexpensive. Tender, smoky barbecue; tomato-based Killer Sauce.

4 RIVERS SMOKEHOUSE 1047 S. Dillard St., Winter Garden; ☎ 407-474-8377; **4rsmokehouse.com;** inexpensive. Award-winning beef brisket; fried pickles, cheese grits, fried okra, and collard greens.

CHINESE

MING COURT 9188 International Dr., Orlando; ☎ 407-351-9988; inexpensive. Authentic Chinese, including dim sum, crispy roast pork, and roast duck.

CUBAN/SPANISH

COLUMBIA 649 Front St., Celebration; ☎ 407-566-1505; **columbia restaurant.com;** moderate. Cuban/Spanish creations such as paella and the 1905 Salad.

FRENCH

LE COQ AU VIN* 4800 S. Orange Ave., Orlando; ☎ 407-851-6980; **lecoqauvinrestaurant.com;** moderate–expensive. Country French cuisine in a relaxed atmosphere. Reservations suggested.

INDIAN

MEMORIES OF INDIA 7625 Turkey Lake Rd., Orlando; ☎ 407-370-3277; **memoriesofindiacuisine.com;** inexpensive–moderate. Classic tandoori dishes, samosas, *tikka masala,* and Sunday Champagne brunch with buffet.

RAGA 7559 W. Sand Lake Rd., Orlando; ☎ 407-985-2900; **raga restaurant.com;** moderate. Blend of Indian, Pakistani, and Middle Eastern cuisines prepared with locally sourced ingredients.

ITALIAN

ANTHONY'S COAL-FIRED PIZZA 8031 Turkey Lake Rd., Orlando; ☎ 407-363-9466; **anthonyscoalfiredpizza.com;** inexpensive. Pizza, eggplant, pasta, beer and wine.

BICE ORLANDO RISTORANTE Loews Portofino Bay, 5601 Universal Blvd., Orlando; ☎ 407-503-1415; **orlando.bicegroup.com;** expensive. Authentic Italian; great wines.

JAPANESE/SUSHI

AMURA 7786 W. Sand Lake Rd., Orlando; ☎ 407-370-0007; **amura .com;** moderate. A favorite sushi bar for locals. The tempura is popular too.

NAGOYA SUSHI 7600 Dr. Phillips Blvd., Ste. 66, in the very rear of The Marketplace at Dr. Phillips; ☎ 407-248-8558; **nagoyasushi.com;** moderate. A small, intimate restaurant with great sushi and an extensive menu.

*20 minutes or more from Walt Disney World

(Continued on next page)

Where to Eat Outside Walt Disney World

HANAMIZUKI 8255 International Dr., Orlando; ☎ 407-363-7200; **hanamizuki.us;** moderate–expensive. Pricey but authentic.

MEXICAN

CANTINA LAREDO 800 Via Dellagio Way, Orlando; ☎ 407-345-0186; **cantinalaredo.com;** moderate–expensive. Authentic Mexican, upscale setting.

CHEVYS FRESH MEX 12547 FL 535, Lake Buena Vista; ☎ 407-827-1052; **chevys.com;** inexpensive–moderate. Across from the FL 535 entrance to WDW.

EL PATRON 12167 S. Apopka–Vineland Rd., Orlando; ☎ 407-238-5300; **elpatronrestaurantcantina.com;** inexpensive. Family-owned restaurant serving freshly prepared Mexican dishes. Full bar.

MOE'S SOUTHWEST GRILL 7541-D W. Sand Lake Rd., Orlando; ☎ 407-264-9903; **moes.com;** inexpensive. Dependable Southwestern fare.

TAQUITOS JALISCO 1041 S. Dillard St., Winter Garden; ☎ 407-654-0363; inexpensive. Low-key. Flautas, chicken *mole,* fajitas, burritos, good vegetarian.

SEAFOOD

BONEFISH GRILL 7830 W. Sand Lake Rd., Orlando; ☎ 407-355-7707; **bonefishgrill.com;** moderate. Casual setting along busy Restaurant Row on Sand Lake Road. Choose your fish; then choose a sauce to accompany.

CELEBRATION TOWN TAVERN 721 Front St., Celebration; ☎ 407-566-2526; **thecelebrationtowntavern.com;** moderate. Popular hangout for locals, with New England–style seafood. Clam chowder is a big hit.

STEAK/PRIME RIB

BULL & BEAR Waldorf Astoria Orlando, 14200 Bonnet Creek Resort Ln., Orlando; ☎ 407-597-5500; **waldorfastoriaorlando.com/dining/bull -and-bear;** expensive. Classic steakhouse with a clubby ambience.

TEXAS DE BRAZIL 5259 International Dr., Orlando; ☎ 407-355-0355; **texasdebrazil.com;** expensive. All-you-can-eat Brazilian-style *churrascaria.* Ribs, filet mignon, chicken, lamb, and salad bar.

VITO'S CHOP HOUSE 8633 International Dr., Orlando; ☎ 407-354-2467; **vitoschophouse.com;** moderate. Upscale meat house with a taste of Tuscany.

THAI

THAI SILK 6803 S. Kirkman Rd. at International Dr., Orlando; ☎ 407-226-8997; **thaisilkorlando.com;** moderate. Acclaimed by Orlando dining critics for its authentic Thai dishes. Delicious vegetarian options; impressive wine list.

for actual tables, reservations fill time slots. The number of slots available is based on the average length of time that guests occupy a table at a particular restaurant, adjusted for seasonality. Disney tries to fill every time slot for every seat in the restaurant. No seats—repeat, none—are reserved for walk-ins.

Some Disney restaurants charge a hefty no-show fee and are booked every day according to their actual capacity. This has reduced the no-show rate to virtually zero, meaning that walk-ins stand only a small shot of getting a seat. If you walk in during busier seasons, expect to either wait 40–75 minutes or be told that no tables are available. (If you want to try for a walk-in, go between 2:00 and 4:30 p.m. Your chances improve during less-busy seasons and cold/rainy days during busier seasons.)

Dinner reservations are generally easy to get within 60 days at most full-service restaurants as long as you're not particular about the time you eat. But for breakfast and lunch at such wildly popular venues such as **Be Our Guest Restaurant** (for which reservations are snapped up as soon as they're available) and **Cinderella's Royal Table** at the Magic Kingdom, you'll need to book anywhere from 7 weeks to 180 days ahead. To make Advance Reservations, call ☎ 407-WDW-DINE or go to **disneyworld.disney.go.com/dining**.

WALT DISNEY WORLD RESTAURANT CATEGORIES

IN GENERAL, FOOD AND BEVERAGE offerings at Walt Disney World are defined by service, price, and convenience:

FULL-SERVICE RESTAURANTS Full-service restaurants are in all Disney resorts (except the All-Star complex, Port Orleans French Quarter, Pop Century, and Art of Animation), all major theme parks, and Disney Springs. Advance Reservations are recommended for all full-service restaurants except those in the Downtown Disney Resort Area, which are operated independently of Disney. The restaurants accept American Express, Carte Blanche, Diners Club, Japan Credit Bureau, MasterCard, and Visa.

BUFFETS AND FAMILY-STYLE RESTAURANTS Many of these have Disney characters in attendance, and most have a separate children's menu featuring dishes such as hot dogs, burgers, chicken nuggets, pizza, macaroni and cheese, and spaghetti and meatballs. In addition to the buffets, several restaurants serve a family-style, all-you-can-eat, fixed-price meal. Advance Reservations are required for character buffets and recommended for all other buffets and family-style restaurants. Most major credit cards are accepted.

If you want to eat a lot but don't feel like standing in yet another line, then consider one of the all-you-can-eat family-style restaurants. These feature platters of food brought to your table in courses by a server. You can sample everything on the menu and eat as much as you like. You can even go back to a favorite appetizer after you finish the main course.

Family-style all-you-can-eat service is available at **Captain's Grille** at the Yacht Club Resort (breakfast only); **Cinderella's Royal Table** (breakfast only) and the **Liberty Tree Tavern** (dinner only) in the Magic Kingdom; **'Ohana** at the Polynesian Village Resort; and **Trail's End Restaurant** (breakfast and dinner only) and **Whispering Canyon Cafe** at the Wilderness Lodge.

FOOD COURTS Featuring a collection of counter-service eateries under one roof, food courts can be found at the Moderate resorts (Coronado Springs, Caribbean Beach, Port Orleans) and Value resorts (All-Star, Art of Animation, and Pop Century). (The closest thing to a food court you'll find at the theme parks is **Sunshine Seasons** at Epcot.) Advance Reservations are neither required nor available at these restaurants.

COUNTER SERVICE Counter-service fast food is available in all theme parks, the BoardWalk, and Disney Springs. The food compares in quality with Captain D's, McDonald's, or Taco Bell but is more expensive, though often served in larger portions.

FAST CASUAL Somewhere between burgers and formal dining are the establishments in Disney's "fast casual" category, including three in the theme parks: **Be Our Guest** in the Magic Kingdom, **Sunshine Seasons** in Epcot, and **Studio Catering Co.** in Disney's Hollywood Studios. Fast-casual restaurants feature menu choices a cut above what you would normally find at a typical counter-service location. (At Sunshine Seasons, for example, you can choose from rotisserie chicken or pork, tasty noodle bowls, or large sandwiches made with artisanal breads. Be Our Guest's dishes include a tasty tuna niçoise salad (with seared tuna). Entrees cost about $2 more on average than traditional counter service, but the variety and food quality more than make up for the difference.

VENDOR FOOD Vendors abound at the theme parks, Disney Springs Marketplace, Disney Springs West Side, and the BoardWalk. Offerings include popcorn, ice-cream bars, churros (Mexican pastries), soft drinks, bottled water, and (in the theme parks) fresh fruit.

SAVE MONEY, SAVE TIME

EVERY TIME YOU BUY A SODA AT THE THEME PARKS, it's going to set you back about $3, and everything else is comparably high. What's more, you lose a lot of touring time getting food, even if you confine your meals to vendors and counter service.

You can say, "Oh well, I'm on vacation" and throw prudence out the window, or you can plan ahead and not only save big bucks

THE COST OF COUNTER-SERVICE FOOD	
Bagel or muffin	$2.79–$2.99
Brownie	$2.99–$3.99
Burrito	$7.09–$7.59
Cake or pie	$3.59–$5.19
Cereal with milk	$3.19–$3.69
Cheeseburger with fries	$8.79–$11.49
Chicken breast sandwich	$9.19–$9.99
Chicken nuggets with fries	$7.59–$9.29
Children's meal (various)	$5.49–$5.99
Chips	$2.79–$3.25
Cookies	$2.50–$3.99
Fish (fried) basket with fries	$7.99–$9.49
French fries	$2.99
Fruit (whole)	$1.69–$3.59
Fruit cup/fruit salad	$3.79–$3.99
Hot dog	$5.75–$10.29
Ice cream/frozen novelties	$3.99–¢4.99
Nachos with cheese	$3.99–$7.69
PB&J sandwich	$5.49 (kids' meal)
Pizza (personal)	$9.19–$10.69
Popcorn	$3.50–$5.50
Pretzel	$2.95–$4.79
Salad (entrée)	$7.99–$11.69
Salad (side)	$3.29
Smoked turkey leg	$10.50–$13.29
Soup/chili	$3.29–$7.99
Sub/deli sandwich	$7.50–$10.49
Taco salad	$8.19
Veggie burger	$8.59–$9.99

but minimize the time you spend hunting and gathering. Here's how to do it:

1. Eat breakfast before you arrive. Restaurants outside the World offer some outstanding breakfast specials. Plus, some hotels furnish small refrigerators in their guest rooms, or you can rent a fridge or bring a cooler. If you can get by on cold cereal, pastries, fruit, and juice, this will save you a ton of money as well as time.

2. Stuff some snacks in a fanny pack and take them with you to the parks. Carry water bottles, or rely on drinking fountains for water.

3. Make lunch your main meal. Entrées are similar to those on the dinner menu, but prices are significantly lower.

THE COST OF COUNTER-SERVICE DRINKS		
DRINKS	**SMALL**	**LARGE**
Beer	$5.75-$7.00	$7.50-$12.50
Bottled water	$2.50-$4.00	$2.50-$4.00
Latte *(one size)*	$3.99	$3.99-$5.19
Coffee *(one size)*	$2.29	$2.29
Float/milkshake/sundae *(one size)*	$4.49-$5.39	$4.49-$5.39
Fruit juice	$2.59-$2.99	$3.29-$3.79
Hot tea and cocoa *(one size)*	$2.09-$2.29	$2.09-$2.29
Milk	$1.79	$2.39-$2.59
Soft drinks, iced tea, and lemonade	$2.59-$2.99	$2.99

Refillable souvenir mugs cost $16.49 (free refills) at Disney resorts and $11 at water parks. Each person on a Disney Dining Plan gets a free mug, refillable only at his/her Disney resort.

4. All theme park restaurants are busiest between 11:30 a.m. and 2:15 p.m. for lunch and 6 and 9 p.m. for dinner. For shorter lines and faster service, don't eat during these hours, especially 12:30–1:30 p.m.

5. Many counter-service restaurants sell cold sandwiches. Buy a cold lunch minus drinks before 11:30 a.m., and carry it in small plastic bags until you're ready to eat (within an hour or so of purchase). Ditto for dinner. Buy drinks at the appropriate time from any convenient vendor.

6. Most fast-food eateries have more than one service window. Regardless of the time of day, check the lines at all windows before queuing. Sometimes a window that's staffed but out of the way will have a much shorter line or none at all. Note, however, that some windows may offer only certain items.

7. If you're short on time and the park closes early, stay until closing and eat dinner outside Disney World before returning to your hotel. If the park stays open late, eat dinner about 4 or 4:30 p.m. at the restaurant of your choice. You should sneak in just ahead of the dinner crowd.

DRESS

DRESS IS INFORMAL at most theme park restaurants, but Disney has a "business casual" dress code for some of its resort restaurants: khakis, dress slacks, jeans, or dress shorts with a collared shirt for men and capris, skirts, dresses, jeans, and dress shorts for women. Restaurants with this dress code are **Jiko—The Cooking Place** at Animal Kingdom Lodge & Villas, the **Flying Fish Cafe** at the BoardWalk, the **California Grill** at the Contemporary Resort, **Monsieur Paul** at Epcot's France Pavilion, **Cítricos** and **Narcoossee's** at the Grand

Floridian, **Artist Point** at Wilderness Lodge & Villas, **Yachtsman Steakhouse** at the Yacht Club Resort, **Todd English's bluezoo** and **Shula's Steak House** at the Dolphin, and **Il Mulino New York Trattoria** at the Swan. **Victoria & Albert's** at the Grand Floridian is the only Disney restaurant that requires men to wear a jacket to dinner.

Also, be aware that smoking is banned at all restaurants and lounges on Walt Disney World property. Diners who puff must feed their nicotine fix outdoors—and in the theme parks, that might also mean going to a designated smoking area.

A FEW CAVEATS

BEFORE YOU BEGIN EATING your way through the World, you need to know:

1. Theme park restaurants rush their customers in order to make room for the next group of diners. Dining at high speed may appeal to a family with young, restless children, but for people wanting to relax, it's more like eating in a pressure chamber than fine dining.

2. Disney restaurants have comparatively few tables for parties of two, and servers are generally disinclined to seat two guests at larger tables. If you're a duo, you might have to wait longer to be seated.

3. At full-service Disney restaurants, an automatic gratuity of 18% is added to your tab—even at buffets where you get your own food.

4. Disney occasionally adds a surcharge of $4 per adult and $2 per child to certain popular restaurants during weeks of peak attendance, including Presidents Day, Spring Break, Easter, mid-December–New Year's Eve, and every day from early June to early August. The following restaurants participate in the gouging: **Akershus Royal Banquet Hall** (Princess Storybook Dining), **Biergarten, Boma—Flavors of Africa** (breakfast and dinner), **Cape May Cafe** (breakfast and dinner buffet), **Chef Mickey's** (breakfast and dinner), **Cinderella's Royal Table, The Crystal Palace, Garden Grill Restaurant, Hollywood & Vine** (Play 'n Dine character buffets), **Liberty Tree Tavern** (dinner), **1900 Park Fare** (Supercalifragilistic Breakfast and Cinderella's Happily Ever After Dinner), **'Ohana** (breakfast and dinner), the *Spirit of Aloha Dinner Show,* **Trail's End Restaurant** at Fort Wilderness (an exception: $2 extra for adults and $1 for kids), and **Tusker House Restaurant.**

DISNEY DINING SUGGESTIONS

FOLLOWING ARE SUGGESTIONS FOR DINING at each of the major theme parks. If you're interested in trying a theme park full-service restaurant, be aware that the restaurants continue to serve after the park's official closing time. For example, we showed up at

The Hollywood Brown Derby just as Disney's Hollywood Studios closed at 8 p.m. We were seated almost immediately and enjoyed a leisurely dinner while the crowds cleared out. Incidentally, don't worry if you're depending on Disney transportation: Buses, boats, and monorails run 1–2 hours after closing.

THE MAGIC KINGDOM

OF THE PARK'S six full-service restaurants, **Be Our Guest** (dinner) in Fantasyland is the best, followed by **Liberty Tree Tavern** in Liberty Square and **The Plaza Restaurant** on Main Street. **Cinderella's Royal Table** in the castle and **The Crystal Palace** on Main Street serve decent-but-expensive buffets chaperoned by Disney characters. Avoid **Tony's Town Square Restaurant** on Main Street. You'll need to make Advance Reservations before you leave home if you want to eat at Cinderella's Royal Table or Be Our Guest.

EPCOT

unofficial **TIP**
Many Epcot eateries are overpriced, most conspicuously **Monsieur Paul** (France) and **Coral Reef Restaurant** (The Seas).

FOR THE MOST PART, Epcot's restaurants have always served decent food, although World Showcase restaurants have occasionally been timid about delivering an honest representation of the host nation's cuisine. While these eateries have struggled with authenticity and have sometimes shied away from challenging the meat-and-potatoes palate of the average tourist, they are bolder now, encouraged by America's expanding appreciation of ethnic dining. True, the less adventuresome can still find sanitized and homogenized meals, but the same kitchens will serve up the real thing for anyone with a spark of curiosity. Representing decent value with their combination of attractive ambience and well-prepared food are **Via Napoli** (Italy), **Biergarten** (Germany), and **La Hacienda de San Angel** (Mexico). Biergarten (along with **Restaurant Marrakesh** in Morocco) offers live entertainment.

unofficial **TIP**
Flame Tree Barbecue in Safari Village is our pick of the Animal Kingdom litter, both in terms of food quality and atmosphere.

DISNEY'S ANIMAL KINGDOM

ANIMAL KINGDOM OFFERS A LOT OF counter-service fast food, along with **Tusker House,** a buffet-style restaurant, and **Yak & Yeti,** a table-service restaurant, in Asia. You'll find plenty of traditional Disney-theme-park food—hot dogs, hamburgers, and the like—but even the fast food is superior to typical Disney fare. Our two counter-service favorites: **Flame Tree Barbecue** in Discovery Island, with its waterfront dining pavilions, and **Yak & Yeti Local Food Cafes** (just outside the full-service Yak & Yeti) for casual Asian dishes from egg rolls to crispy honey chicken.

The third full-service restaurant in Animal Kingdom, the **Rainforest Cafe,** has entrances both inside and outside the park (you don't have to buy park admission to eat there). Both Rainforest Cafes (the other is at Disney Springs Marketplace) accept Advance Reservations.

DISNEY'S HOLLYWOOD STUDIOS

DINING AT DHS is more interesting than at the Magic Kingdom and less international than at Epcot. The park has five restaurants where Advance Reservations are recommended: **The Hollywood Brown Derby, 50's Prime Time Cafe, Sci-Fi Dine-In Theater Restaurant, Mama Melrose's Ristorante Italiano,** and the **Hollywood & Vine** buffet. The upscale Brown Derby is by far the best restaurant at the Studios. For simple Italian food, including pizza, Mama Melrose's is fine. At the Sci-Fi Dine-In, you eat in little cars at a simulated drive-in movie from the 1950s. Though you won't find a more entertaining restaurant in Walt Disney World, the food is quite disappointing. Somewhat better is the 50's Prime Time Cafe, where you sit in Mom's fabulous midcentury kitchen and scarf down meat loaf while watching clips of classic TV sitcoms. Hollywood & Vine features Disney Channel characters during breakfast and lunch.

WALT DISNEY WORLD RESTAURANTS
At a Glance

TO HELP YOU MAKE YOUR DINING CHOICES, we've compiled a quick-reference list of full-service restaurants at Disney World. Here you can check the restaurant's cuisine, location, overall rating, cost range, quality rating, and value rating. Restaurants are grouped by cuisine and listed within each category from the highest overall star rating to the lowest.

OVERALL RATING The overall rating represents the entire dining experience: style, service, and ambience, in addition to taste, presentation, and quality of food. Five stars is the highest rating and indicates that the restaurant offers the best of everything. Four-star restaurants are above average, and three-star restaurants offer good, though not necessarily memorable, meals. Two-star restaurants serve mediocre fare, and one-star restaurants are below average. Our star ratings don't correspond to ratings awarded by AAA, Mobil, Zagat, or other restaurant reviewers.

COST RANGE The next rating tells how much a full-service entree will cost. Appetizers, sides, soups/salads, desserts,

Inexpensive	**$15 or less per person**
Moderate	**$15–$28 per person**
Expensive	**More than $28 per person**

drinks, and tips aren't included. We've classified costs as inexpensive, moderate, or expensive.

QUALITY RATING The food quality is rated on a scale of one to five stars, five being the best rating attainable. The quality rating is based expressly on the taste, freshness of ingredients, preparation, presentation, and creativity of food served. There is no consideration of price. If you are a person who wants the best food available and cost is not an issue, you need look no further than the quality ratings.

VALUE RATING If, on the other hand, you are looking for both quality and value, then you should check the value rating, also expressed as stars. The greater the stars, the more you get for your dining dollar.

WDW Restaurants by Cuisine

CUISINE	LOCATION	OVERALL RATING	COST	QUALITY RATING	VALUE RATING
AFRICAN					
Jiko—The Cooking Place	Animal Kingdom Lodge/Jambo House	★★★★½	EXP	★★★★½	★★★½
Boma—Flavors of Africa	Animal Kingdom Lodge/Jambo House	★★★★	EXP	★★★★	★★★★½
Sanaa	Animal Kingdom Villas–Kidani Village	★★★★	EXP	★★★★	★★★★
Tusker House Restaurant	Animal Kingdom	★★★	MOD	★★★	★★★
AMERICAN					
California Grill	Contemporary	★★★★½	EXP	★★★★½	★★★
The Hollywood Brown Derby	DHS	★★★★	EXP	★★★★	★★★
Artist Point	Wilderness Lodge	★★★½	EXP	★★★★	★★★
Cape May Café	Beach Club	★★★½	MOD	★★★½	★★★★
Whispering Canyon Café	Wilderness Lodge	★★★	MOD	★★★½	★★★★
Captain's Grille	Yacht Club	★★★	MOD	★★★½	★★★
The Crystal Palace	Magic Kingdom	★★★	MOD	★★★½	★★★
House of Blues	Disney Springs	★★★	MOD	★★★½	★★★
50's Prime Time Café	DHS	★★★	MOD	★★★	★★★
Liberty Tree Tavern	Magic Kingdom	★★★	MOD	★★★	★★★
Tusker House Restaurant	Animal Kingdom	★★★	MOD	★★★	★★★
Cinderella's Royal Table	Magic Kingdom	★★★	EXP	★★★	★★
Olivia's Cafe	Old Key West	★★★	MOD	★★★	★★
T-REX	Disney Springs	★★★	MOD	★★	★★
The Wave . . . of American Flavors	Contemporary	★★★	MOD	★★	★★
ESPN Club	BoardWalk	★★½	MOD	★★★	★★★

WDW Restaurants by Cuisine (continued)

CUISINE	LOCATION	OVERALL RATING	COST	QUALITY RATING	VALUE RATING
AMERICAN (continued)					
ESPN Wide World of Sports Grill	ESPN Wide World of Sports Complex	★★½	MOD	★★★	★★★
Hollywood & Vine	DHS	★★½	MOD	★★★	★★★
1900 Park Fare	Grand Floridian	★★½	MOD	★★★	★★★
Chef Mickey's	Contemporary	★★½	EXP	★★★	★★★
Boatwright's Dining Hall	Port Orleans	★★½	MOD	★★★	★★
Grand Floridian Cafe	Grand Floridian	★★½	MOD	★★★	★★
Beaches & Cream Soda Shop	Beach Club	★★½	INEXP	★★½	★★½
Fresh Mediterranean Market	Dolphin	★★½	MOD	★★½	★★
Splitsville	Disney Springs	★★½	MOD	★★½	★★
Planet Hollywood	Disney Springs	★★½	MOD	★★	★★
Rainforest Cafe	Animal Kingdom and Disney Springs	★★½	MOD	★★	★★
Garden Grove	Swan	★★	MOD	★★★	★★
Las Ventanas	Coronado Springs	★★	MOD	★★½	★★
Sci-Fi Dine-In Theater Restaurant	DHS	★★	MOD	★★½	★★
Turf Club Bar & Grill	Saratoga Springs	★★	MOD	★★★	★★
Garden Grill Restaurant	Epcot	★★	EXP	★★	★★★
Big River Grille & Brewing Works	BoardWalk	★★	MOD	★★	★★
The Fountain	Dolphin	★★	MOD	★★	★★
The Plaza Restaurant	Magic Kingdom	★★	MOD	★★	★★
Trail's End Restaurant	Fort Wilderness Resort	★★	MOD	★★	★★
Wolfgang Puck Grand Cafe	Disney Springs	★★	EXP	★½	★½
Maya Grill	Coronado Springs	★	EXP	★	★
BUFFET					
Boma—Flavors of Africa	Animal Kingdom Lodge	★★★★	EXP	★★★★	★★★★½
Cape May Café	Beach Club	★★★½	MOD	★★★½	★★★★
The Crystal Palace	Magic Kingdom	★★★	MOD	★★★½	★★★
Tusker House Restaurant	Animal Kingdom	★½	MOD	★	★★
Chef Mickey's	Contemporary	★★½	EXP	★★★	★★★
Hollywood & Vine	DHS	★★½	MOD	★★★	★★★
1900 Park Fare	Grand Floridian	★★½	MOD	★★★	★★★
Garden Grove	Swan	★★	MOD	★★★	★★
Akershus Royal Banquet Hall	Epcot	★★	EXP	★★	★★★★
Biergarten	Epcot	★★	EXP	★★	★★★★
Trail's End Restaurant	Fort Wilderness Resort	★★	MOD	★★	★★
CAJUN					
Boatwright's Dining Hall	Port Orleans	★★½	MOD	★★★	★★
CHINESE					
Nine Dragons Restaurant	Epcot	★★★	MOD	★★★	★★
CUBAN					
Bongos Cuban Cafe	Disney Springs	★★	MOD	★★	★★
ENGLISH					
Rose & Crown Dining Room	Epcot	★★★	MOD	★★★½	★★

WDW Restaurants by Cuisine *(continued)*

CUISINE	LOCATION	OVERALL RATING	COST	QUALITY RATING	VALUE RATING
FRENCH					
Monsieur Paul	Epcot	★★★★	EXP	★★★★½	★★★
Be Our Guest Restaurant	Magic Kingdom	★★★★	EXP	★★★★	★★★★
Les Chefs de France	Epcot	★★★	EXP	★★★	★★★
GERMAN					
Biergarten	Epcot	★★	EXP	★★	★★★★
GLOBAL					
Paradiso 37	Disney Springs	★★½	INEXP	★★★	★★★
GOURMET					
Victoria & Albert's	Grand Floridian	★★★★★	EXP	★★★★★★	★★★★
INDIAN					
Sanaa	Animal Kingdom Villas–Kidani Village	★★★★	EXP	★★★★	★★★★
IRISH					
Raglan Road Irish Pub & Restaurant	Disney Springs	★★★★	MOD	★★★½	★★★
ITALIAN					
Tutto Italia Ristorante	Epcot	★★★★	EXP	★★★★	★★★
Via Napoli	Epcot	★★★★	MOD	★★★½	★★★
Trattoria Al Forno	BoardWalk	★★★½	MOD	★★★½	★★
Ravello	Four Seasons	★★★	MOD	★★★	★★★
Il Mulino New York Trattoria	Swan	★★★	EXP	★★★	★★
Mama Melrose's Ristorante Italiano	DHS	★★½	MOD	★★★	★★
Portobello	Disney Springs	★★½	EXP	★★★	★★
Tony's Town Square Restaurant	Magic Kingdom	★★½	MOD	★★★	★★
JAPANESE/SUSHI					
Kimonos	Swan	★★★★	MOD	★★★★½	★★★
Teppan Edo	Epcot	★★★½	EXP	★★★★	★★★
Tokyo Dining	Epcot	★★★	MOD	★★★★	★★★
Benihana	Hilton	★★★	MOD	★★★½	★★★
MEDITERRANEAN					
Citricos	Grand Floridian	★★★½	EXP	★★★★½	★★★
Fresh Mediterranean Market	Dolphin	★★½	MOD	★★½	★★
MEXICAN					
La Hacienda de San Angel	Epcot	★★★	EXP	★★★½	★★½
San Angel Inn Restaurante	Epcot	★★★	EXP	★★	★★
Maya Grill	Coronado Springs	★	EXP	★	★
MOROCCAN					
Restaurant Marrakesh	Epcot	★★	MOD	★★½	★★

WDW Restaurants by Cuisine (continued)

CUISINE	LOCATION	OVERALL RATING	COST	QUALITY RATING	VALUE RATING
NORWEGIAN					
Akershus Royal Banquet Hall	Epcot	★★★	EXP	★★★	★★★★
POLYNESIAN/PAN-ASIAN					
'Ohana	Polynesian Village	★★★	MOD	★★★½	★★★
Kona Cafe	Polynesian Village	★★★	MOD	★★★	★★★★
Trader Sam's Grog Grotto	Polynesian Village	★★★	MOD	★★★	★★★
Yak & Yeti Restaurant	Animal Kingdom	★★	EXP	★★½	★★
SEAFOOD					
Narcoossee's	Grand Floridian	★★★★½	EXP	★★★½	★★
Flying Fish Café	BoardWalk	★★★★	EXP	★★★★	★★★
Artist Point	Wilderness Lodge	★★★½	EXP	★★★★	★★★
Todd English's bluezoo	Dolphin	★★★	EXP	★★★	★★
The Boathouse	Disney Springs	★★	MOD	★★½	★★
Fulton's Crab House	Disney Springs	★★½	EXP	★★★½	★★
Shutters at Old Port Royale	Caribbean Beach	★★	MOD	★★½	★★
STEAK					
Capa	Four Seasons	★★★★	EXP	★★★★	★★
Shula's Steak House	Dolphin	★★★★	EXP	★★★★	★★
Le Cellier Steakhouse	Epcot	★★★½	EXP	★★★½	★★★
Yachtsman Steakhouse	Yacht Club	★★★	EXP	★★★½	★★
Shutters at Old Port Royale	Caribbean Beach	★★	MOD	★★½	★★

PART FIVE

WALT DISNEY WORLD *with* KIDS

RECOMMENDATIONS *for* MAKING *the* DREAM COME TRUE

WHEN PLANNING A DISNEY WORLD vacation with young children, consider the following:

AGE Although the color and festivity of Disney World will excite all children, and specific attractions delight toddlers and preschoolers, Disney entertainment is generally oriented to older kids and adults. Children should be a fairly mature 7 years old to *appreciate* the Magic Kingdom and Disney's Animal Kingdom, and a year or two older to get much out of Epcot or Disney's Hollywood Studios.

TIME OF YEAR TO VISIT Avoid the hot, crowded summer months, especially if you have preschoolers. Go in October, November (except Thanksgiving), early December, January, February, or May. If you have children of varied ages and they're good students, take the older ones out of school and visit during the cooler, less congested off-season. Arrange special assignments relating to the educational aspects of Disney World. If your children can't afford to miss school, take your vacation as soon as the school year ends in late May or early June. Alternatively, try late August before school starts. But understand that you don't have to visit during one of the more ideal times of year to have a great vacation.

BUILD NAPS AND REST INTO YOUR ITINERARY The theme parks are huge; don't try to see everything in one day. Tour in early morning and return to your hotel around 11:30 a.m. for lunch, a swim, and a nap. Even during off-season when the crowds are smaller and the temperatures more pleasant, the size of the major theme parks will exhaust most children under age 8 by lunchtime. Return to the park in late afternoon or early evening and continue touring. If you plan to return to your hotel in midday and would like your room made up, let the housekeeping staff know.

*un**official*** **TIP**
Naps and relief from the frenetic pace of the theme parks, even during the off-season, are indispensable.

WHERE TO STAY The time and hassle involved in commuting to and from the theme parks will be lessened if you stay in a hotel close to the theme parks. We should point out that this doesn't necessarily mean you have to lodge at a hotel in Walt Disney World. Because Walt Disney World is so geographically dispersed, many off-property hotels are actually closer to the theme parks than some Disney resorts. Regardless of whether you stay in or out of the World, it's imperative that you take young children out of the parks each day for a few hours of rest. Neglecting to relax is the best way we know to get the whole family in a snit and ruin the day (or the vacation).

If you have young children, you must plan ahead. Make sure your hotel is within 20 minutes of the theme parks. It's true you can revive somewhat by retreating to a Disney hotel for lunch or by finding a quiet restaurant in the theme parks, but there's no substitute for returning to the familiarity and comfort of your own hotel. Regardless of what you have heard, children too large to sleep in a stroller won't relax unless you take them back to your hotel. If it takes renting a car to make returning to your hotel practicable, rent the car.

If you're traveling with children 12 years old and younger and you want to stay in the World, we recommend the **Polynesian Village, Grand Floridian,** or **Wilderness Lodge** (in that order), if they fit your budget. For less expensive rooms, try **Port Orleans French Quarter.** The least expensive on-site rooms are available at the **All-Star Resorts.** In addition to standard hotel rooms, the **All-Star Music** and **Art of Animation Resorts** offer two-room family suites that can sleep as many as six and provide kitchenettes. Log cabins at **Fort Wilderness Resort & Campground** and the DVC resorts are options for families who need a little more space. Outside the World, check our top hotels for families, starting on page 49.

BE IN TOUCH WITH YOUR FEELINGS When you or your children get tired and irritable, call time out and regroup. Trust your instincts. What would feel best—another ride, an ice-cream break, or going back to the room for a nap? The way to protect your considerable investment in your Disney vacation is to stay happy and have a good time. You don't have to meet a quota for experiencing attractions. Do what *you* want.

LEAST COMMON DENOMINATORS Somebody is going to run out of steam first, and when he or she does, the whole family will be affected. Sometimes a snack break will revive the flagging member. Sometimes, however, it's better to just return to your hotel. Pushing the tired or discontented beyond their capacity will spoil the day for them—and you. Accept that energy levels vary and be prepared to respond to members of your group who poop out.

BUILDING ENDURANCE Though most children are active, their normal play usually doesn't condition them for the exertion that's required to tour a Disney theme park. We recommend starting a program of family walks four to six weeks before your trip to get in shape.

SETTING LIMITS AND MAKING PLANS Avoid arguments and disappointment by establishing guidelines for each day, and get everybody committed.

BE FLEXIBLE Any day at Walt Disney World includes some surprises; be prepared to adjust your plan. Listen to your intuition.

OVERHEATING, SUNBURN, AND DEHYDRATION These are the most common problems of younger children at Disney World. Carry and use sunscreen. Be sure to put some on children in strollers, even if the stroller has a canopy. To avoid overheating, rest regularly in the shade or in an air-conditioned restaurant or show. Keep little ones hydrated by carrying plastic bottles of water (bottles with screw caps are sold in all major parks for about $3).

BLISTERS AND SORE FEET Everyone should wear comfortable, well-broken-in shoes. If you or your children are susceptible to blisters, bring along blister bandages, available at most drugstores (and at First Aid in the parks, if you didn't heed our warnings)—they offer excellent protection, stick well, and won't sweat off. When you feel a "hot spot" starting, stop, air out your foot, and place a bandage over the area before a blister forms. Young children may not tell their parents about a developing blister until it's too late, so inspect the feet of preschoolers two or more times a day.

FIRST AID Each major theme park has a **First Aid Center**. In the Magic Kingdom, it's at the end of Main Street to your left, between Casey's Corner and The Crystal Palace. At Epcot, it's on the World Showcase side of Odyssey Center. At Disney's Hollywood Studios, it's in the Guest Relations Building inside the main entrance. At Disney's Animal Kingdom, it's in Discovery Island, on your left just before you cross the bridge to Africa, across from the ice-cream stand. And in all four parks, First Aid and the Baby Care Center are right next to each other. If you or your children have a medical problem, go to a First Aid Center. They're friendlier than most doctor's offices and are accustomed to treating everything from paper cuts to allergic reactions.

KIDS WITH ADHD Some parents of children prescribed Ritalin or similar medication let their child take a "drug holiday" when school lets out. If you've cut your child's dosage or discontinued her medication altogether, be aware that she might experience sensory overload at Disney World. Consult your child's physician before altering his or her drug regimen.

SUNGLASSES If you want your younger children to wear sunglasses, put a strap or string on the frames so that the glasses will stay on during rides and can hang from the child's neck while you're indoors.

THINGS YOU FORGOT OR RAN OUT OF Rain gear, diapers, baby formula, sunburn treatments, memory cards, and other sundries are sold at all major theme parks and at Typhoon Lagoon, Blizzard Beach, and Disney Springs. If you don't see something you need, ask if it's in stock. Basic over-the-counter meds are often available free in small quantities at the First Aid Centers in the parks.

INFANTS AND TODDLERS AT THE THEME PARKS The major parks have **Baby Care Centers.** Everything necessary for changing diapers, preparing formulas, and warming bottles and food is available. Supplies are sold, and rockers and special chairs for nursing mothers are provided. At the Magic Kingdom, the Baby Care Center is next to The Crystal Palace at the end of Main Street. At Epcot, it's in the Odyssey Center, between Test Track in Future World and Mexico in World Showcase. At Disney's Hollywood Studios, it's in the Guest Relations Building, left of the main entrance. At Disney's Animal Kingdom, the Baby Care Center is behind First Aid, near the Discovery Island entrance to Africa. Dads are welcome at the centers and can use most services. In addition, many men's restrooms in the major parks have changing stations.

Babies and toddlers are allowed to experience any attraction that doesn't have minimum height or age restrictions. If you think you might try nursing during a theater attraction, be advised that most shows run about 17–20 minutes. Exceptions are *The Hall of Presidents* at the Magic Kingdom and *The American Adventure* at Epcot, which run 23 and 29 minutes, respectively.

Strollers are available for rent at all four theme parks and Disney Springs area (single stroller, $15 per day with no deposit, $13 per day for the entire stay; double stroller, $31 per day with no deposit, $27 per day for the entire stay; stroller rentals at Disney Springs require a $100 credit card deposit; double strollers not available at Disney Springs). Strollers are welcome at Blizzard Beach and Typhoon Lagoon, but no rentals are available. With multiday rentals, you can skip the rental line entirely after your first visit—just head over to the stroller-handout area, show your receipt, and you'll be wheeling out of there in no time. If you rent a stroller at the Magic Kingdom and you decide to go to Epcot, Disney's Animal Kingdom, or Disney's Hollywood Studios, turn in your Magic Kingdom stroller and present your receipt at the next park. You'll be issued another stroller at no additional charge.

You can pay in advance for stroller rentals—this allows you to bypass the "paying" line and head straight for the "pickup" line. Disney resort guests can pay in advance at their resort's gift shop. Save receipts! Obtain strollers at the Magic Kingdom entrance, to the left of Epcot's Entrance Plaza and at Epcot's International Gateway, and at Oscar's Super Service just inside the entrance of Disney's Hollywood Studios. At Disney's Animal Kingdom, they're at Garden Gate Gifts, to the right just inside the entrance. Returning the stroller is a breeze. You can ditch your rental stroller anywhere in the park when you're ready to leave. To see what the rental strollers look like, Google "rental strollers at Walt Disney World."

Well-marked stroller parking is available in all the "lands" of every park. If you leave your stroller in front of an attraction instead of a designated parking area, it will be moved.

unofficial **TIP**
Kingdom Strollers (☎ 800-271-5301; **kingdomstrollers .com**) and **Orlando Stroller Rentals** (☎ 800-281-0884; **orlandostrollerrentals.com**) offer strollers of higher quality than Disney's. Both will also deliver to and pick up from your hotel.

If you need to go to your hotel for a break and intend to return to the park, leave your rental stroller by an attraction near the park entrance, marking it with something personal like a bandana. When you return, you'll know in an instant which one is yours.

Rental strollers are too large for all infants and many toddlers. If you plan to rent a stroller for your baby or toddler, bring pillows, cushions, or rolled towels to buttress her in.

It's OK to bring your own stroller, but only collapsible strollers are allowed on monorails, parking-lot trams, and buses.

DISNEY, KIDS, AND SCARY STUFF

MONSTERS AND SPECIAL EFFECTS AT Disney's Hollywood Studios are more real and sinister than those in the other parks. If your child has difficulty coping with the ghouls of The Haunted Mansion, think twice about exposing him to machine-gun battles, earthquakes, and the creature from *Alien* on The Great Movie Ride.

Small-Child Fright-Potential Chart

This is a quick reference to identify attractions to be wary of, and why. The chart represents a generalization, and all kids are different. It relates specifically to kids ages 3–7. On average, children at the younger end of the range are more likely to be frightened than children in their sixth or seventh year.

THE MAGIC KINGDOM

Sorcerers of the Magic Kingdom Loud but not frightening.

MAIN STREET, U.S.A.

Main Street Vehicles Not frightening in any respect.

Town Square Meet and Greets Not frightening in any respect.

Walt Disney World Railroad Not frightening in any respect.

ADVENTURELAND

Jungle Cruise Moderately intense, some macabre sights. A good test attraction for little ones.

Pirates of the Caribbean Slightly intimidating queuing area; intense boat ride with gruesome (though humorously presented) sights and a short, unexpected slide down a flume.

The Magic Carpets of Aladdin Much like Dumbo. A favorite of most young children.

Swiss Family Treehouse May not be suitable for kids (or adults) who are afraid of heights.

Walt Disney's Enchanted Tiki Room A thunderstorm, loud volume level, and simulated explosions frighten some preschoolers.

FRONTIERLAND

Big Thunder Mountain Railroad Visually intimidating from outside, with moderately intense visual effects. The roller coaster is wild enough to frighten many adults, particularly seniors. Switching-off option provided (see page 93).

Country Bear Jamboree Not frightening in any respect.

Frontierland Shootin' Arcade Could be frightening to children who are scared of guns and loud noises.

Splash Mountain Visually intimidating from outside, with moderately intense visual effects. The ride culminates in a 52-foot plunge down a steep chute. Switching-off option provided (see page 93).

Tom Sawyer Island and Fort Langhorn Some very young children are intimidated by dark walk-through tunnels that can be easily avoided.

LIBERTY SQUARE

The Hall of Presidents Not frightening, but boring for young ones.

The Haunted Mansion Name raises anxiety, as do sounds and sights of waiting area. Intense attraction with humorously presented macabre sights. The ride itself is gentle.

Liberty Belle Riverboat Not frightening in any respect.

FANTASYLAND

Ariel's Grotto Not frightening in any respect.

The Barnstormer May frighten some preschoolers.

Small-Child Fright-Potential Chart (cont'd.)

THE MAGIC KINGDOM (cont'd.)

FANTASYLAND (continued)

Dumbo the Flying Elephant A tame midway ride; a great favorite of most young children.

Enchanted Tales with Belle Not frightening in any respect.

It's a Small World Not frightening in any respect.

Mad Tea Party Midway-type ride can induce motion sickness in all ages.

Mickey's PhilarMagic Some preschoolers may be a little scared at first, but taking the 3-D glasses off tones down the effect.

The Many Adventures of Winnie the Pooh Frightens a small percentage of preschoolers.

Peter Pan's Flight Not frightening in any respect.

Pete's Silly Sideshow Not frightening in any respect.

Prince Charming Regal Carrousel Not frightening in any respect.

Princess Fairytale Hall Long lines may have parents running for the hills.

Seven Dwarfs Mine Train May frighten some preschoolers.

Under the Sea: Journey of the Little Mermaid Animatronic octopus character frightens some preschoolers.

TOMORROWLAND

Astro Orbiter Visually intimidating from the waiting area, but the ride is relatively tame.

Buzz Lightyear's Space Ranger Spin Dark ride with cartoonlike aliens. May frighten some preschoolers.

Monsters, Inc. Laugh Floor May frighten a small percentage of preschoolers.

Space Mountain Very intense roller coaster in the dark; the Magic Kingdom's wildest ride and a scary roller coaster by any standard. Switching-off option provided (see page 93).

Stitch's Great Escape! Very intense. May frighten children age 9 and younger. Switching-off option provided (see page 93).

Tomorrowland Speedway Noise of waiting area slightly intimidates preschoolers; otherwise, not frightening.

Tomorrowland Transit Authority PeopleMover Not frightening in any respect.

Walt Disney's Carousel of Progress Not frightening in any respect.

EPCOT

FUTURE WORLD

Sum of All Thrills Intense roller-coaster simulator may frighten some kids.

Imagination!: *Captain EO* Extremely intense visual effects and loudness frighten many young children.

Journey into Imagination with Figment Loud noises and unexpected flashing lights startle younger children.

The Land: *The Circle of Life* Not frightening in any respect.

Small-Child Fright-Potential Chart (cont'd.)

The Land: Living with the Land Not frightening in any respect.

The Land: Soarin' May frighten kids age 7 and younger, or anyone with a fear of heights. Otherwise a very mellow ride.

Mission: Space Extremely intense space-simulation ride that has been known to frighten guests of all ages. Preshow may also frighten some children. Switching-off option provided (see page 93).

The Seas: The Seas with Nemo & Friends Very sweet but may frighten some toddlers.

The Seas: Main Tank and Exhibits Not frightening in any respect.

The Seas: Turtle Talk with Crush Not frightening in any respect.

Spaceship Earth Dark, imposing presentation intimidates a few preschoolers.

Test Track Intense thrill ride may frighten guests of any age. Switching-off option provided (see page 93).

Universe of Energy: *Ellen's Energy Adventure* Dinosaur segment frightens some preschoolers; visually intense, with some intimidating effects.

WORLD SHOWCASE

Agent P's World Showcase Adventure Not frightening in any respect.

Canada: *O Canada!* Not frightening, but audience must stand.

China: *Reflections of China* Not frightening in any respect.

France: *Impressions de France* Not frightening in any respect.

Frozen Ever After Dark. The previous ride ended with a plunge down a 20-foot flume, which, if it was kept, may frighten a few preschoolers.

Germany Not frightening in any respect.

Italy Not frightening in any respect.

Japan Not frightening in any respect.

Mexico: Gran Fiesta Tour Not frightening in any respect.

Morocco Not frightening in any respect.

Royal Sommerhus Meet and Greet Not frightening in any respect.

United Kingdom Not frightening in any respect.

United States: *The American Adventure* Not frightening in any respect.

DISNEY'S ANIMAL KINGDOM

The Oasis Not frightening in any respect.

Rafiki's Planet Watch Not frightening in any respect.

DISCOVERY ISLAND

Meet Disney Pals at Adventurers Outpost Not frightening in any respect.

Small-Child Fright-Potential Chart (cont'd.)

DISNEY'S ANIMAL KINGDOM (cont'd.)

DISCOVERY ISLAND (continued)

The Tree of Life: *It's Tough to Be a Bug!* Very intense and loud, with special effects that startle viewers of all ages and potentially terrify little kids.

Wilderness Explorers Not frightening in any respect.

AFRICA

Festival of the Lion King A bit loud, but otherwise not frightening.

Kilimanjaro Safaris A "collapsing" bridge and the proximity of real animals make a few young children anxious.

Pangani Forest Exploration Trail Not frightening in any respect.

Wildlife Express Train Not frightening in any respect.

ASIA

Expedition Everest Can frighten guests of all ages. Switching-off option provided (see page 93).

Flights of Wonder Swooping birds alarm a few small children.

Kali River Rapids Potentially frightening and certainly wet for guests of all ages. Switching-off option provided (see page 93).

Maharajah Jungle Trek Some children may balk at the bat exhibit.

DINOLAND U.S.A.

The Boneyard Not frightening in any respect.

Dinosaur High-tech thrill ride rattles riders of all ages. Switching-off option provided (see next page).

Primeval Whirl A beginner roller coaster. Most children age 7 and older will take it in stride. Switching-off option provided (see next page).

Theater in the Wild: *Finding Nemo—The Musical* Not frightening in any respect, albeit loud.

TriceraTop Spin A midway-type ride that will frighten only a small percentage of younger children.

DISNEY'S HOLLYWOOD STUDIOS

HOLLYWOOD BOULEVARD

The Great Movie Ride Intense in parts, with very realistic special effects and some visually intimidating sights. Frightens many preschoolers.

SUNSET BOULEVARD

Fantasmic! Terrifies some preschoolers.

Rock 'n' Roller Coaster The wildest coaster at Walt Disney World. May frighten guests of any age. Switching-off option provided (see next page).

Theater of the Stars: *Beauty and the Beast—Live on Stage* Not frightening in any respect.

The Twilight Zone Tower of Terror Visually intimidating to young children; contains intense and realistic special effects. The plummeting elevator at the ride's end frightens many adults as well as kids. Switching-off option provided (see next page).

Small-Child Fright-Potential Chart (cont'd.)

ECHO LAKE

Indiana Jones Epic Stunt Spectacular! An intense show with powerful special effects, including explosions, but young kids generally handle it well.

Star Tours—The Adventures Continue Too visually intense for children under age 8. Switching-off option provided (see below).

STREETS OF AMERICA

Honey, I Shrunk the Kids Movie Set Adventure Not scary (though oversized).

Jim Henson's Muppet-Vision 3-D Intense and loud, but not frightening.

Lights, Motors, Action! Extreme Stunt Show Super stunt spectacular; intense with loud noises and explosions, but not threatening in any way.

PIXAR PLACE

Toy Story Mania! Dark ride may frighten some preschoolers.

MICKEY AVENUE

Walt Disney: One Man's Dream Not frightening in any respect.

ANIMATION COURTYARD

Disney Junior—Live on Stage! Not frightening in any respect.

Voyage of the Little Mermaid Some kids are creeped out by Ursula.

Preschoolers should start with Dumbo and work up to the Jungle Cruise in late morning, after being revved up and before getting hungry, thirsty, or tired. Pirates of the Caribbean is out for preschoolers. You get the idea.

SWITCHING OFF (a.k.a. The Baby Swap)

SEVERAL ATTRACTIONS HAVE MINIMUM HEIGHT and/or age requirements. Some couples with children too small or too young forgo these attractions, while others take turns to ride. Missing some of Disney's best rides is an unnecessary sacrifice, and waiting in line twice for the same ride is a tremendous waste of time.

Instead, take advantage of "switching off," also known as "The Baby Swap" or "The Rider Swap" (or "The Baby/Rider Switch"). To switch off, there must be at least two adults. Adults and children wait in line together. When you reach a cast member, say you want to switch off. The cast member will allow everyone, including young children, to enter the attraction. When you reach the loading area, one adult rides while the other exits with the kids. Then the riding adult disembarks and takes charge of the children while the other adult rides. A third member of the party, either an adult or an older child, can ride twice, once with each switching-off adult, so that the switching-off adults don't have to ride alone.

On most FastPass+ attractions, when you tell the cast member that you want to switch off, you'll get a special "rider exchange" FastPass good for three people. One parent and the nonriding child (or children) will at that point be asked to leave the line. When those riding reunite with those waiting, the waiting adult and two others from the party can ride using the special FastPass. This eliminates confusion at the boarding area while sparing the nonriding adult and child the tedium of waiting in line.

ATTRACTIONS WHERE SWITCHING OFF IS COMMON	
THE MAGIC KINGDOM	**DISNEY'S ANIMAL KINGDOM**
Big Thunder Mountain Railroad	DINOSAUR
Seven Dwarfs Mine Train	Expedition Everest
Space Mountain	Kali River Rapids
Splash Mountain	Primeval Whirl
Stitch's Great Escape!	**DISNEY'S HOLLYWOOD STUDIOS**
EPCOT	Rock 'n' Roller Coaster
Mission: Space	Star Tours—The Adventures Continue
Test Track	The Twilight Zone Tower of Terror

If your young child gets cold feet just before boarding a ride where there's no age or height requirement, you usually can arrange a switch-off with the loading attendant. (This happens frequently in Pirates of the Caribbean's dungeon waiting area.)

No law says you have to ride. If you reach the boarding area and someone is unhappy, tell an attendant you've changed your mind and you'll be shown the way out.

The DISNEY CHARACTERS

WATCHING CHARACTERS HAS BECOME A PASTIME. Families once were content to meet a character occasionally. They now pursue them relentlessly, armed with autograph books and cameras. Because some characters are only rarely seen, character watching has become character collecting. (To cash in on character collecting, Disney sells autograph books throughout Disney World.) Mickey, Minnie, and Goofy are a snap to bag; they seem to be everywhere. But some characters, like the Queen of Hearts and Friar Tuck, seldom come out, and quite a few appear only in parades or stage shows. Other characters appear only in a location consistent with their starring role. The Fairy Godmother is often near Cinderella Castle in Fantasyland, while Buzz Lightyear appears close to his eponymous attraction in Tomorrowland.

WDW CHARACTER-GREETING VENUES

DISNEY HAS CREATED many permanent greeting locations intended to satisfy guests' inexhaustible desire to meet characters. The chart below and on the next page lists them by park and character.

THE MAGIC KINGDOM

MICKEY AND HIS POSSE

Chip 'n' Dale Frontierland

Daisy, Donald, Goofy, Minnie Pete's Silly Sideshow (FastPass+)

Mickey Town Square Theater (FastPass/FastPass+)

Pluto Town Square

DISNEY ROYALTY

Aladdin, Jasmine Adventureland

Anna and Elsa Princess Fairytale Hall (FastPass+)

Ariel Ariel's Grotto

Aurora, Belle *Enchanted Tales with Belle* (FastPass+)

Cinderella, Rapunzel Princess Fairytale Hall (FastPass+)

The Fairy Godmother, the Tremaines In Cinderella Castle

Gaston Fountain outside Gaston's Tavern

Merida Fairytale Garden

Naveen, Tiana Liberty Square

Snow White Liberty Square

FAIRIES

Tinker Bell and Friends Town Square Theater (FastPass+)

MISCELLANEOUS

***ALICE IN WONDERLAND* Alice, the White Rabbit** Mad Tea Party

***THE ARISTOCATS* Marie** Town Square

***LILO AND STITCH* Stitch** Tomorrowland

***PETER PAN* Peter, Wendy** Adventureland

***TOY STORY* Buzz Lightyear** Tomorrowland
  Woody Frontierland near Splash Mountain

EPCOT

MICKEY AND HIS POSSE

Chip 'n' Dale Outside on the Land side of the Epcot Character Spot

Donald Mexico, at the Mexico Promenade

Goofy, Minnie, Mickey Epcot Character Spot

Pluto On the right as you enter Epcot through the main turnstiles

Characters are subject to change; check the *Times Guide* or **kennythepirate.com** for the latest information.

EPCOT (continued)

DISNEY ROYALTY

Aladdin, Jasmine Morocco **Aurora, The Beast, Belle** France

Anna, Elsa, *Frozen* characters Norway (in 2016)

Mulan China **Snow White** Germany

MISCELLANEOUS

Alice, Mary Poppins and Bert, Pooh, Tigger, Eeyore United Kingdom

Duffy the Disney Bear World Showcase Plaza

DISNEY'S ANIMAL KINGDOM

MICKEY AND HIS POSSE

Chip 'n' Dale Rafiki's Planet Watch at Conservation Station and The Oasis, just past the entrance turnstiles and to the right

Daisy Discovery Island near the bridge to Africa

Donald DinoLand U.S.A., to the left of the DINOSAUR exit on Cretaceous Trail

Goofy, Pluto DinoLand U.S.A., near Primeval Whirl

Mickey, Minnie Adventurers Outpost on Discovery Island (FastPass+)

DISNEY ROYALTY

Pocahontas Discovery Island trails that run behind The Tree of Life

MISCELLANEOUS

***THE JUNGLE BOOK* King Louie and Baloo** At Upcountry Landing on the walkway between Asia and Africa

***THE LION KING* Rafiki** Rafiki's Planet Watch, at Conservation Station

***UP* Dug, Russell:** By *It's Tough to Be a Bug!*

DISNEY'S HOLLYWOOD STUDIOS

MICKEY AND HIS POSSE

Chip 'n' Dale, Daisy, Donald, Goofy, Pluto In front of The Great Movie Ride

Minnie In front of The Great Movie Ride and Center Stage Courtyard

Sorcerer Mickey Streets of America near Studio Catering Co.

DISNEY CHANNEL STARS

Phineas and Ferb: Streets of America

Sofia the First, Jake (Jake and the Never Land Pirates) Animation Courtyard near *Disney Junior—Live on Stage!*

MISCELLANEOUS

***MONSTERS, INC.* Mike, Sulley:** Streets of America (Backlot)

***TOY STORY* Buzz, Woody:** Pixar Place

CHARACTER DINING

FRATERNIZING WITH CHARACTERS is so popular that Disney offers character breakfasts, brunches, and dinners where families can dine in the presence of Mickey, Minnie, Goofy, and assorted princesses. Besides grabbing customers from Denny's and Hardee's, character meals provide a familiar, controlled setting in which young children can warm gradually to characters. All meals are attended by several characters. Adult prices apply to persons ages 10 or older, children's prices to ages 3–9; little ones under age 3 eat free. For additional information on character dining, call ☎ 407-939-3463 (WDW-DINE).

Because of the incredible popularity of character dining, reservations can be hard to come by if you wait until a couple of months before your vacation to book your choices, so arrange Advance Reservations by calling WDW-DINE as far in advance as possible. To book a character meal, you must provide Disney with a credit card number. Your card will be charged $10 *per person* if you no-show or cancel your reservation less than 24 hours in advance; you may, however, reschedule with no penalty.

> *unofficial* **TIP**
> Many children particularly enjoy meals with "face characters" such as Snow White, Belle, Jasmine, Cinderella, and Ariel, who speak and are thus able to engage children in a way not possible for the mute animal characters.

At very popular character meals like the breakfast at Cinderella's Royal Table, you're required to make a for-real reservation and guarantee it with a for-real deposit.

How to Choose a Character Meal

We receive a lot of mail asking for advice about character meals. Some *are* better than others, sometimes much better. Here's what we look for when we evaluate character meals:

1. THE CHARACTERS The various meals offer a diverse assortment of Disney characters. Selecting a meal that features your children's special favorites is a good first step. Check the Character-Meal Hit Parade chart on the following pages to see which characters are assigned to each meal.

2. ATTENTION FROM THE CHARACTERS In all character meals, the characters circulate among the guests hugging children, posing for pictures, and signing autographs. How much time a character spends with you and your children will depend primarily on the ratio of characters to guests. The more characters and fewer guests the better. Because many character meals never fill to capacity, the character–guest ratios found in our Character-Meal Hit Parade chart have been adjusted to reflect an average attendance as opposed to a sellout crowd. Even so, there's quite a range.

3. THE SETTING Some character meals are in exotic settings. For others, moving the event to an elementary-school cafeteria would be an improvement. Our chart rates each meal's setting with the familiar scale of zero (worst) to five (best) stars. Two restaurants,

Character-Meal Hit Parade

1. CINDERELLA'S ROYAL TABLE MAGIC KINGDOM

MEALS SERVED DAILY Breakfast, lunch, and dinner

SETTING ★★★★

CHARACTERS Cinderella, Ariel, Aurora, Jasmine, Snow White

TYPE OF SERVICE Fixed menu

FOOD VARIETY & QUALITY ★★★

NOISE LEVEL Quiet **CHARACTER–GUEST RATIO** 1:26

2. AKERSHUS ROYAL BANQUET HALL EPCOT

MEALS SERVED Breakfast, lunch, and dinner

SETTING ★★★★

CHARACTERS 4–6 characters chosen from Ariel, Belle, Jasmine, Mary Poppins, Mulan, Sleeping Beauty, Snow White

TYPE OF SERVICE Family-style and menu (all you care to eat)

FOOD VARIETY & QUALITY ★★★½

NOISE LEVEL Quiet **CHARACTER–GUEST RATIO** 1:54

3. CHEF MICKEY'S CONTEMPORARY

MEALS SERVED Breakfast, dinner **SETTING** ★★★

SETTING ★★★

CHARACTERS *Breakfast, lunch, and dinner:* Mickey, Minnie, Donald, Goofy, Pluto (sometimes Chip 'n' Dale)

TYPE OF SERVICE Buffet

FOOD VARIETY & QUALITY Breakfast ★★★ Dinner ★★★½

NOISE LEVEL Loud **CHARACTER–GUEST RATIO** 1:56

4. THE CRYSTAL PALACE MAGIC KINGDOM

MEALS SERVED Breakfast, lunch, and dinner **SETTING** ★★★

CHARACTERS Pooh, Eeyore, Piglet, Tigger

TYPE OF SERVICE Buffet

FOOD VARIETY & QUALITY Breakfast ★★½ Lunch and dinner ★★★

NOISE LEVEL Very loud

CHARACTER–GUEST RATIO Breakfast 1:67 Lunch and dinner 1:89

5. 1900 PARK FARE GRAND FLORIDIAN

MEALS SERVED Breakfast, dinner **SETTING** ★★★

CHARACTERS *Breakfast:* Mary Poppins, Alice, Mad Hatter, Pooh, Tigger *Dinner:* Cinderella, Prince Charming, Lady Tremaine, the two stepsisters

TYPE OF SERVICE Buffet

FOOD VARIETY & QUALITY Breakfast ★★★ Dinner ★★★½

NOISE LEVEL Moderate

CHARACTER–GUEST RATIO Breakfast 1:54 Dinner 1:44

6. GARDEN GRILL RESTAURANT   EPCOT

MEAL SERVED Dinner   **SETTING** ★★★★½

CHARACTERS Mickey, Pluto, Chip 'n' Dale

TYPE OF SERVICE Family-style   **FOOD VARIETY & QUALITY** ★★★½

NOISE LEVEL Very quiet   **CHARACTER–GUEST RATIO** 1:46

7. TUSKER HOUSE RESTAURANT   DISNEY'S ANIMAL KINGDOM

MEALS SERVED Breakfast, lunch   **SETTING** ★★★

CHARACTERS Donald, Daisy, Mickey, Goofy

TYPE OF SERVICE Buffet   **FOOD VARIETY & QUALITY** ★★★

NOISE LEVEL Very loud   **CHARACTER–GUEST RATIO** 1:112

8. CAPE MAY CAFE   BEACH CLUB

MEAL SERVED Breakfast   **SETTING** ★★★

CHARACTERS Goofy, Donald, Minnie   **TYPE OF SERVICE** Buffet

FOOD VARIETY & QUALITY ★★½   **NOISE LEVEL** Moderate

CHARACTER–GUEST RATIO 1:67

9. 'OHANA   POLYNESIAN

MEAL SERVED Breakfast   **SETTING** ★★

CHARACTERS Lilo and Stitch, Mickey, Pluto

TYPE OF SERVICE Family-style   **FOOD VARIETY & QUALITY** ★★½

NOISE LEVEL Moderate   **CHARACTER–GUEST RATIO** 1:57

10. HOLLYWOOD & VINE   DISNEY'S HOLLYWOOD STUDIOS

MEALS SERVED Breakfast, lunch   **SETTING** ★★½

CHARACTERS Handy Manny, Sofia the First, Doc McStuffins, Jake (*Jake and the Never Land Pirates*)

TYPE OF SERVICE Buffet   **FOOD VARIETY & QUALITY** ★★★

NOISE LEVEL Moderate   **CHARACTER–GUEST RATIO** 1:71

11. GARDEN GROVE   SWAN

MEALS SERVED Breakfast (Sat & Sun only), dinner   **SETTING** ★★★

CHARACTERS Chip 'n' Dale, Goofy, Pluto   **TYPE OF SERVICE** Buffet

FOOD VARIETY & QUALITY ★★★½   **NOISE LEVEL** Moderate

NOISE LEVEL Moderate

CHARACTER–GUEST RATIO 1:198, but often much better

11. RAVELLO   FOUR SEASONS

MEALS SERVED Breakfast (Thurs & Sun only), dinner   **SETTING** ★★★

CHARACTERS Goofy and pals   **TYPE OF SERVICE** Buffet

FOOD VARIETY & QUALITY ★★★½   **NOISE LEVEL** Moderate

NOISE LEVEL Moderate

CHARACTER–GUEST RATIO 1:39

Cinderella's Royal Table in the Magic Kingdom and Garden Grill Restaurant in the Land Pavilion at Epcot, deserve special mention. Cinderella's Royal Table is on the first and second floors of Cinderella Castle in Fantasyland, offering guests a look inside the castle. Garden Grill is a revolving restaurant overlooking several scenes from the Living with the Land boat ride. Also at Epcot, the popular Princess Storybook Meals are held in the castlelike Akershus Royal Banquet Hall. Though Chef Mickey's at the Contemporary Resort is rather sterile in appearance, it affords a great view of the monorail running through the hotel. Themes and settings of the remaining character-meal venues, while apparent to adults, will be lost on most children.

4. THE FOOD Although some food served at character meals is quite good, most is average—in other words, palatable but nothing to get excited about. In terms of variety, consistency, and quality, restaurants generally do a better job with breakfast than with lunch or dinner (if served). Some restaurants offer a buffet, while others opt for "one-skillet" family-style service, in which all the hot items on the bill of fare are served from the same pot or skillet. To help you sort it out, we rate the food at each character meal in our chart using the tried-and-true five-star scale.

5. THE PROGRAM Some larger restaurants stage modest performances where the characters dance, head a parade around the room, or lead songs and cheers. For some guests, these activities give the meal a celebratory air; for others, they turn what was already mayhem into absolute chaos. Either way, the antics consume time the characters could spend with families at their table.

6. NOISE If you want to eat in peace, character meals are a bad choice. That said, some are much noisier than others. Once again, our chart gives you some idea of what to expect.

7. WHICH MEAL? Although character breakfasts seem to be the most popular, character lunches and dinners are usually more practical because they do not interfere with your early-morning touring. During hot weather especially, a character lunch at midday can be heavenly.

8. COST Dinners cost more than lunches and lunches more than breakfasts. Prices for meals (except at Cinderella Castle) vary considerably from the least expensive to the most expensive restaurant. Breakfasts run $27–$58 for adults and $15–$38 for kids ages 3–9. For character lunches, expect to pay $31–$61 for adults and $16–$38 for kids. Dinners are $31–$73 for adults and $16–$43 for children. Little ones age 2 years and younger eat free. The meals at the high end of the price range are at **Cinderella's Royal Table** in the Magic Kingdom and **Akershus Royal Banquet** Hall at Epcot. The reasons for the sky-high prices: (1) Cinderella's Royal Table is small but in great demand and (2) both Akershus and Cindy's are Disney-princess central.

9. ADVANCE RESERVATIONS Disney makes Advance Reservations for character meals 180 days before you wish to dine (Disney resort guests can reserve 190 days out, or 10 additional days in advance); moreover, Disney resort guests can make Advance Reservations for all meals during their stay. Advance Reservations for most character meals are easy to obtain even if you call only a couple of weeks before you leave home. Meals at Be Our Guest and Cinderella's Royal Table are another story; they are without doubt among the very hottest tickets at Disney World.

10. CHECKING IT TWICE Disney occasionally shuffles the characters and theme of a character meal. If your little one's heart is set on Pooh and Piglet, getting Hook and Mr. Smee is just a waste of time and money. Reconfirm all character-meal Advance Reservations three weeks or so before you leave home by calling ☎ 407-WDW-DINE.

11. "FRIENDS" For some venues, Disney has stopped specifying characters scheduled for a particular meal. Instead, they say it's a given character "and friends"—for example, "Pooh and friends," meaning Eeyore, Piglet, and Tigger, or some combination thereof, or "Mickey and friends" with some assortment chosen among Minnie, Goofy, Pluto, Donald, Daisy, Chip, and Dale.

12. THE BUM'S RUSH Most character meals are leisurely affairs, and you can usually stay as long as you want. An exception is Cinderella's Royal Table. Because Cindy's is in such high demand, the restaurant does everything short of pre-chewing your food to move you through.

BABYSITTING

CHILD-CARE CENTERS Child care isn't available inside the theme parks, but two Magic Kingdom resorts connected by monorail or boat (**Polynesian Village & Villas** and **Wilderness Lodge & Villas**), four Epcot resorts (the **Yacht & Beach Club Resorts**, the **Swan**, and the **Dolphin**), and **Animal Kingdom Lodge,** along with the **Hilton Orlando at Lake Buena Vista,** have child-care centers for potty-trained children age 3 and older (see chart on the next page). Services vary, but children generally can be left between 5 p.m. and midnight. Milk and cookies and blankets and pillows are provided at all centers, and dinner is provided at most. Play is supervised but not organized, and toys, videos, and games are plentiful. Guests at any Disney resort or campground may use the services.

WALT DISNEY WORLD CHILD-CARE CLUBS*

HOTEL	NAME OF PROGRAM	AGES	PHONE
Animal Kingdom Lodge			
Simba's Cubhouse		3–12	☎ 407-938-4785
Dolphin and Swan			
Camp Dolphin		4–12	☎ 407-934-4241
Polynesian Village Resort			
Lilo's Playhouse		3–12	☎ 407-824-2000
Yacht & Beach Club Resorts			
Sandcastle Club		3–12	☎ 407-934-3750
Wilderness Lodge & Villas			
Cub's Den		3–12	☎ 407-824-1083

*Child-care clubs operate afternoons and evenings. Before 4 p.m., call the hotels rather than the numbers listed above. All programs require reservations; call ☎ 407-WDW-DINE (939-3463).

The most elaborate of the child-care centers (or "clubs" or "camps") is **Lilo's Playhouse** at the Polynesian Village Resort. The rate for ages 3–12 is $15 per hour, per child (2-hour minimum).

All the clubs accept reservations (some six months in advance!) with a credit card guarantee. Call the club directly, or reserve through Disney at ☎ 407-WDW-DINE. Most clubs require a 24-hour cancellation notice and levy a hefty penalty of 2 hours' time or $30 per child for no-shows. A limited number of walk-ins are usually accepted on a first-come, first-served basis.

If you're staying in a Disney resort that doesn't offer a child-care club and you *don't* have a car, then you're better off using in-room babysitting. Trying to take your child to a club in another hotel by Disney bus requires a 50- to 90-minute trip each way. By the time you've deposited your little one, it will almost be time to pick him or her up again.

IN-ROOM BABYSITTING Three local companies provide in-room sitting in Walt Disney World and surrounding areas: **Kid's Nite Out** (☎ 407-828-0920 or 800-696-8105; **kidsniteout.com**), and, yes, **Fairy Godmothers** (☎ 407-277-3724). Kid's Nite Out also serves hotels in the greater Orlando area, including downtown. All three provide sitters older than age 18 who are insured, bonded, screened, reference-checked, police-checked, and trained in CPR. In addition to caring for your kids in your room, the sitters will, if you direct (and pay), take your children to the theme parks or other venues. All three services offer bilingual sitters.

PART SIX

SPECIAL TIPS *for* SPECIAL PEOPLE

WALT DISNEY WORLD *for* SINGLES

WALT DISNEY WORLD IS GREAT FOR SINGLES. It's safe, clean, and low-pressure. If you're looking for a place to relax without being hit on, Disney World is perfect. Bars, lounges, and nightclubs are the most laid-back and friendly you're likely to find anywhere. In many, you can hang out and not even be asked to buy a drink (or asked to let someone buy a drink for you). Parking lots are well lit and constantly patrolled. For women alone, safety and comfort are unsurpassed.

There's also no need to while away the evening hours alone in your hotel room. Between the BoardWalk and Disney Springs, nightlife options abound. If you drink more than you should and are a Disney resort guest, Disney buses will return you safely to your hotel.

unofficial **TIP**
Virtually every type of entertainment performed fully clothed is available at amazingly reasonable prices at Disney nightspots.

WALT DISNEY WORLD *for* COUPLES

WEDDINGS AND HONEYMOONS

SO MANY COUPLES TIE THE KNOT or honeymoon in the World that Disney has a dedicated department to help them arrange the day of their dreams. **Disney's Fairy Tale Weddings & Honeymoons** (☎ 321-939-4610; **disneyweddings.com**) offers a range of ceremony venues and services, plus honeymoon planning and registries. Wedding packages start at $2,495.

Most packages include a bouquet, a cake and Champagne toast (not included in the basic Memories Collection package), live music, photography, limo service, a wedding-planning website, a wedding coordinator, and Annual Passes to Disney World for the happy couple (not part of the Memories Collection). The officiant and marriage certificate cost extra. Disney has a list of local officiants from which to choose, or the couple can bring their own.

ROMANTIC GETAWAYS

DISNEY WORLD IS A FAVORITE GETAWAY FOR COUPLES, but not all Disney hotels are equally romantic. Some are too family-oriented; others swarm with convention-goers. For romantic (though expensive) lodging, we recommend **Animal Kingdom Lodge & Villas, Bay Lake Tower** at the Contemporary, the **Polynesian Village, Wilderness Lodge & Villas,** the **Grand Floridian, BoardWalk Inn & Villas,** and the **Yacht & Beach Clubs.** The **Alligator Bayou** section at **Port Orleans Riverside,** a Moderate Disney resort, also has secluded rooms.

QUIET, ROMANTIC PLACES TO EAT

RESTAURANTS WITH GOOD FOOD *and* a couple-friendly ambience are rare in the parks. Only a handful of dining locales satisfy both requirements: **Coral Reef Restaurant,** an alfresco table at **Tutto Italia Ristorante,** the terrace at the **Rose & Crown Dining Room,** and the upstairs tables at the France Pavilion's **Monsieur Paul,** all in Epcot; and the corner booths at **The Hollywood Brown Derby** in Disney's Hollywood Studios. Waterfront (though not necessarily quiet or romantic) dining is available at **Fulton's Crab House, Paradiso 37,** and **Portobello** at Disney Springs and **Narcoossee's** at the Grand Floridian.

Victoria & Albert's at the Grand Floridian is the World's showcase gourmet restaurant; expect to pay big bucks. Other good choices for couples include **Artist Point** at Wilderness Lodge, **Yachtsman Steakhouse** at the Yacht Club, **Shula's Steak House** at the Dolphin, **Jiko—The Cooking Place** at Animal Kingdom Lodge, and **Flying Fish Cafe** at the BoardWalk.

Eating later in the evening and choosing a restaurant we've mentioned will improve your chances for intimate dining; nevertheless, children—well behaved or otherwise—are everywhere at Walt Disney World, and there's no way to escape them.

WALT DISNEY WORLD *for* SENIORS

MOST SENIORS WE INTERVIEW ENJOY Disney World much more when they tour with folks their own age. If, however, you're considering going to Disney World with your grandchildren, we recommend an orientation visit without them first. If you know first-hand what to expect, it's much easier to establish limits, maintain control, and set a comfortable pace when you visit with the youngsters.

If you're determined to take the grandkids, read carefully those sections of this book that discuss family touring. Because seniors are a varied and willing lot, there aren't any attractions we would suggest they avoid. For seniors, as with other Disney visitors, personal taste is more important than age. We hate to see mature visitors pass up an exceptional attraction like Splash Mountain because younger visitors call it a "thrill ride." A full-blown adventure, Splash Mountain gets its appeal more from music and visual effects than from the thrill of the ride. Because you must choose among attractions that might interest you, we provide facts to help you make informed decisions.

GETTING AROUND

MANY SENIORS LIKE TO WALK, but a 7-hour visit to a theme park includes 4–10 miles on foot. If you're not up to that, let someone push you in a rented wheelchair (theme parks: $12 per day with no deposit, $10 per day for multiday rentals; Disney Springs: free with $100 refundable deposit; Disney resorts: $315 deposit). The theme parks also offer fun-to-drive electric carts (electric convenience vehicles, or ECVs) for $50 per day, with a $20 refundable deposit. If you're looking to save money on an ECV, **Buena Vista Scooters** (**buenavistascooters.com**) rents them for $30 per day with delivery and pick up at your Disney resort.

Your rental deposit slip is good for a replacement wheelchair in any park during the same day. You can rent a chair at the Magic Kingdom in the morning, return it, go to Epcot, present your deposit slip, and get another chair at no additional charge.

LODGING

IF YOU CAN AFFORD IT, stay in Walt Disney World. If you're concerned about the quality of your accommodations or the availability of transportation, staying inside the Disney complex will ease your mind. The rooms are some of the nicest in the Orlando area and are always clean and well maintained. Plus, transportation is always available to any destination in Disney World at no additional cost.

Disney hotels reserve rooms closer to restaurants and transportation for guests of any age who can't tolerate much walking. They also provide golf carts to pick up from and deliver guests to their rooms. Cart service can vary dramatically depending on the time of day and the number of guests requesting service. At check-in time (around 3 p.m.), for example, the wait for a ride can be as long as 40 minutes.

Seniors intending to spend more time at Epcot and Disney's Hollywood Studios than at the Magic Kingdom or Disney's Animal Kingdom should consider the **Yacht & Beach Club Resorts,** the **Swan,** the **Dolphin,** or BoardWalk Inn & Villas.

The **Contemporary Resort** and the adjacent **Bay Lake Tower** are good choices for seniors who want to be on the monorail system. So are the **Grand Floridian** and the **Polynesian Village,** though they cover many acres, necessitating a lot of walking. For a restful, rustic feeling, choose **Wilderness Lodge & Villas.** If you want a kitchen and the comforts of home, book **Old Key West Resort,** the **Beach Club Villas, Animal Kingdom Villas,** or **BoardWalk Villas.** If you enjoy watching animals, try **Animal Kingdom Lodge & Villas.** Try **Saratoga Springs** for golf.

RV-ers will find pleasant surroundings at Disney's **Fort Wilderness Resort & Campground.** Several independent campgrounds are within 30 minutes of Disney World. None offers the wilderness setting or amenities that Disney does, but they cost less.

DINING

EAT BREAKFAST AT YOUR HOTEL RESTAURANT, or save money by having juice and pastries in your room. Although you aren't allowed to bring food into the parks, fruit, juices, and soft drinks are sold throughout Disney World. Follow with an early dinner and be out of the restaurants, rested and ready for evening touring and fireworks, long before the main crowd begins to think about

unofficial **TIP**
Make your dining Advance Reservations for before noon to avoid the lunch crowds.

dinner. We recommend fitting dining and rest times into the day. Plan lunch as your break in the day. Sit back, relax, and enjoy. Then return to your hotel for a nap or a swim.

WALT DISNEY WORLD *for* GUESTS *with* SPECIAL NEEDS

DISNEY WORLD IS SO ATTUNED TO GUESTS with physical challenges that unscrupulous people have been known to fake a disability in order to take unfair advantage. If you have a disability, even a restricted diet, Disney World is prepared to meet your needs.

Valuable trip-planning information is available at **disneyworld .com.** Each major theme park offers a free booklet that describes disabled services and facilities; get it when entering the theme and water parks, at resort front desks, and at wheelchair-rental locations in the theme parks. Printable PDF versions of the guides are available online at **tinyurl.com/wdwguestswithdisabilities.** For specific requests, such as those regarding special accommodations at hotels or on the Disney transportation system, call ☎ 407-939-7807 (voice) or 407-939-7670 (TTY). When the recorded menu comes up, press *1.*

VISITORS WITH DISABILITIES

WHOLLY OR PARTIALLY NONAMBULATORY guests may rent wheelchairs. Most rides, shows, attractions, restrooms, and restaurants accommodate the nonambulatory disabled. If you're in a park and need assistance, go to Guest Relations.

A limited number of electric carts, ECVs (electric convenience vehicles), and ESVs (electric standing vehicles) are available for rent. Easy to drive, they give nonambulatory guests tremendous freedom and mobility.

All Disney lots have close-in parking for disabled visitors; ask for directions when you pay your parking fee. All monorails and most rides, shows, restrooms, and restaurants accommodate wheelchairs.

Even if an attraction doesn't accommodate wheelchairs, nonambulatory guests still may ride if they can transfer from their wheelchair to the ride's vehicle. Disney staff, however, aren't trained or permitted to assist in transfers. Guests must be able to board the ride unassisted or have a member of their party assist them. Either way, members of the nonambulatory guest's party will be permitted to go along on the ride.

Because waiting areas of most attractions won't accommodate wheelchairs, nonambulatory guests and their party should request boarding instructions from a Disney attendant as soon as they arrive at an attraction. Almost always, the entire group will be allowed to board without a lengthy wait.

DIETARY RESTRICTIONS Disney works hard to accommodate guests with special dietary needs. When you make a dining reservation online or by phone, you'll be asked about food allergies and the like. The host or hostess and your server will also ask about this and send the chef out to discuss the menu; if you're not asked, just talk to your server when you're seated. For more information, e-mail **special .diets@disneyworld.com** or visit **tinyurl.comwdwspecialdiets.**

SIGHT- AND/OR HEARING-IMPAIRED GUESTS Guest Relations at the parks provides free assistive-technology devices to visually and hearing-impaired guests ($25 refundable deposit, depending on the device). Sight-impaired guests can customize the given information (such architectural details, restroom locations, and descriptions of attractions and restaurants) through an interactive audio menu that is guided by a GPS system in the device. Hearing-impaired guests can benefit from amplified audio and closed-captioning for attractions loaded into the same device.

Braille guidebooks are available from Guest Relations at all parks ($25 refundable deposit). Closed captioning is provided on some rides, while many theater attractions provide reflective captioning. A sign-language interpreter performs at some live-theater presentations; for show information, call ☎ 407-824-4321 (voice) or 407-939-8255 (TTY).

Disney's Disability Access Service (DAS)

Disney revised its procedures for assisting disabled guests in late 2013, in response to media reports that its then-current Guest Assistance Card (GAC) program was being abused rampantly.

The updated program, called Disability Access Service (DAS), is still designed to accommodate guests who can't wait in regular standby lines. You must still obtain a DAS card at the Guest Relations window of the first theme park you visit. The same card works in every subsequent park you visit.

When you get to Guest Relations, you'll need to present identification and describe your or your family member's limitations. You don't need to disclose a disease or medical condition—what Disney's looking for is a description of how the condition affects you in the parks. Disney's goal here is to get you the right level of assistance, not to obligate you to prove that you or your family member qualifies.

Be as detailed as possible in describing limitations. For instance, if your child is on the autism spectrum and has trouble waiting in long lines or sensory issues that make it difficult for him or her to stand or be subjected to loud noises, you need to let the cast member know each of these things. "He doesn't wait in lines" isn't enough to go on.

DAS cards are good for parties of up to six people. For parties of more than six, all members of the party must be present when the card is used. DAS cards are good (1) for the duration of your vacation, (2) for 14 days, or (3) until the back of the card is full, whichever of these times is shortest. If you fill your card, you must return to Guest Relations and get another.

Finally, note that you can use FastPass+ while you're using the DAS. In fact, cast members will suggest that you do so. It may take some extra planning on the front end, but using FastPass+ helps your DAS access.

PART SEVEN

ARRIVING *and* GETTING AROUND

GETTING THERE

DIRECTIONS

YOU CAN DRIVE to any Walt Disney World destination via **World Drive** off US 192; via **Epcot Center Drive** off Interstate 4; via **FL 536** and **Osceola Parkway West** from FL 417/Central Florida GreeneWay; or from the **Western Way** interchange off FL 429, also known as the Western Beltway (see the map on the following page).

> *unofficial* **TIP**
> Interstate 4 is technically an east–west highway, but it actually runs diagonally (northeast–southwest) across Florida. In metro Orlando, it runs mostly north–south— and that can complicate getting your bearings if you're not familiar with the area. Most highways branching off I-4 run east and west here, not north and south as logic might suggest.

FROM INTERSTATE 10 Take I-10 east across Florida to I-75 southbound at Exit 296A/Tampa, and then take Florida's Turnpike (a toll road) southbound at Exit 328 (on the left) toward Orlando. Take FL 429 (another toll road) to Exit 267A/Tampa southbound off the turnpike. Leave FL 429 at Exit 8, the Western Way interchange, in the direction of Walt Disney World, and follow the signs to your Disney destination. Also use these directions to reach hotels along US 192 (Irlo Bronson Memorial Highway).

FROM INTERSTATE 75 SOUTHBOUND Take I-75 south onto Florida's Turnpike via Exit 328 (on the left) toward Orlando. Take FL 429 (toll) southbound off the turnpike. Leave FL 429 at Exit 8, the Western Way interchange, in the direction of Walt Disney World, and follow the signs to your Disney destination. Also use these directions to reach hotels along US 192 (Irlo Bronson Memorial Highway).

FROM INTERSTATE 95 SOUTHBOUND Exit I-95 onto I-4 west toward Orlando and Tampa. Outside of rush hour, continue on I-4

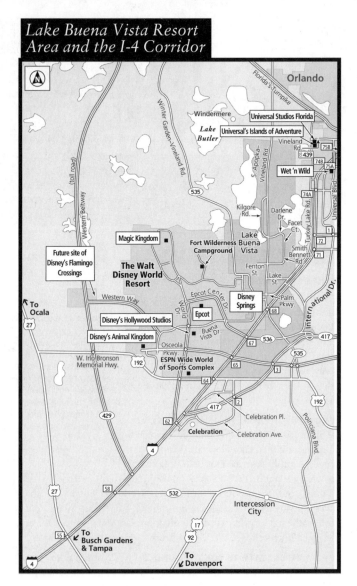

Lake Buena Vista Resort Area and the I-4 Corridor

through downtown Orlando to Walt Disney World Exit 64, 65, 67, or 68, depending on your Disney World destination. During rush hour, take I-4 Exit 101B just south of Seminole Town Center onto FL 417/Central Florida GreeneWay. Skirt Orlando to the southwest and continue on FL 417 to Exit 6/FL 536, marked for Epcot/Downtown Disney.

FROM ORLANDO INTERNATIONAL AIRPORT Two routes lead from the airport to Walt Disney World (see the South Orlando and Walt Disney World Area map on pages 22 and 23). Both routes take almost exactly the same time to drive except during rush-hour traffic, when Route One via FL 417 is far less congested than Route Two via the Beachline Expressway. Also, Route One eliminates the need to drive on I-4, which is always very congested.

Route One: Drive southwest on FL 417/Central Florida GreeneWay, a toll road. Take Exit 6/International Drive toward FL 535. FL 536 will cross I-4 and become Epcot Center Drive. From here, follow the signs to your Walt Disney World destination. If you're going to a hotel on US 192 (Irlo Bronson Memorial Highway), follow the same route until you reach I-4. Take I-4 west toward Tampa. Take the first US 192 exit if your hotel is on West Irlo Bronson, the second exit if your hotel is on East Irlo Bronson. If your hotel is in Lake Buena Vista, take Exit 6 onto FL 536 as described previously, then turn right on FL 535 to the Lake Buena Vista area. If you're headed to Animal Kingdom, Animal Kingdom Lodge, Pop Century, Art of Animation, the All-Star Resorts, or ESPN Wide World of Sports, the quickest route is to take Exit 3/ Osceola Parkway and follow the signs to your destination.

unofficial **TIP**
Both routes require money for tolls. Some exits are unmanned and require exact change, so be sure you have at least $2 in quarters. Also, note that while the manned toll booths take bills up to $20, they don't accept credit cards. For details, see **sunpass.com.**

Route Two: Take FL 528/Beachline Expressway, a toll road, west for about 19 miles to the intersection with I-4. Go west on I-4 to Exit 67/FL 536, marked Epcot/Downtown Disney, and then follow the signs to your Walt Disney World destination. This is also the route to take if your hotel is on International Drive or Universal Boulevard, near Universal Studios, near SeaWorld, or near the Orange County Convention Center. For these destinations, take I-4 east toward Orlando.

FROM MIAMI, FORT LAUDERDALE, AND SOUTHEASTERN FLORIDA Head north on Florida's Turnpike to Exit 249/Osceola Parkway West, and follow the signs.

FROM TAMPA AND SOUTHWESTERN FLORIDA Take I-75 northbound to I-4; then drive east on I-4, take Exit 64 onto US 192 West, and follow the signs.

Walt Disney World Exits Off I-4

East to west (from Orlando to Tampa), five I-4 exits serve Walt Disney World.

EXIT 68 (FL 535/LAKE BUENA VISTA) primarily serves the Downtown Disney Resort Area and Disney Springs, including the Marketplace and the West Side. It also serves non-Disney hotels with a Lake Buena Vista address. This exit puts you on a road with lots of traffic signals. Avoid it unless you're headed to one of the preceding destinations.

EXIT 67 (FL 536/EPCOT/DOWNTOWN DISNEY) delivers you to a four-lane expressway into the heart of Disney World. It's the fastest and most convenient way for westbound travelers to access almost all Disney destinations except Disney's Animal Kingdom and ESPN Wide World of Sports Complex.

EXIT 65 (OSCEOLA PARKWAY) is the best exit for westbound travelers to access Disney's Animal Kingdom, Animal Kingdom Lodge, Pop Century Resort, Art of Animation Resort, the All-Star Resorts, and ESPN Wide World of Sports Complex.

EXIT 64 (US 192/MAGIC KINGDOM) is the best route for eastbound travelers to all Disney destinations.

EXIT 62 (DISNEY WORLD/CELEBRATION) is the first Disney exit you'll encounter heading east. This four-lane, controlled-access highway connects to the Walt Disney World Maingate. Accessing Disney World via the next exit, Exit 64, also routes you through the main entrance.

TRANSPORTATION TO WALT DISNEY WORLD FROM THE AIRPORT

IF YOU FLEW INTO MCO, you have four basic options for getting to Walt Disney World:

1. TAXI Taxis carry four to eight passengers (depending on vehicle type). Rates vary according to distance. If your hotel is in the World, your fare will be about $48–$65, plus tip. For the US 192 Maingate area, it will cost about $55. To International Drive or downtown Orlando, expect to pay in the neighborhood of $38–$50.

2. SHUTTLE SERVICE Mears Transportation Group (☎ 855-463-2776; **mearstransportation.com**) provides your transportation if your vacation package includes airport transfers. Nonpackage travelers can also use the service. The shuttles collect passengers until they fill a van (or bus). They're then dispatched. Mears charges *per-person* rates (children under age 3 ride free). One-way and round-trip services are available.

From your hotel to the airport, you're likely to ride in a van (unless you're part of a tour group, for which Mears might send a bus). Because shuttles make several pickups, you must leave much earlier than if you were taking a cab or returning a rental car.

FROM THE AIRPORT TO:	ONE-WAY ADULT/CHILD	ROUND-TRIP ADULT/CHILD
INTERNATIONAL DRIVE	$20/$15	$32/$24
DOWNTOWN ORLANDO	$19/$15	$31/$23
WALT DISNEY WORLD–LAKE BUENA VISTA	$22/$17	$36/$27
US 192 MAINGATE AREA	$22/$17	$36/$27

3. TOWN-CAR SERVICE Like a taxi, town-car service will transport you directly from the airport to your hotel. The driver will usually be waiting for you in your airline's baggage-claim area. If saving time and hassle is worth the money, book a town car.

Tiffany Towncar Service (☎ 888-838-2161 or 407-370-2196; **tiffanytowncars.com**) provides a prompt, clean ride. The round-trip fee to a Disney or non-Disney resort in a town car is $130–$140 plus tip; one-way is about $75–$80. Tiffany offers a free 30-minute stop at a Publix supermarket en route to your hotel.

Quicksilver Tours & Transportation (☎ 888-GO-TO-WDW [468-6939] or 407-299-1434; **quicksilver-tours.com**) offers 8-person limos and 10-person vans as well as 4-person town cars. Round-trip town-car rates range from $125 to $130, depending on location; round-trip van rates range from $140 to $145; round-trip limo rate is $240.

Mears Transportation Group (☎ 855-463-2776; **mearstrans portation.com**) also offers a town-car service for around $180 round-trip.

4. RENTAL CARS These are readily available at MCO, both short- and long-term. If you don't want a car for your entire stay, most rental companies allow you to drop it off at certain hotels or one of their subsidiary locations in the Walt Disney World area. Likewise, you can pick up a car at any time during your stay at the same hotels and locations without trekking back to the airport.

5. RIDE-SHARING SERVICES For now, **Uber** and **Lyft** can save you as much as $10 or more versus a regular cab. (At press time, both were negotiating with the city of Orlando to charge their lower fares rather than have to charge the same fares as local taxis.)

DISNEY'S MAGICAL EXPRESS

THIS FREE BUS SERVICE runs between MCO and most Walt Disney World hotels. Guests staying at Disney-owned and -operated resorts are eligible. (Guests staying at the Swan, the Dolphin, Shades of Green, and the hotels of the Downtown Disney Resort Area are not.) In addition to transportation, Magical Express provides free luggage-delivery service between your airline and your Disney hotel, except if your flight arrives between 10 p.m. and 5 a.m., in which case you'll need to pick up your stuff from baggage claim.

To use the service, register your flight information with your resort reservation, either at the time of booking or as soon as you've booked your flights, by calling ☎ 866-599-0951 or using **mydisneyexperience.com.**

US and Canadian travelers will receive their Magical Express paperwork in the mail 20–40 days before they arrive. The packet contains instructions for getting around the airport, bus vouchers, and luggage tags (two per traveler); **MagicBands** (see page 10) also work as bus vouchers. You'll check your bags as you normally would and plan to see them again in your hotel room.

Non-Canadian international travelers won't get their vouchers or tags in the mail—instead, they'll need to go through Customs with bags in hand. Disney will collect the bags for transport at the Magical Express Welcome Center, where international guests will also receive their bus vouchers.

The Magical Express Welcome Center is on the B side of the airport's lower level. Cast members are stationed throughout the area to help you find your way. You can pick them out by their nautical costumes, the signs they're holding, and the big white Mickey gloves they wear.

If you already have your bus vouchers or MagicBands, just head straight to the bus check-in. A cast member will scan your vouchers/bands and direct you to a holding area for your resort's bus line. If you've lost or accidentally packed your vouchers/bands or you need other assistance, you'll be directed to the Welcome Center desk.

The day before you check out, you'll get a notification with your return information on it. This will include a time for you to board your bus back to MCO.

RENTING A CAR

READERS PLANNING TO STAY IN THE WORLD frequently contact us asking if they will need to rent a car. If your plans don't include restaurants, attractions, or other destinations outside of Disney World, our answer to that question is a very qualified no. That said . . .

unofficial **TIP**
The website **Zalyn (zalyn.com)** knows virtually every discount and coupon available for every car-rental agency, and it will apply all of them to see which gives you the lowest overall cost. With a little effort, you can often get a great deal.

You Should Plan to Rent a Car:

1. If your hotel is outside Walt Disney World.

2. If your hotel is in Walt Disney World and you want to dine someplace other than the theme parks and your own hotel.

3. If you plan to return to your hotel for naps or swimming during the day.

4. If you plan to visit other area theme parks or water parks.

GETTING ORIENTED

A GOOD MAP

READERS FREQUENTLY COMPLAIN about the signs and maps provided by Disney. While it's easy to find the major theme parks, locating other destinations can be challenging: Many Disney-supplied maps are stylized and hard to read, while others provide incomplete information. Your best bet, in addition to the maps in this guide, is **Alamo Rent A Car**'s road map of Walt Disney World. Get it from the front desk or concierge at the resorts.

Another very good map of the Orlando–Kissimmee–Disney World area is available free at the **Car Care Center** operated by Goodyear, near the Magic Kingdom parking lot.

HOW *to* TRAVEL *Around the* WORLD

TRANSPORTATION TRADE-OFFS FOR GUESTS: LODGING OUTSIDE WALT DISNEY WORLD

DISNEY DAY GUESTS (those not staying inside Walt Disney World) can use the monorail system, the bus system, and the boat system. If, for example, you go to Disney's Hollywood Studios in the morning, then decide to go to Epcot for lunch, you can take a bus directly there. The most important advice we can give day guests is to park their cars in the lot of the theme park or other Disney destination where they plan to finish their day. This is critical if you stay at a park until closing time.

ALL YOU NEED TO KNOW ABOUT DRIVING TO THE THEME PARKS

1. POSITIONING OF THE PARKING LOTS Disney's Animal Kingdom, Disney's Hollywood Studios, and Epcot parking lots are adjacent to each park's entrance. The Magic Kingdom parking lot is adjacent to the Transportation and Ticket Center (TTC). From the TTC you take either a ferry or the monorail to the Magic Kingdom entrance.

2. PAYING TO PARK Disney resort guests and Annual Pass holders park free. All others pay $17 per day.

3. FINDING YOUR CAR WHEN IT'S TIME TO GO Jot down, text, or take a phone picture of the section and row where you've parked. If

*un*official **TIP**
Once you've paid to park in any major theme park lot, show your receipt and you'll be admitted into another park's lot on the same day without further charge.

WALT DISNEY WORLD GPS ADDRESSES AND COORDINATES
MAGIC KINGDOM PARKING LOT 3111 World Dr., Lake Buena Vista, FL 32830 N28° 25.124′, W81° 34.871′
EPCOT PARKING LOT 200 Epcot Center Dr., Lake Buena Vista, FL 32830 N28° 22.869′, W81° 32.964
ANIMAL KINGDOM PARKING LOT 2801 Osceola Pkwy., Lake Buena Vista, FL 32380 N28° 21.480′, W81° 35.426′
Disney's Hollywood Studios Parking Lot 351 S. Studio Dr., Lake Buena Vista, FL 32830 N28° 21.425′, W81° 33.618′
BLIZZARD BEACH PARKING LOT 1534 Blizzard Beach Dr., Lake Buena Vista, FL 32830 N28° 21.338′, W81° 34.384′
TYPHOON LAGOON PARKING LOT 1145 Buena Vista Dr., Lake Buena Vista, FL 32830 N28° 22.162′, W81° 31.576′
DISNEY SPRINGS PARKING LOT 1490 E. Buena Vista Dr., Lake Buena Vista, FL 32830 N28° 22.064′, W81° 31.167′

you're driving a rental car, note the license-plate number. (You wouldn't believe how many white rental cars there are.)

4. GETTING FROM YOUR CAR TO THE PARK ENTRANCE Each lot provides trams to the park entrance or, at the Magic Kingdom, to the TTC. If you arrive early in the morning, it may be faster to walk to the entrance (or TTC) than to take the tram. At the TTC, Disney has added digital wait-time boards, showing you how long the wait is to board the express monorail to the Magic Kingdom or board the ferry. Choose the shorter of the two lines.

5. GETTING TO ANIMAL KINGDOM FOR PARK OPENING If you're staying on-property and are planning to be at this theme park when it opens, take a Disney bus from your resort instead of driving. Animal Kingdom's parking lot frequently opens 15 minutes before the park itself—which doesn't leave enough time to park, hop on a tram, and pass through security before park opening.

6. HOW MUCH TIME TO ALLOT FOR PARKING AND GETTING TO THE PARK ENTRANCE For Epcot and Disney's Animal Kingdom, it takes 10–15 minutes to pay, park, and walk or ride to the park entrance. At Disney's Hollywood Studios, allow 8–12 minutes; at the Magic Kingdom, it's 10–15 minutes to get to the TTC and another 20–30 to reach the park entrance via the monorail or the ferry. Allot another 10–20 minutes if you didn't buy your park admission in advance.

7. COMMUTING FROM PARK TO PARK You can commute to the other theme parks via Disney bus, or to and from the Magic Kingdom and Epcot by monorail. You can also, of course, commute via your own car. Using Disney transportation or your own car, allow 45–60 minutes entrance-to-entrance one-way. Again, **leave your car in the lot of the park where you'll finish the day.**

8. LEAVING THE PARK AT THE END OF THE DAY If you stay at a park until closing, expect the parking-lot trams, monorails, and ferries to be mobbed. (The Magic Kingdom has wait-time displays showing the lines for the monorail and ferry.) If the wait for the tram is unacceptable, walk to your car, or walk to the first stop on the tram route and wait there for a tram. When someone gets off, you can get on.

9. DINNER AND A QUICK EXIT One way to beat closing crowds at the Magic Kingdom is to arrange an Advance Reservation for dinner at one of the restaurants at the Contemporary Resort. When you leave the Magic Kingdom to go to dinner, move your car from the TTC lot to the Contemporary Resort. After dinner, either walk (8–10 minutes) or take the monorail back to the Magic Kingdom. When the park closes and everyone else is fighting their way onto the monorail or ferry, you can stroll leisurely back to the Contemporary, pick up your car, and be on your way. You can pull the same trick at Epcot by arranging an Advance Reservation at one of the Epcot resorts. After *IllumiNations* when the park closes, simply exit the park by the International Gateway and walk back to the resort where your car is parked.

10. CAR TROUBLE All the parking lots have security patrols that circulate through the lots. If you have a dead battery or some other automotive problem, the security patrols will help get you going. If you have more-serious trouble, the **Car Care Center** (☎ 407-824-0976), operated by Goodyear and located in Walt Disney World near the Magic Kingdom parking lot, will help you. Prices are comparable to what you'd pay at home for most services. The Car Center stays pretty busy, so expect to leave your car for a while unless the fix is simple. Hours are Monday–Friday, 7 a.m.–7 p.m.; Saturday, 7 a.m.–4 p.m.; and Sunday, 8 a.m.–3 p.m.

11. SCORING A GREAT PARKING PLACE Anytime you arrive at a park after noon, there will be some empty spots up front vacated by early arriving guests who have already departed.

Taking a Shuttle Bus from Your Out-of-the-World Hotel

MANY INDEPENDENT HOTELS AND MOTELS in the Walt Disney World area provide trams and buses. They deposit you near the theme park entrances, saving you parking fees. The rub is that they might not get you there as early as you desire (a critical point if you take our touring advice) or be available when you wish to return to your lodging. Also, some shuttles go directly to Disney World, while others stop at additional area lodgings.

If you're depending on shuttles, you'll want to leave the park at least 45 minutes before closing. If you stay until closing and lack the energy to mess with the shuttle, take a cab. Cab stands are near the Bus Information buildings at Disney's Animal Kingdom, Epcot, Disney's Hollywood Studios, and the TTC. If no cabs are on hand, staff at Bus Information will call one for you.

THE DISNEY TRANSPORTATION SYSTEM

IN THE MOST BASIC TERMS, the Disney Transportation System is a "hub and spoke" system. Hubs include the TTC, Disney Springs, and all four major theme parks (from 2 hours before official opening time to 1 hour after closing). Although there are some exceptions, there is direct service from Disney resorts to the major theme parks and to Disney Springs, and from park to park. If you want to go from resort to resort or most anywhere else, you will have to transfer at one of the hubs.

If a hotel offers boat or monorail service, its bus service will be limited; you'll have to transfer at a hub for many destinations. If you're staying at a Magic Kingdom resort served by monorail (**Polynesian Village, Contemporary–Bay Lake Tower, Grand Floridian**), you'll be able to commute efficiently to the Magic Kingdom. If you want to visit Epcot, you must take the monorail to the TTC and transfer to the Epcot monorail. (Guests at the Polynesian Village can eliminate the transfer by walking 5–10 minutes to the TTC and catching the direct monorail to Epcot.)

Walt Disney World Bus Service

Disney buses have an illuminated panel above the windshield that flashes the bus's destination. Also, theme parks have designated waiting areas for each Disney destination. To catch the bus to the Caribbean Beach Resort from Disney's Hollywood Studios, for example, go to the bus stop and wait in the area marked TO THE CARIBBEAN BEACH RESORT. At the resorts, go to any bus stop and wait for the bus displaying your destination on the illuminated panel. Directions to Disney destinations are available when you check in or at your hotel's Guest Relations desk.

Service from resorts to major theme parks is fairly direct. You may have intermediate stops, but you won't have to transfer. Service to the water parks and other Disney World hotels sometimes requires transfers.

Buses begin service to the theme parks at about 7:30 a.m. on days when the parks' official opening time is 9 a.m. Generally, buses run every 20 minutes. Buses to all four parks deliver you to the park entrance.

To be on hand for actual opening time (when official opening is 9 a.m.), catch direct buses to Epcot, Disney's Animal Kingdom, and Disney's Hollywood Studios between 7:30 and 8 a.m. Catch direct buses to the Magic Kingdom between 8 and 8:15 a.m. If you must transfer to reach your park, leave 15–20 minutes earlier. On days when official opening is 7 or 8 a.m., move up your departure time accordingly.

For your return bus trip in the evening, leave the park 40 minutes to an hour before closing to avoid the rush. If you're caught in the exodus, you may be inconvenienced, but you won't be stranded. Buses and and boats continue to operate for 1 hour after the parks close.

Walt Disney World Monorail Service

Picture the monorail system as three loops. Loop A is an express route that runs counterclockwise connecting the Magic Kingdom with the TTC. Loop B runs clockwise alongside Loop A, making all stops, with service to (in this order) the TTC, Polynesian Resort, Grand Floridian Resort & Spa, Magic Kingdom, Contemporary Resort and Bay Lake Tower, and back to the TTC. The long Loop C dips southeast, connecting the TTC with Epcot. The hub for all loops is the TTC (where you usually park to visit the Magic Kingdom).

unofficial **TIP**
Monorails run for 1 hour after the Magic Kingdom and Epcot close. If a train is too crowded or you need transportation after the monorails have stopped, catch a bus or boat.

The monorail serving Magic Kingdom resorts usually starts an hour and a half before official opening. If you're staying at a Magic Kingdom resort and wish to be among the first in the park when official opening is 9 a.m., board the monorail at these times:

From the Contemporary and Bay Lake Tower	7:45–8 a.m.
From the Polynesian	7:50–8:05 a.m.
From the Grand Floridian	8–8:10 a.m.

If you're a day guest, you'll be allowed on the monorail at the TTC between 8:15 and 8:30 a.m. when official opening is 9 a.m. If you want to board earlier, walk from the TTC to the Polynesian Resort and board there.

The monorail connecting Epcot and the TTC begins operating at 7:30 a.m. when Epcot's official opening is 9 a.m. To be at Epcot when it opens, catch the Epcot monorail at the TTC by 8:05 a.m.

PART EIGHT

BARE NECESSITIES

❚❚ CREDIT CARDS *and* MONEY

CREDIT CARDS AND MOBILE PAYMENTS

ACCEPTED THROUGHOUT WALT DISNEY WORLD are **American Express, Diners Club, Discover, Japan Credit Bureau, MasterCard,** and **Visa,** along with **Apple Pay** (requires iPhone 6 or newer).

BANKING SERVICES

BANK SERVICE AT THE THEME PARKS is limited to ATMs, which are marked on the park maps and are plentiful throughout Walt Disney World; most MasterCard and Visa cards are accepted. To use an American Express card, you must sign an agreement with Amex before your trip. If your credit card doesn't work in the ATMs, a teller at any **SunTrust Bank** full-service location will process your transaction. The SunTrust closest to Disney World is at 1675 E. Buena Vista Dr., across from Disney Springs Marketplace; for other Orlando-area branches, visit **suntrust.com.**

A LICENSE TO PRINT MONEY

ONE OF DISNEY'S MORE SUBLIME PLOYS for separating you from your money is the printing and issuing of **Disney Dollars.** Available throughout Disney World or by phone (☎ 407-566-4985) in denominations of $1, $5, $10, and $50, each emblazoned with a Disney character, the colorful cash can be used for purchases in Disney World, Disneyland, and Disney Stores nationwide. Disney Dollars can also be exchanged one-for-one with US currency, but only while you're in Disney World. Also, you need your sales receipt to exchange for US dollars. Disney money is sometimes a perk (for which you're charged dollar-for-dollar) offered with Walt Disney World travel packages.

PROBLEMS *and* HOW *to* SOLVE THEM

ATTRACTIONS CLOSED FOR REPAIRS

FIND OUT IN ADVANCE what rides and attractions may be closed during your visit. For complete refurbishment schedules, check online at **touringplans.com** or use our mobile app, **Lines.**

CAR TROUBLE

SECURITY PATROLS WILL HELP if you lock the keys in your parked car or find the battery dead. For more-serious problems, the closest repair facility is the **Car Care Center** near the Magic Kingdom parking lot (☎ 407-824-0976).

The nearest off-World repair center is **Maingate Citgo** (7424 W. Irlo Bronson Memorial Hwy., west of Interstate 4; ☎ 407-396-2721). Disney security can help you find it. Farther away but highly recommended by one of our Orlando-area researchers is **Riker's Automotive & Tire** (5700 Central Florida Pkwy., near Sea-World; ☎ 407-238-9800; **rikersauto.com**). "They do great work," our source reports, "and they're the only car place that has never tried to get extra money out of me because I'm a woman and I know nothing about cars."

CELL PHONE SNAFUS

READERS REPORT THAT MOBILE RECEPTION in Walt Disney World can be frustratingly spotty. The problem is compounded by crowd noise and the ambient music played throughout the parks. Even if you have a good signal, it's an exasperating challenge to find someplace quiet enough to have a conversation. When possible, opt for texting instead.

GASOLINE

THERE ARE THREE **Hess** gas stations on Disney property. One station is adjacent to the Car Care Center, on the exit road from the Transportation and Ticket Center (Magic Kingdom) parking lot. It's also convenient to the Shades of Green, Grand Floridian, and Polynesian resorts. Most centrally located is the Hess station at the corner of Buena Vista Drive and Epcot Resorts Boulevard, near the BoardWalk Inn. A third station, also on Buena Vista Drive, is across from the area formerly known as Pleasure Island in Disney Springs.

LOST AND FOUND

IF YOU LOSE (OR FIND) SOMETHING in the **Magic Kingdom,** go to **City Hall.** At **Epcot,** go to the **Entrance Plaza.** At **Disney's Hollywood Studios,** go to **Hollywood Boulevard Guest Relations;** at **Disney's Animal Kingdom,** go to **Guest Relations** at the main entrance. See page 10 for a list of phone numbers for each park; if you're still on-site, it's easiest to call the main number (☎ 407-824-4245) and ask to be transferred to the specific park's Lost and Found.

MEDICAL MATTERS

HEADACHE RELIEF Aspirin and other sundries are sold at the **Emporium** on Main Street, U.S.A., in the Magic Kingdom (behind the counter; you have to ask); at most retail shops in Epcot's Future World and World Showcase, Disney's Hollywood Studios, and Disney's Animal Kingdom; and at each Disney resort's gift shop.

ILLNESSES REQUIRING MEDICAL ATTENTION A **Centra Care** walk-in clinic is at 12500 South Apopka–Vineland Rd. (☎ 407-934-CARE). It's open 8 a.m.–midnight weekdays and 8 a.m.–8 p.m. weekends. Centra Care also operates a 24-hour physician-house-call service and runs a free shuttle (☎ 407-938-0650). **Buena Vista Urgent Care** (8216 World Center Dr., Suite D; ☎ 407-465-1110) is highly recommended by *Unofficial Guide* readers.

   The Medical Concierge (☎ 855-932-5252; **themedicalconcierge .com**) has board-certified physicians available 24-7 for house calls to your hotel room. They offer in-room X-rays and IV therapy service as well as same-day dental and specialist appointments. They also rent medical equipment. Insurance receipts, insurance billing, and foreign-language interpretation are provided. Walk-in clinics are also available.

   DOCS (Doctors on Call Service; ☎ 407-399-DOCS; **doctors oncallservice.com**) offers 24-hour house-call service.

   Physician Room Service (☎ 407-238-2000; **physicianroom service.com**) provides board-certified doctor house calls to Walt Disney World–area guest rooms for adults and children.

DENTAL EMERGENCIES Call **Celebration Dental Group** (☎ 407-566-2222).

PRESCRIPTION MEDICINE Two drugstores nearby are **Walgreens** (12100 S. Apopka–Vineland Rd.; ☎ 407-238-0600) and **Turner Drugs** (12500 S. Apopka–Vineland Rd.; ☎ 407-828-8125; **turner drug.com**). Turner Drugs charges $7.50 to deliver a filled prescription to your Disney hotel's front desk, $10–$15 for non-Disney hotels. The fee is charged to your hotel account.

RAIN

WEATHER BAD? Go to the parks anyway. The crowds are lighter on rainy days, and most attractions and waiting areas are under cover. Showers, especially during the warmer months, usually don't last very long.

Ponchos cost about $8, umbrellas about $12. All ponchos sold at Disney World are made of clear plastic, so picking out somebody in your party on a rainy day can be tricky. Amazon sells an inexpensive orange poncho that will make your family pumpkin-colored beacons in a plastic-covered sea of humanity.

unofficial **TIP**
Rain gear isn't always displayed in shops, so you'll have to ask for it.

SERVICES

MESSAGES

MESSAGES LEFT AT CITY HALL IN THE Magic Kingdom, Guest Relations at Epcot, Hollywood Boulevard Guest Relations at Disney's Hollywood Studios, or Guest Relations at Disney's Animal Kingdom can be retrieved at any of the four.

PHONE CHARGING

CHARGING STATIONS IN THE THEME PARKS are listed as follows in each park chapter: Magic Kingdom, page 132; Epcot, page 172; Animal Kingdom, page 207, and DHS, page 231.

LOCKERS AND PACKAGE PICK-UP

LOCKERS ARE AVAILABLE ON THE GROUND FLOOR of the Main Street railroad station in the Magic Kingdom, to the right of Spaceship Earth in Epcot, and on the Transportation and Ticket Center's east and west ends. At DHS, lockers are to the right of the park entrance at Oscar's Super Service; Animal Kingdom lockers are to the left inside the entrance. Cost is $8 a day for small lockers and $10 a day for large lockers; prices include a $5 refundable deposit. Lockers at Blizzard Beach and Typhoon Lagoon water parks cost the same.

Package Pick-Up is available at each of the major parks. Ask the salesperson to send your purchases to Package Pick-Up, and when you leave the park, they'll be waiting for you. Epcot has two exits, thus two Package Pick-Ups; specify the main entrance or the International Gateway. If you're staying at a Disney resort, you can also have the packages delivered to your resort's gift shop for pickup the following day. If you're leaving Orlando within 24 hours, however, take them with you or use the in-park pickup location.

PHOTO NEEDS

Camera Centers at the parks sell disposable point-and-shooters with flash for around $18 plus tax ($21 for a waterproof version). Memory cards run $40–$60, so bring yours from home. Film developing is unavailable at Walt Disney World.

Disney's **Memory Maker** photo service costs $169 if you buy it in advance, $199 if you buy it in the parks. Memory Maker is a repository for photos of you and your family taken by roving Disney photographers around the parks, as well as by automated cameras on rides. Because Memory Maker is linked to your My Disney Experience account, you're also able to see photos of friends and family you've linked to there. Choose the images you want to keep, customize them with text and colorful borders, order photo CDs, and so on. Go to **disneyworld.disney.go.com/memory -maker** for more information.

As of 2015, Walt Disney World no longer includes photo packages in the cost of character meals.

GROCERY STORES

FOR REASONABLE PRICES, try the **Publix** at 7880 Winter Garden– Vineland Rd. (☎ 407-876-0605), just north of the intersection of Silverlake Park Drive and FL 535, or the **Winn-Dixie** on 11957 Apopka–Vineland Rd. (☎ 407-465-8600), about a mile north of the Crossroads Shopping Center. Avoid the **Gooding's** in the Crossroads Shopping Center, across FL 535 from the Disney World entrance. Its location makes it undeniably convenient, but its selection is poor and you'll find the prices more frightening than the Tower of Terror.

If you don't have a car or you don't want to take the time to go to the supermarket, **GardenGrocer** (**gardengrocer.com**) will shop for you and deliver your groceries. The best way to compile your order is on GardenGrocer's website before you leave home. It's simple, and the selection is huge. If there's something you want that's not on their list of available items, they'll try to find it for you. Delivery arrangements are per your instructions. If you're staying at a hotel, you can arrange for your groceries to be left with bell services. If you can't get online, you can order by phone (☎ 866-855-4350). For orders of $200 or more, there's no delivery charge; for orders less than $200, the delivery charge is $12; a minimum order of $40 is required. Note that Garden Grocer doesn't deliver to the Swan or Dolphin as of this writing, and their delivery schedule may fill completely over the holidays.

Wine and beer are sold in grocery stores. The best range of adult beverages is sold at the **ABC Fine Wine & Spirits** store less than a mile north of the Crossroads shopping center (11951 S. Apopka– Vineland Rd.; ☎ 407-239-0775).

PART NINE

The MAGIC KINGDOM

OPENED IN 1971, THE MAGIC KINGDOM was the first built of Walt Disney World's four theme parks. It is undoubtedly what most people think of when they think of Disney World.

ARRIVING

IF YOU DRIVE, THE MAGIC KINGDOM **Ticket and Transportation Center (TTC)** parking lot opens about 2 hours before the park does. After paying a fee, you are directed to a parking space, then transported by tram to the TTC, where you catch a monorail or ferry to the entrance.

If you're staying at the Bay Lake Tower, Contemporary, Grand Floridian, or Polynesian Village Resort, you can commute to the Magic Kingdom by monorail (guests at the Contemporary and Bay Lake Tower can walk there more quickly). If you stay at Wilderness Lodge and Villas or Fort Wilderness Campground, you can take a boat or bus. Guests at other Disney resorts can reach the park by bus. Disney lodging guests are deposited at the park's entrance, bypassing the TTC.

GETTING ORIENTED

AT THE MAGIC KINGDOM, stroller, wheelchair, and ECV/ESV rentals are in the train station; you'll find lockers on the right, just inside the entrance. On your left as you enter **Main Street, U.S.A.** is **City Hall,** the theme park's center for information, lost and found, guided tours, and entertainment schedules.

unofficial **TIP**
If you don't already have a handout guide map of the park, get one at City Hall.

The Magic Kingdom

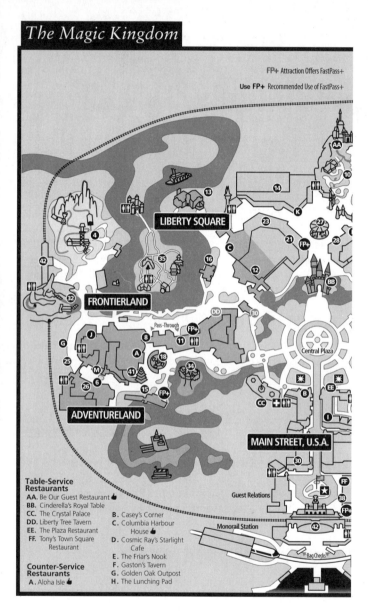

FP+ Attraction Offers FastPass+

Use FP+ Recommended Use of FastPass+

LIBERTY SQUARE

FRONTIERLAND

Central Plaza

Pass-Through

ADVENTURELAND

MAIN STREET, U.S.A.

Guest Relations

Monorail Station

Bag Check

Table-Service Restaurants
AA. Be Our Guest Restaurant
BB. Cinderella's Royal Table
CC. The Crystal Palace
DD. Liberty Tree Tavern
EE. The Plaza Restaurant
FF. Tony's Town Square Restaurant

Counter-Service Restaurants
A. Aloha Isle

B. Casey's Corner
C. Columbia Harbour House
D. Cosmic Ray's Starlight Cafe
E. The Friar's Nook
F. Gaston's Tavern
G. Golden Oak Outpost
H. The Lunching Pad

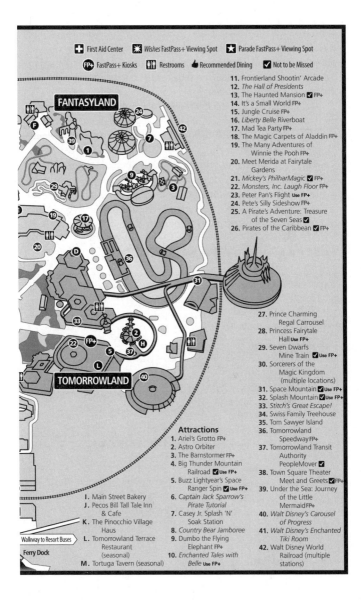

Key (legend):
- ➕ First Aid Center
- ❌ *Wishes* FastPass+ Viewing Spot
- ⭐ Parade FastPass+ Viewing Spot
- 🅕🅟+ FastPass+ Kiosks
- 🚻 Restrooms
- 🍴 Recommended Dining
- ☑ Not to be Missed

Map labels: FANTASYLAND, TOMORROWLAND, Walkway to Resort Buses, Ferry Dock

11. Frontierland Shootin' Arcade
12. *The Hall of Presidents*
13. The Haunted Mansion ☑ FP+
14. It's a Small World FP+
15. Jungle Cruise FP+
16. *Liberty Belle* Riverboat
17. Mad Tea Party FP+
18. The Magic Carpets of Aladdin FP+
19. The Many Adventures of Winnie the Pooh FP+
20. Meet Merida at Fairytale Gardens
21. Mickey's PhilharMagic ☑ FP+
22. *Monsters, Inc. Laugh Floor* FP+
23. Peter Pan's Flight Use FP+
24. Pete's Silly Sideshow FP+
25. A Pirate's Adventure: Treasure of the Seven Seas ☑
26. Pirates of the Caribbean ☑ FP+
27. Prince Charming Regal Carrousel
28. Princess Fairytale Hall Use FP+
29. Seven Dwarfs Mine Train ☑ Use FP+
30. Sorcerers of the Magic Kingdom (multiple locations)
31. Space Mountain ☑ Use FP+
32. Splash Mountain ☑ Use FP+
33. *Stitch's Great Escape!*
34. Swiss Family Treehouse
35. Tom Sawyer Island
36. Tomorrowland Speedway FP+
37. Tomorrowland Transit Authority PeopleMover ☑
38. Town Square Theater Meet and Greets ☑ FP+
39. Under the Sea: Journey of the Little Mermaid FP+
40. *Walt Disney's Carousel of Progress*
41. *Walt Disney's Enchanted Tiki Room*
42. Walt Disney World Railroad (multiple stations)

Attractions
1. Ariel's Grotto FP+
2. Astro Orbiter
3. The Barnstormer FP+
4. Big Thunder Mountain Railroad ☑ Use FP+
5. Buzz Lightyear's Space Ranger Spin ☑ Use FP+
6. *Captain Jack Sparrow's Pirate Tutorial*
7. Casey Jr. Splash 'N' Soak Station
8. *Country Bear Jamboree*
9. Dumbo the Flying Elephant FP+
10. *Enchanted Tales with Belle* Use FP+

I. Main Street Bakery
J. Pecos Bill Tall Tale Inn & Cafe
K. The Pinocchio Village Haus
L. Tomorrowland Terrace Restaurant (seasonal)
M. Tortuga Tavern (seasonal)

The guide map found there lists all attractions, shops, and eating places; provides information about first aid, baby care, and assistance for the disabled; and gives tips for good photos. It also lists times for the day's special events, live entertainment, and parades; it also tells when and where to find Disney characters. The guide map is supplemented by a daily entertainment schedule known as the *Times Guide.*

Main Street ends at the **Central Plaza,** a hub from which branch the entrances to five other sections of the Magic Kingdom: **Adventureland, Frontierland, Liberty Square, Fantasyland,** and **Tomorrowland.**

Cinderella Castle, at the entrance to Fantasyland, is the Magic Kingdom's architectural icon and visual center. If you start in Adventureland and go clockwise around the Magic Kingdom, the castle spires will always be roughly on your right; if you start in Tomorrowland and go counterclockwise through the park, the spires will always be roughly on your left.

FASTPASS+ IN THE MAGIC KINGDOM

ADVENTURELAND
- Jungle Cruise
- The Magic Carpets of Aladdin
- Pirates of the Caribbean

FANTASYLAND
- Ariel's Grotto
- The Barnstormer
- Dumbo the Flying Elephant
- *Enchanted Tales with Belle*
- It's a Small World
- Mad Tea Party
- The Many Adventures of Winnie the Pooh
- *Mickey's PhilharMagic*
- Peter Pan's Flight
- Princess Fairytale Hall
- Seven Dwarfs Mine Train
- Under the Sea: Journey of the Little Mermaid

FRONTIERLAND
- Big Thunder Mountain Railroad
- Splash Mountain

LIBERTY SQUARE
- The Haunted Mansion

MAIN STREET, U.S.A.
- Town Square Theater Meet and Greets (Mickey, Tinker Bell)

TOMORROWLAND
- Buzz Lightyear's Space Ranger Spin
- *Monsters, Inc. Laugh Floor*
- Space Mountain
- Tomorrowland Speedway

ENTERTAINMENT & PARADES
- *Celebrate the Magic*
- Festival of Fantasy Parade
- Main Street Electrical Parade
- *Wishes* Fireworks

WHILE THE MAGIC KINGDOM offers FastPass+ for more than two dozen attractions (see table above), our touring plan software

NOT TO BE MISSED AT THE MAGIC KINGDOM
ADVENTURELAND • Pirates of the Caribbean
FANTASYLAND • Peter Pan's Flight • *Mickey's PhilharMagic* • Seven Dwarfs Mine Train
FRONTIERLAND • Big Thunder Mountain Railroad • Splash Mountain
LIBERTY SQUARE • The Haunted Mansion
SPECIAL EVENTS • Evening Parade • *Celebrate the Magic* • *Wishes*
TOMORROWLAND • Space Mountain

identifies only five as frequently needing FastPass+: **Peter Pan's Flight, *Enchanted Tales with Belle*, Big Thunder Mountain Railroad, Splash Mountain,** and **Space Mountain.** Note that we haven't included the popular **Anna and Elsa Meet and Greet** at Princess Fairytale Hall among our FastPass+ musts. Lines do get incredibly long—approaching 4 hours in some cases!—but hourly capacity is only around 45–50 families, or roughly 500–600 people per day. You definitely need FastPass+, but your chances of scoring reservations are very low.

On the other hand, six Magic Kingdom attractions *never* seem to need FastPass+, either because our touring plans get you to them before long lines develop or because the attractions rarely see long waits: **The Barnstormer, It's a Small World, Mad Tea Party, The Magic Carpets of Aladdin, *Mickey's PhilharMagic,*** and ***Monsters, Inc. Laugh Floor.***

FastPass+ kiosk locations in the Magic Kingdom are as follows (also see the map on pages 126 and 127):

- In the walkway between Adventureland and Liberty Square, near the Diamond Horseshoe Saloon and the Swiss Family Treehouse
- At the entrance to Jungle Cruise in Adventureland
- Outside *Mickey's PhilharMagic* in Fantasyland
- Near *Stitch's Great Escape!* in Tomorrowland

Same-Day FastPass+ Availability

The preceding advice tells you which attractions to focus on when making your *advance* FastPass+ reservations before you get to the park. Once you're in the park, you can make more FastPass+ reservations once your advance reservations have been used or have expired (you must cancel your expired FastPass+ before you can book another). The table on the next page shows which attractions are likely to have day-of FastPasses available, and the approximate times at which they'll run out.

MAGIC KINGDOM
When Same-Day FP+ Runs Out, by Crowd Level

ATTRACTION	HIGH CROWDS*	MODERATE CROWDS*	HIGH CROWDS*
Ariel's Grotto	5 p.m.	6-9 p.m.	9-10 p.m.
The Barnstormer	6-7 p.m.	8-9 p.m.	10-11 p.m.
Big Thunder Mountain	4-6 p.m.	5 p.m.	2-3 p.m.
Buzz Lightyear's Space Ranger Spin	5-6 p.m.	7-8 p.m.	6-8 p.m.
Dumbo the Flying Elephant	6-7 p.m.	8-9 p.m.	10-11 p.m.
Enchanted Tales with Belle	5-6 p.m.	6-7 p.m.	7-9 p.m.
Festival of Fantasy Parade	3 p.m.	Unlikely day-of availability	Unlikely day-of availability
The Haunted Mansion	6 p.m.	7-8 p.m.	5-8 p.m.
It's a Small World	6-7 p.m.	8-9 p.m.	9-10 p.m.
Jungle Cruise	5-6 p.m.	7-9 p.m.	8-10 p.m.
Monsters, Inc. Laugh Floor	5-6 p.m.	8-9 p.m.	9-10 p.m.
Mad Tea Party	6-7 p.m.	8-9 p.m.	10-11 p.m.
The Magic Carpets of Aladdin	6-7 p.m.	8-9 p.m.	11 p.m.
Main Street Electrical Parade	Noon-3 p.m.	Until first performance	Unlikely day-of availability
The Many Adventures of Winnie the Pooh	6-7 p.m.	8-9 p.m.	10-11 p.m.
Peter Pan's Flight	2-3 p.m.	3-4 p.m.	1-3 p.m.
Mickey's PhilharMagic	6-7 p.m.	7 p.m.	8-9 p.m.
Pirates of the Caribbean	5-6 p.m.	7-8 p.m.	3-5 p.m.
Princess Fairytale Hall: Cinderella and Rapunzel	5 p.m.	Unlikely day-of availability	Unlikely day-of availability
Princess Fairytale Hall: Anna and Elsa	5 p.m.	Unlikely day-of availability	Unlikely day-of availability
Seven Dwarfs Mine Train	1 p.m.	Unlikely day-of availability	Unlikely day-of availability
Splash Mountain	2-4 p.m.	3-6 p.m.	2-4 p.m.
Tomorrowland Speedway	5-6 p.m.	6-9 p.m.	7-9 p.m.
Town Square Mickey Mouse Meet and Greet	5-6 p.m.	5-9 p.m.	9-11 p.m.
Town Square Tinker Bell Meet and Greet	6 p.m.	8-10 p.m.	9-11 p.m.
Under the Sea: Journey of the Little Mermaid	5-6 p.m.	7-9 p.m.	8-9 p.m.
Wishes	3 p.m.	Until first performance	Unlikely day-of availability

* LOW CROWDS (Levels 1-3 on TouringPlans.com Crowd Calendar)

* MODERATE CROWDS (Levels 4-7 on TouringPlans.com Crowd Calendar)

* HIGH CROWDS (Levels 8-10 on TouringPlans.com Crowd Calendar)

MAIN STREET, *U.S.A.*

MAIN STREET IS A DISNEYFIED turn-of-the-19th-century small-town American street. Its buildings are real, not elaborate props. Attention to detail is exceptional: Furnishings and fixtures are true to the period. Along the street are shops, eating places, **City Hall,** and a fire station. Occasionally, horse-drawn trolleys, fire engines, and horseless carriages transport visitors along Main Street to the **Central Plaza.**

Main Street Characters

DESCRIPTION AND COMMENTS Colorful characters, including the mayor of Main Street, roam the area for photos, autographs, and lively conversation. Not as engaging as the characters who populate Hollywood Boulevard in Disney's Hollywood Studios, but still fun.

TOURING TIPS Characters are usually available from park opening until around 2 p.m. They're fun to talk to if you're in the area, but don't make a special trip.

Sorcerers of the Magic Kingdom ★★★

Appeal by Age	PRESCHOOL ★★★★	GRADE SCHOOL ★★★★½	TEENS ★★★★½
YOUNG ADULTS ★★★★		OVER 30 ★★★★	SENIORS ★★★½

What it is Interactive video game. **Scope and scale** Minor attraction. **When to go** Before 11 a.m. or after 8 p.m. **Special comments** Long lines to play. **Authors' rating** Great idea; ★★★. **Duration of presentation** About 2 minutes per step, 4 or 5 steps per game. **Probable waiting time per step** 10–15 minutes.

DESCRIPTION AND COMMENTS Sorcerers of the Magic Kingdom combines aspects of role-playing games such as Dungeons and Dragons with Disney characters and theme park attractions. Your objective: to help the wizard Merlin keep evildoers from taking over the Magic Kingdom. Merlin sends you on adventures in different parts of the park to fight these villains. Each land hosts a different adventure within the game.

This free game is played with a set of trading cards—similar to baseball cards or Magic: The Gathering cards—with a different Disney character on each card. Each character possesses special properties that help it fight certain villains. Pick up the cards, plus a map showing where in the park you can play the game, at either the Fire Station on Main Street, U.S.A., or across from Sleepy Hollow Refreshments in Liberty Square.

You'll need your park ticket or MagicBand to pick up your first set of cards and start the game. One card, known as your "key," is special because it links you to your game. You'll need to present your key card when you pick up a set of cards to start your next adventure.

When you pick up your first set of cards, you'll view an instructional video explaining how to use them and the object of the game. Then you'll be sent to another location to start your first adventure. Each location in the park is associated with a unique symbol: an eye, a feather, a dragonfly, or something along those lines. Look for these symbols on the map to find the best route to your starting point.

Main Street Services

Most park services are centered on Main Street, U.S.A., including:

BABY CARE CENTER Next to The Crystal Palace, left around the Central Plaza (toward Adventureland)

BANKING SERVICES ATMs underneath the Main Street railroad station

FIRST AID Next to The Crystal Palace, left around the Central Plaza (toward Adventureland)

LIVE-ENTERTAINMENT AND PARADE INFORMATION
City Hall, at the railroad-station end of Main Street

LOST AND FOUND City Hall   **LOST PERSONS** City Hall

CELL PHONE CHARGING In Fantasyland, near the *Tangled*-themed restrooms between It's a Small World and The Haunted Mansion, and behind Big Top Treats in Storybook Circus

STORAGE LOCKERS Underneath the Main Street railroad station

WHEELCHAIR, ECV/ESV, AND STROLLER RENTALS Ground floor of the railroad station at the end of Main Street

Each adventure consists of four or five stops in a particular land. At each stop, another story will play on a computer screen, outlining what your villain is trying to do. Merlin will ask you to cast a spell, using your character cards, to stop the villain. Hold one or more of your cards up to the video display to cast your spell. Cameras in the display read your card, deploy the spell, and show you the results.

The game has three levels: easy, medium, and hard. The easy version is the default and is appropriate for small children; holding up any one of your character cards is enough to defeat any villain. In more-advanced levels of the game, you need to display two or more character cards in specific combinations to defeat a particular villain. Different card combinations produce different spells, and only some spells work on certain characters in those advanced levels.

The audio at each step holds clues to which cards you should use against advanced villains. For example, if a villain says something like "Don't toy with me!" then you should look for cards with characters that are toys, such as the *Toy Story* characters; references to "being spotted" suggest using cards with characters from *101 Dalmatians;* and so on.

TOURING TIPS You'll probably encounter a line of 5–10 people ahead of you at each portal, especially if you play during the afternoon. One complete adventure should take about 30–60 minutes to play, depending on how crowded the park is. If the line to pick up cards is too long at the Main Street Fire Station, try the Liberty Square distribution point.

Town Square Theater Meet and Greets: Mickey Mouse, Tinker Bell and Friends (FastPass+) ★★★★

Appeal by Age	PRESCHOOL ★★★★★	GRADE SCHOOL ★★★★★	TEENS ★★★★½
YOUNG ADULTS ★★★★	OVER 30 ★★★★½		SENIORS ★★★★½

What it is Character-greeting venue. **Scope and scale** Minor attraction. **When to go** Before 10 a.m. or after 4 p.m., or use FastPass+. **Special comments** Mickey and the fairies have 2 separate queues, requiring 2 separate waits in line. **Authors' rating** It all started with this mouse; ★★★★. **Duration of experience** 2 minutes per character. **Probable waiting time** 15–25 minutes. **Queue speed** Slow.

DESCRIPTION AND COMMENTS Meet Mickey, along with Tinker Bell and her Pixie Hollow friends, throughout the day at the Town Square Theater on Main Street, to your right as you enter the park.

TOURING TIPS Lines usually drop off after the afternoon parade. Oddly enough, meeting Mickey rarely requires FastPass+.

Transportation Rides

DESCRIPTION AND COMMENTS Trolleys, buses, and the like that add color to Main Street.

TOURING TIPS Will save you a walk to the hub. Not worth a wait.

Walt Disney World Railroad ★★½

Appeal by Age	PRESCHOOL ★★★★	GRADE SCHOOL ★★★★	TEENS ★★★★
YOUNG ADULTS ★★★½	OVER 30 ★★★★		SENIORS ★★★★

What it is Scenic railroad ride around the perimeter of the Magic Kingdom; provides transportation to Frontierland and Fantasyland. **Scope and scale** Minor attraction. **When to go** Anytime. **Special comments** Main Street is usually the least congested station. **Authors' rating** Plenty to see; ★★★. **Duration of ride** About 20 minutes for a complete circuit. **Average wait in line per 100 people ahead of you** 8 minutes; assumes 2 or more trains operating. **Loading speed** Moderate.

DESCRIPTION AND COMMENTS Blends an unusual variety of sights and experiences with an energy-saving way to get around the park. The train provides a glimpse of all lands except Adventureland.

TOURING TIPS Save the train until after you've seen the featured attractions, or use it when you need transportation. On busy days, lines form at the Frontierland Station but rarely at the Main Street Station. Wheelchair access is available at the Frontierland and Fantasyland Stations.

Only folded strollers are permitted on board, so you can't ride with your rented Disney stroller. You can, however, get a replacement stroller at your destination. Just take your personal belongings, stroller name card, and rental receipt with you on the train.

Finally, note that the railroad shuts down immediately before and during parades. Check your park map or *Times Guide* for parade times. Needless to say, this is not the time to queue up for the train.

■⌐ ADVENTURELAND

ADVENTURELAND IS THE FIRST LAND to the left of Main Street. It combines an African-safari theme with elements of old New Orleans and the Caribbean. A new restaurant is scheduled to open here in late 2015 or early 2016, in the area across from Swiss Family Treehouse. The working name is **Skipper's Cantina,** and the theme is reportedly tied to the Jungle Cruise.

Captain Jack Sparrow's Pirate Tutorial ★★★½

Appeal by Age	PRESCHOOL ★★★★½	GRADE SCHOOL ★★★★½	TEENS ★★★½
YOUNG ADULTS ★★★½	OVER 30 ★★★½		SENIORS ★★★½

What it is Outdoor stage show with guest participation. **Scope and scale** Diversion. **When to go** See *Times Guide* for show schedule. **Authors' rating** Sign us up; ★★★½. **Duration of presentation** About 20 minutes.

DESCRIPTION AND COMMENTS Outside Pirates of the Caribbean, Cap'n Jack and a crew member teach would-be knaves the skills needed for a career in piracy. Some kids go on stage to train in the finer points of dueling, similar to *Jedi Training Academy* at Hollywood Studios (see page 239). The show finishes with everyone taking the probably-not-legally-binding pirate's oath and singing a rousing round of "A Pirate's Life for Me." If you or your kids are fans of the Pirates ride or the movie series, this show is worth a look as well.

TOURING TIPS The shows attract decent crowds, but the first and last show seem to be the least popular. Standing-room-only outdoors.

Jungle Cruise (*FastPass+*) ★★★

Appeal by Age PRESCHOOL ★★★★ GRADE SCHOOL ★★★★ TEENS ★★★½
YOUNG ADULTS ★★★★ OVER 30 ★★★★ SENIORS ★★★★

What it is Outdoor safari-themed boat ride. **Scope and scale** Major attraction. **When to go** Before 10:30 a.m., during the last 2 hours before closing, or use FastPass+. **Special comments** Fun to ride at night! **Authors' rating** A classic, but kinda long in the tooth; ★★★½. **Duration of ride** 8–9 minutes. **Average wait in line per 100 people ahead of you** 3½ minutes; assumes 10 boats operating. **Loading speed** Moderate.

DESCRIPTION AND COMMENTS An outdoor cruise through jungle water-ways. Passengers encounter animatronic elephants, lions, hostile natives, and a menacing hippo. Boatman's spiel adds to the fun. The technology now seems dated and worn, but in the Jungle Cruise's defense, you can always depend on the robotic critters being present as you motor past.

TOURING TIPS A convoluted queuing area makes it difficult to estimate the length of your wait. Fortunately, the Jungle Cruise is a FastPass+ attrac-tion. Before you obtain a FastPass, however, ask a cast member what the estimated wait in the standby line is.

The Magic Carpets of Aladdin ★★★

Appeal by Age PRESCHOOL ★★★★½ GRADE SCHOOL ★★★★ TEENS ★★★½
YOUNG ADULTS ★★★½ OVER 30 ★★★ SENIORS ★★★½

What it is Elaborate midway ride. **Scope and scale** Minor attraction. **When to go** Before 11 a.m. or after 7 p.m. **Authors' rating** A visually appealing children's ride; ★★★½. **Duration of ride** 1½ minutes. **Average wait in line per 100 people ahead of you** 16 minutes. **Loading speed** Slow.

DESCRIPTION AND COMMENTS A midway ride like Dumbo, except with magic carpets instead of elephants. A spitting camel is positioned to spray jets of water on carpet riders. Riders can maneuver their carpets up and down to spit back and side to side to avoid getting wet.

TOURING TIPS Like Dumbo, this ride has great eye appeal but extremely limited capacity (that is, it loads slowly). Try to get younger kids on during the first 30 minutes the park is open, or try just before park closing.

A Pirate's Adventure: Treasure of the Seven Seas ★★½

Appeal by Age PRESCHOOL ★★★½ GRADE SCHOOL ★★★★½ TEENS ★★★★
YOUNG ADULTS ★★★½ OVER 30 ★★★½ SENIORS ★★★★

What it is Interactive game. **Scope and scale** Diversion. **When to go** Anytime. **Authors' rating** Simple, fast, and fun—especially at night; not to be missed; ★★★½. **Duration of experience** About 20 minutes to play the entire game.

DESCRIPTION AND COMMENTS Similar to Agent P's World Showcase Adventure at Epcot (page 183), A Pirate's Adventure features interactive areas with physical props and narrations that lead guests through a quest to find lost treasure.

The journey begins at an old cartography shop near Golden Oak Outpost. Groups of up to six people are given a talisman (an RFID card) that will help them on their journey. Guests use the talisman to activate a TV screen, which will assign them one of five different missions. Your group is then given a map and sent off to find your first location. Once there, a member of your party touches the talisman to the symbol at the station, and the animation begins.

Each adventure has four or five stops throughout Adventureland, and each stop contains 30–45 seconds of activity. No strategy or action is required: You watch what unfolds on the screen, get your next destination, and head off.

TOURING TIPS The effects are better at night. While we think everyone should try A Pirate's Adventure, it isn't a must if time is tight.

Pirates of the Caribbean *(FastPass+)* ★★★★

| Appeal by Age | PRESCHOOL ★★★½ | GRADE SCHOOL ★★★★ | TEENS ★★★★½ |
| YOUNG ADULTS ★★★★ | OVER 30 ★★★★½ | | SENIORS ★★★★½ |

What it is Indoor pirate-themed boat ride. **Scope and scale** Headliner. **When to go** Before 11 a.m., after 7 p.m., or use FastPass+. **Special comments** Frightens some kids. **Authors' rating** Disney Audio-Animatronics at their best; not to be missed; ★★★★. **Duration of ride** About 7½ minutes. **Average wait in line per 100 people ahead of you** 3 minutes; assumes one FastPass+ line, one standby line. **Loading speed** Fast.

DESCRIPTION AND COMMENTS An indoor cruise through a series of sets that depict a pirate raid on an island settlement, from bombardment of the fortress to debauchery after the victory. One of the most influential theme park attractions ever created, the Magic Kingdom's version retains the elaborate queuing area, grand scale, and detailed scenes that have awed audiences since its debut in Disneyland in 1967. The *Pirates of the Caribbean* movie series has boosted the ride's popularity, and guests' demands led to the addition of animatronic figures of the film's Captain Jack Sparrow and Captain Barbossa in scenes.

TOURING TIPS A timeless attraction. Engineered to move large crowds in a hurry, Pirates is a good attraction to see during late afternoon. It has two covered waiting lines.

Swiss Family Treehouse ★★★

| Appeal by Age | PRESCHOOL ★★★½ | GRADE SCHOOL ★★★½ | TEENS ★★★ |
| YOUNG ADULTS ★★★ | OVER 30 ★★★½ | | SENIORS ★★★ |

What it is Outdoor walk-through treehouse. **Scope and scale** Minor attraction. **When to go** Anytime. **Special comments** Requires climbing a lot of stairs. **Authors' rating** Incredible detail and execution; ★★★. **Duration of tour** 10–15 minutes. **Average wait in line per 100 people ahead of you** 7 minutes.

DESCRIPTION AND COMMENTS An immense replica of the shipwrecked Swiss Family Robinson's arboreal abode. With its multiple stories and mechanical wizardry, it's the queen of all treehouses.

TOURING TIPS A self-guided walk-through tour involves a lot of stairs up and down, but no ropes, ladders, or anything fancy. People who stop for extra-long looks or to rest sometimes create bottlenecks that slow the crowd flow. Visit in late afternoon or early evening if you're on a one-day tour, or in the morning of your second day.

Walt Disney's Enchanted Tiki Room ★★★½

Appeal by Age	PRESCHOOL ★★★½		GRADE SCHOOL ★★★½	TEENS ★★★
YOUNG ADULTS ★★★		OVER 30 ★★★½		SENIORS ★★★★

What it is Audio-Animatronic Pacific-island musical-theater show. **Scope and scale** Minor attraction. **When to go** Before 11 a.m. or after 3:30 p.m. **Special comments** Frightens some preschoolers. **Authors' rating** Very, very . . . unusual; ★★★½. **Duration of presentation** 15½ minutes. **Preshow entertainment** Talking birds. **Probable waiting time** 15 minutes.

DESCRIPTION AND COMMENTS The current show here is a shortened version of the original attraction, which premiered at Disneyland in 1963. It stars four singing, wisecracking parrots (José, Fritz, Michael, and Pierre) and remains a favorite of many, including us. It can frighten some younger kids, though.

TOURING TIPS Usually not too crowded. We go in the late afternoon, when we appreciate sitting in air-conditioned comfort with our brains in "park."

FRONTIERLAND

FRONTIERLAND ADJOINS ADVENTURELAND as you move clockwise around the Magic Kingdom. The focus is on the Old West, with stockade-type structures and pioneer trappings.

Big Thunder Mountain Railroad (FastPass+) ★★★★

Appeal by Age	PRESCHOOL ★★★½	GRADE SCHOOL ★★★★½	TEENS ★★★★½
YOUNG ADULTS ★★★★½		OVER 30 ★★★★½	SENIORS ★★★★

What it is Tame western-mining-themed coaster. **Scope and scale** Headliner. **When to go** Before 10 a.m., in the hour before closing, or use FastPass+. **Special comments** Must be 40″ tall to ride; children younger than age 7 must ride with an adult. Switching-off option provided (see page 93). **Authors' rating** Great effects; relatively tame ride; not to be missed; ★★★★. **Duration of ride** About 3½ minutes. **Average wait in line per 100 people ahead of you** 2½ minutes; assumes 5 trains operating. **Loading speed** Moderate-fast.

DESCRIPTION AND COMMENTS Roller coaster through and around a Disney "mountain." The idea is that you're on a runaway mine train during the Gold Rush. This roller coaster is about 5 on a "scary scale" of 10. First-rate examples of Disney creativity are showcased: realistic mining town, falling rocks, and an earthquake, all humorously animated with swinging possums, petulant buzzards, and the like.

TOURING TIPS A superb Disney experience, but more mild than wild. Emphasis is more on the sights than on the thrill of the ride.

Nearby Splash Mountain affects traffic flow to Big Thunder Mountain Railroad—adventuresome guests ride Splash Mountain first, then go next door to ride Big Thunder. All this means large crowds in Frontierland all day and long waits for Big Thunder. The best way to experience the Magic Kingdom's "mountains" is to ride Seven Dwarfs Mine Train and Space Mountain one morning as soon as the park opens, then Splash Mountain and Big Thunder Mountain the next morning. If you have only one day, the order should be (1) Seven Dwarfs, (2) Splash Mountain, (3) Big Thunder, and (4) Space Mountain.

Country Bear Jamboree ★★★

Appeal by Age	PRESCHOOL ★★★½	GRADE SCHOOL ★★★½	TEENS ★★★
YOUNG ADULTS ★★★	OVER 30 ★★★½		SENIORS ★★★★

What it is Audio-Animatronic country hoedown. **Scope and scale** Major attraction. **When to go** Anytime. **Authors' rating** Old and worn but pure Disney; ★★★½. **Duration of presentation** 11 minutes. **Preshow entertainment** None. **Probable waiting time** It's not terribly popular but has a comparatively small capacity. Waiting time between noon and 5:30 p.m. on a busy day will average 11–22 minutes.

DESCRIPTION AND COMMENTS A charming cast of animatronic bears sing and stomp in a Western-style revue. Recent editing has cut a few minutes from the show, quickening its pace somewhat. However, most songs remain the same, and the geriatric bears seem a step away from assisted living.

TOURING TIPS During hot summer afternoons, rainy days, and busy times, the show draws large crowds from midmorning on.

Frontierland Shootin' Arcade ★½

Appeal by Age	PRESCHOOL ★★★½	GRADE SCHOOL ★★★½	TEENS ★★★★½
YOUNG ADULTS ★★★★	OVER 30 ★★★½		SENIORS ★★★★

What it is Electronic shooting gallery. **Scope and scale** Diversion. **When to go** Whenever convenient. **Special comments** Costs $1 per play. **Authors' rating** Very nifty shooting gallery; ★½.

DESCRIPTION AND COMMENTS One of a few attractions not included in Magic Kingdom admission. Would-be gunslingers get around 30 shots per $1 play. Each shot is followed by a short delay before the next shot can be taken—this prevents small children from accidentally using all 30 shots in 5 seconds.

TOURING TIPS Not a place to waste time if you're on a tight schedule. The fun is entirely in the target practice—no prizes can be won.

Splash Mountain (FastPass+) ★★★★★

Appeal by Age	PRESCHOOL ★★★★†	GRADE SCHOOL ★★★★½	TEENS ★★★★½
YOUNG ADULTS ★★★★½	OVER 30 ★★★★½		SENIORS ★★★★½

† Many preschoolers are too short to meet the height requirement, and others are visually intimidated when they see the ride from the waiting line. Among preschoolers who actually ride, most give the attraction high marks.

Wet

What it is Indoor/outdoor water-flume adventure ride. **Scope and scale** Super-headliner. **When to go** As soon as the park opens, during afternoon or evening parades, just before closing, or use FastPass+. **Special comments** 40" minimum height requirement; children younger than age 7 must ride with an adult. Switching-off option provided (see page 93). **Authors' rating** A soggy delight, and not to be missed; ★★★★★. **Duration of ride** About 10 minutes. **Average wait in line per 100 people ahead of you** 3½ minutes; assumes ride is operating at full capacity. **Loading speed** Moderate.

DESCRIPTION AND COMMENTS Splash Mountain combines steep chutes and animatronics with at least one special effect for each of the senses. The ride covers more than half a mile, splashing through swamps, caves, and backwoods bayous before climaxing in a five-story plunge and Br'er Rabbit's triumphant return home. More than a hundred Audio-Animatronic characters, including Br'er Rabbit, Br'er Bear, and Br'er Fox, regale riders with songs, including "Zip-a-Dee-Doo-Dah."

TOURING TIPS This happy, exciting, adventuresome ride vies with Space Mountain in Tomorrowland as the park's most popular attraction. Crowds build fast in the morning, and waits of more than 2 hours can be expected once the park fills. Get in line first thing, certainly no later than 45 minutes after the park opens. Long lines will persist all day.

If you have only a day to see the Magic Kingdom, make FastPass+ reservations in advance for around 9:30 a.m. at Big Thunder Mountain Railroad and around 3:30 p.m. at Space Mountain. On the day of your visit, ride Seven Dwarfs Mine Train as soon as the park opens, then hotfoot it to Splash Mountain to ride immediately. Your FastPass+ reservation for Big Thunder will be valid by the time you're done, and you'll have experienced three of the park's four headliners in about an hour.

If you have two mornings, do the Fantasyland and Frontierland attractions—Seven Dwarfs Mine Train, Splash Mountain, and Big Thunder Mountain Railroad—on one day and Space Mountain the next. Spreading your visits over two mornings eliminates a lot of walking.

As with Space Mountain, hundreds are poised to dash to Splash Mountain when the park opens. The best strategy is to go to the end of Main Street and turn left at The Crystal Palace restaurant. In front of the restaurant is a bridge that provides a shortcut to Adventureland. Stake out a position at the barrier rope. When the park opens, move as fast as you comfortably can and cross the bridge to Adventureland.

Another shortcut: Just past the first group of buildings on your right, roughly across from the Swiss Family Treehouse, is a small passageway containing restrooms and phones. Easy to overlook, it connects Adventureland to Frontierland. Go through here into Frontierland and take a hard left. As you emerge along the waterfront, Splash Mountain is straight ahead. If you miss the passageway, don't fool around looking for it. Continue straight through Adventureland to Splash Mountain.

Less exhausting in the morning is commuting to Splash Mountain via the Walt Disney World Railroad. Board at Main Street Station and wait for the park to open. The train will pull out of the station a few minutes after the rope drops at the Central Plaza end of Main Street. Ride to Frontierland Station and disembark. As you come down the stairs at the station, the entrance to Splash Mountain will be on your left.

If you ride in front, you'll almost certainly get wet. Since you don't know which seat you'll be assigned, go prepared: On a cool day, carry a plastic garbage bag. Tear holes in the bottom and sides to make a water-resistant poncho (tuck the bag under your bottom). Leave your phone or camera with a nonriding member of your group, or wrap it in plastic. Alternatively. store a change of clothes and shoes in a rental locker. Wear waterproof sandals, such as Tevas, and change back to regular shoes after the ride.

The steep chute you see when standing in line seems scary, but the drop looks worse than it is. Still, many children wig out when they see it.

Tom Sawyer Island and Fort Langhorn ★★★

**Appeal by Age   PRESCHOOL ★★★★   GRADE SCHOOL ★★★★½   TEENS ★★★★
YOUNG ADULTS ★★★½   OVER 30 ★★★½   SENIORS ★★★**

What it is Outdoor walk-through exhibit and rustic playground. **Scope and scale** Minor attraction. **When to go** Midmorning–late afternoon. **Special comments** Closes at dusk. **Authors' rating** Great for rambunctious kids; ★★★.

DESCRIPTION AND COMMENTS Tom Sawyer Island is a getaway within the park. It has hills to climb; a cave, windmill, and pioneer stockade (Fort Langhorn) to explore; a tipsy barrel bridge to cross; and paths to follow. You can watch riverboats chug past. It's a delight for adults and a godsend for children who have been in tow and closely supervised all day.

TOURING TIPS Tom Sawyer Island isn't one of the Magic Kingdom's more celebrated attractions, but it certainly is well conceived: Attention to detail is excellent, and kids love the frontier ambience. It's a must for families with children ages 5–15. If your group consist of adults, visit on your second day or on your first day after you've seen the attractions you most wanted to see.

Although children could spend a whole day on the island, plan on at least 20 minutes. Access is by raft from Frontierland; two operate simultaneously, and the trip is pretty efficient, although you may have to stand in line to board both ways.

Walt Disney World Railroad

DESCRIPTION AND COMMENTS Stops in Frontierland on its circle tour of the park. See page 133 for additional details.

TOURING TIPS Feet-saving link to Main Street and Fantasyland, but the Frontierland Station is more congested than those stations.

◧ LIBERTY SQUARE

LIBERTY SQUARE re-creates America at the time of the American Revolution. The architecture is Federal or Colonial. The **Liberty Tree,** a live oak more than 130 years old, lends dignity and grace to the setting.

The Hall of Presidents ★★★½

Appeal by Age	PRESCHOOL ★★½	GRADE SCHOOL ★★★	TEENS ★★★½
YOUNG ADULTS ★★★½	OVER 30 ★★★★		SENIORS ★★★★½

What it is Audio-Animatronic historical theater presentation. **Scope and scale** Major attraction. **When to go** Anytime. **Authors' rating** Impressive and moving; ★★★½. **Duration of presentation** Almost 23 minutes. **Preshow entertainment** None. **Probable waiting time** The lines for this attraction look intimidating once you're inside the lobby, but they're swallowed up as the theater exchanges audiences. It would be exceptionally unusual not to be admitted to the next show.

DESCRIPTION AND COMMENTS George Washington joins Presidents Lincoln and Obama as the only chief executives with speaking parts; Morgan Freeman narrates. Revamped roughly every decade, the presentation remains inspirational and patriotic, highlighting milestones in American history. Very moving; one of Disney's best and most ambitious animatronic efforts.

TOURING TIPS Detail and costuming are masterly. This is one of the park's most popular attractions among older visitors. Don't be put off by long lines. The theater holds more than 700 people, thus swallowing large lines at a single gulp when visitors are admitted.

The Haunted Mansion *(FastPass+)* ★★★★½

Appeal by Age PRESCHOOL ★★★½   GRADE SCHOOL ★★★★   TEENS ★★★★½
YOUNG ADULTS ★★★★½   OVER 30 ★★★★½   SENIORS ★★★★½

What it is Haunted-house dark ride. **Scope and scale** Major attraction. **When to go** Before 11 a.m. or during the last 2 hours before closing. **Special comments** Frightens some very young children. **Authors' rating** A masterpiece of detail and not to be missed; ★★★★½. **Duration of ride** 7-minute ride plus a 1½-minute preshow. **Average wait in line per 100 people ahead of you** 2½ minutes; assumes both "stretch rooms" operating. **Loading speed** Fast.

DESCRIPTION AND COMMENTS Only slightly scarier than a whoopee cushion, The Haunted Mansion serves up some of the Magic Kingdom's best visual effects. "Doom Buggies" on a conveyor belt transport you through the house from parlor to attic, then through a graveyard. Some children become overly anxious about what they think they'll see. Almost nobody is scared by the actual sights.

TOURING TIPS Lines here ebb and flow more than those at most other Magic Kingdom hot spots because the Mansion is near *The Hall of Presidents* and the *Liberty Belle* Riverboat. These two attractions disgorge 700 and 450 people, respectively, when each show or ride ends, and many of these folks head straight for the Mansion. If you can't go before 11:30 a.m. or after 8 p.m., try to slip in between crowds. If you're touring the Magic Kingdom in a single day, you'll find that FastPass+ saves more time at other attractions than it does here. On the other hand, you may find it useful if you're touring over two or more days.

Liberty Belle Riverboat ★★½

Appeal by Age PRESCHOOL ★★★½   GRADE SCHOOL ★★★½   TEENS ★★★
YOUNG ADULTS ★★★½   OVER 30 ★★★½   SENIORS ★★★★

What it is Outdoor scenic boat ride. **Scope and scale** Major attraction. **When to go** Anytime. **Authors' rating** Relaxing and scenic; ★★½. **Duration of ride** About 16 minutes. Average wait to board 10–14 minutes.

DESCRIPTION AND COMMENTS Large-capacity paddle-wheel riverboat navigates the waters around Tom Sawyer Island and Fort Langhorn, passing settler cabins, old mining paraphernalia, an Indian village, and a small menagerie of animatronic wildlife. A beautiful craft, the *Liberty Belle* provides a lofty perspective of Frontierland and Liberty Square.

TOURING TIPS A good attraction for the busy middle of the day. If you encounter huge crowds, chances are that the attraction has been inundated by a wave of guests coming from a just-concluded performance of *The Hall of Presidents.*

◧ FANTASYLAND

FANTASYLAND IS THE HEART OF THE MAGIC KINGDOM, an enchanting place spread gracefully like a miniature Alpine village beneath the steepled towers of **Cinderella Castle.**

Fantasyland is divided into three distinct sections. Directly behind Cinderella Castle and set upon a snowcapped mountain is **Beast's Castle,** part of a *Beauty and the Beast*–themed area. Most of this section holds dining and shopping, such as **Be Our Guest Restaurant; Gaston's Tavern,** a small quick-service eatery; and a gift shop. The far-right corner of Fantasyland—including **Dumbo, The Barnstormer** kiddie coaster, and the Fantasyland train station—is called **Storybook Circus** as an homage to Disney's *Dumbo* film. These are low-capacity rides appropriate for younger children. A covered seating area with plush chairs, electrical outlets, and USB chargers is available behind **Big Top Souvenirs.**

The middle of Fantasyland holds the headliners, including **Under the Sea** and **Seven Dwarfs Mine Train.** The placement of these two attractions allows good traffic flow either to the left for dining, to the right for attractions geared to smaller children, or back to the original part of Fantasyland for classic attractions such as **Peter Pan's Flight** and **The Many Adventures of Winnie the Pooh.**

The original part of Fantasyland also hosts the incredibly popular **Princess Fairytale Hall** meet and greet, with waits of 5 hours or more to meet *Frozen*'s Anna and Elsa. Even so, Len's daughter, Hannah, thinks it's the best character-greeting venue in Walt Disney World. (Lines for the B-list princesses are shorter.)

Finally, when nature (or your mother-in-law) calls, don't miss the ***Tangled*-themed restrooms and outdoor seating** (with phone-charging stations), near Peter Pan's Flight and It's a Small World.

Ariel's Grotto ★★★

Appeal by Age PRESCHOOL ★★★★½ GRADE SCHOOL ★★★★½ TEENS ★★★★
YOUNG ADULTS ★★★★ OVER 30 ★★★½ SENIORS ★★★★

What it is Character-greeting venue. **Scope and scale** Minor attraction. **When to go** Before 10:30 a.m. or during the last 2 hours before closing. **Authors' rating** Not as themed as other character greetings; ★★★. **Duration of experience** About 30–90 seconds. **Probable waiting time** 45 minutes. **Queue speed** Slow.

DESCRIPTION AND COMMENTS Ariel's elaborate home is next to Under the Sea: Journey of the Little Mermaid, in the base of the seaside cliffs under Prince Eric's Castle. Ariel (in mermaid form) greets guests from a seashell throne.

TOURING TIPS May close an hour before the rest of the park. The greeting area is set up almost as if to encourage guests to linger, which keeps the line long. The queue isn't air-conditioned—surprising for a venue that's supposed to store fish.

The Barnstormer (*FastPass+*) ★★

Appeal by Age PRESCHOOL ★★★★ GRADE SCHOOL ★★★★ TEENS ★★★½
YOUNG ADULTS ★★★ OVER 30 ★★★ SENIORS ★★★½

Lose Things

What it is Small roller coaster. **Scope and scale** Minor attraction. **When to go** Before 11 a.m., during parades, during the last 2 hours before closing, or use FastPass+. **Special comments** 35" minimum height requirement. **Authors' rating** Great for little ones, but not worth the wait for adults; ★★. **Duration of ride** About 53 seconds. **Average wait in line per 100 people ahead of you** 7 minutes. **Loading speed** Slow.

DESCRIPTION AND COMMENTS The Barnstormer is a very small roller coaster. The ride is zippy but supershort. In fact, of the 53 seconds the ride is in motion, 32 seconds are consumed in leaving the loading area, being ratcheted up the first hill, and braking into the off-loading area. The actual time you spend careering around the track is 21 seconds.

The Barnstormer is a benign introduction to the roller-coaster genre and a predictably positive way to help your children step up to more-adventuresome rides. Simply put, a few circuits will increase your little one's confidence and improve his or her chances for enjoying Disney's more adult attractions.

TOURING TIPS The cars of this dinky coaster are too small for most adults and tend to whiplash taller people. Parties without children should skip this one. If The Barnstormer is high on your children's hit parade, try to ride within the first hour that Fantasyland is open.

Casey Jr. Splash 'N' Soak Station ★★★

Appeal by Age	PRESCHOOL ★★★★½	GRADE SCHOOL ★★★★½	TEENS ★★★
YOUNG ADULTS ★★½		OVER 30 ★★½	SENIORS ★★★

What it is Opportunity to get wet. **Scope and scale** Diversion. **When to go** When it's hot. **Authors' rating** Great way to cool off; ★★★.

DESCRIPTION AND COMMENTS Casey Jr., the circus train from *Dumbo*, plays host to an absolutely drenching experience outside the Fantasyland Train Station in the Storybook Circus area. Expect a cadre of captive circus beasts to spray water on you in this elaborate water-play area.

TOURING TIPS Puts all other theme park splash areas to soaking shame. Bring a change of clothes and a big towel.

Dumbo the Flying Elephant *(FastPass+)* ★★★

Appeal by Age	PRESCHOOL ★★★★½	GRADE SCHOOL ★★★★	TEENS ★★★
YOUNG ADULTS ★★★½		OVER 30 ★★★½	SENIORS ★★★

What it is Disneyfied midway ride. **Scope and scale** Minor attraction. **When to go** Before 10:30 a.m., after 3 p.m., or use FastPass+. **Authors' rating** Disney's signature ride for children; ★★★½. **Duration of ride** 1½ minutes. **Average wait in line per 100 people ahead of you** 10 minutes. **Loading speed** Slow.

DESCRIPTION AND COMMENTS A tame, happy ride based on the lovable flying pachyderm. Parents and children sit inside small fiberglass "elephants" mounted on long metal arms, which spin around a central axis. Controls inside each vehicle allow you to raise the arm, making you spin higher off the ground. Despite being little different from your average carnival ride, Dumbo is a favorite of many younger children.

As part of the Fantasyland expansion, Dumbo moved to the upper-right corner of the land. The attraction's capacity has doubled with the addition of a second ride—a clone of the first. These two changes, along with the addition of the newer Fantasyland attractions, have drastically reduced waits to ride. If you do find yourself with a wait, Dumbo also includes a covered queue featuring interactive elements (read: things your kids can play with to pass the time in line).

TOURING TIPS If Dumbo is essential to your child's happiness, ride within the first 2 hours the park is open or after dinner—not only are crowds smaller at night, but the lighting and effects make the ride much prettier then. Or try Dumbo following the afternoon parade.

Enchanted Tales with Belle (FastPass+) ★★★★

Appeal by Age PRESCHOOL ★★★★½ GRADE SCHOOL ★★★★½ TEENS ★★★½
YOUNG ADULTS ★★★★ OVER 30 ★★★★ SENIORS ★★★★

What it is Interactive character show. **Scope and scale** Minor attraction. **When to go** As soon as the park opens, during the last 2 hours before closing, or use FastPass+. **Authors' rating** The prettiest meet-and-greet location in the park; ★★★★. **Duration of presentation** About 20 minutes. **Preshow entertainment** As described below. **Probable waiting time** 25 minutes. **Queue speed** Slow.

DESCRIPTION AND COMMENTS A multiscene *Beauty and the Beast* experience that takes guests into Maurice's workshop, through a magic mirror, and into Beast's library, where the audience shares a story with Belle.

Enter the attraction by walking through Maurice's cottage, where you see mementos tracing Belle's childhood, including her favorite books, and lines drawn on one wall showing how fast Belle grew every year. From there you'll enter Maurice's workshop at the back of the cottage. An assortment of Maurice's odd wood gadgets covers every inch of the floor, walls, and ceiling. Take a moment to peruse the gadgets, then focus your attention on the mirror on the wall to the left of the entry door.

Soon enough, the room gets dark and the mirror begins to sparkle. Through magic and some really good carpentry skills, the mirror turns into a full-size doorway, through which guests enter into a wardrobe room. Once you're in the wardrobe room, the attraction's premise is explained: you're supposed to re-enact the story of *Beauty and the Beast* for Belle on her birthday, and guests are chosen to act out key parts in the play.

Once the parts are cast, everyone walks into the castle's library and takes a seat. Cast members explain how the play will take place and introduce Belle, who gives a short speech about how thrilled she is for everyone to be there. The play is acted out within a few minutes, and the actors get a chance to take photos with Belle and receive a small bookmark as a memento.

Enchanted Tales with Belle is the prettiest and most elaborate meet-and-greet station in Walt Disney World. For the lucky few who get to act in the play, it's also a chance to interact with Belle in a way that isn't possible in other character encounters. You may endure a 30-minute wait for a 3-minute show, but it's the best of its kind in Orlando. Your kids will love it.

TOURING TIPS *Enchanted Tales* is the new Dumbo, with long lines from the time the park opens. Since it's slow-loading, make *Enchanted Tales* the first thing on your touring plan if you want to see it. Alternatively, try to visit during the last 2 hours the park is open, or use FastPass+.

It's a Small World *(FastPass+)* ★★★½

Appeal by Age PRESCHOOL ★★★★½ GRADE SCHOOL ★★★★ TEENS ★★★
YOUNG ADULTS ★★★½ OVER 30 ★★★½ SENIORS ★★★★

What it is World brotherhood–themed indoor boat ride. **Scope and scale** Major attraction. **When to go** Before 11 a.m., during parades, after 7 p.m., or use FastPass+ **Authors' rating** Exponentially "cute"; ★★★½. **Duration of ride** About 11 minutes. **Average wait in line per 100 people ahead of you** 3½ minutes; assumes busy conditions with 30 or more boats operating. **Loading speed** Fast.

DESCRIPTION AND COMMENTS It's a Small World is a relentlessly upbeat indoor attraction with a mind-numbing tune that only a backhoe can dislodge from your brain. Small boats carry visitors on a tour around the world, with singing and dancing dolls showcasing the costumes and cultures of different nations. One of Disney's oldest entertainment offerings, Small World first unleashed its brainwashing song and lethally cute dolls on the real world at the 1964 New York World's Fair. We think it ranks with the *Enchanted Tiki Room* in the "What were they smokin'?" category.

TOURING TIPS Cool off here during the heat of the day. Lines are usually 30 minutes or less. If you wear a hearing aid, *turn it off*.

Mad Tea Party *(FastPass+)* ★★

Appeal by Age PRESCHOOL ★★★★½ GRADE SCHOOL ★★★★½ TEENS ★★★★
YOUNG ADULTS ★★★½ OVER 30 ★★★½ SENIORS ★★½

What it is Midway-type spinning ride. **Scope and scale** Minor attraction. **When to go** Before 11 a.m., after 5 p.m., or use FastPass+. **Special comments** You can make the teacups spin faster by turning the wheel in the center of the cup. **Authors' rating** Not worth the wait; ★★. **Duration of ride** 1½ minutes. **Average wait in line per 100 people ahead of you** 7½ minutes. **Loading speed** Slow.

Queasy

DESCRIPTION AND COMMENTS Riders whirl feverishly in big teacups. *Alice in Wonderland*'s Mad Hatter provides the theme. Teens are fond of luring adults onto the teacups, then turning the wheel in the middle (making the cup spin faster), until the adults are plastered against the sides and on the verge of throwing up. Don't even *think* about getting on this ride with anyone younger than 21.

TOURING TIPS Mad Tea Party is notoriously slow-loading. Ride the morning of your second day if your schedule is more relaxed. Not a good choice for FastPass+.

The Many Adventures of Winnie the Pooh *(FastPass+)* ★★★½

Appeal by Age PRESCHOOL ★★★★½ GRADE SCHOOL ★★★★ TEENS ★★★½
YOUNG ADULTS ★★★½ OVER 30 ★★★½ SENIORS ★★★★

What it is Indoor track ride. **Scope and scale** Minor attraction. **When to go** Before 10 a.m., in last hour park is open, or use FastPass+. **Authors' rating** As cute as the Pooh Bear himself; ★★★½. **Duration of ride** About 4 minutes. **Average wait in line per 100 people ahead of you** 4 minutes. **Loading speed** Moderate.

DESCRIPTION AND COMMENTS Pooh is sunny, upbeat, and fun. You ride a "Hunny Pot" through the pages of a huge picture book into the Hundred Acre Wood, where you encounter Pooh, Piglet, Eeyore, Owl, Rabbit, Tigger, Kanga, and Roo as they contend with a blustery day. There's even a dream sequence with Heffalumps and Woozles.

TOURING TIPS Pooh is a good choice for FastPass+ if you have small children and you're touring over two or more days.

Mickey's PhilharMagic *(FastPass+)* ★★★★

Appeal by Age PRESCHOOL ★★★★ GRADE SCHOOL ★★★★½ TEENS ★★★★½
YOUNG ADULTS ★★★★½ OVER 30 ★★★★½ SENIORS ★★★★½

What it is 3-D movie. **Scope and scale** Major attraction. **When to go** Before 11 a.m., during parades, or use FastPass+. **Authors' rating** A zany masterpiece, not to be missed; ★★★★. **Duration of presentation** About 12 minutes. **Probable waiting time** 12–30 minutes.

DESCRIPTION AND COMMENTS *Mickey's PhilharMagic* features an odd collection of Disney characters, mixing Mickey and Donald with Simba and Ariel as well as Jasmine and Aladdin. Presented in a theater large enough to accommodate a 150-foot-wide screen—huge by 3-D movie standards—the 3-D movie is augmented by an arsenal of special effects built into the theater. The plot involves Mickey, as the conductor of the *PhilharMagic*, leaving the theater to solve a mystery. In his absence Donald appears and attempts to take charge, with disastrous results.

The attraction is one of Disney's best 3-D efforts. Brilliantly conceived, furiously paced, and laugh-out-loud funny, *PhilharMagic* incorporates a hit parade of Disney's most beloved characters in a production that will leave you grinning.

TOURING TIPS Proceed cautiously if you have kids under age 5 in your group, but it's the rare child who is frightened. The theater is large, so don't be alarmed to see a gaggle of people in the lobby. *PhilharMagic* never needs FastPass+.

Peter Pan's Flight *(FastPass+)* ★★★★

Appeal by Age PRESCHOOL ★★★½ **GRADE SCHOOL** ★★★½ **TEENS** ★★★½
YOUNG ADULTS ★★★★   **OVER 30** ★★★★   **SENIORS** ★★★★

What it is Indoor track ride. **Scope and scale** Minor attraction. **When to go** First or last 30 minutes the park is open, or use FastPass+. **Authors' rating** Nostalgic, mellow, and well done; not to be missed; ★★★★. **Duration of ride** A little over 3 minutes. **Average wait in line per 100 people ahead of you** 5½ minutes. **Loading speed** Moderate–slow.

DESCRIPTION AND COMMENTS Though not a major attraction, Peter Pan's Flight is an absolutely delight, its happy theme uniting some favorite Disney characters, beautiful effects, and charming music. An indoor attraction, Peter Pan's Flight offers a relaxing ride in a "flying pirate ship" over old London and thence to Never-Never Land, where Peter saves Wendy from walking the plank and Captain Hook rehearses for *Dancing with the Stars* on the snout of the ubiquitous crocodile. Unlike some dark rides, this won't frighten young children.

TOURING TIPS Count on long lines all day. Fortunately, the new queue runs under the roof of the building, out of direct sun and rain, and has tons of new art and interactive games to help pass the time. Ride in the first 30 minutes the park is open, during a parade, just before the park closes, or use FastPass+.

Pete's Silly Sideshow *(FastPass+)* ★★★½

Appeal by Age PRESCHOOL ★★★★½ **GRADE SCHOOL** ★★★★½ **TEENS** ★★★★
YOUNG ADULTS ★★★★   **OVER 30** ★★★★   **SENIORS** ★★★

What it is Character-greeting venue. **Scope and scale** Minor attraction. **When to go** Before 11 a.m., during the last 2 hours before closing, or use FastPass+. **Authors' rating** Well themed, with unique costumes; ★★★½. **Duration of experience** 7 minutes per character. **Probable waiting time** 25 minutes. **Queue speed** Slow.

DESCRIPTION AND COMMENTS Pete's Silly Sideshow is a circus-themed character-greeting area in the Storybook Circus area. The characters' costumes are distinct from the ones normally seen around the parks. Characters include Goofy as The Great Goofini, Donald Duck as The Astounding Donaldo, Daisy Duck as Madame Daisy Fortuna, and Minnie Mouse as Minnie Magnifique.

TOURING TIPS On non–Extra Magic Hour days, Pete's opens 45 minutes later than the rest of the park and usually closes at the same time as the first *Wishes* fireworks show. The queue is indoors and air-conditioned. There's one queue for Goofy and Donald and a second queue for Minnie and Daisy; you can meet two characters at once, but you have to line up twice to meet all four. Rarely a good use of FastPass+.

Prince Charming Regal Carrousel ★★★

Appeal by Age	PRESCHOOL ★★★★½	GRADE SCHOOL ★★★★	TEENS ★★★
YOUNG ADULTS ★★★		OVER 30 ★★★½	SENIORS ★★★½

What it is Merry-go-round. **Scope and scale** Minor attraction. **When to go** Anytime. **Authors' rating** A beautiful ride for children; ★★★. **Duration of ride** About 2 minutes. **Average wait in line per 100 people ahead of you** 5 minutes. **Loading speed** Slow.

DESCRIPTION AND COMMENTS One of the most elaborate and beautiful merry-go-rounds you'll ever see, especially when its lights are on.
TOURING TIPS The carousel, while lovely, loads and unloads very slowly.

Princess Fairytale Hall *(FastPass+)* ★★★

Appeal by Age	PRESCHOOL ★★★★★	GRADE SCHOOL ★★★★½	TEENS ★★★★
YOUNG ADULTS ★★★★		OVER 30 ★★★½	SENIORS ★★★½

What it is Character-greeting venue. **Scope and scale** Minor attraction. **When to go** Before 10:30 a.m., after 4 p.m., or use FastPass+. **Authors' rating** You want princesses? Disney's got 'em! ★★★. **Duration of experience** About 7–10 minutes. **Average wait in line per 100 people ahead of you** About 35 minutes. **Loading speed** Slow.

DESCRIPTION AND COMMENTS Princess Fairytale Hall is Disney-princess central in the Magic Kingdom. Inside are two greeting venues, with each holding a small reception area for two princesses. Rapunzel usually leads one side, typically paired with Snow White, Cinderella, or another princess, while Anna and Elsa from *Frozen* hold forth on the other side. Around 5–10 guests at a time are admitted to each greeting area, where there's plenty of time for small talk, a photo, and a hug from each princess.
TOURING TIPS Anna and Elsa are the hottest character-greeting ticket in all of Walt Disney World. If your child absolutely must meet them, use FastPass+ or head to Fairytale Hall first thing in the morning. Understand, though, that even if you're on hand at park opening, waits can easily top 2 hours—and often much, much more than that.

Seven Dwarfs Mine Train *(FastPass+)* ★★★★

Appeal by Age	PRESCHOOL ★★★★	GRADE SCHOOL ★★★★½	TEENS ★★★★
YOUNG ADULTS ★★★★		OVER 30 ★★★★	SENIORS ★★★★½

What it is Indoor/outdoor roller coaster. **Scope and scale** Major attraction. **When to go** As soon as the park opens, or use FastPass+. **Special comments** 38" minimum height requirement. **Authors' rating** Great family coaster; not to be missed; ★★★★. **Duration of ride** About 2 minutes. **Average wait in line per 100 people ahead of you** About 4½ minutes. **Loading speed** Fast.

DESCRIPTION AND COMMENTS In the pantheon of Disney coasters, Seven Dwarfs Mine Train fits somewhere between The Barnstormer and Big Thunder Mountain Railroad—that is, it's geared to older grade-school kids who've been on amusement park rides before. There are no loops, inversions, or rolls in the track, and no massive hills or steep drops; rather, the Mine Train's trick is that your ride vehicle's seats swing side-to-side as you go through turns. And—what a coincidence!—Disney has designed a curvy track with steep turns. There's also an elaborate indoor section showing the Seven Dwarfs' underground operation.

The exterior design includes waterfalls, forests, and landscaping and is meant to join together all of the surrounding Fantasyland's various locations, including France and Germany. The swinging effect is more noticeable the farther back you're seated in the train.

TOURING TIPS If you have only a day to see the Magic Kingdom, make FastPass+ reservations in advance for around 9:30 a.m. at Big Thunder Mountain Railroad and around 3:30 p.m. at Space Mountain. On the day of your visit, ride Seven Dwarfs Mine Train as soon as the park opens, then hurry to Splash Mountain to ride immediately. Your FastPass+ reservation for Big Thunder Mountain will be valid by the time you're done, and you'll have experienced three of the park's four headliners in about an hour.

If you have two mornings, do the Fantasyland and Frontierland attractions—Seven Dwarfs Mine Train, Splash Mountain, and Big Thunder Mountain Railroad—on one day and Space Mountain the next.

Under the Sea: Journey of the Little Mermaid
(FastPass+) ★★★½

Appeal by Age PRESCHOOL ★★★★½ GRADE SCHOOL ★★★★ TEENS ★★★½
YOUNG ADULTS ★★★★ OVER 30 ★★★★ SENIORS ★★★½

What it is Dark ride retelling the film's story. **Scope and scale** Major attraction. **When to go** Before 10:30 a.m., during the last 2 hours before closing, or use FastPass+. **Authors' rating** Colorful, but most effects are too simple for an attraction this big; ★★★½. **Duration of ride** About 5½ minutes. **Average wait in line per 100 people ahead of you** 3 minutes. **Loading speed** Fast.

DESCRIPTION AND COMMENTS Under the Sea takes riders through almost a dozen scenes retelling the story of *The Little Mermaid,* this time with Audio-Animatronics, video effects, and a vibrant 3-D set the size of a small theater.

Guests board a clamshell-shaped ride vehicle running along a continuously moving track (similar to The Haunted Mansion's). Then the ride "descends" under water, past Ariel's grotto and on to King Triton's undersea kingdom. The most detailed animatronic is of Ursula the Sea Witch, and she's a beauty. Other scenes hit the film's highlights, including Ariel meeting Prince Eric, her deal with Ursula to become human, and, of course, the couple's happy ending.

The attraction's exterior is attractive, with detailed rock work, water, and story elements. That said, most of the effects are unimaginative, such as starfish that do nothing but spin on a central axis or lobsters that simply turn left and right, and virtually the entire second half of the story is condensed into a handful of small scenes crammed together at the end of the ride.

TOURING TIPS Expect long waits throughout most of the day. If you can, ride early in the morning, late at night, or use FastPass+.

Walt Disney World Railroad

DESCRIPTION AND COMMENTS Stops in Fantasyland on its circuit of the park. See page 133 for additional details.

▪▐ TOMORROWLAND

AT VARIOUS POINTS IN ITS HISTORY, Tomorrowland's attractions presented life's possibilities in adventures ranging from the modern-day (If You Had Wings' round-the-world travel in the 1970s) to the distant future (Mission to Mars). The problem that stymied Disney repeatedly was that the future came faster and looked different than what they'd envisioned. Today, Tomorrowland's theme makes the least sense of any area in any Disney park. It's not so much a vision of the future as it is a collection of attractions that don't fit anywhere else in the Magic Kingdom.

Astro Orbiter ★★

Appeal by Age PRESCHOOL ★★★★ GRADE SCHOOL ★★★½ TEENS ★★★½
YOUNG ADULTS ★★★ OVER 30 ★★★ SENIORS ★★½

Queasy

What it is Buck Rogers-style rockets revolving around a central axis. **Scope and scale** Minor attraction. **When to go** Before 11 a.m. or during the last hour before closing. **Special comments** Not as innocuous as it appears. **Authors' rating** Not worth the wait; ★★. **Duration of ride** 1½ minutes. **Average wait in line per 100 people ahead of you** 13½ minutes. **Loading speed** Slow.

DESCRIPTION AND COMMENTS Though visually appealing, the Astro Orbiter is still a slow-loading carnival ride: The fat little rocket ships simply fly in circles, though you do get a nice view when you're aloft.

TOURING TIPS Expendable on any schedule. If you ride with preschoolers, seat them first, then board. The Astro Orbiter flies higher and faster than Dumbo and frightens some young children (and adults).

Buzz Lightyear's Space Ranger Spin *(FastPass+)* ★★★★

Appeal by Age PRESCHOOL ★★★★½ GRADE SCHOOL ★★★★½ TEENS ★★★★
YOUNG ADULTS ★★★★ OVER 30 ★★★★ SENIORS ★★★★

What it is Whimsical space travel–themed indoor ride. **Scope and scale** Minor attraction. **When to go** First or last hour the park is open, or use FastPass+. **Authors' rating** Surreal shooting gallery; ★★★★. **Duration of ride** About 4½ minutes. **Average wait in line per 100 people ahead of you** 3 minutes. **Loading speed** Fast.

DESCRIPTION AND COMMENTS This attraction is based on the space-commando character of Buzz Lightyear from the film *Toy Story.* The marginal storyline has you and Buzz Lightyear trying to save the universe from the evil Emperor Zurg. You can spin your car and shoot simulated "laser cannons" at Zurg and his minions. The first room's mechanical claw and red robot contain high-value targets, so aim for these.

TOURING TIPS Each car is equipped with two laser cannons and a score-keeping display. Each display is independent, so you can compete with your riding partner. A joystick allows you to spin the car to line up the various targets. Each time you pull the trigger, you'll release a red laser beam that you can see hitting or missing the target. Most folks' first ride is occupied with learning how to use the equipment and figuring out how the targets work. The next ride (like certain potato chips, one is not enough), you'll surprise yourself by how much better you do. *Unofficial* readers are unanimous in their praise of Buzz Lightyear. Some, in fact, spend hours riding it again and again.

Experience Buzz Lightyear after riding Space Mountain first thing in the morning, or use FastPass+.

Monsters, Inc. Laugh Floor *(FastPass+)* ★★★½

Appeal by Age PRESCHOOL ★★★½ GRADE SCHOOL ★★★★½ TEENS ★★★★
YOUNG ADULTS ★★★★ OVER 30 ★★★★ SENIORS ★★★★

What it is Interactive animated comedy show. **Scope and scale** Major attraction. **When to go** Before 11 a.m., after 4 p.m., or use FastPass+. **Special comments** Audience members may be asked to participate in skits. **Authors' rating** Good concept, but the jokes are hit-and-miss; ★★★½. **Duration of presentation** About 15 minutes.

DESCRIPTION AND COMMENTS We learned in Disney/Pixar's *Monsters, Inc.* that children's screams could be converted into electricity, which was used to power a town inhabited by monsters. During the film, the monsters discovered that children's laughter was an even better source of energy. In this attraction, the monsters have set up a comedy club to capture as many laughs as possible. Mike Wazowski, the one-eyed character from the film, emcees the club's three comedy acts. Each consists of an animated monster (most not seen in the film) trying out various bad puns, corny jokes, and Abbott and Costello–like routines. Using the same cutting-edge technology as Epcot's popular *Turtle Talk with Crush,* behind-the-scenes Disney cast members voice the characters and often interact with audience members during the skits. As with any comedy club, some performers are funny and some are not. Disney has shown a willingness to try new material, though, so the show should remain fresh to repeat visitors.

TOURING TIPS The theater holds several hundred people, so there's no need to rush here first thing in the morning. Try to arrive late in the morning after you've visited other Tomorrowland attractions, or after the afternoon parade when guests start leaving the park.

Space Mountain *(FastPass+)* ★★★★

Appeal by Age PRESCHOOL ★★½† GRADE SCHOOL ★★★★ TEENS ★★★★★
YOUNG ADULTS ★★★★½ OVER 30 ★★★★½ SENIORS ★★★½

†Some preschoolers love Space Mountain; others are frightened by it.

What it is Roller coaster in the dark. **Scope and scale** Super-headliner. **When to go** When the park opens or use FastPass+. **Special comments** Great fun and action; much wilder than Big Thunder Mountain Railroad. 44" minimum height requirement; children younger than age 7 must be accompanied by an adult. Switching-off option provided (see page 93). **Authors' rating** Not to be missed; ★★★★. **Duration of ride** Almost 3 minutes. **Average wait in line per 100 people ahead of you** 3 minutes; assumes 2 tracks, with 1 dedicated to FastPass+ riders, dispatching at 21-second intervals. **Loading speed** Moderate-fast.

Queasy

DESCRIPTION AND COMMENTS Totally enclosed in a mammoth futuristic structure, Space Mountain has always been the Magic Kingdom's most popular attraction. The theme is a space flight through dark recesses of the galaxy. Effects are superb, and the ride is the fastest and wildest in the Magic Kingdom. As a coaster, Space Mountain is much zippier than Big Thunder Mountain Railroad, but much tamer than the Rock 'n' Roller Coaster at Disney's Hollywood Studios or Expedition Everest at Disney's Animal Kingdom.

As a headliner, Space Mountain goes through periodic refurbishments to add effects and maintain ride quality. Past improvements include new lighting and effects, an improved sound system and soundtrack, and interactive games in the queue to help pass the time in line.

TOURING TIPS People who can handle a fairly wild roller-coaster ride will take Space Mountain in stride. What sets Space Mountain apart is that cars plummet through darkness, with only occasional lighting. Half the fun is not knowing where the car will go next.

Space Mountain is a favorite of many Magic Kingdom visitors ages 7–60. Each morning before opening, particularly during summer and holidays, several hundred Space Mountain junkies await the signal to head to the ride's entrance. To get ahead of the competition, be one of the first in the park. Proceed to the end of Main Street and wait at the entrance to Tomorrowland.

Seats are one behind another, as opposed to side by side—meaning parents can't sit next to their kids if they meet the height requirement.

If you don't catch Space Mountain first thing in the morning, use Fast-Pass+ or try again during the 30 minutes before closing.

Stitch's Great Escape! ★★

Appeal by Age PRESCHOOL ★★½   **GRADE SCHOOL** ★★½   **TEENS** ★★½
YOUNG ADULTS ★★½   **OVER 30** ★★   **SENIORS** ★★½

What it is Theater-in-the-round sci-fi adventure show. **Scope and scale** Minor attraction. **When to go** Before 11 a.m. or after 6 p.m.; try during parades. **Special comments** Frightens children of all ages; 40" minimum height requirement. Switching-off option provided (see page 93). **Authors' rating** It stinks—literally; ★★. **Duration of presentation** About 12 minutes. **Preshow entertainment** About 6 minutes. **Probable waiting time** 5–15 minutes.

DESCRIPTION AND COMMENTS Stitch's Great Escape! stars the havoc-wreaking little alien from the feature film Lilo & Stitch. Here, he's a prisoner of the galactic authorities and is being transferred to a processing facility en route to his final place of incarceration. He manages to escape by employing an efficient though gross trick, knocking out power to the facility in the process. (One wonders why an alien civilization smart enough to master teleportation hasn't yet invented a backup power source.) The rest of the attraction consists of Stitch lumbering around in the dark while cheap sound and odor effects are unleashed upon the audience. Unofficial Guide readers usually rate Stitch's Great Escape! as their least favorite of all Walt Disney World attractions.

TOURING TIPS Stitch is more than enough to scare the pants off many kids ages 6 and younger. Parents, take note: You're held in your seat by overhead restraints that will will prevent you from leaving your seat to comfort your child if the need arises.

Tomorrowland Speedway (FastPass+) ★★

Appeal by Age PRESCHOOL ★★★★   **GRADE SCHOOL** ★★★★   **TEENS** ★★★½
YOUNG ADULTS ★★½   **OVER 30** ★★★   **SENIORS** ★★½

What it is Drive-'em-yourself miniature cars. **Scope and scale** Major attraction. **When to go** Before 10 a.m., during the last 2 hours before closing, or use FastPass+. **Special comments** Kids must be 54" tall to drive unassisted. **Authors' rating** Boring for adults (★★); great for preschoolers. **Duration of ride** About 4¼ minutes. **Average wait in line per 100 people ahead of you** 4½ minutes; assumes 285-car turnover every 20 minutes. **Loading speed** Slow.

Queasy

DESCRIPTION AND COMMENTS An elaborate miniature raceway with gas-powered cars that travel up to 7 mph. The cars poke along on a guide rail, leaving the driver with little to do, but teenagers and many adults still enjoy it.

TOURING TIPS The 9-and-under crowd loves this ride; adults can skip it. If your child is too short to drive, ride along and allow the child to steer the car while you work the foot pedal. The line snakes across a pedestrian bridge to the loading areas. For a shorter wait, turn right off the bridge to the first loading area (rather than continuing to the second).

Tomorrowland Transit Authority PeopleMover ★★★½

Appeal by Age	PRESCHOOL ★★★★	GRADE SCHOOL ★★★★	TEENS ★★★½
YOUNG ADULTS ★★★★		OVER 30 ★★★★	SENIORS ★★★★

What it is Scenic tour of Tomorrowland. **Scope and scale** Minor attraction. **When to go** Anytime, but especially during hot, crowded times of day (11:30 a.m.–4:30 p.m.). **Special comments** A good way to check out the line at Space Mountain and the Speedway. **Authors' rating** Scenic and relaxing; ★★★½. **Duration of ride** 10 minutes. **Average wait in line per 100 people ahead of you** 1½ minutes; assumes 39 trains operating. **Loading speed** Fast.

DESCRIPTION AND COMMENTS The PeopleMover's tramlike cars carry riders on a leisurely tour of Tomorrowland, including a peek inside Space Mountain. In ancient times, the attraction was called the WEDway PeopleMover ("WED" being the initials of one Walter Elias Disney).

TOURING TIPS Lines move quickly and you seldom have to wait.

Walt Disney's Carousel of Progress ★★★

Appeal by Age	PRESCHOOL ★★★½	GRADE SCHOOL ★★★½	TEENS ★★★½
YOUNG ADULTS ★★★★		OVER 30 ★★★★	SENIORS ★★★★

What it is Audio-Animatronic theater production. **Scope and scale** Major attraction. **When to go** Anytime. **Authors' rating** Nostalgic and warm; ★★★. **Duration of presentation** 21 minutes. **Preshow entertainment** Documentary on the attraction's long history. **Probable waiting time** Less than 10 minutes.

DESCRIPTION AND COMMENTS *Walt Disney's Carousel of Progress* offers a nostalgic look at how technology and electricity have changed the lives of an animatronic family over several generations, from about 1900 to 1990. Adults will be amused by the references to laser discs and car phones; kids will be confused.

TOURING TIPS The *Carousel* handles big crowds effectively and is a good choice during busier times of day. Because of its age, Carousel seems to have more minor operational glitches than most attractions, but it is air-conditioned.

LIVE ENTERTAINMENT *in* *the* MAGIC KINGDOM

FOR SPECIFIC EVENTS THE DAY YOU VISIT, check the entertainment schedule in your Disney guide map (free as you enter the Magic Kingdom or at City Hall) or the *Times Guide*, available along with the guide map.

Our one-day touring plans exclude live performances in favor of seeing as much of the park as time permits (parades and shows divert crowds from rides). Nonetheless, the high quality of Magic Kingdom entertainment presents a persuasive argument for a second day of touring. Here's a list of regular performances and events:

BAY LAKE AND SEVEN SEAS LAGOON FLOATING ELECTRICAL PAGEANT ★★★★ Usually performed at nightfall (9 p.m. at the Polynesian Village Resort, 9:15 at the Grand Floridian Resort & Spa, and 10:15 at the Contemporary Resort) on Seven Seas Lagoon and Bay Lake, this is one of our favorites among the Disney extras, but it's necessary to leave the Magic Kingdom to view it. The pageant is a stunning electric-light show aboard small barges and set to nifty electronic music. Leave the Magic Kingdom and take the monorail to the Polynesian Village, Grand Floridian, or Contemporary.

CASTLE FORECOURT STAGE ★★★½ The 20-minute *Dream-Along with Mickey* live show features Mickey, Minnie, Donald, Goofy, and a peck of princesses and other secondary characters, plus human backup dancers, in a show built around the premise that—*quelle horreur!*—Donald doesn't believe in the power of dreams. Crisis is averted through a frenetic whirlwind of song and dance.

CELEBRATE THE MAGIC ★★★★½ In one of the most imaginative shows yet, videos and special effects are set to music and projected nightly onto Cinderella Castle. The effects are tremendous, and Disney regularly updates the show's content to keep it fresh (read: the *Frozen* princesses appear). We rate this as not to be missed.

For the winter holidays, *Celebrate the Magic* gets a *Frozen*-inspired retheming. Titled *A Frozen Holiday Wish,* the castle's projections include Anna, Elsa, Olaf, and other stars from that blockbuster, plus the usual cavalcade of classic Disney characters.

DISNEY-CHARACTER SHOWS AND APPEARANCES A number of characters are usually on hand to greet guests when the park opens. Because they snarl pedestrian traffic and stop most children dead in their tracks, this is sort of a mixed blessing. Most days, a character is on duty for photos and autographs 9 a.m.–10 p.m. next to City Hall. Mickey, Tinker Bell, and miscellaneous fairies can be found in Main Street's Town Square Theater, to the right as you enter the park; Disney princesses are found in Fairytale Hall in Fantasyland. Check the daily *Times Guide* for character-greeting locations and times.

FLAG RETREAT At 5 p.m. daily at Town Square (Walt Disney World Railroad end of Main Street). Sometimes performed with large college marching bands, sometimes with a smaller Disney band.

MAGIC KINGDOM BANDS Banjo, Dixieland, steel-drum, marching, and fife-and-drum bands play daily throughout the park.

MOVE IT! SHAKE IT! DANCE AND PLAY IT! STREET PARTY ★★★½ Starting at the Walt Disney World Railroad end of Main Street, U.S.A., and working toward the Central Plaza, this short walk incorporates about a dozen guests with a handful of floats, Disney characters (including Mickey, Minnie, and Goofy), and entertainers. The parade's soundtrack, updated in late 2014, includes recent pop hits by Disney and non-Disney artists, there's a good amount of interaction between the entertainers and the crowd. Unless you're already on Main Street, however, or too pooped for anything else, we don't recommend making a special trip to view this parade.

TINKER BELL'S FLIGHT This special effect in the sky above Cinderella Castle heralds the beginning of *Wishes* (see below).

TOMORROWLAND FORECOURT STAGE This two-story space behind the Astro Orbiter occasionally hosts DJ-led dance parties. Not worth a special trip, but a nice diversion if you're passing by.

***WISHES* FIREWORKS SHOW *FASTPASS+*/★★★★★** Memorable vignettes and music from beloved Disney films combine with a stellar fireworks display while Jiminy Cricket narrates a lump-in-your-throat story about making wishes come true. (See page 155 for good viewing spots.) A spot we'd previously recommended, in the Tomorrowland Terrace area, was apparently so good that Disney decided to start charging for it. To view *Wishes* from this location now costs $49 per adult and $29 per child. The event includes a dessert buffet and nonalcoholic beverages. Reservations can be made 60 days in advance by calling ☎ 407-WDW-DINE (939-3463).

***WISHES* FIREWORKS CRUISE** For a different view, you can watch the fireworks from Seven Seas Lagoon aboard a chartered pontoon boat. The charter costs $293 for up to 8 people and just under $350 for 10 (tax included). Chips, soda, and water are provided; more-substantial food items may be arranged through reservations. Your Disney captain will take you for a little cruise and then position the boat in a perfect place to watch the fireworks. Because this is a private charter rather than a tour, only your group will be aboard. Life jackets are provided, but wearing them is at your discretion. To reserve a charter, call ☎ 407-WDW-PLAY (939-7529) at exactly 7 a.m. Eastern time about 180 days before the day you want to cruise. We recommend phoning about 185 days out to have a Disney agent specify the exact morning to call for reservations.

PARADES

unofficial **TIP**
Be advised that the Walt Disney World Railroad shuts down during parades, making it impossible to access other lands by train.

PARADES AT THE MAGIC KINGDOM ARE full-fledged spectaculars with dozens of Disney characters and amazing special effects. We rate the afternoon parade as outstanding and the evening parade as not to be missed.

In addition to providing great entertainment, parades lure guests away from the attractions. If getting on rides appeals to you more than watching a parade, you'll find substantially shorter lines just before and during parades. Because the parade route doesn't pass through Adventureland, Tomorrowland, or Fantasyland, attractions in these lands are particularly good bets. Be forewarned: Parades disrupt traffic in the Magic Kingdom. It's nearly impossible, for example, to get to Adventureland from Tomorrowland, or vice versa, during one.

AFTERNOON PARADE

USUALLY STAGED AT 3 P.M., this parade features bands, floats, and marching characters. A new production, **Festival of Fantasy** (★★★★), debuted in 2014, with an original score and new floats paying tribute to *The Little Mermaid, Brave,* and *Frozen,* among other Disney films. The most talked-about float is Maleficent (the villain from *Sleeping Beauty,* and the star of her own feature film) in dragon form—she spits actual fire at a couple of points along the route.

EVENING PARADE(S)

THIS HIGH-TECH AFFAIR employs electroluminescent and fiber-optic technologies, light-spreading thermoplastics (don't try this at home!), and clouds of underlit liquid-nitrogen smoke. For those who flunked chemistry and physics, the parade also offers music, Mickey Mouse, and twinkling lights. Evening-parade performances vary by season, happening as often as twice a night during the busy times of year, to two or three times a week during less busy seasons. We rate it as not to be missed.

The **Main Street Electrical Parade** (**MSEP;** ★★★★) is the current nightly cavalcade at the Magic Kingdom. Its soundtrack—*Baroque Hoedown*—is a synthesizer-heavy testament to what prog rock might have been with access to modern technology and antidepressants. In our opinion, the Electrical Parade is the standard against which everything else is judged. Disney is known to swap out parades and may do so at any time. If you're at Disney World while MSEP is running (call ☎ 407-824-4321 before you go to check), make a special trip to see it.

PARADE ROUTE AND VANTAGE POINTS

MAGIC KINGDOM PARADES CIRCLE TOWN SQUARE, head down Main Street, go around the Central Plaza, and cross the bridge to Liberty Square. In Liberty Square, they follow the waterfront and end in Frontierland. Sometimes they begin in Frontierland and run the route in the opposite direction. Most guests watch from the Central Plaza or from Main Street. One of the best and most popular vantage points is the upper platform of the Walt Disney World Railroad station at the Town Square end of Main Street. Problem is, you have to stake out your position 30–60 minutes before the events begin.

Because most spectators pack Main Street and the Central Plaza, we recommend watching the parade from Liberty Square or Frontierland. Great vantage points frequently overlooked are as follows:

1. Sleepy Hollow snack-and-beverage shop, immediately to your right as you cross the bridge into Liberty Square. You'll have a perfect view of the parade as it crosses Liberty Square Bridge, but only when the parade begins on Main Street.

2. The path on the Liberty Square side of the moat from Sleepy Hollow snack-and-beverage shop to Cinderella Castle. Any point along this path offers a clear and unobstructed view as the parade crosses Liberty Square Bridge. Once again, this spot works only for parades coming from Main Street.

3. The covered walkway between Liberty Tree Tavern and The Diamond Horseshoe Saloon. This elevated vantage point is perfect (particularly on rainy days).

4. Elevated wooden platforms in front of the Frontierland Shootin' Arcade, Frontier Trading Post, and the building with the sign reading FRONTIER MERCANTILE. These spots usually get picked off 10–12 minutes before parade time.

5. Benches on the perimeter of the Central Plaza, between the entrances to Liberty Square and Adventureland. Usually unoccupied until after the parade begins, they offer a comfortable resting place and unobstructed (though somewhat distant) view of the parade as it crosses Liberty Square Bridge.

6. Liberty Square and Frontierland dockside areas.

7. The elevated porch of Tony's Town Square Restaurant on Main Street provides an elevated viewing platform and an easy path to the park exit when the fireworks are over.

Assuming it starts on Main Street (evening parades normally do), the parade takes 16–20 minutes to reach Liberty Square or Frontierland. On evenings when the parade runs twice, the first parade draws a huge crowd, siphoning guests from attractions. Many folks leave the park after the early parade, with many more departing following the fireworks (which are scheduled on the hour between the two parades).

Continue to tour after the fireworks. This is a particularly good time to ride Space Mountain and enjoy attractions in Adventureland. If you're touring Adventureland and the parade begins on Main Street, you won't have to assume your viewing position in Frontierland until 15 minutes after the parade kicks off. If you watch from the Splash Mountain side of the street and head for the attraction as the last float passes, you'll be able to ride with only a couple minutes' wait.

MAGIC KINGDOM TOURING PLANS

STARTING ON PAGE 159, our step-by-step touring plans are field-tested for seeing *as much as possible* in one day with a minimum of time wasted in lines. They're designed to help you avoid crowds and bottlenecks on days of moderate-to-heavy attendance. Understand, however, that there's more to see in the Magic Kingdom than can be experienced in one day. Since we first began covering the Magic Kingdom, four headliner attractions have been added and an entire land created and destroyed.

On days of lighter attendance (see "Selecting the Time of Year for Your Visit," page 13s), our plans will save you time, but they won't be as critical to successful touring as on busier days.

To help with FastPass+, we've listed the approximate return times for which you should try to make reservations. (The plans should work with anything close to the times shown.) Because Disney limits how many FastPass+ reservations you can get, we've listed which attractions are most likely to need FastPass+, too. Check **touringplans.com** for the latest information.

CHOOSING THE APPROPRIATE TOURING PLAN

WE PRESENT FIVE MAGIC KINGDOM TOURING PLANS:

- Magic Kingdom One-Day Touring Plan for Adults
- Authors' Selective Magic Kingdom One-Day Touring Plan for Adults
- Magic Kingdom One-Day Touring Plan for Parents with Small Children
- Magic Kingdom Dumbo-or-Die-in-a-Day Touring Plan for Parents with Small Children
- Magic Kingdom Two-Day Touring Plan

If you have two days (or two mornings) at the Magic Kingdom, the Two-Day Touring Plan is *by far* the most relaxed and efficient. It takes advantage of early morning, when lines are short and the park hasn't filled with guests.

If you only have one day but wish to see as much as possible, use the One-Day Touring Plan for Adults. It's exhausting, but it packs in the maximum. If you prefer a more relaxed visit, use the Authors' Selective One-Day Touring Plan. It includes the best the park has to offer (in the authors' opinion) and weeds out less impressive attractions.

If you have children younger than age 8, adopt the One-Day Touring Plan for Parents with Small Children. It's a compromise, blending the preferences of younger children with those of older siblings and adults. The plan includes many children's rides in Fantasyland but omits roller coaster rides and other attractions that frighten young children or are off-limits because of height requirements.

The Dumbo-or-Die-in-a-Day Touring Plan for Parents with Small Children is designed for parents who will withhold no sacrifice for the children. On the Dumbo-or-Die plan, adults generally stand around, sweat, wipe noses, pay for stuff, and watch the children enjoy themselves. It's great!

"NOT A TOURING PLAN" TOURING PLANS

FOR THE TYPE-B READER, these touring plans avoid detailed step-by-step strategies for saving every last minute in line—they're more guidelines than actual rules. Use these to avoid the longest waits in line while having maximum flexibility to see what interests you.

FOR PARENTS OF SMALL CHILDREN WITH ONE DAY TO TOUR, ARRIVING AT PARK OPENING *Note:* Use FastPass+ wherever you can get it. See Fantasyland first, starting with Seven Dwarfs Mine Train and Peter Pan's Flight. See Frontierland and some of Adventureland, and then take a midday break. Return to the park and complete your tour of Adventureland. Next, meet characters at the Town Square Theater and tour Tomorrowland. End on Main Street for parades and fireworks.

FOR ADULTS WITH ONE DAY TO TOUR, ARRIVING AT PARK OPENING *Note:* Use FastPass+ for attractions in the late morning and midafternoon, especially in Frontierland and Tomorrowland. See Seven Dwarfs Mine Train and Peter Pan's Flight in Fantasyland, and then head to Liberty Square. Tour Frontierland, Adventureland, and Tomorrowland next. End on Main Street for parades and fireworks.

FOR PARENTS AND ADULTS WITH TWO DAYS TO TOUR *Note:* Day One works great for Disney resort guests on Extra Magic

Hours mornings. Use FastPass+ where you can. Start Day One with Seven Dwarfs Mine Train in Fantasyland; then tour Liberty Square and Frontierland before leaving the park around midday. Begin Day Two in Tomorrowland; then tour Adventureland. End on Main Street for parades and fireworks.

FOR PARENTS AND ADULTS WITH AN AFTERNOON AND A FULL DAY *Note:* The full day works great for Disney resort guests on Extra Magic Hours mornings. For the afternoon, tour Frontierland, Adventureland, and Tomorrowland (get FastPass+ reservations for Splash and Space Mountains and Big Thunder Mountain Railroad). On your full day of touring, see Fantasyland, Liberty Square, and Tomorrowland again (for any missed attractions from the previous afternoon). End on Main Street for parades and fireworks.

PRELIMINARY INSTRUCTIONS FOR ALL MAGIC KINGDOM TOURING PLANS

ON DAYS OF MODERATE-TO-HEAVY ATTENDANCE, follow your chosen touring plan exactly, deviating only as follows:

1. When you aren't interested in an attraction it lists. For example, if the plan tells you to ride Space Mountain and you don't like roller coasters, just skip this step and proceed to the next.

2. When you encounter a very long line at an attraction the touring plan calls for. For example, if you arrive at The Haunted Mansion and find extremely long lines, skip it and go to the next step, returning later.

PARK-OPENING PROCEDURES

YOUR SUCCESS DURING your first hour of touring will be affected somewhat by the opening procedure Disney uses that day:

A. Guests are held at the turnstiles until the park opens. Hustle past Main Street and head for the first attraction on your plan.

B. Guests are admitted to Main Street a half-hour to an hour before the remaining lands open. Access to other lands will be blocked by a rope barrier at the Central Plaza end of Main Street. Once admitted, stake out a position at the rope barrier as follows:

If you're going to Frontierland or Adventureland first, stand in front of The Crystal Palace, on the left at the Central Plaza end of Main Street. Wait next to the rope barrier blocking the walkway to Adventureland. When the rope drops, head to Frontierland by way of Adventureland.

If you're going to Tomorrowland first, wait at the entrance of the Tomorrowland bridge. When the rope drops, cross quickly.

If you're going to Fantasyland or Liberty Square first, go to the end of Main Street and line up left of center at the rope.

BEFORE YOU GO

1. Call ☎ 407-824-4321 the day before to confirm opening time.

2. Purchase admission and make FastPass+ reservations before you arrive.

3. Familiarize yourself with park-opening procedures (above).

THE TOURING PLANS

Magic Kingdom One-Day Touring Plan for Adults

FOR Adults without young children.

ASSUMES Willingness to experience all major rides (including roller coasters) and shows.

START TIMES FOR FASTPASS+ Seven Dwarfs Mine Train, 9 a.m.; Big Thunder Mountain Railroad, 10 a.m.; Peter Pan's Flight, 11 a.m.

Our recommendations for day-of FastPass+ reservations: Around noon, make a Haunted Mansion reservation for around 2 p.m. Around 3 p.m., make a Space Mountain reservation for around 7 p.m. After 7 p.m., check for reservations for *Wishes*.

1. Arrive at the Magic Kingdom entrance 50 minutes (Disney resort guests) to 70 minutes (non–Disney resort guests) before opening. Get guide maps and the *Times Guide*.

2. As soon as the park opens, head to Fantasyland and ride The Many Adventures of Winnie the Pooh.

3. Ride Under the Sea: Journey of the Little Mermaid.

4. Ride Seven Dwarfs Mine Train.

5. In Frontierland, ride Splash Mountain.

6. Ride Big Thunder Mountain Railroad.

7. Ride It's a Small World in Fantasyland.

8. Ride Peter Pan's Flight.

9. In Frontierland, see *Country Bear Jamboree*.

10. Eat lunch.

11. In Liberty Square, ride the *Liberty Belle* Riverboat.

12. Experience *The Hall of Presidents*.

13. In Fantasyland, see *Mickey's PhilharMagic*.

14. In Liberty Square, see The Haunted Mansion.

15. See *Monsters, Inc. Laugh Floor* in Tomorrowland.

16. Ride the Tomorrowland Transit Authority PeopleMover.

17. See *Walt Disney's Carousel of Progress.*

18. Ride Buzz Lightyear's Space Ranger Spin.

19. Eat dinner.

20. Ride Space Mountain.

21. In Adventureland, explore the Swiss Family Treehouse.

22. See *Walt Disney's Enchanted Tiki Room.*

23. Play A Pirate's Adventure.

24. Ride Pirates of the Caribbean.

25. Take the Jungle Cruise.

26. See the evening parade on Main Street.

27. See the evening castle light show and fireworks on Main Street. A good viewing spot is somewhere between The Plaza Restaurant and Tomorrowland Terrace.

Authors' Selective Magic Kingdom One-Day Touring Plan for Adults

FOR Adults touring without young children.

ASSUMES Willingness to experience all major rides (including roller coasters) and shows.

START TIMES FOR FASTPASS+ Seven Dwarfs Mine Train, 9 a.m.; Big Thunder Mountain, 10 a.m.; Peter Pan's Flight, 11 a.m.

Our recommendations for day-of FastPass+ reservations: Around noon, make a Haunted Mansion reservation for around 2 p.m. Around 3 p.m., make a Space Mountain reservation for around 7 p.m. After 7 p.m., check for reservations for *Wishes.*

1. Arrive at the Magic Kingdom entrance 50 minutes (Disney resort guests) to 70 minutes (non–Disney resort guests) before opening. Get guide maps and the *Times Guide.*

2. As soon as the park opens, head to Fantasyland and ride The Many Adventures of Winnie the Pooh.

3. Ride Under the Sea: Journey of the Little Mermaid.

4. Ride Seven Dwarfs Mine Train.

5. In Frontierland, ride Splash Mountain.

6. ide Big Thunder Mountain Railroad.

7. Ride It's a Small World in Fantasyland.

8. Ride Peter Pan's Flight.

9. In Frontierland, see *Country Bear Jamboree.*

10. Eat lunch.

11. In Liberty Square, ride the *Liberty Belle* Riverboat.

12. Experience *The Hall of Presidents.*

13. In Liberty Square, see The Haunted Mansion.

14. In Fantasyland, see *Mickey's PhilharMagic*.

15. See *Monsters, Inc. Laugh Floor* in Tomorrowland.

16. Ride the Tomorrowland Transit Authority PeopleMover.

17. Ride Buzz Lightyear's Space Ranger Spin.

18. Eat dinner.

19. Ride Space Mountain.

20. In Adventureland, explore the Swiss Family Treehouse.

21. Take the Jungle Cruise.

22. See *Walt Disney's Enchanted Tiki Room*.

23. Ride Pirates of the Caribbean.

24. Play A Pirate's Adventure.

25. See the evening parade on Main Street.

26. See the evening castle light show and fireworks on Main Street. A good viewing spot is somewhere between The Plaza Restaurant and Tomorrowland Terrace.

Magic Kingdom One-Day Touring Plan for Parents with Small Children

FOR Parents with children younger than age 8.

ASSUMES Periodic stops for rest, restrooms, and refreshments.

START TIMES FOR FASTPASS+ Seven Dwarfs Mine Train, 9 a.m.; Peter Pan's Flight, 10 a.m.; *Enchanted Tales with Belle*, 11 a.m.

Our recommendations for day-of FastPass+ reservations: Around lunchtime, make a Buzz Lightyear's Space Ranger Spin reservation for around 3:30 p.m. Make a Pirates of the Caribbean reservation for around 8 p.m. After you've used your last FastPass, check for reservations for *Wishes*.

1. Arrive at the Magic Kingdom entrance 50 minutes (Disney resort guests) to 70 minutes (non-Disney resort guests) before opening. Rent strollers before the park opens. Get guide maps and the *Times Guide*.

2. As soon as the park opens, head to Fantasyland and ride The Many Adventures of Winnie the Pooh.

3. Ride Under the Sea: Journey of the Little Mermaid.

4. Ride Seven Dwarfs Mine Train.

5. Ride The Barnstormer.

6. Ride Dumbo the Flying Elephant.

7. See *Mickey's PhilharMagic*.

8. Ride Peter Pan's Flight.

9. Ride It's a Small World.

10. See *Enchanted Tales with Belle*.

11. Eat lunch.

12. Meet Mickey Mouse at Town Square Theater on MainStreet.

13. Take a midday break.

14. Ride Buzz Lightyear's Space Ranger Spin in Tomorrowland.

15. See *Monsters, Inc. Laugh Floor*.

16. Explore the Swiss Family Treehouse in Adventureland.

17. In Frontierland, take the raft over to Tom Sawyer Island. Allow at least 30 minutes to explore.

18. See *Country Bear Jamboree*.

19. Eat dinner.

20. In Liberty Square, see The Haunted Mansion.

21. In Adventureland, take the Jungle Cruise.

22. Ride Pirates of the Caribbean.

23. Play A Pirate's Adventure.

24. See the evening parade on Main Street.

25. See the evening castle light show and fireworks on Main Street. A good viewing spot is somewhere between The Plaza Restaurant and Tomorrowland Terrace.

TO CONVERT THIS ONE-DAY TOURING PLAN TO A TWO-DAY TOURING PLAN For Day 1, make FastPass+ reservations well in advance for Peter Pan's Flight around 11 a.m., The Many Adventures of Winnie the Pooh around 6:15 p.m., and *Enchanted Tales with Belle* around 7:15 pm. When the park opens, ride Seven Dwarfs Mine Train immediately, followed by Under the Sea. See the Storybook Circus attractions next, then Splash Mountain and The Haunted Mansion, before riding Peter Pan and leaving the park for lunch. Return to the park and work in the Frontierland and Liberty Square attractions around your FastPass+ reservations.

For Day 2, ride Buzz Lightyear, Astro Orbiter, and the Tomorrowland Speedway as soon as the park opens, then visit the Adventureland attractions, starting with the Magic Carpets of Aladdin. End your day with the PeopleMover and *Monsters, Inc.*, show in Tomorrowland, followed by the evening parade and fireworks.

Magic Kingdom Dumbo-or-Die-in-a-Day Touring Plan for Parents with Small Children

FOR Parents with a martyr complex, or rich folks who are paying someone else to squire their kids around. The plan is designed for days when the park doesn't close until 9 p.m. or later.

ASSUMES Frequent stops for rest, restrooms, and refreshments.

START TIMES FOR FASTPASS+ Seven Dwarfs Mine Train, 9 a.m.; Peter Pan's Flight, 10 a.m.; *Enchanted Tales with Belle,* 11 a.m.

Our recommendations for day-of FastPass+ reservations: Make a Pirates of the Caribbean FastPass+ reservation for around 3:30 p.m. Make a Haunted Mansion reservation for around 6 p.m. After you've used your last FastPass, check for FastPass+ reservations for *Wishes.*

1. Arrive at the Magic Kingdom entrance 50 minutes (Disney resort guests) to 70 minutes (non-Disney resort guests) before opening. Rent strollers before the park opens. Get guide maps and the *Times Guide.*

2. As soon as the park opens, head to Fantasyland and ride Seven Dwarfs Mine Train.

3. Ride Under the Sea: Journey of the Little Mermaid.

4. Ride Dumbo the Flying Elephant. Ride again. (*Tip:* Stand in line about 48 people behind the other parent and child. When the first parent is done riding, hand the child to the second parent in line.)

5. Ride The Barnstormer.

6. In Tomorrowland, ride the Astro Orbiter.

7. Take the Jungle Cruise in Adventureland.

8. Return to Fantasyland to ride Peter Pan's Flight.

9. In Liberty Square, see The Haunted Mansion.

10. See *Enchanted Tales with Belle.*

11. Eat lunch and take a midday break of at least 3 hours outside the park.

12. In Frontierland, take the raft over to Tom Sawyer Island. Allow at least 30 minutes to explore.

13. In Adventureland, ride Pirates of the Caribbean.

14. Ride The Magic Carpets of Aladdin.

15. See *Walt Disney's Enchanted Tiki Room.*

16. In Frontierland, see Country Bear Jamboree.

17. In Fantasyland, see *Mickey's PhilharMagic.*

18. Eat dinner.

19. Ride Buzz Lightyear's Space Ranger Spin in Tomorrowland.

20. Take a spin on the Tomorrowland Speedway.

21. Back in Fantasyland, ride The Many Adventures of Winnie the Pooh.

22. Ride the Prince Charming Regal Carrousel.

23. Ride It's a Small World.

24. Meet Mickey Mouse at Town Square Theater on Main Street.

25. See the evening parade on Main Street.

26. See the evening castle light show and fireworks on Main Street. A good viewing spot is somewhere between The Plaza Restaurant and Tomorrowland Terrace.

TO CONVERT THIS ONE-DAY TOURING PLAN TO A TWO-DAY TOURING PLAN The idea is to split the park in half over an afternoon and a full day, so that Tomorrowland, Storybook Circus, and a few of the other Fantasyland attractions are on the second day:

For the day of your afternoon visit, make FastPass+ reservations well in advance for Splash Mountain around 4 p.m., Pirates of the Caribbean around 5 p.m., and Jungle Cruise around 6:30 p.m. Work in the other rides, shows, and dinner around these, and end the day with the evening parade.

For your full-day visit, make FastPass+ reservations well in advance for Peter Pan's Flight around 10:30 a.m., *Enchanted Tales with Belle* around 6:30 p.m., and Buzz Lightyear around 8 p.m. Ride Seven Dwarfs Mine Train as soon as the park opens, then Winnie the Pooh on the way to Astro Orbiter and Tomorrowland Speedway. Visit Storybook Circus as you loop back to Under the Sea, then continue clockwise through Fantasyland before leaving the park for a midday break. Return to the park for dinner before your *Enchanted Tales* reservation, then see *Mickey's PhilharMagic*, the *Monsters, Inc.,* show in Tomorrowland, and Buzz Lightyear. See the parade and fireworks if you've not already done so, and try to get same-day FastPass+ reservations after you've used your first three or four.

Magic Kingdom Two-Day Touring Plan

FOR Anyone wishing to spread his or her Magic Kingdom visit over two days.

ASSUMES Willingness to experience all major rides (including roller coasters) and shows.

START TIMES FOR FASTPASS+ *Day One:* Big Thunder Mountain Railroad: 10:30 a.m.; Peter Pan's Flight, noon; The Haunted Mansion, 1 p.m. Check for FastPass+ reservations for *Wishes* fireworks after you've used your first three FastPasses or after 4 p.m. (whichever is later). Note that Day Two does not require FastPass+.

Day One

1. Arrive at the Magic Kingdom entrance 50 minutes (Disney resort guests) to 70 minutes (non–Disney resort guests) before opening. Get guide maps and the *Times Guide.*

2. As soon as the park opens, ride Seven Dwarfs Mine Train.

3. Ride The Many Adventures of Winnie the Pooh.

4. Ride Under the Sea: Journey of the Little Mermaid.

5. Meet Goofy and Donald at Pete's Silly Sideshow.

6. Take the WDW Railroad from Fantasyland to Frontierland.

7. In Frontierland, ride Splash Mountain.

8. Ride Big Thunder Mountain Railroad.

9. Eat lunch.

10. Ride Peter Pan's Flight in Fantasyland.

11. See *Mickey's PhilharMagic*.

12. Ride It's a Small World.

13. In Liberty Square, see The Haunted Mansion.

14. Ride the *Liberty Belle Riverboat*.

15. Experience *The Hall of Presidents*.

16. In Frontierland, see *Country Bear Jamboree*.

17. Take the raft over to Tom Sawyer Island. Allow at least 30 minutes to explore.

18. In Adventureland, play A Pirate's Adventure.

19. Ride Pirates of the Caribbean.

20. See the evening parade on Main Street.

21. See the evening castle light show and fireworks on Main Street. A good viewing spot is somewhere between The Plaza Restaurant and Tomorrowland Terrace.

Day Two

1. Arrive at the Magic Kingdom entrance 50 minutes (Disney resort guests) to 70 minutes (non–Disney resort guests) before opening. Get guide maps and the *Times Guide*.

2. In Tomorrowland, ride Space Mountain.

3. Ride Buzz Lightyear's Space Ranger Spin.

4. In Adventureland, explore the Swiss Family Treehouse.

5. Take the Jungle Cruise.

6. See *Walt Disney's Enchanted Tiki Room*.

7. Return to Tomorrowland to see *Monsters, Inc. Laugh Floor*.

8. Ride the Tomorrowland Transit Authority PeopleMover.

9. See *Walt Disney's Carousel of Progress*.

10. Eat lunch.

11. Tour and meet characters on Main Street (check the *Times Guide* for locations and times), or shop, see live entertainment, and revisit favorite attractions.

PART TEN

EPCOT

EDUCATION, INSPIRATION, AND CORPORATE IMAGERY are the focus at Epcot, the most adult of the Disney theme parks. Some people find the attempts at education to be superficial, while others want more entertainment and less education. Most visitors, however, find plenty of both.

Epcot is more than twice as big as either the Magic Kingdom or Disney's Hollywood Studios and, though smaller than Disney's Animal Kingdom, has more territory to be covered on foot. Epcot rarely sees the congestion so common to the Magic Kingdom, but it has lines every bit as long as those at the Jungle Cruise or Space Mountain. Visitors must come prepared to do considerable walking among attractions and a comparable amount of standing in line.

Epcot's size means you can't see it all in one day without skipping an attraction or two and giving others a cursory glance. A major difference between Epcot and the other parks, however, is that some Epcot attractions can be savored slowly or skimmed, depending on personal interests. For example, the first section of General Motors' Test Track is a thrill ride, the second a collection of walk-through exhibits.

The EPCOT ACRONYM

WHEN IT OPENED IN 1982, Epcot was EPCOT Center. Before that, Walt Disney envisioned a utopian working city of the future that he called EPCOT, an acronym for *Experimental Prototype Community of Tomorrow.* Corporate Disney ultimately altered Walt's vision, and the city became a theme park, with only the name remaining. Because EPCOT Center had virtually nothing in common with the original concept, *EPCOT* eventually became *Epcot.*

OPERATING HOURS

EPCOT HAS TWO THEMED AREAS: **Future World** and **World Showcase.** Each has its own operating hours. Future World always opens before World Showcase in the morning and usually closes before World Showcase in the evening. Most of the year, World Showcase opens 2 hours later than Future World. For exact hours during your visit, call ☎ 407-824-4321 or visit **disneyworld.com.**

ARRIVING

PLAN TO ARRIVE AT THE TURNSTILES 30–40 minutes prior to official opening time. Give yourself an extra 10 minutes or so to park and make your way to the entrance.

If you're staying at an Epcot resort, it will take you about 20–30 minutes to walk from your hotel to Future World via the International Gateway (the back entrance of Epcot). Instead of walking, you can catch a boat from your resort to the International Gateway and walk about 8 minutes to the Future World section. To reach the front (Future World) entrance of Epcot from the resorts, take a boat from your hotel to Disney's Hollywood Studios and transfer to an Epcot bus, take a bus to Disney Springs and transfer to an Epcot bus, or best of all, take a cab.

unofficial **TIP**
Epcot has its own parking lot and, unlike at the Magic Kingdom, there's no need to take a monorail or ferry to reach the entrance.

Arriving by car is easy—walk or take a tram from the parking lot to the front gate. Monorail service connects Epcot with the Transportation and Ticket Center, the Magic Kingdom (transfer required), and the Magic Kingdom resorts (transfer required).

Getting through entrance security at Epcot takes longer than at the other parks. A second, often overlooked, security checkpoint is on the other (east) side of the main checkpoint.

GETTING ORIENTED

EPCOT'S THEMED AREAS ARE DISTINCTLY DIFFERENT. **Future World** combines Disney creativity and major corporations' technological resources to examine where mankind has come from and

Epcot

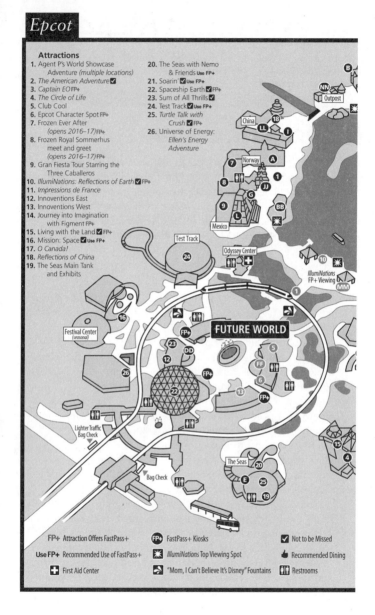

Attractions

1. Agent P's World Showcase Adventure *(multiple locations)*
2. *The American Adventure* ☑
3. *Captain EO* FP+
4. *The Circle of Life*
5. Club Cool
6. Epcot Character Spot FP+
7. Frozen Ever After *(opens 2016–17)* FP+
8. Frozen Royal Sommerhus meet and greet *(opens 2016–17)* FP+
9. Gran Fiesta Tour Starring the Three Caballeros
10. *IllumiNations: Reflections of Earth* ☑ FP+
11. *Impressions de France*
12. Innoventions East
13. Innoventions West
14. Journey into Imagination with Figment FP+
15. Living with the Land ☑ FP+
16. Mission: Space ☑ Use FP+
17. *O Canada!*
18. *Reflections of China*
19. The Seas Main Tank and Exhibits
20. The Seas with Nemo & Friends Use FP+
21. Soarin' ☑ Use FP+
22. Spaceship Earth ☑ FP+
23. Sum of All Thrills ☑
24. Test Track ☑ Use FP+
25. Turtle Talk with Crush ☑ FP+
26. Universe of Energy: *Ellen's Energy Adventure*

FP+ Attraction Offers FastPass+   (FP+) FastPass+ Kiosks   ☑ Not to be Missed

Use FP+ Recommended Use of FastPass+   ✳ *IllumiNations* Top Viewing Spot   🍖 Recommended Dining

➕ First Aid Center   ➥ "Mom, I Can't Believe It's Disney" Fountains   🚻 Restrooms

WORLD SHOWCASE LAGOON

Germany · Italy · America Gardens Theatre · Japan · Morocco · France · International Gateway Entrance · United Kingdom · Walkway to Epcot Resorts & Disney's Hollywood Studios · Canada · World ShowPlace Events Pavilion · Imagination! · The Land

Table-Service Restaurants

A. Akershus Royal Banquet Hall
B. Biergarten Restaurant
C. Le Cellier Steakhouse
D. Chefs de France
E. Coral Reef Restaurant
F. Garden Grill Restaurant
G. La Hacienda de San Angel
H. Monsieur Paul
I. Nine Dragons Restaurant
J. Restaurant Marrakesh
K. Rose & Crown Pub & Dining Room
L. San Angel Inn Restaurante
M. Spice Road Table
N. Teppan Edo
O. Tokyo Dining
P. Tutto Italia Ristorante
Q. Via Napoli Ristorante e Pizzeria

Counter-Service Restaurants

AA. L'Artisan des Glaces
BB. La Cantina de San Angel
CC. Crêpes des Chefs de France
DD. Electric Umbrella
EE. Fife & Drum Tavern
FF. Fountain View
GG. Les Halles Boulangerie–Pâtisserie
HH. Kabuki Cafe
II. Katsura Grill
JJ. Kringla Bakeri og Kafe
KK. Liberty Inn
LL. Lotus Blossom Cafe
MM. Promenade Refreshments
NN. Refreshment Cool Post
OO. Refreshment Port
PP. Sommerfest
QQ. Sunshine Seasons
RR. Tangierine Cafe
SS. Yorkshire County Fish Shop

where it's going. **World Showcase** features landmarks, cuisine, and culture of almost a dozen nations.

At Epcot, the architectural symbol is **Spaceship Earth.** This 180-foot geosphere is visible from almost everywhere in the park. Like Cinderella Castle at the Magic Kingdom, Spaceship Earth can help you keep track of where you are in Epcot. But it's in a high-traffic area and isn't centrally located, so it isn't a good meeting place.

Any of the distinctive national pavilions in World Showcase makes a good meeting place, but be specific. "Hey, let's meet in Japan!" sounds fun, but each pavilion is a mini-town with buildings, monuments, gardens, and plazas. Pick a specific place in Japan—the sidewalk side of the pagoda, for example.

FASTPASS+ IN EPCOT

EPCOT OFFERS FASTPASS+ for 11 attractions in two tiers:

TIER A *(Choose one per day)*	TIER B *(Choose two per day)*
• *IllumiNations*	• *Captain EO*
• Living with the Land	• Epcot Character Spot
• Soarin'	• Journey into Imagination
• Test Track	• Mission: Space (Green or Orange)
	• Spaceship Earth
	• The Seas with Nemo & Friends
	• *Turtle Talk with Crush*

(*Note:* **Frozen Ever After** and the **Royal Sommerhus Meet and Greet** will most likely be FastPass+ attractions as well, but at press time we didn't know which tier they'd be assigned to.)

Because the tiers limit the number and combinations of Fast-Pass+ attractions you can experience, much of our Epcot touring strategy is dictated by the popular **Soarin'** and **Test Track** in Tier A—long lines at these two mean that you'll want to get one of them out of the way first thing in the morning. (**Living with the Land,** also in Tier A, is rarely a good use of FastPass+ as it doesn't get the same crowds as the other two.)

Our most frequent FastPass+ recommendation is for **Spaceship Earth** in Future World, usually around lunch. Because wait times can reach 30–40 minutes, it's one of the best choices in Tier B.

On the other hand, we've identified four attractions for which FastPass+ is *never* necessary: *Captain EO,* **Journey into Imagination with Figment,** the nonspinning **Mission: Space (Green),** and **Epcot Character Spot.** In addition to these four, *IllumiNations* (or its successor) is a must-see, and FastPass+ gets you into a special viewing area for the show, but you still have to arrive a good 30–40 minutes in advance to get a good spot. What's more, there are so many

EPCOT
When Same-Day FP+ Runs Out, by Crowd Level

ATTRACTION	LOW CROWDS*	MODERATE CROWDS*	HIGH CROWDS*
Captain EO (if open)	6 p.m.		Until 6-7 p.m.
Epcot Character Spot	4-5 p.m. (all crowd levels)		
IllumiNations (or replacement)	1-2 p.m.	Noon-1 p.m.	11 a.m.-noon
Journey into Imagination	6 p.m.	5-6 p.m.	4-5 p.m.
Living with the Land	6 p.m. (all crowd levels)		
Mission: Space (Orange)	1-3 p.m.	11 a.m.-noon	10 a.m.-noon
The Seas with Nemo & Friends	6-7 p.m.		3-5 p.m.
Soarin'	1-3 p.m.	Noon-1 p.m.	11 a.m.
Spaceship Earth	6-7 p.m.	4-5 p.m.	Noon-1 p.m.
Test Track	1-3 p.m.	Noon-1 p.m.	10 a.m.-noon
Turtle Talk with Crush	6-7 p.m. (all crowd levels)		
* LOW CROWDS (Levels 1-3 on TouringPlans.com Crowd Calendar)			
* MODERATE CROWDS (Levels 4-7 on TouringPlans.com Crowd Calendar)			
* HIGH CROWDS (Levels 8-10 on TouringPlans.com Crowd Calendar)			

other good viewing spots around World Showcase Lagoon that it's difficult to recommend FastPass+ for *IllumiNations*.

Look for Epcot FastPass+ kiosks in the following locations (also see the map on pages 168 and 169):

- At the Soarin' entrance, downstairs in The Land
- At the MyMagic+ Service Center, between Spaceship Earth and Innoventions East
- At the International Gateway entrance to the park
- In the Future World East walkway, on the way to Mission: Space
- In the Future World West walkway, on the way to The Land

Same-Day FastPass+ Availability

The preceding advice tells you which attractions to focus on when making your *advance* FastPass+ reservations before you get to the park. Once you're in the park, you can make more FastPass+ reservations once your advance reservations have been used or have expired (you must cancel your expired FastPass+ before you can book another). The table above shows which attractions are likely to have day-of FastPasses available, and the approximate times at which they'll run out.

FUTURE WORLD

GLEAMING, FUTURISTIC STRUCTURES OF immense proportions define the first themed area you encounter at Epcot. Broad thoroughfares are punctuated with billowing fountains—all reflected in shining, space-age facades. Everything, including landscaping, is sparkling-clean and seems bigger than life. Pavilions dedicated to mankind's past, present, and future technological accomplishments form the perimeter of Future World. Front and center is **Spaceship Earth,** flanked by **Innoventions East and West.**

Future World Services

Epcot's service facilities in Future World include the following:

BABY CARE CENTER On the World Showcase side of the Odyssey Center

BANKING SERVICES ATMs outside the main entrance, on the Future World bridge, and in Germany, World Showcase

CELL PHONE CHARGING Outlets available in The Seas, upstairs near the women's restroom; in The Land, upstairs near the Garden Grill; and in Mexico, near the bench against the ramp that leads to the market

DINING RESERVATIONS At Guest Relations, to the left of Spaceship Earth

FIRST AID Next to the Baby Care Center on the World Showcase side of the Odyssey Center

LIVE-ENTERTAINMENT INFORMATION At Guest Relations

LOST AND FOUND At the main entrance at the gift shop

LOST PERSONS At Guest Relations and the Baby Care Center on the World Showcase side of the Odyssey Center

WHEELCHAIR, ECV, ESV, AND STROLLER RENTALS Inside the main entrance and to the left, toward the rear of the Entrance Plaza

Most services are concentrated in Future World's Entrance Plaza, near the main gate.

GUEST RELATIONS

GUEST RELATIONS, left of the geosphere, is Epcot's equivalent of the Magic Kingdom's City Hall, serving as park headquarters and the primary information center. If you wish to eat in one of Epcot's sit-down restaurants and you haven't made a reservation by phone (☎ 407-WDW-DINE) or online, you can make a reservation at Guest Relations or at any other sit-down restaurant in any of the parks. If you're near one of these locations, in-person is often faster than calling.

Spaceship Earth *(FastPass+)* ★★★★

**Appeal by Age   PRESCHOOL ★★★★   GRADE SCHOOL ★★★★   TEENS ★★★★
YOUNG ADULTS ★★★★   OVER 30 ★★★★   SENIORS ★★★★½**

What it is Educational dark ride through past, present, and future. **Scope and scale** Headliner. **When to go** Before 10 a.m., after 4 p.m., or use FastPass+. **Special comments** If lines are long when you arrive, try again after 4 p.m. **Authors' rating** One of Epcot's best; not to be missed; ★★★★. **Duration of ride** About 16 minutes. **Average wait in line per 100 people ahead of you** 3 minutes. **Loading speed** Fast.

DESCRIPTION AND COMMENTS This ride spirals through the 18-story interior of Epcot's premier landmark, taking visitors past Audio-Animatronic scenes depicting mankind's developments in communications, from cave painting to printing to television to space communications and computer networks. The ride shows an amazing use of the geodesic sphere's interior. Scenes are periodically redone to keep things fresh. Interactive video screens on the ride vehicles allow you to customize the ride's ending animated video.

TOURING TIPS Because it's near Epcot's main entrance, Spaceship Earth attracts arriving guests throughout the morning. If you want to ride Soarin' and Test Track, try to get a FastPass+ reservation for around 1 p.m. You should be almost done with Future World's attractions by then and ready to head to World Showcase. Or, if you plan on spending the afternoon in Future World and don't want to use FastPass+, try Spaceship Earth after 3 p.m.

Innoventions East and West ★★½

**Appeal by Age   PRESCHOOL ★★★½   GRADE SCHOOL ★★★★   TEENS ★★★½
YOUNG ADULTS ★★★   OVER 30 ★★★½   SENIORS ★★★½**

What it is Static and hands-on exhibits relating to products and technologies of the near future. **Scope and scale** Minor diversion. **When to go** On your second day at Epcot or after you've seen all the major attractions. **Special comments** Most exhibits demand time and participation to be rewarding. **Authors' rating** We're hoping for a spectacular refurbishment; ★★½.

Note: At press time, all of Innoventions West and a good chunk of Innoventions East were closed for refurbishment, with no reopening date announced.

DESCRIPTION AND COMMENTS Dynamic, interactive, and forward-looking, Innoventions resembles a high-tech trade show. Electronics and entertainment technology exhibits play a prominent role, as do ecology and "how things work" displays.

The problem that Disney faces with Innoventions is the same one it faces with Tomorrowland in the Magic Kingdom: The future arrives faster and different than expected. In the case of Innoventions, this means that exhibits based on cutting-edge technology will have approximately the same shelf life as a sesame bagel. As a result, large chunks of Innoventions are either closed or somewhat outdated.

Some exhibits are definitely worth stopping for, however. Our favorite is Raytheon's **Sum of All Thrills,** a roller-coaster simulator in which you design the coaster track on a tabletop computer, then climb aboard a giant robotic arm to experience your creation. We also like **Habit Heroes,** which requires you to do calisthenics to save the planet from sloth and gluttony (not kidding).

TOURING TIPS Spend time at Innoventions on your second day at Epcot. If you have only one day, visit late if you have the time and endurance. (The one exception to this is Sum of All Thrills, which you should visit in the morning after Soarin', Test Track, and Mission: Space.)

TOURING TIPS Spend time at Innoventions on your second day at Epcot. If you have only one day, visit late if you have the time and endurance. (The exception is Sum of All Thrills, which you should visit in the morning after Soarin', Test Track, and Mission: Space.) Skip exhibits with waits of more than 10 minutes, or experience them first thing in the morning on your second day, when there are no lines.

CLUB COOL

DESCRIPTION AND COMMENTS Attached to the fountain side of Innoventions West is this combination retail space and soda fountain. It doesn't look like much, but inside, this Coca-Cola–sponsored exhibit provides free unlimited samples of soft drinks from around the world (some of them kind of strange). Because it's centrally located in Future World, it's a good meeting or break place.

SUM OF ALL THRILLS ★★★★

Appeal by Age	PRESCHOOL ★★★½	GRADE SCHOOL ★★★★½	TEENS ★★★★½
YOUNG ADULTS ★★★★½		OVER 30 ★★★★½	SENIORS ★★★★

What it is Hands-on exhibit and ride simulator. **Scope and scale** Minor attraction. **When to go** Before 10:30 a.m. or after 5 p.m. **Special comments** 48" minimum height requirement, 54" for track designs with inversions. **Authors' rating** Not to be missed; ★★★★. **Duration of attraction** 15 minutes. **Average wait in line per 100 people ahead of you** 40 minutes; assumes all simulators operating. **Loading speed** Slow.

DESCRIPTION AND COMMENTS Sum of All Thrills is a design-your-own-roller-coaster simulator in which you use a computer program to specify the drops, curves, and loops of a coaster track before boarding a robotic arm to experience your creation. Three vehicle options are available: bobsled, roller coaster, and jet aircraft. You can program actual loops into both the coaster and jet courses, and the robot arm will swing you upside down. In addition to the vehicle, you also select the kinds of turns, loops, and hills in your track design. Using computer-design tools, you can further customize these components by changing the height and width of each piece as you go.

TOURING TIPS Not a high-capacity attraction, but also not on most guests' radar. Ride as early in the morning as possible.

Epcot Character Spot *(FastPass+)*   ★★★

Appeal by Age	PRESCHOOL ★★★★½	GRADE SCHOOL ★★★★½	TEENS ★★★★
YOUNG ADULTS ★★★★		OVER 30 ★★★★	SENIORS ★★★

What it is Character-greeting venue. **Scope and scale** Diversion. **When to go** Before 11 a.m., or use FastPass+. **Authors' rating** Indoors and air-conditioned; ★★★. **Duration of experience** 8 minutes. **Probable waiting time** 20–40 minutes. **Queue speed** Slow.

DESCRIPTION AND COMMENTS In Future World West, to the right of The Fountain restaurant, Epcot Character Spot offers the chance to meet Disney characters indoors, in air-conditioned comfort. Characters on hand typically include Mickey Mouse, Minnie Mouse, and Pluto. You may also find Chip 'n' Dale nearby outside.

TOURING TIPS The Character Spot should be your first stop if you have small children. Make FastPass+ reservations for Soarin' for around 9:30 a.m. so you can proceed there directly after getting autographs. The venue typically stays open until 9 p.m., even when other Future World attractions close at 7 p.m., and usually until around 10:45 p.m. during evening Extra Magic Hours, when Epcot is open until 11 p.m. or later.

Universe of Energy: *Ellen's Energy Adventure* ★★★★

Appeal by Age	PRESCHOOL ★★★	GRADE SCHOOL ★★★½	TEENS ★★★
YOUNG ADULTS ★★★½		OVER 30 ★★★	SENIORS ★★★★

What it is Combination ride and theater presentation about energy. **Scope and scale** Major attraction. **When to go** Before 11:15 a.m. or after 4:30 p.m. **Special comments** Don't be dismayed by long lines; 580 people enter the pavilion each time the theater changes audiences. **Authors' rating** The most unique theater in Walt Disney World; ★★★★. **Duration of presentation** About 26½ minutes. **Preshow entertainment** 8 minutes. **Probable waiting time** 20-40 minutes.

DESCRIPTION AND COMMENTS This attraction begins with a preshow film starring Ellen DeGeneres. While watching TV, Ellen dozes off and dreams that she's competing on *Jeopardy!* against her know-it-all former college roommate Judy (Jamie Lee Curtis). All of the categories deal with energy, and unfortunately for Ellen, Judy has a PhD in the subject. Luckily, Ellen's next-door neighbor happens to be Bill Nye the Science Guy, who convinces Ellen—along with everyone else in the audience—to take a time-traveling crash course in the history of energy.

You move from the preshow hall to what appears to be an ordinary theater to watch another film, this one about energy sources. Then the seats divide into six 97-passenger traveling cars that carry you from the Big Bang to the swamps and animatronic dinosaurs of a prehistoric forest.

The dialogue between DeGeneres and Nye is humorous and upbeat, but the script was written almost 20 years ago. Don't expect to hear calls to action on climate change or carbon footprints, or much more than a passing reference to alternative energy sources.

The dinosaurs frighten some preschoolers, and kids of all ages lose the thread during the educational segments.

TOURING TIPS Because the theater has a ride component, the line doesn't move while the show is in progress. When the theater empties, however, a large chunk of the line disappears as people are admitted for the next show. Because of this, waits are generally tolerable.

Mission: Space *(FastPass+)* ★★★★

Appeal by Age	PRESCHOOL ★★★½	GRADE SCHOOL ★★★★½	TEENS ★★★★
YOUNG ADULTS ★★★★		OVER 30 ★★★★	SENIORS ★★★½

What it is Space-flight-simulator ride. **Scope and scale** Super-headliner. **When to go** First or last hour the park is open, or use FastPass+. **Special comments** Not recommended for pregnant women or people prone to motion sickness or claustrophobia; 44" minimum height requirement; a gentler nonspinning version is also available. **Authors' rating** Not to be missed; ★★★★. **Duration of ride** About 5 minutes plus preshow. **Average wait in line per 100 people ahead of you** 4 minutes. **Loading speed** Moderate-fast.

DESCRIPTION AND COMMENTS Mission: Space was one of the most popular rides at Disney World until two guests died after riding it in 2005 and 2006. While neither death was linked directly to the attraction, the negative publicity caused many guests to skip it entirely. In response, Disney added a tamer nonspinning version of Mission: Space in 2006. Even before you walk into the building, you're asked whether you want your ride with or without spin. Choose the spinning version and you're on the Orange team; the Green team trains on the no-spin side.

Guests for both versions of the attraction enter the NASA Mission: Space Training Center, where they are introduced to the deep-space exploration program and then divided into groups for flight training. After orientation, they are strapped into space capsules for a simulated flight, where, of course, the unexpected happens. Each capsule accommodates a crew consisting of a group commander, pilot, navigator, and engineer, with a guest functioning in each role. The crew's skill and finesse (or, more often, lack thereof) in handling their respective responsibilities have no effect on the outcome of the flight. The capsules are small, and both ride versions are amazingly realistic. The nonspinning version does not subject your body to g-forces, but it does bounce and toss you around in a manner roughly comparable to other Disney motion simulators.

TOURING TIPS In minutes, Disney can reconfigure the ride's four centrifuges to either version of the attraction based on guest demand. In general, the kinder, gentler version has a wait time of about half that of its more harrowing counterpart.

Having experienced the industrial-strength version of Mission: Space under a variety of circumstances, we've always felt icky when riding it on an empty stomach, especially first thing in the morning. We came up with a number of potential explanations for this phenomenon, involving everything from low blood sugar and inner-ear disorders to some of us just not being astronaut material. Understandably disturbed by the latter possibility, we looked around for an expert opinion to explain what we were feeling. The number of organizations with experience studying the effects of high-g (high-gravity) forces on humans is limited to a select few: NASA, the Air Force, and Mad Tea Party cast members were the first to come to mind. As NASA is a codeveloper of Mission: Space, we called them. Amazingly, a spokesman told us that NASA no longer does much high-g training these days. And the agency was reluctant to pass along anything resembling medical advice to the general public.

Hit the john before you get in line—you'll think your bladder really has been to Mars and back before you get out of this attraction. We recommend securing a midmorning FastPass+ reservation for Mission: Space (Orange).

TEST TRACK PAVILION

DESCRIPTION AND COMMENTS Sponsored by Chevrolet, this pavilion consists of the **Test Track** attraction and **Inside Track,** a collection of transportation-themed exhibits and multimedia presentations. The pavilion is the last on the left before the World Showcase. Many readers tell us that Test Track "is one big commercial" for Chevrolet. We agree that promotional hype is more heavy-handed here than in most other business-sponsored attractions. But Test Track is nonetheless one of the most creatively conceived attractions in Disney World.

Test Track *(FastPass+)* ★★★★

**Appeal by Age PRESCHOOL ★★★★   GRADE SCHOOL ★★★★★   TEENS ★★★★★
YOUNG ADULTS ★★★★½   OVER 30 ★★★★½   SENIORS ★★★★½**

What it is Auto-test-track simulator ride. **Scope and scale** Super-headliner.
When to go The first 30 minutes the park is open or just before closing, or use
FastPass+. **Special comments** 40" minimum height requirement. **Authors' rating**
Not to be missed; ★★★★. **Duration of ride** About 4 minutes. **Average wait in
line per 100 people ahead of you** 4½ minutes. **Loading speed** Moderate–fast.

DESCRIPTION AND COMMENTS Test Track takes guests through the process of designing a new vehicle and then "testing" their car in a high-
speed drive through and around the pavilion.

Guests entering the pavilion walk past displays of futuristic concept
cars. Throughout the queue's walls are glossy video screens where engi-
neers discuss the work of car design and consumers explain the characteristics of their perfect car.

After hearing about auto design, guests are admitted into the Chevrolet Design Studio to create their own concept car using a large touchscreen (like a giant iPad). Next, they board a six-seat ride vehicle that's
attached to a track on the ground, for an actual drive through Chevrolet's
test track. The idea here is that guests are taking part in a computer simulation designed to test their vehicle's performance characteristics. Tests
include braking, cornering, and acceleration, culminating in a spin around
the outside of the pavilion at speeds of up to 65 miles per hour. The postshow area continues the creative process by allowing guests to craft
commercials for their cars. Farther into the pavilion are displays of actual
Chevys, many of which you can sit in.

TOURING TIPS It's always been a challenge to keep Test Track running,
especially in humid or wet weather. But when it works, it's one of Epcot's
better attractions.

Be aware that FastPass+ reservations often run out by afternoon. In
that case, try the single-rider line. Because most groups are unwilling to
split up, this line is usually much shorter than the regular (standby) line.

IMAGINATION! PAVILION

DESCRIPTION AND COMMENTS Multiattraction pavilion on the west side
of Innoventions West and down the walk from The Land. Outside is an
"upside-down waterfall" and one of our favorite Future World landmarks, the "jumping water," a fountain that hops over the heads of
unsuspecting passersby.

TOURING TIPS We recommend early-morning or late-evening touring. See
the individual attractions for specifics.

Captain EO *(FastPass+)* ★★★

**Appeal by Age   PRESCHOOL ★★★   GRADE SCHOOL ★★★   TEENS ★★★
YOUNG ADULTS ★★½   OVER 30 ★★½   SENIORS ★★★**

What it is 3-D film and 1980s pop-culture artifact with special effects. **Scope and
scale** Headliner. **When to go** When it's playing, anytime—FastPass+ is unnecessary.
Special comments The high decibels frighten some young children. **Authors'
rating** ★★★. **Duration of presentation** About 17 minutes. **Preshow entertainment** 8 minutes. **Probable waiting time** 15 minutes.

DESCRIPTION AND COMMENTS In response to Michael Jackson's death in 2009, Disney brought back his space-themed 3-D musical film *Captain EO,* which originally ran in Epcot from 1986 to 1994, for a "limited" engagement in its theme parks. In early 2015, Disney preempted *EO* to show previews of upcoming theatrical releases. *EO* returned for the summer of 2015, but at press time its long-term status was tenuous.

We think *Captain EO* is still worth seeing if it's playing. It hasn't aged as well as Jackson's other long-form video work, notably *Thriller,* but it's still one of the ultimate 1980s-era music videos. Directed by Francis Ford Coppola, it's a 3-D space fantasy with lasers, fiber optics, cannons, and other special effects in the theater, plus some audience participation.

TOURING TIPS Shows usually begin on the hour and half-hour. The sound level is earsplitting, frightening some young children. Avoid seats in the first several rows; if you sit too close to the screen, the 3-D images don't focus properly. The theater rarely fills, making FastPass+ unnecessary.

Journey into Imagination with Figment *(FastPass+)* ★★½

Appeal by Age	PRESCHOOL ★★★★	GRADE SCHOOL ★★★½	TEENS ★★★
YOUNG ADULTS ★★★½		OVER 30 ★★★	SENIORS ★★★

What it is Dark fantasy-adventure ride. **Scope and scale** Major-attraction wannabe. **When to go** Anytime. **Authors' rating** ★★½. **Duration of ride** About 6 minutes. **Average wait in line per 100 people ahead of you** 2 minutes. **Loading speed** Fast.

DESCRIPTION AND COMMENTS Journey into Imagination takes you on a tour of the zany Imagination Institute. Sometimes you're a passive observer and sometimes you're a test subject as the ride provides a glimpse of the fictitious lab's inner workings. Stimulating all your senses and then some, it hits you with optical illusions, an experiment in which noise generates colors, a room that defies gravity, and other brain teasers. All along the way, Figment (a purple dragon) makes surprise appearances. After the ride, you can adjourn to an interactive exhibit area offering the latest in unique, hands-on imagery technology.

Pleasant rather than exciting, the ride falls short of the promise suggested by its name. Will you go to sleep? No. Will you find it amusing? Probably. Will you remember it tomorrow? Only Figment knows.

TOURING TIPS The standby wait for this attraction rarely exceeds 20 minutes, so no need for FastPass+ here. You can enjoy the interactive postshow exhibit without taking the ride, so save it for later in the day.

THE LAND PAVILION

DESCRIPTION AND COMMENTS The Land is a huge pavilion that contains three attractions and several restaurants. Its emphasis has shifted from farming to environmental concerns.

TOURING TIPS This is a good place to grab a fast-food lunch. If you're here to see the attractions, however, don't go during mealtimes. Note that strollers aren't allowed inside.

The Circle of Life ★★★½

APPEAL BY AGE	PRESCHOOL ★★★½	GRADE SCHOOL ★★★½	TEENS ★★★½
YOUNG ADULTS ★★★½		OVER 30 ★★★	SENIORS ★★★½

What it is Film exploring humans' relationship with the environment. **Scope and scale** Minor attraction. **When to go** Anytime. **Authors' rating** Inspiring and enlightening; ★★★½. **Duration of presentation** About 20 minutes. **Preshow entertainment** Ecological slide show and trivia. **Probable waiting time** 10–15 minutes.

DESCRIPTION AND COMMENTS This playful yet educational film, starring Pumbaa, Simba, and Timon from *The Lion King,* spotlights the environmental interdependency of all creatures, demonstrating how easily the ecological balance can be upset. The message is sobering but enlightening.

TOURING TIPS To stay ahead of the crowd, see this in late afternoon.

Living with the Land *(FastPass+)* ★★★★

Appeal by Age	PRESCHOOL ★★★½	GRADE SCHOOL ★★★½	TEENS ★★★★
YOUNG ADULTS ★★★★		OVER 30 ★★★★	SENIORS ★★★★½

What it is Indoor boat ride chronicling the past, present, and future of farming and agriculture in the United States. **Scope and scale** Major attraction. **When to go** Before 11 a.m., after 1 p.m., or use FastPass+. **Special comments** Go early in the morning and save other Land attractions (except for Soarin') for later in the day. The ride is on the pavilion's lower level. **Authors' rating** Informative without being dull; not to be missed; ★★★★. **Duration of ride** About 14 minutes. **Average wait in line per 100 people ahead of you** 3 minutes; assumes 15 boats operating. **Loading speed** Moderate.

DESCRIPTION AND COMMENTS This boat ride takes you through swamps, past inhospitable farm environments, and through a futuristic greenhouse where real crops are grown using the latest agricultural technologies.

TOURING TIPS See this attraction before the lunch crowd hits The Land's restaurants. Living with the Land is rarely a good use of FastPass+.If you really enjoy Living with the Land or you have a special interest in the agricultural techniques demonstrated, take the **Behind the Seeds** tour. It's a 1-hour guided walk behind the scenes that examines advanced and experimental growing methods in-depth. The tour costs $20 for adults and $16 for children ages 3–9. Reservations are made on a space-available basis at the guided-tour waiting area near the entrance to Soarin'. This tour can also be reserved in advance by calling ☎ 407-WDW-TOUR.

Soarin' *(FastPass+)* ★★★★½

Appeal by Age	PRESCHOOL ★★★★½	GRADE SCHOOL ★★★★★	TEENS ★★★★½
YOUNG ADULTS ★★★★½		OVER 30 ★★★★★	SENIORS ★★★★★

What it is Flight simulator ride. **Scope and scale** Super-headliner. **When to go** First 30 minutes the park is open, or use FastPass+. **Special comments** May induce motion sickness; 40" minimum height requirement. Switching-off option provided (see page 93). **Authors' rating** Thrilling and mellow at the same time; not to be missed; ★★★★½. **Duration of ride** 5½ minutes. **Average wait in line per 100 people ahead of you** 4 minutes; assumes 2 concourses operating. **Loading speed** Moderate.

DESCRIPTION AND COMMENTS Soarin' is a thrill ride for all ages, as exhilarating as a hawk on the wing yet as mellow as swinging in a hammock. If you've ever experienced flying dreams, you'll have some sense of how Soarin' feels.

Once you enter the main theater, you're secured in a seat not unlike those on inverted roller coasters. When everyone is in place, the rows of seats swing into position, making you feel as if the floor has dropped away, and you're suspended with your legs dangling. Thus hung out to dry, you embark on a simulated hang glider tour, with IMAX-quality images projected all around you and with the flight simulator moving in sync with the movie. The images are well chosen and drop-dead beautiful. Special effects include wind, sound, and even smell. The ride itself is thrilling but perfectly smooth. We think Soarin' is a must-experience for guests of any age who are tall enough to ride. And yes, senior citizens have told us they tried it and were crazy about it. On the other hand, a few readers who are afraid of heights have reported feeling anxious on Soarin'.

A new ride film is expected to debut at Soarin' in 2016, along with a third ride theater to increase ride capacity by 50%. We hear the new ride film will incorporate flyover sequences from around the world, possibly with different, random sequences each time you ride.

TOURING TIPS Having Soarin' opposite Test Track and Mission: Space in Future World takes some crowd pressure off both sides of the park. Keep in mind, however, that Test Track and Mission: Space serve up a little too much thrill for some guests. Soarin', conversely, is an almost platonic ride for any age. For that reason, it's at the top of the hit parade. See it before 9:30 a.m. or book FastPass+ reservations up to 60 days in advance; expect same-day reservations to be gone by 1 p.m. on days of moderate attendance or as early as 11 a.m. on busier days.

THE SEAS WITH NEMO & FRIENDS PAVILION

THIS AREA ENCOMPASSES one of America's top marine aquariums, a ride that tunnels through the aquarium, an interactive animated film, and a number of first-class educational walk-through exhibits. It's a stunning package, one we rate as not to be missed. A comprehensive makeover featuring characters from Disney/Pixar's *Finding Nemo* has brought whimsy and much-needed levity to what theretofore was educationally brilliant but somewhat staid.

The Seas Main Tank and Exhibits ★★★½

Appeal by Age	PRESCHOOL ★★★★½	GRADE SCHOOL ★★★★½	TEENS ★★★★
YOUNG ADULTS ★★★★		OVER 30 ★★★★	SENIORS ★★★★

What it is A huge saltwater aquarium, plus exhibits on oceanography, ocean ecology, and sea life. **Scope and scale** Major attraction. **When to go** Before 11:30 a.m. or after 5 p.m., especially on Extra Magic Hours evenings. **Authors' rating** Excellent; ★★★½. **Average wait in line per 100 people ahead of you** 3½ minutes. **Loading speed** Fast.

DESCRIPTION AND COMMENTS The Seas is among Future World's most ambitious offerings. Scientists and divers conduct actual marine experiments in a 200-foot-diameter, 27-foot-deep main tank containing fish, mammals, and crustaceans in a simulation of an ocean ecosystem. Visitors can watch the activity through 8-inch-thick windows below the surface (including some in the Coral Reef Restaurant). On entering The Seas, you're directed to the loading area for The Seas with Nemo & Friends, an attraction that conveys you via a Plexiglas tunnel through The Seas' main tank. Following the ride, you disembark at Sea Base Alpha, where you can enjoy the attractions mentioned previously. (If the wait for the ride is too long, it's possible to head straight for the exhibits by going through the pavilion's exit, around back, and to the left of the main entrance.)

The Seas' fish population is substantial, but the strength of this attraction lies in the dozen or so exhibits offered after the ride. Visitors can view fish-breeding experiments, watch short films about sea life, and more. A delightful exhibit showcases clownfish (Nemo), regal blue tang (Dory), and other species featured in *Finding Nemo*. Other highlights include a haunting, hypnotic jellyfish tank; a sea horse aquarium; a stingray exhibit; and a manatee tank.

About two-thirds of the main aquarium is home to reef species, including sharks, rays, and a number of fish that you've seen in quiet repose on your dinner plate. The other third, separated by an inconspicuous divider, houses bottle-nosed dolphins and sea turtles. As you face the main aquarium, the most glare-free viewing windows for the dolphins are on the ground floor to the left by the escalators. For the reef species, it's the same floor on the right by the escalators. Stay as long as you wish.

TOURING TIPS With The Seas with Nemo & Friends and *Turtle Talk with Crush*, The Seas is one of Epcot's more popular venues. We recommend experiencing the ride and *Turtle Talk* in the morning before the park gets crowded, saving the excellent exhibits for later. The Seas is uncrowded during evening Extra Magic Hours, making it a perfect time to have large swaths of the aquarium to yourself.

The Seas with Nemo & Friends *(FastPass+)* ★★★

Appeal by Age PRESCHOOL ★★★★½ GRADE SCHOOL ★★★★ TEENS ★★★½
YOUNG ADULTS ★★★½ OVER 30 ★★★½ SENIORS ★★★★

What it is Ride through a tunnel in The Seas' main tank. **Scope and scale** Major attraction. **When to go** Before 10:30 a.m., after 3 p.m., or use FastPass+. **Authors' rating** ★★★. **Duration of ride** 4 minutes. **Average wait in line per 100 people ahead of you** 3½ minutes. **Loading speed** Fast.

DESCRIPTION AND COMMENTS The Seas with Nemo & Friends is a high-tech ride featuring characters from the animated hit Finding Nemo. The ride likewise deposits you at the heart of The Seas, where the exhibits, *Turtle Talk with Crush,* and viewing platforms for the main aquarium are.

Upon entering The Seas, you're given the option of experiencing the ride or proceeding directly to the exhibit area. If you choose the ride, you'll be ushered to its loading area, where you'll be made comfortable in a "clamobile" for your journey through the aquarium. The attraction features technology that makes it seem as if the animated characters are swimming with live fish. Very cool.

Almost immediately you meet Mr. Ray and his class and learn that Nemo is missing. The remainder of the odyssey consists of finding Nemo with the help of Dory, Bruce, Marlin, Squirt, and Crush, all characters from the animated feature. Unlike the film, however, the ride ends with a musical finale.

TOURING TIPS The earlier you ride, the better. If waits are too much, come back after 3 p.m. or so, or use FastPass+.

Turtle Talk with Crush *(FastPass+)* ★★★★

Appeal by Age PRESCHOOL ★★★★½ GRADE SCHOOL ★★★★½ TEENS ★★★★
YOUNG ADULTS ★★★★ OVER 30 ★★★★ SENIORS ★★★★

What it is Interactive animated film. **Scope and scale** Minor attraction. **When to go** Before 11 a.m., after 3 p.m., or use FastPass+. **Authors' rating** A real spirit-lifter; not to be missed; ★★★★. **Duration of presentation** 17 minutes. **Preshow entertainment** None. **Probable waiting time** 10–20 minutes.

DESCRIPTION AND COMMENTS *Turtle Talk with Crush* is an interactive theater show starring the 153-year-old surfer-dude turtle from *Finding Nemo*. Although it starts like a typical Disney-theme-park movie, *Turtle*

Talk quickly turns into a surprise interactive encounter as the on-screen Crush begins to have actual conversations with guests in the audience. Real-time computer graphics are used to accurately move Crush's mouth when forming words, and he's voiced by a guy who went to the Jeff Spicoli School of Diction.

TOURING TIPS It's unusual to wait more than one or two shows to get in. If you find long lines in the morning, try back after 3 p.m. when more of the crowd has moved on to World Showcase, or use FastPass+.

The "Mom, I Can't Believe It's Disney!" Fountains ★★★★

Appeal by Age	PRESCHOOL ★★★★★	GRADE SCHOOL ★★★★★	TEENS ★★★★
YOUNG ADULTS ★★★★		OVER 30 ★★★★	SENIORS ★★★★★

What it is Combination fountain and shower. **When to go** When it's hot. **Scope and scale** Diversion. **Special comments** Secretly installed by Martians during *IllumiNations*. **Authors' rating** Yes! ★★★★. **Duration of experience** Indefinite. **Probable waiting time** None.

DESCRIPTION AND COMMENTS These simple fountains—one on the walkway linking Future World to World Showcase, the other in Future World East, on the way to Test Track—aren't much to look at, but they offer a truly spontaneous experience: a rarity in Walt Disney World.

Spouts of water erupt randomly from the sidewalk. You can frolic in the water or let it cascade down on you or blow up your britches. On a broiling Florida day, when you think you might suddenly combust, fling yourself into the fountain and do decidedly un-Disney things. Dance, skip, sing, jump, splash, cavort, roll around, stick your toes down the spouts, or catch the water in your mouth as it descends. You can do all of this with your clothes on or, depending on your age, with your clothes off. It's hard to imagine so much personal freedom at Disney World and almost unthinkable to contemplate soggy people slogging and squishing around the park, but there you have it. Hurrah!

TOURING TIPS We don't know if the fountain's creator has been drummed out of the corps by the Disney Tribunal of People Who Sit on Sticks, but we're all grateful for his courage in introducing one thing that's not super-controlled. We do know your kids will be right in the middle of this thing before your brain sounds the alert. Our advice: pack a pair of dry shorts and turn the kids loose. You might even want to bring a spare pair for yourself. Or perhaps not.

▌▌ WORLD SHOWCASE

EPCOT'S SECOND THEMED AREA, World Showcase is an ongoing World's Fair encircling a picturesque 40-acre lagoon. The cuisine, culture, history, and architecture of almost a dozen countries are permanently displayed in individual national pavilions spaced along a 1.2-mile promenade. The pavilions replicate familiar landmarks and present representative street scenes from the host countries.

World Showcase features some of the loveliest gardens in the United States. In Germany, France, United Kingdom, Canada, and, to a lesser extent, China, they're sometimes tucked away and out of sight of pedestrian traffic on the World Showcase Promenade.

Most adults enjoy World Showcase, but many children find it boring. To make it more interesting to children, most Epcot retail shops sell **Passport Kits** for about $11. Each kit contains a blank passport and stamps for every World Showcase country. As kids accompany their folks to each country, they tear out the appropriate stamp and stick it in the passport. The kit also contains basic information on the nations and a Mickey Mouse button.

unofficial **TIP**
To get your kids interested in World Showcase, buy them a Passport Kit and let them collect stamps from each Epcot country.

Children also enjoy **Kidcot Fun Stops,** designed to make World Showcase more interesting for the 5- to 12-year-old crowd. So simple and uncomplicated that you can't believe Disney people thought it up, the Fun Stops usually are nothing more than a large table on the sidewalk at each pavilion. Each table is staffed by a Disney cast member who stamps passports and supervises children in modest craft projects relating to the host country. Reports from parents about both the Passport Kits and the Fun Stops are uniformly positive.

Agent P's World Showcase Adventure ★★★★

Appeal by Age	PRESCHOOL ★★★½	GRADE SCHOOL ★★★★	TEENS ★★★★½
YOUNG ADULTS ★★★½		OVER 30 ★★★½	SENIORS ★★★½

What it is Interactive scavenger hunt in select World Showcase pavilions. **Scope and scale** Minor attraction. **When to go** Anytime. **Authors' rating** One of our favorite additions to the parks; ★★★★. **Duration of presentation** Allow 30 minutes per adventure. **Preshow entertainment** None. **Probable waiting time** None.

DESCRIPTION AND COMMENTS In their eponymous Disney Channel show, Phineas and Ferb have a pet platypus named Perry. In the presence of humans, Perry doesn't do a whole lot. (To be fair, we're not experts on typical platypus behavior, but read on.) When the kids aren't looking, though, Perry takes on the role of Agent P—a fedora-wearing, James Bond–esque secret agent who battles the evil Dr. Doofenshmirtz to prevent world domination (or at least domination of the tri-state area in which the show is based).

In Agent P's World Showcase Adventure, you're a secret agent helping Perry, and you receive a cell phone–like device before you're dispatched on a mission to your choice of seven World Showcase pavilions. Once you arrive at the pavilion, the device's video screen and audio provide various clues to help you solve a set of simple puzzles necessary for defeating Dr. Doofenshmirtz's plan. As you discover each clue, you'll find special effects such as talking statues and flaming lanterns, plus live "secret agents" stationed in the pavilions just for this attraction. For example, in a prior version of the game you were instructed to utter the phrase "Danger is my cup of tea" to someone working behind the counter at the United Kingdom's tea shop; he or she would respond by handing you a Twinings tea packet on which was printed a clue to solve a puzzle.

Agent P makes static World Showcase pavilions more interactive and kid-friendly. The adventures have simple clues, fast pacing, and neat rewards for solving the puzzles.

TOURING TIPS Playing the game is free, and no deposit is required for the device. You'll need a valid theme park ticket to sign up before you play, and you can choose both the time and location of your adventure. Register at Future World's Innoventions East or West building, or along the Odyssey Bridge connecting Future World to World Showcase. Before heading off to your chosen country, pick up your device at the Italy, Norway, or United Kingdom Pavilion or the east side of the main walkway from Future World to World Showcase.

Each group can have up to three devices for the same adventure. Because you're working with a device about the size of a mobile phone, it's best to have one device for every two people in your group.

NOW, MOVING CLOCKWISE around the World Showcase Promenade, here are the nations represented and their attractions.

MEXICO PAVILION

DESCRIPTION AND COMMENTS Pre-Columbian pyramids dominate the architecture of this exhibit. One forms the pavilion's facade, and the other overlooks the restaurant and plaza alongside the boat ride—**Gran Fiesta Tour**—inside the pavilion.

TOURING TIPS A romantic and exciting testimony to Mexico's charms, the pyramids contain a large number of authentic and valuable artifacts. Many people zip past these treasures without stopping to look. The village scene inside the pavilion is beautiful and exquisitely detailed. A retail shop occupies most of the left half of the inner pavilion, while Mexico's Kidcot stop is in the first entryway inside the pyramid. On the opposite side of the main floor is **La Cava de Tequila,** a bar serving more than 100 varieties of tequila as well as margaritas and mezcal.

Gran Fiesta Tour Starring the Three Caballeros ★★½

**Appeal by Age PRESCHOOL ★★★★ GRADE SCHOOL ★★★½ TEENS ★★★½
YOUNG ADULTS ★★★ OVER 30 ★★★½ SENIORS ★★★½**

What it is Indoor scenic boat ride. **Scope and scale** Minor attraction. **When to go** Before noon or after 5 p.m. **Authors' rating** Visually appealing, light, and relaxing; ★★½. **Duration of ride** About 7 minutes (plus 1½-minute wait to disembark). **Average wait in line per 100 people ahead of you** 4½ minutes; assumes 16 boats in operation. **Loading speed** Moderate.

DESCRIPTION AND COMMENTS The Gran Fiesta Tour incorporates animated versions of Donald Duck, José Carioca, and Panchito—an avian singing group called The Three Caballeros, from Disney's 1944 animated musical of the same name—to spice up what has been characterized as a slower-paced Mexican-style It's a Small World.

The ride's premise is that the Caballeros are scheduled to perform at a fiesta, but Donald has gone missing. Large video screens show Donald playing hooky, enjoying Mexico's pyramids, monuments, and watersports while José and Panchito search other Mexican points of interest. Everyone is reunited in time for a rousing concert near the end of the ride. Along the way, guests are treated to detailed scenes in eye-catching colors, and an impressive music system.

At the risk of sounding like the Disney geeks we are, we must point out that Panchito is technically the only Mexican Caballero; José Carioca is from Brazil, and Donald is from Burbank. In any case, more of the ride's visuals seem to be on the left side of the boat; have small children sit nearer the left to keep their attention, and listen for Donald's humorous monologue as you wait to disembark at the end of the ride.

TOURING TIPS If the line looks longer than 5 minutes, grab a margarita at La Cava del Tequila and come back in 15.

"NORWAY" PAVILION

DESCRIPTION AND COMMENTS This pavilion encapsulates both everything we love about Epcot and everything we hate about corporate Disney. Parts of the pavilion—those based on the actual country of Norway—are complex, beautiful, and diverse. Highlights include replicas of the 14th-century Akershus Castle in Oslo and a miniature version of a stave church built in 1212 in Gol, Norway (go inside—the doors open!).

For years after it was built, Epcot's Norway sat in a state of mostly benign neglect. The boat ride, Maelstrom, was a relatively short and lightly themed float-through of the country's history. But at least it was based on an actual country, at an actual point in time.

Fast-forward to today and the monster hit that is 2013's *Frozen,* set in the mythical Scandinavian-ish kingdom of Arendelle. Disney's bean counters, who couldn't design a pavilion if given Walt's own cryogenically preserved brain, must have looked at all the money *Frozen* made, seen Epcot's need to attract more customers, and decided that whatever World Showcase *really* is, it should include a made-up country whose main attraction is a hastily repurposed boat ride. If you ask us, this *Frozen* stuff should have gone in Disney's Hollywood Studios instead.

Frozen Ever After *(opens 2016)*

What it is Indoor boat ride and Disney film–shilling vehicle. **Scope and scale** Major attraction. **When to go** Before noon., after 7 p.m., or use FastPass+. **Special comments** Expect long waits from the moment it opens. **Authors' rating** N/A. **Duration of ride** About 4½ minutes. **Average wait in line per 100 people ahead of you** 4 minutes; assumes 12 or 13 boats operating. **Loading speed** Fast.

DESCRIPTION AND COMMENTS Frozen Ever After replaces the Maelstrom boat ride. Expect to see all of the major *Frozen* characters, including Marshmallow, Olaf, Sven, and Wandering Oaken. Scenes in the ride will include Troll Valley and, of course, Elsa belting out "Let It Go."

TOURING TIPS Epcot hasn't opened many major new rides in recent years, and because this one is based on a wildly successful film, you should expect Frozen Ever After to be mobbed from the day it opens. Your likely best bet will be to arrive as soon as World Showcase opens, then backtrack to Mexico; otherwise, use FastPass+.

Royal Sommerhus Meet and Greet *(opens 2016)*

What it is Meet and greet with the *Frozen* princesses. **Scope and scale** Minor attraction. **When to go** Before noon, after 7 p.m., or use FastPass+. **Special comments** Expect long waits at the outset that should moderate over time. **Authors' rating** N/A. **Duration of greeting** N/A. **Average wait in line per 100 people ahead of you** N/A. **Loading speed** N/A.

DESCRIPTION AND COMMENTS Scheduled to open in 2016 along with Frozen Ever After is a character greeting for Anna and Elsa. While *Frozen* wasn't explicitly set in Norway, Disney alleges the meet and greet will feature traditional Norwegian architecture and crafts.

TOURING TIPS We've heard that this meet and greet will have multiple rooms with Anna and Elsa operating simultaneously. This, coupled with Epcot's lower average attendance, means that once the initial crowds die down after opening, waits should be somewhat shorter than those to see the same princesses at the Magic Kingdom's Princess Fairytale Hall.

CHINA PAVILION

DESCRIPTION AND COMMENTS A half-sized replica of the Temple of Heaven in Beijing identifies this pavilion. Gardens and reflecting ponds simulate those found in Suzhou, and an art gallery features a lotus-blossom gate and formal saddle roofline. The China Pavilion offers two restaurants: the quick-service **Lotus Blossom Cafe** and the full-service **Nine Dragons Restaurant,** (Advance Reservations recommended) which serves lamentably lackluster Chinese food in a lovely setting. **The Joy of Tea,** a tea stand and specialty-drink vendor, will feed your caffeine addiction until you can make it to Morocco's espresso bar.

The pavilion also hosts exhibits on Chinese history and culture. Past exhibits have covered everything from China's indigenous peoples to the layout of Hong Kong Disneyland. The current exhibit displays scaled-down replicas of the terra-cotta "tomb warriors" buried with the Qin Dynasty emperor in the second century B.C. to guard him in the afterlife.

Reflections of China ★★★½

Appeal by Age	PRESCHOOL ★★★	GRADE SCHOOL ★★★½	TEENS ★★★★
YOUNG ADULTS ★★★★	OVER 30 ★★★★		SENIORS ★★★★½

What it is Film about the Chinese people and country. **Scope and scale** Major attraction. **When to go** Anytime. **Special comments** Audience stands throughout the performance. **Authors' rating** A beautifully produced film; ★★★½. **Duration of presentation** About 14 minutes. **Preshow entertainment** None. **Probable waiting time** 10 minutes.

DESCRIPTION AND COMMENTS Pass through the Hall of Prayer for Good Harvest to view the Circle-Vision 360 film *Reflections of China*. Warm and appealing, it's a brilliant (albeit politically sanitized) introduction to the people and the natural beauty of China.

TOURING TIPS The pavilion is truly beautiful—serene yet exciting. *Reflections of China* plays in a theater where guests must stand, but the film can usually be enjoyed anytime without much waiting.

GERMANY PAVILION

DESCRIPTION AND COMMENTS A clock tower, adorned with boy and girl figures, rises above the *platz* (plaza) marking the Germany Pavilion. Dominated by a fountain depicting St. George's victory over the dragon, the platz is encircled by buildings in the style of traditional German architecture. The main attraction is the **Biergarten,** a buffet that serves traditional German food and beer (Advance Reservations are required). Yodeling, folk dancing, and oompah-band music are part of the festivities.

The biggest draw in Germany may be **Karamell-Küche** ("Caramel Kitchen"), offering small caramel-covered sweets including apples, fudge, and cupcakes. We love coming here for a midday snack to tide us over before dinner. Also be sure to check out the large and elaborate model railroad just beyond the restrooms as you walk from Germany toward Italy.

TOURING TIPS The pavilion is pleasant and festive. Anytime is good for touring.

ITALY PAVILION

DESCRIPTION AND COMMENTS The entrance to Italy is marked by an 83-foot-tall campanile (bell tower) said to mirror the tower in St. Mark's Square in Venice. Left of the campanile is a replica of the 14th-century Doge's Palace, also in the famous square. The pavilion has a waterfront on the lagoon where gondolas are tied to striped moorings.

TOURING TIPS Streets and courtyards in the Italy Pavilion are among the most realistic in World Showcase. For a quick lunch, **Via Napoli** occasionally offers pizza by the slice; **Tutto Gusto Wine Cellar** serves appetizer plates along with libations. There's no film or ride, so you can tour the rest of the pavilion at any hour.

UNITED STATES PAVILION

The American Adventure ★★★★

Appeal by Age	PRESCHOOL ★★½	GRADE SCHOOL ★★★½	TEENS ★★★½
YOUNG ADULTS ★★★★		OVER 30 ★★★★	SENIORS ★★★★½

What it is Patriotic mixed-media and Audio-Animatronic theater presentation on US history. **Scope and scale** Headliner. **When to go** Anytime. **Authors' rating** Disney's best historic/patriotic attraction; not to be missed; ★★★★. **Duration of presentation** About 29 minutes. **Preshow entertainment** Voices of Liberty chorale singing. **Probable waiting time** 16 minutes.

DESCRIPTION AND COMMENTS The United States Pavilion consists of a fast-food restaurant (the **Liberty Inn**) and a patriotic show.

The presentation is a composite of everything Disney does best. Located in an imposing brick structure reminiscent of Colonial Philadelphia, the 29-minute production is a stirring, but sanitized, rendition of American history narrated by an animatronic Mark Twain (who carries a smoking cigar) and Ben Franklin (who climbs a set of stairs to visit Thomas Jefferson). Behind a stage (almost half the size of a football field) is a 28-by-155–foot rear-projection screen (the largest ever used) on which motion-picture images are interwoven with action on stage.

TOURING TIPS *The American Adventure* is the best patriotic attraction in the Disney repertoire. It usually plays to capacity audiences from around 1:30 to 3:30 p.m., but it isn't hard to get into: Because of the theater's large capacity, it's highly unusual for guests not to be admitted to the next performance.

JAPAN PAVILION

DESCRIPTION AND COMMENTS The five-story, blue-roofed pagoda, inspired by a 17th-century shrine in Nara, sets this pavilion apart. A hill garden behind it features waterfalls, rocks, flowers, lanterns, paths, and rustic bridges. The building on the right (as one faces the entrance) was inspired by the ceremonial and coronation hall at the Imperial Palace at Kyoto. It contains restaurants and a US outpost of Japan's **Mitsukoshi** department store. Through the center entrance and to the left is **Bijutsu-kan Gallery,** exhibiting colorful displays from Japanese pop culture.

A new meet-and-greet area opened in early 2015, behind the pagoda, on the small hill in front of Katsura Grill. Here, female cast members wearing offbeat street fashion answer questions about Japan's youth culture, especially that of Tokyo's Harajuku district. Check the *Times Guide* for a schedule.

TOURING TIPS Tasteful and elaborate, the pavilion creatively blends simplicity, architectural grandeur, and natural beauty. Tour anytime.

MOROCCO PAVILION

DESCRIPTION AND COMMENTS A bustling market, winding streets, lofty minarets, and stuccoed archways re-create the romance and intrigue of Marrakesh and Casablanca. The pavilion also has a museum of Moorish art and **Restaurant Marrakesh,** featuring North African specialties. **Spice Road Table** serves up tapas-style Mediterranean dishes and excellent views of *IllumiNations,* along with high prices.

TOURING TIPS Morocco has neither a ride nor theater, so tour it anytime.

FRANCE PAVILION

DESCRIPTION AND COMMENTS A replica of the Eiffel Tower is, *naturellement,* this pavilion's centerpiece.A replica of the Eiffel Tower is, *naturellement,* this pavilion's centerpiece. The streets recall La Belle Époque, France's "beautiful time" between 1870 and 1910. The restaurants, along with the bakery and ice-cream shop, are very popular—you wouldn't be the first visitor to buy a croissant to tide you over until your next real meal. Readers rank France as the best World Showcase pavilion.

Impressions de France ★★★½

Appeal by Age	PRESCHOOL ★★★½	GRADE SCHOOL ★★★½	TEENS ★★★½
YOUNG ADULTS ★★★★	OVER 30 ★★★★		SENIORS ★★★★½

What it is Film essay on the French people and country. **Scope and scale** Major attraction. **When to go** Anytime. **Authors' rating** Exceedingly beautiful film; not to be missed; ★★★½. **Duration of presentation** About 18 minutes. **Preshow entertainment** None. **Probable waiting time** 15 minutes (at suggested times).

DESCRIPTION AND COMMENTS *Impressions de France* is an 18-minute movie projected over 200 degrees onto five screens. Unlike at China and Canada, you sit to view this well-made film introducing France's people, cities, and natural wonders.

TOURING TIPS The film usually begins on the hour and half-hour. Detail and the evocation of a bygone era enrich the atmosphere of this pavilion. Streets are small and become quite congested when visitors queue for the film.

UNITED KINGDOM PAVILION

DESCRIPTION AND COMMENTS A variety of period architecture attempts to capture Britain's city, town, and rural atmospheres. One street alone has a thatched-roof cottage, a four-story timber-and-plaster building, a pre-Georgian plaster building, a formal Palladian exterior of dressed stone, and a city square with a Hyde Park bandstand (whew!).

The pavilion is mostly shops. The **Rose & Crown Pub and Dining Room** is the only World Showcase full-service restaurant with dining on the water side of the promenade. For fast food, try the **Yorkshire County Fish Shop.**

TOURING TIPS There are no attractions here, so tour anytime. Alice in Wonderland, Mary Poppins, and/or Pooh meet fans in the character-greeting area; check the *Times Guide* for a schedule. Advance Reservations aren't required for the Rose & Crown Pub, making it a nice place to stop for a beer.

CANADA PAVILION

DESCRIPTION AND COMMENTS Canada's cultural, natural, and architectural diversity are reflected in this large and impressive pavilion. Thirty-foot-tall totem poles embellish an American Indian village at the foot of a magnificent château-style hotel. Nearby is a rugged stone building said to be modeled after a famous landmark near Niagara Falls and that reflects Britain's influence on Canada. **Le Cellier,** a steakhouse on the pavilion's lower level, is one of Disney World's highest-rated restaurants. It almost always requires Advance Reservations; you'd have to be incredibly lucky to get a walk-in spot, but it doesn't hurt to ask. Lunch is easier to arrange.

O Canada! ★★★½

Appeal by Age	PRESCHOOL ★★★	GRADE SCHOOL ★★★	TEENS ★★★★
YOUNG ADULTS ★★★★		OVER 30 ★★★★	SENIORS ★★★★

What it is Film essay on the Canadian people and their country. **Scope and scale** Major attraction. **When to go** Anytime. **Special comments** Audience stands during performance. **Authors' rating** Makes you want to catch the first plane to Canada; ★★★½. **Duration of presentation** About 15 minutes. **Preshow entertainment** None. **Probable waiting time** 9 minutes.

DESCRIPTION AND COMMENTS Starring Martin Short, *O Canada!* showcases Canada's natural beauty and population diversity and demonstrates the immense pride Canadians have in their country. Visitors leave the theater through **Victoria Gardens,** inspired by British Columbia's famed Butchart Gardens.

TOURING TIPS *O Canada!,* a large-capacity theater attraction (guests must stand), gets fairly heavy late-morning attendance because Canada is the first pavilion encountered as one travels counterclockwise around World Showcase Lagoon.

LIVE ENTERTAINMENT *in* EPCOT

LIVE ENTERTAINMENT IN EPCOT IS MORE diverse than it is in the Magic Kingdom. In World Showcase, it reflects the nations represented. Future World provides a perfect setting for new and experimental offerings. Information about live entertainment on the day you visit is contained in the Epcot guide map you obtain upon entry or at Guest Relations.

Here are some of the performers and performances you're apt to encounter:

AMERICA GARDENS THEATRE This large amphitheater, near the US Pavilion, faces World Showcase Lagoon. It hosts pop and oldies musical acts throughout much of the year, as well as Epcot's popular **Candlelight Processional** for the Christmas holidays, and sometimes the **Voices of Liberty** (see below).

AROUND WORLD SHOWCASE Impromptu performances take place in and around the pavilions. Among the acts are a strolling mariachi group in Mexico; a flag corps and juggler in Italy; two singing groups (**Voices of Liberty** and **American Music Machine**) at the US Pavilion; traditional songs, drums, and dances in Japan; more traditional music in Morocco; acrobats in France; a Scottish folk group in the United Kingdom; and a lumberjack show in Canada. Performances occur about every half-hour.

DINNER AND LUNCH SHOWS Restaurants in World Showcase serve up healthy portions of live entertainment with the victuals. Find folk dancing and an oompah band in Germany, singing waiters in Italy, and belly dancers in Morocco. Shows take place only at dinner in Italy and Morocco but at both lunch and dinner in Germany. Advance Reservations are required.

DISNEY CHARACTERS Characters appear at the Epcot Character Spot (see page 174), elsewhere throughout the park (see pages 95 and 96), and in live shows at America Gardens Theatre and the Showcase Plaza between Mexico and Canada. Times are listed in the *Times Guide*. Finally, **Garden Grill Restaurant** in The Land and **Akershus Royal Banquet Hall** in Norway offer character meals.

IN FUTURE WORLD A musical crew of drumming janitors works near the front entrance and at Innoventions Plaza (between the two Innoventions buildings and by the fountain) according to the daily entertainment schedule. They're occasionally complemented by an electric-keyboard band playing oldies tunes.

INNOVENTIONS FOUNTAIN SHOW Numerous times each day, the fountain situated between the two Innoventions buildings comes alive with pulsating, arching plumes of water synchronized to a musical score.

IllumiNations: Reflections of Earth (FastPass+) ★★★★½

Appeal by Age	PRESCHOOL ★★★½	GRADE SCHOOL ★★★★½	TEENS ★★★★½
YOUNG ADULTS ★★★★½		OVER 30 ★★★★½	SENIORS ★★★★½

What it is Nighttime fireworks and laser show at World Showcase Lagoon. **Scope and scale** Super-headliner. **Fright potential** Not frightening in any respect. **Bottleneck rating** 7 when leaving. **When to go** Stake out a viewing position 60–100 minutes before the show (45–90 minutes during less-busy periods); FastPass+ not recommended except as noted on the following page. **Special comments** Showtime is listed in the daily entertainment schedule (*Times Guide*); audience

stands. **Authors' rating** Epcot's most impressive entertainment event; ★★★★½.
Duration of show About 18 minutes.

DESCRIPTION AND COMMENTS Epcot's great outdoor spectacle inte-
grates fireworks, laser lights, neon, and music in a stirring tribute to the
nations of the world. It's the climax of every Epcot day, and not to be
missed.

This enchanting and ambitious show (it tells the history of the universe starting with the big bang) is well worth keeping the kids up late.
The best places to view the show are from the lakeside veranda of **La
Hacienda de San Angel** at the Mexico Pavilion, **Spice Road Table** in
Morocco, or the **Rose & Crown Pub** at the UK Pavilion. Come early and
relax with a drink or snack. The drawback is—you guessed it—that you
will have to claim this spot at least 90 minutes before *IllumiNations.*

As noted earlier, FastPass+ gets you into a special viewing area for
the show—in **Showcase Plaza,** on the south shore of World Showcase
Lagoon, directly north of Future World—but you still have to arrive a
good half hour or so in advance to get a good spot. What's more, there
are so many other good viewing spots around the lagoon that *Illumi-
Nations* really isn't a good use of FastPass+—the consequence is an
hour-long wait at either Soarin' or Test Track. The one exception is if
you're visiting World Showcase for an evening, as there are no other Tier
A attractions here.

For other great viewing spots, check out the map on page 321. Note
that the boat dock opposite Germany may be exposed to a lot of smoke
from the fireworks because of Epcot's prevailing winds.

IllumiNations is the climax of every day at Epcot, so keep in mind
that once the show is over, you'll be leaving the park and so will almost
everybody else. For suggested exit strategies, see below.

Word around the lagoon is that a new nighttime extravaganza will
replace *IllumiNations* sometime in late 2015 or early 2016. While we don't
know the plot, we're reasonably sure it'll contain lasers, fireworks, and
music. There are hints that it'll contain some sort of interactive element.

For a really good view of the show, you can charter a pontoon boat
for about $350. Captained by a Disney cast member, the boat holds up
to 10 guests. Your captain will take you for a little cruise and then position the boat in a perfect place to watch *IllumiNations.* For more information, call ☎ 407-WDW-PLAY.

Getting out of Epcot after IllumiNations (Read This Before Selecting a Viewing Spot)

IllumiNations ends the day at Epcot. When it's over, only a couple
of gift shops remain open. Because there's nothing to do, everyone
leaves at once. This creates a great snarl at Package Pick-Up, the
Epcot monorail station, and the Disney bus stop. It also pushes to
the limit the tram system hauling guests to their cars in the parking
lot. It's important, then, to decide how quickly you want to leave
the park after the show, and then pick your vantage point.

If you're staying at an Epcot resort (Swan, Dolphin, Yacht
& Beach Club Resorts, and BoardWalk Inn & Villas), watch
the show from somewhere on the southern (US Pavilion) half of
World Showcase Lagoon, then leave through the International

Gateway between France and the United Kingdom. You can walk or take a boat back to your hotel from the International Gateway. If you have a car and you're visiting Epcot in the evening for dinner and *IllumiNations,* park at the Yacht Club or Beach Club. After the show, duck out the International Gateway and be on the road to your hotel in 15 minutes.

If you're staying at any other Disney hotel and you don't have a car, the fastest way home is to join the mass exodus through the main gate after *IllumiNations* and catch a bus or the monorail.

Those who have a car in the Epcot lot have a more problematic situation. To beat the crowd, find a viewing spot at the end of World Showcase Lagoon nearest Future World (and the exits). Leave as soon as the show concludes, trying to exit ahead of the crowd (note that thousands of people will be doing exactly the same thing). To get a good vantage point between Mexico and Canada on the northern end of the lagoon, stake out your spot 60–100 minutes before the show (45–90 minutes during less-busy periods), or use FastPass+. Otherwise, you may squander more time holding your spot before *IllumiNations* than you would if you watched from the less-congested southern end of the lagoon and took your chances with the crowd upon departure.

More groups get separated and more kids get lost following *IllumiNations* than at any other time. In summer, you'll be walking in a throng of up to 30,000 people. If you're heading for the parking lot, anticipate this congestion and preselect a point in the Epcot entrance area where you can meet if someone gets separated from the group. We recommend the fountain just inside the main entrance.

For those with a car, the main problem is reaching the parking lot. Once you're there, traffic leaves the parking lot pretty well. If you paid close attention to where you parked, consider skipping the tram and walking. If you walk, watch your children closely and hang on to them for all they're worth—the parking lot is pretty wild at this time of night, with hundreds of moving cars.

Good Locations for Viewing IllumiNations *and Other World Showcase Lagoon Performances*

The best place to be for any presentation on World Showcase Lagoon is in a seat on the lakeside veranda of **La Cantina de San Angel** in the Mexico Pavilion. Come early (at least 90 minutes before *IllumiNations* starts) and relax with a cold drink or snack while you wait for the show.

La Hacienda de San Angel in Mexico, the **Rose & Crown Pub** in the United Kingdom, and **Spice Road Table** in Morocco also have lagoonside seating. Because of a small wall at the Rose & Crown, however, the view isn't quite as good as from the Cantina. If you want to combine dinner at either location with *IllumiNations*, make a dinner reservation for about 1 hour and 15 minutes before showtime. Report a few minutes early for your seating and tell the host you want a table outside where you can view *IllumiNations* during or after dinner. In our experience, the staff will bend over backward to accommodate you. If you can't get a table outside, eat inside, then hang out until showtime. When the lights dim to indicate the start of *IllumiNations*, you'll be allowed to join the diners in watching it.

Because most guests run for the exits after a presentation, and because islands in the southern (US Pavilion) half of the lagoon block the view from some places, the most popular spectator positions are along the northern waterfront from Norway and Mexico to Canada and the United Kingdom.

If you're late finishing dinner or you don't want to spend an hour-plus standing by a rail, here are some good viewing spots along the southern perimeter (moving counterclockwise from the UK to Germany) that often go unnoticed until 10–30 minutes before showtime:

1. **International Gateway Island** The pedestrian bridge across the canal near International Gateway spans an island that offers great viewing. This island normally fills 30 minutes or more before showtime.

2. **Second-floor (restaurant-level) deck of the Mitsukoshi building in Japan** An Asian arch slightly blocks your sightline, but this covered deck offers a great vantage point, especially if the weather is iffy. Only the Hacienda de San Angel in Mexico is more protected.

3. **Gondola landing at Italy** An elaborate waterfront promenade offers excellent viewing positions. Claim your spot at least 30 minutes before showtime.

4. **Boat dock opposite Germany** Another good vantage point, the dock generally fills 30 minutes before *IllumiNations*.

5. **Waterfront promenade by Germany** Views are good from the 90-foot-long lagoonside walkway between Germany and China.

None of the viewing locations are reservable, and good spots go early on busier nights. But speaking personally, we refuse to hold down a slab of concrete for 2 hours before *IllumiNations* as some people do. Most nights, you can find an acceptable vantage point 15–30 minutes before the show.

unofficial **TIP**
It's important not to position yourself under a tree, an awning, or anything else that blocks your overhead view.

IllumiNations and FastPass+

We don't recommend *IllumiNations* as a good use of one of your first three advance FastPass+ reservations, but if you have only one day to tour Epcot and you're using our standard touring plan, you should be able to pick up a same-day FastPass+ reservation for *IllumiNations* just after 1 p.m., after you've experienced all of Epcot's headliners.

The new *Frozen*-themed boat ride and princess meet and greet in Norway (see page 560), scheduled to open in 2016, will likely both be FastPass+ attractions. That could make for some tough choices under the current FastPass+ system: Reservations for *IllumiNations* generally run out by 1–2 p.m., but it's unlikely that most guests would be finished with their Norway FastPass+ experiences by then. However, plenty of excellent *IllumiNations*-viewing locations that don't require FastPass+ can be found around World Showcase Lagoon, so it's not critical to have a reservation.

IllumiNations *Cruise*

For a *really* good view, you can charter a pontoon boat for $346 with tax. Captained by a Disney cast member, the boat holds up to 10 guests. Your captain will take you for a little cruise and then position the boat in a perfect place to watch *IllumiNations*. Chips, soda, and water are provided; sandwiches and more-substantial food items may be arranged through Disney reservations or Yacht Club Private Dining (☎ 407-934-3160.) Cruises depart from Bayside Marina. A major indirect benefit of the charter is that you can enjoy *IllumiNations* without fighting the mob afterward. Because this is a private charter rather than a tour, only your group will be aboard. Life jackets are provided, but you can wear them at your discretion. Because there are few boats, charters sell out fast. To reserve, call ☎ 407-WDW-PLAY (939-7529) at exactly 7 a.m. 180 days before the day you want to charter. We recommend phoning about 185 days out to have a Disney agent specify the exact morning to call for reservations. Similar charters are available on the Seven Seas Lagoon to watch the Magic Kingdom fireworks.

▐▌ EPCOT TOURING PLANS

OUR EPCOT TOURING PLANS ARE FIELD-TESTED, step-by-step itineraries for seeing all major attractions at Epcot with a minimum of waiting in line. They're designed to keep you ahead of the crowds while the park is filling in the morning, and to place you at the less crowded attractions during Epcot's busier hours. They assume you would be happier doing a little extra walking rather than a lot of extra standing in line.

Touring Epcot is much more strenuous and demanding than touring the other theme parks, requiring about twice as much walking. Our plans will help you avoid crowds and bottlenecks on days of moderate-to-heavy attendance, but they can't shorten the distance you have to walk. (Wear comfortable shoes.) On days of lighter attendance, when the crowd conditions aren't a critical factor, the plans will help you organize your tour.

unofficial **TIP**
Unlike the Magic Kingdom, Epcot has no effective in-park transportation; wherever you want to go, it's always quicker to walk.

To help with FastPass+, we've listed the approximate return times for which you should attempt to make reservations. (The touring plan should work with anything close to the times shown.) Check **touringplans.com** for the latest information.

We offer four touring plans:

EPCOT ONE-DAY TOURING PLAN This plan packs as much as possible into one long day and requires a lot of hustle and stamina. You'll be doing a lot of walking and some backtracking in order to avoid long waits in line. You might not complete the tour—how far you get depends on how quickly you move from attraction to attraction, how many times you rest and eat, how quickly the park fills, and what time it closes.

This plan is not recommended for families with very young children. If you're touring with young children and have only one day, use the Authors' Selective Epcot One-Day Touring Plan. Break after lunch and then relax at your hotel, returning to the park in late afternoon. If you can allocate two days to Epcot, use one of the Epcot two-day touring plans.

AUTHORS' SELECTIVE EPCOT ONE-DAY TOURING PLAN This plan eliminates what are, in the authors' opinion, some lesser attractions and offers a somewhat more relaxed tour if you have only one day. While the plan includes only what the authors believe is the best Epcot has to offer, exclusion of a particular attraction doesn't mean it isn't worthwhile.

Families with children younger than age 8 using this touring plan should review Epcot attractions in the Small-Child Fright-Potential Chart (pages 89–93). Rent a stroller for any child small enough to fit in one, and take your young children back to the hotel for a nap after lunch. If you can allocate two days to seeing Epcot, try one of the Epcot two-day touring plans.

EPCOT ONE-DAY TOURING PLAN FOR PARENTS WITH SMALL CHILDREN This touring plan is for parents and kids who want to experience Epcot's best attractions in a single day. It's the most popular Epcot touring plan at **touringplans.com.**

The plan includes a midday break of 3–4 hours. Make time for this break by skipping intense attractions such as Test Track and Mission: Space and by forgoing many World Showcase exhibits.

Families with children younger than age 8 using this touring plan should review Epcot attractions in our Small-Child Fright-Potential Chart in Part Five (see pages 89–93), and rent a stroller for any child small enough to fit in one.

EPCOT TWO-DAY EARLY-RISER TOURING PLAN This is the most efficient Epcot touring plan, eliminating 90% of the backtracking and extra walking required by the others while still providing a comprehensive tour. Most folks will complete each day of the plan by midafternoon. While the plan doesn't include *IllumiNations* or other evening festivities, these activities, along with dinner at an Epcot restaurant, can be added to the itinerary at your discretion.

As with the previous touring plans, families with children younger than age 8 using this plan should review Epcot attractions in the Small-Child Fright-Potential Chart (pages 89–93). Rent a stroller for any child small enough to fit.

"NOT A TOURING PLAN" TOURING PLANS

FOR PARENTS AND ADULTS WITH ONE DAY TO TOUR, ARRIVING AT PARK OPENING Ride Test Track and then Mission: Space Orange (FastPass+ suggested start time: 9 a.m.). Next, ride Sum of All Thrills, Soarin' (FastPass+ suggested start time: 11 a.m.), and Spaceship Earth; tour other Future World East and West attractions as you come to them and as you desire. Then tour World Showcase clockwise, starting in Mexico (FastPass+ suggested start time for the Frozen Ever After boat ride or the Royal Sommerhus meet and greet in Norway, both opening in 2016: 2 p.m.). End the day with *IllumiNations*.

FOR PARENTS AND ADULTS WITH ONE DAY TO TOUR, ARRIVING LATE MORNING Tour Future World West except for Soarin'. Tour World Showcase counterclockwise, starting in Canada (FastPass+ suggested start time for the Frozen Ever After boat ride or the Royal Sommerhus meet and greet in Norway: 3 p.m.). Tour Future World East; then ride Spaceship Earth. Now ride Soarin' (FastPass+ suggested start time: 6:30 p.m.)—or, if FastPass+ is unavailable for that, try to get reservations for Test Track instead. End the day with *IllumiNations*.

FOR PARENTS AND ADULTS WITH TWO DAYS TO TOUR On Day One, start with Test Track and Mission: Space Orange (FastPass+

suggested start times: 9 a.m. and 10 a.m., respectively), and then ride Sum of All Thrills. See the rest of Future World as desired, and then tour Mexico through the United States in World Showcase (Fast-Pass+ suggested start time for the Frozen Ever After boat ride or the Royal Sommerhus meet and greet in Norway: 2 p.m.). On Day Two, ride Soarin' (FastPass+ suggested start time: 9 a.m.), and then tour Canada through Japan in World Showcase. End the day with *IllumiNations* (use FastPass+).

PRELIMINARY INSTRUCTIONS FOR ALL EPCOT TOURING PLANS

1. Call ☎ 407-824-4321 for the hours of operation on the day of your visit.

2. Make Advance Reservations at the Epcot full-service restaurant(s) of your choice before your visit.

3. Make FastPass+ reservations 60 or 30 days in advance.

THE TOURING PLANS

Epcot One-Day Touring Plan

FOR Adults and children ages 8 or older.

ASSUMES Willingness to experience all major rides and shows.

START TIMES FOR FASTPASS+ Test Track, 9:15 a.m.; Mission: Space (Orange), 10:15 a.m.; Frozen Ever After, 3 p.m. Check for FastPass+ reservations for *IllumiNations* after you've used your first three FastPasses or after 3 p.m. (whichever is later).

1. Arrive 40 minutes before opening. Get guide maps and the *Times Guide*.

2. As soon as the park opens, ride Soarin' in The Land.

3. Ride Living with the Land.

4. In Future World East, ride Test Track.

5. Ride Sum of All Thrills.

6. Ride Mission: Space (Orange).

7. Experience *Ellen's Energy Adventure*.

8. Eat lunch (we recommend Sunshine Seasons in The Land).

9. Ride Spaceship Earth.

10. See The Seas with Nemo & Friends and *Turtle Talk with Crush*.

11. In Imagination!, experience Journey into Imagination.

12. Tour Mexico and ride the Gran Fiesta Tour.

13. Try the new Frozen Ever After boat ride and visit the stave church in Norway.

14. Play a game of Agent P's World Showcase Adventure. Sign up between the Mexico and Norway Pavilions.

15. Tour China and watch *Reflections of China.*

16. Tour Germany.

17. Visit Italy.

18. See *The American Adventure.*

19. Eat dinner.

20. Explore Japan.

21. Tour Morocco.

22. Visit France and see *Impressions de France.*

23. Tour the United Kingdom.

24. Tour Canada and see *O Canada!*

25. See *IllumiNations.* Prime viewing spots are along the lagoon between Canada and France. You could also try for a lagoon-side table at La Cantina de San Angel or La Hacienda de San Angel in Mexico (Advance Reservations needed at the latter), or Spice Road Table in Morocco.

Authors' Selective Epcot One-Day Touring Plan

FOR All parties.

ASSUMES Willingness to experience major rides and shows.

START TIMES FOR FASTPASS+ Test Track, 9:30 a.m.; Mission: Space (Orange), 10:30 a.m.; Frozen Ever After, 2:45 p.m. Check for FastPass+ reservations for *IllumiNations* after you've used your first three FastPasses or after 3 p.m. (whichever is later).

1. Arrive 40 minutes before opening. Get guide maps and the *Times Guide.*

2. As soon as the park opens, ride Soarin' in The Land.

3. Ride Living with the Land.

4. In Future World East, ride Test Track.

5. Ride Sum of All Thrills.

6. Ride Mission: Space (Orange).

7. Experience *Ellen's Energy Adventure.*

8. Eat lunch (we recommend Sunshine Seasons in The Land).

9. Ride Spaceship Earth.

10. See The Seas with Nemo & Friends and *Turtle Talk with Crush.*

11. Tour Mexico and ride the Gran Fiesta Tour.

12. Try the new Frozen Ever After boat ride and visit the stave church in Norway.

13. Play a game of Agent P's World Showcase Adventure. Sign up between the Mexico and Norway Pavilions.

14. Tour China and watch *Reflections of China.*

15. Tour Germany.

16. Visit Italy.

17. See *The American Adventure.*

18. Eat dinner.

19. Explore Japan.

20. Tour Morocco.

21. Visit France and see *Impressions de France.*

22. Tour the United Kingdom.

23. Tour Canada and see *O Canada!*

24. See *IllumiNations.* Prime viewing spots are along the lagoon between Canada and France. You could also try for a lagoon-side table at La Cantina de San Angel or La Hacienda de San Angel in Mexico (Advance Reservations needed at the latter), or Spice Road Table in Morocco.

Epcot One-Day Touring Plan for Parents with Small Children

FOR Parents with kids younger than age 8.

START TIMES FOR FASTPASS+ Soarin', 9 a.m.; Spaceship Earth, 11 a.m.; Frozen Ever After, 6 p.m. Check for FastPass+ reservations for *IllumiNations* after you've used your first three FastPasses or after 6 p.m. (whichever is later).

1. Arrive 40 minutes before opening. Rent strollers if needed. Get guide maps and the *Times Guide.*

2. As soon as the park opens, head to the Epcot Character Spot in Innoventions West.

3. Ride Soarin' in The Land.

4. See *The Circle of Life.*

5. In the Imagination! Pavilion, experience Journey into Imagination with Figment.

6. Ride Spaceship Earth.

7. Eat lunch and take a midday breakback at your hotel.

8. Experience *Ellen's Energy Adventure.*

9. See The Seas with Nemo & Friends and *Turtle Talk with Crush.*

10. Ride Living with the Land.

11. Tour Mexico and ride the Gran Fiesta Tour.

12. Try the new Frozen Ever After boat ride and visit the stave church in Norway.

13. Play a game of Agent P's World Showcase Adventure. Sign up between the Mexico and Norway Pavilions.

14. Eat dinner.

15. See *The American Adventure.*

16. Tour Canada and see *O Canada!*

17. See *IllumiNations.* Prime viewing spots are along the lagoon between Canada and France. You could also try for a lagoon-side table at La Cantina de San Angel or La Hacienda de San Angel in Mexico (Advance Reservations needed at the latter), or Spice Road Table in Morocco.

Epcot Two-Day Early-Riser Touring Plan

FOR All parties.

START TIMES FOR FASTPASS+ *Day One:* Soarin', 9 a.m.; Spaceship Earth, 11 a.m.; Frozen Ever After, 6 p.m. Check for FastPass+ reservations for *IllumiNations* after you've used your first three FastPasses or after 6 p.m. (whichever is later). *Day Two:* Test Track, 9 a.m.; Mission: Space (Orange), 10 a.m.; Spaceship Earth: 11 a.m. Check for FastPass+ reservations for *IllumiNations* after you've used your first three FastPasses or after 1 p.m. (whichever is later).

DAY ONE

1. Arrive 40 minutes before opening. Rent strollers if needed. Get guide maps and the *Times Guide.*

2. As soon as the park opens, see The Seas with Nemo & Friends and *Turtle Talk with Crush.*

3. In the Imagination! Pavilion, experience Journey into Imagination with Figment.

4. Ride Soarin' in The Land.

5. See *The Circle of Life.*

6. Eat lunch (we recommend Sunshine Seasons in The Land).

7. Ride Living with the Land.

8. Tour Mexico and ride the Gran Fiesta Tour.

9. Try the new Frozen Ever After boat ride and visit the stave church in Norway.

10. Watch *Reflections of China.*

11. Tour Germany.

12. Visit Italy.

13. See *The American Adventure.*

14. Explore Japan.

DAY TWO

1. Arrive 40 minutes before opening. Rent strollers if needed. Get guide maps and the *Times Guide*.

2. As soon as the park opens, ride Test Track.

3. Ride Sum of All Thrills.

4. Experience *Ellen's Energy Adventure*.

5. Ride Mission: Space (Orange).

6. Tour Innoventions East.

7. Ride Spaceship Earth.

8. Eat lunch.

9. Tour Canada and see *O Canada!*

10. Tour the United Kingdom.

11. Play Agent P's World Showcase Adventure. Sign up between the UK and France Pavilions.

12. Visit France and see *Impressions de France*.

13. Tour Morocco.

14. See *IllumiNations*. Prime viewing spots are along the lagoon between Canada and France. You could also try for a lagoon-side table at La Cantina de San Angel or La Hacienda de San Angel in Mexico (Advance Reservations needed at the latter), or Spice Road Table in Morocco.

PART ELEVEN

DISNEY'S ANIMAL KINGDOM

AT 500 ACRES, DISNEY'S ANIMAL KINGDOM is five times the size of the Magic Kingdom and more than twice the size of Epcot, but most of its vast geography is accessible only on guided tours or as part of attractions. At 500 acres, Animal Kingdom is five times the size of the Magic Kingdom and almost twice the size of Epcot. But most of Animal Kingdom's vast geography is accessible only on guided tours or as part of attractions. Animal Kingdom consists of five sections, or "lands": **The Oasis, Discovery Island, DinoLand U.S.A., Africa,** and **Asia.**

Its size notwithstanding, Animal Kingdom offers a limited number of attractions. To be exact, there are seven rides, several walk-through exhibits, an indoor theater, three amphitheaters, a conservation exhibit, and a children's playground.

With a decade and a half under its belt, Animal Kingdom has received mixed reviews. Guests complain loudly about the park layout and the necessity of backtracking through Discovery Island in order to access the various themed areas. However, most of the attractions (with one or two notable exceptions) have been well received. Also praised are the natural-habitat animal exhibits as well as the park architecture and landscaping.

ARRIVING

DISNEY'S ANIMAL KINGDOM IS OFF OSCEOLA PARKWAY in the southwest corner of Walt Disney World and is not too far from Blizzard Beach, the Coronado Springs Resort, and the All-Star Resorts. Animal Kingdom Lodge is about a mile away from the park on its northwest side. From Interstate 4, take Exit 64B, US 192, to the Walt Disney World main entrance (World Drive) and follow the signs to Animal Kingdom. The park has its own 6,000-car pay parking lot with close-in parking for guests with disabilities. Once parked, you can walk to the entrance or catch a ride on one of Disney's trademark trams.

Animal Kingdom is connected to other destinations by the Disney bus system. If you're staying at a Disney resort and you plan to arrive at Animal Kingdom entrance before park opening, use Disney transportation rather than taking your own car. The Animal Kingdom parking lot often opens only 15 minutes before the park, causing long lines and frustration for drivers.

> *un**official* **TIP**
> Jot down the location of your car, text yourself a message, or snap a picture of the row you're parked in with your phone or digital camera.

OPERATING HOURS

ANIMAL KINGDOM, NOT UNEXPECTEDLY, hosted tremendous crowds during its early years. Consequently, Disney management has done a fair amount of fiddling and experimenting with operating hours and opening procedures. Animal Kingdom's opening time now roughly corresponds to that of the other parks. Thus, you can expect a 9 a.m. opening during less busy times of the year and an 8 a.m. opening during holidays and high season. Animal Kingdom usually closes well before the other parks—as early as 5 p.m., in fact, during off-season. More common is a 6 or 7 p.m. closing.

Park-opening procedures at Animal Kingdom vary. Sometimes guests arriving prior to the official opening time are admitted to The Oasis and Discovery Island. The remainder of the park is roped off until official opening time. The rest of the time, those arriving early are held at the entrance turnstiles.

During slower or colder times of year, Disney may delay the daily opening of Kali River Rapids in Asia, as well as the Boneyard playground, the Wildlife Express Train, and Conservation Station. These procedures are subject to change, so check the *Times Guide* or our mobile app, **Lines,** for the exact schedule when you arrive. On holidays and other days of projected heavy attendance, Disney will open the park 30–60 minutes early.

Many guests wrap up their tour and leave by 3:30 or 4 p.m. Lines for the major rides and *It's Tough to Be a Bug!* usually thin appreciably between 4 p.m. and closing time. If you arrive at 2 p.m. and take in a couple of stage shows (described later), waits should be tolerable by the time you hit The Tree of Life and the rides.

> *un**official* **TIP**
> Even if you dawdle in the shops and linger over the wildlife exhibits, you should easily be able to take in Animal Kingdom in one day.

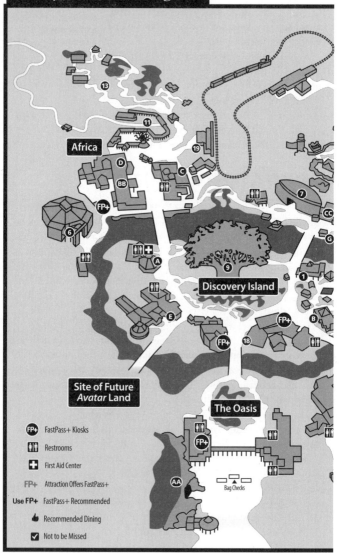

Disney's Animal Kingdom

Africa

Discovery Island

Site of Future *Avatar* Land

The Oasis

Bag Checks

FP+ FastPass+ Kiosks

Restrooms

First Aid Center

FP+ Attraction Offers FastPass+

Use FP+ FastPass+ Recommended

Recommended Dining

✓ Not to be Missed

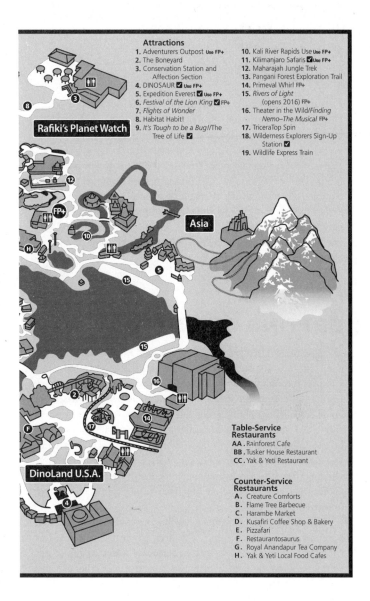

Attractions

1. Adventurers Outpost Use FP+
2. The Boneyard
3. Conservation Station and Affection Section
4. DINOSAUR ☑ Use FP+
5. Expedition Everest ☑ Use FP+
6. *Festival of the Lion King* ☑ FP+
7. *Flights of Wonder*
8. Habitat Habit!
9. *It's Tough to be a Bug!*/The Tree of Life ☑
10. Kali River Rapids Use Use FP+
11. Kilimanjaro Safaris ☑ Use FP+
12. Maharajah Jungle Trek
13. Pangani Forest Exploration Trail
14. Primeval Whirl FP+
15. *Rivers of Light* (opens 2016) FP+
16. Theater in the Wild/*Finding Nemo—The Musical* FP+
17. TriceraTop Spin
18. Wilderness Explorers Sign-Up Station ☑
19. Wildlife Express Train

Rafiki's Planet Watch

Asia

DinoLand U.S.A.

Table-Service Restaurants

AA . Rainforest Cafe
BB . Tusker House Restaurant
CC . Yak & Yeti Restaurant

Counter-Service Restaurants

A . Creature Comforts
B . Flame Tree Barbecue
C . Harambe Market
D . Kusafiri Coffee Shop & Bakery
E . Pizzafari
F . Restaurantosaurus
G . Royal Anandapur Tea Company
H . Yak & Yeti Local Food Cafes

NOT TO BE MISSED AT DISNEY'S ANIMAL KINGDOM	
AFRICA	• Festival of the Lion King • Kilimanjaro Safaris
ASIA	• Expedition Everest
DINOLAND U.S.A.	• Dinosaur • *Finding Nemo—The Musical*
DISCOVERY ISLAND	• *It's Tough to Be a Bug!* • Wilderness Explorers

Animal Kingdom currently holds two morning Extra Magic Hours sessions per week, although we don't think they save you all that much time in line. Our advice is to get an extra hour of sleep and visit when early entry is not in effect.

For now, Kilimanjaro Safaris and the Pangani Forest Exploration Trail close around 30–60 minutes before sunset. Thus, as days get shorter with the change of seasons, the attractions close earlier in the day. At press time, a nighttime version of Kilimanjaro Safaris was expected to open in late 2015 or early 2016; the Pangani Trail may also stay open past dark, though nothing official has been announced at this writing.

In the fall, Animal Kingdom closes all animal exhibits as early as 4:45 p.m.

GETTING ORIENTED

AT THE ENTRANCE PLAZA ARE TICKET KIOSKS fronting the main entrance. To your right, before the turnstiles, is an ATM. After you pass through the turnstiles, wheelchair and stroller rentals are to your right. **Guest Relations**—park headquarters for information, guide maps, entertainment schedules (*Times Guides*), missing persons, and lost and found—is to the left. Nearby are restrooms, public phones, and rental lockers. Beyond the entrance plaza, you enter **The Oasis,** a lushly vegetated network of converging pathways winding through a landscape punctuated with streams, waterfalls, and misty glades and inhabited by what Disney calls "colorful and unusual animals."

The park is arranged somewhat like the Magic Kingdom, in a hub-and-spoke configuration. The lush, tropical Oasis serves as Main Street, funneling visitors to **Discovery Island** at the center of the park. Dominated by the park's central icon, the 14-story hand-carved **Tree of Life,** Discovery Island is the park's retail and dining center. From Discovery Island, guests can access the respective themed areas of **Africa, Asia,** and **DinoLand U.S.A.** Discovery Island additionally hosts a theater attraction in The Tree of Life, and a number of short nature trails.

FASTPASS+ AT DISNEY'S ANIMAL KINGDOM

FASTPASS+ IS OFFERED at 9 (soon to be 10) attractions:

AFRICA
- *Festival of the Lion King*
- Kilimanjaro Safaris

ASIA
- Expedition Everest
- Kali River Rapids
- *Rivers of Light* (opens 2016)

DINOLAND U.S.A.
- Dinosaur
- *Finding Nemo—The Musical*
- Primeval Whirl

DISCOVERY ISLAND
- *It's Tough to Be a Bug!*
- Meet Favorite Disney Pals at Adventurers Outpost

Our touring plans most frequently recommend FastPass+ reservations for **Kali River Rapids** and **Kilimanjaro Safaris**. Using FastPass+ for these lets you experience other important attractions early in the morning, when lines are short, while still giving you relatively short lines at Kali and Safaris to contend with when you arrive.

Dinosaur and the **Adventurers Outpost** character meet and greet show up on our Animal Kingdom touring plans for parents with small children. Using FastPass+ for these will generally save

Disney's Animal Kingdom Services

Most of the park's service facilities are inside the main entrance and on Discovery Island, as follows:

BABY CARE CENTER On Discovery Island, behind the MyMagic+ Service Center

BANKING SERVICES ATMs at the main entrance, by the turnstiles, and near Dinosaur in DinoLand U.S.A.

CAMERA MEMORY CARDS AND SUPPLIES Just inside the main entrance at Garden Gate Gifts, in Africa at Duka La Filimu and Mombasa Marketplace, and at other retail shops throughout the park

CELL PHONE CHARGING Outlets available at Pizzafari, Restaurantosaurus, Tusker House, and Conservation Station

FIRST AID On Discovery Island, next to the MyMagic+ Service Center

GUEST RELATIONS/INFORMATION Inside the main entrance to the left

LIVE-ENTERTAINMENT AND PARADE INFORMATION Included in the park guide map, available free at Guest Relations

LOST AND FOUND Inside the main entrance to the left

LOST PERSONS Can be reported at Guest Relations and at the Baby Care Center on Discovery Island

STORAGE LOCKERS Inside the main entrance to the left

WHEELCHAIR, ECV/ESV, AND STROLLER RENTALS Inside the main entrance, to the right

ANIMAL KINGDOM
When Same-Day FP+ Runs Out, by Crowd Level

ATTRACTION	LOW CROWDS*	MODERATE CROWDS*	HIGH CROWDS*
Dinosaur	3–4 p.m.	4 p.m.	11 a.m.–2 p.m.
Expedition Everest	3–4 p.m.	4 p.m.	11 a.m.–2 p.m.
Festival of the Lion King	2–3 p.m.	2–3 p.m.	1–2 p.m. (Levels 8–9), 5 p.m. (Level 10)
Finding Nemo— The Musical	3–4 p.m.	4 p.m.	1–3 p.m.
It's Tough to Be a Bug!	3–4 p.m.	4–5 p.m.	5–6 p.m.
Kali River Rapids	2–3 p.m.	3–4 p.m.	1–4 p.m.
Kilimanjaro Safaris (daytime version)	1–2 p.m.	1–2 p.m.	Noon–1 p.m.
Meet Mickey and Minnie at Adventurers Outpost	Noon–1 p.m.	Noon–3 p.m.	1–2 p.m.
Primeval Whirl	3–4 p.m.	4–5 p.m.	5–6 p.m.

* LOW CROWDS (Levels 1–3 on TouringPlans.com Crowd Calendar)

* MODERATE CROWDS (Levels 4–7 on TouringPlans.com Crowd Calendar)

* HIGH CROWDS (Levels 8–10 on TouringPlans.com Crowd Calendar)

you more time in line than using it at any other child-friendly attraction in our plans.

Expedition Everest is our least frequently suggested FastPass+ attraction. While posted wait times can average 60–80 minutes during summer and more during holidays, getting to Everest first thing in the morning lets you avoid those lines and save FastPass+ for something else. Plus, it has a single-rider line—a great option if you can't get a FastPass+ reservation and you don't mind splitting up your group to ride.

Opening in 2016, **Rivers of Light** (page 219), a nighttime spectacular combining live music, floating lanterns, water screens, and animal imagery, will likely be a good choice for a day-of FastPass after the initial crowds have dissipated, after you've covered other attractions. If you're visiting right after the show debuts, though, you might be better off reserving FastPass+ before your trip.

FastPass+ kiosk locations in Animal Kingdom are as follows (also see the map on pages 204 and 205):

- To the left of Expedition Everest's entrance in Asia
- Near Dawa Bar in Asia
- In front of the Disney Outfitters store on Discovery Island and across the walkway near Island Mercantile
- In front of the MyMagic+ Service Center, to the left of the entrance at The Oasis

Same-Day FastPass+ Availability

The preceding advice tells you which attractions to focus on when making your *advance* FastPass+ reservations before you get to the park. Once you're in the park, you can make more FastPass+ reservations once your advance reservations have been used or have expired (you must cancel your expired FastPass+ before you can book another). The table opposite shows which attractions are likely to have day-of FastPasses available, and the approximate times at which they'll run out.

The OASIS

THOUGH THE FUNCTIONAL PURPOSE of The Oasis is the same as that of Main Street in the Magic Kingdom (that is, to funnel guests to the center of the park), it also serves as what Disney calls a "transitional experience." In plain English, this means that it sets the stage and gets you into the right mood to enjoy Animal Kingdom. You will know the minute you pass through the turnstiles that this is not just another Main Street. Where Main Street, Hollywood Boulevard, and the Epcot entrance plaza direct you like an arrow straight into the heart of the respective parks, The Oasis immediately envelops you in an environment that is replete with choices. There is not one broad thoroughfare, but rather multiple paths. Each will deliver you to Discovery Island at the center of the park, but which path you choose and what you see along the way is up to you. There is nothing obvious about where you are going, no Cinderella Castle or giant golf ball to beckon you. Instead there's a lush, green, canopied landscape with streams, grottoes, and waterfalls, an environment that promises adventure without revealing its nature.

The natural-habitat zoological exhibits in The Oasis are representative of the ones throughout the park. Although extraordinarily lush and beautiful, the exhibits are primarily designed for the comfort and well-being of the animals. A sign will identify the animal(s) in each exhibit, but there's no guarantee the animals will be immediately visible. Because most habitats are large and provide ample terrain for the occupants to hide, you must linger and concentrate, looking for small movements in the vegetation. When you do spot the animal, you may only make out a shadowy figure, or perhaps only a leg or a tail will be visible. In any event, don't expect the animals to stand out like a lump of coal in the snow. Animal watching Disney-style requires a sharp eye and a bit of effort.

unofficial **TIP**
The Oasis's exhibits are designed for the animals' comfort, so you need to be patient and look closely if you want to see these creatures.

TOURING TIPS The Oasis is a place at which to linger, a place to savor and appreciate. Although this is exactly what the designers intended, it will be largely lost on Disney-conditioned guests who blitz through at warp speed to queue up for the big attractions. If you're a blitzer in the morning, plan to spend some time in The Oasis on your way out of the park. The Oasis usually opens 30 minutes before and closes 30–60 minutes after the rest of the park.

▚ DISCOVERY ISLAND

DISCOVERY ISLAND IS AN ISLAND OF tropical greenery and whimsical equatorial African architecture, executed in vibrant hues of teal, yellow, red, and blue. Connected to the other lands by bridges, the island is the hub from which guests can access the park's various themed areas. A village is arrayed in a crescent around the base of Animal Kingdom's signature landmark, **The Tree of Life.** Towering 14 stories above the village, The Tree of Life is this park's version of Cinderella Castle or Spaceship Earth. Flanked by pools, meadows, and exotic gardens populated by a diversity of birds and animals, The Tree of Life houses a theater attraction inspired by the Disney/Pixar film *A Bug's Life.*

As you enter Discovery Island over the bridge from The Oasis and the park entrance, you'll see The Tree of Life directly ahead, at 12 o'clock. The bridge to Asia is to the right of the tree at 2 o'clock, with the bridge to DinoLand U.S.A. at roughly 4 o'clock. The bridge connecting The Oasis to Discovery Island is at 6 o'clock, the bridge to the future *Avatar* land is at 8 o'clock, and the bridge to Africa is at 11 o'clock.

Discovery Island is also the park's central headquarters for shopping, dining, and services. Here you'll find the **First Aid** and **Baby Care Centers,** plus FastPass+ kiosks. For Disney merchandise, try **Island Mercantile.** Counter-service food and snacks are available, but there are no sit-down eateries—the three full-service restaurants in the park are the **Rainforest Cafe,** to the left of the main entrance; **Tusker House Restaurant,** in Africa; and **Yak & Yeti Restaurant,** in Asia.

DISCOVERY ISLAND TRAILS Winding behind The Tree of Life is a series of walking trails that include around a dozen animal-viewing opportunities, from otters and kangaroos to lemurs, storks, and porcupines. One end of the path begins just before the bridge from Discovery Island to Africa, on the right side of the walkway; the other is to the right of the entrance to The Tree of Life. Besides the animals, you'll find verdant landscaping, waterfalls, and quiet spots to sit and reflect on your relationship with nature. Or nap. As we think Thoreau said, "Not until we have dozed do we begin to understand ourselves."

Meet Favorite Disney Pals at Adventurers Outpost (FastPass+) ★★★½

Appeal by Age PRESCHOOL ★★★★ GRADE SCHOOL ★★★★½ TEENS ★★★★
YOUNG ADULTS ★★★★ OVER 30 ★★★★ SENIORS ★★★★

What it is Character-greeting venue. **Scope and scale** Minor attraction. **When to go** First thing in the morning, after 5 p.m., or use FastPass+. **Authors' rating** Nicely themed (and air-conditioned); ★★★½. **Duration of experience** About 2 minutes. **Probable waiting time** About 20 minutes. **Queue speed** Fast.

DESCRIPTION AND COMMENTS An indoor, air-conditioned character-greeting location for Mickey and Minnie Mouse, Adventurers Outpost is decorated with photos, memorabilia, and souvenirs from the Mouses' world travels.

TOURING TIPS The Outpost features two greeting rooms with two identical sets of characters, so lines move fairly quickly. Good use of FastPass+ if you have kids too small to ride Expedition Everest or Dinosaur.

The Tree of Life / It's Tough to Be a Bug! (FastPass+) ★★★★

Appeal by Age PRESCHOOL ★★★½ GRADE SCHOOL ★★★★ TEENS ★★★★
YOUNG ADULTS ★★★★ OVER 30 ★★★★ SENIORS ★★★★½

What it is 3-D theater show. **Scope and scale** Major attraction. **When to go** Anytime. **Special comments** The theater is inside the tree. **Authors' rating** Zany and frenetic and not to be missed; ★★★★. **Duration of presentation** About 8 minutes. **Probable waiting time** 12–20 minutes.

DESCRIPTION AND COMMENTS The Tree of Life, apart from its size, is quite a work of art. Although from afar it is certainly magnificent and imposing, it is not until you examine the tree at close range that you truly appreciate its rich detail. What appears to be ancient gnarled bark is, in fact, hundreds of carvings that depict all manner of wildlife, each integrated seamlessly into the trunk, roots, and limbs of the tree. A stunning symbol of the interdependence of all living things, The Tree of Life is the most visually compelling structure to be found in any Disney park.

In sharp contrast to the grandeur of the tree is the subject of the attraction housed within its trunk. Called It's Tough to Be a Bug!, this humorous 3-D presentation is about the difficulties of being a very small creature. Contrasting with the relatively serious tone of Disney's Animal Kingdom in general, It's Tough to Be a Bug! stands virtually alone in providing some much-needed levity and whimsy. The show is similar to Mickey's PhilharMagic at the Magic Kingdom in that it combines a 3-D film with an arsenal of tactile and visual special effects. We rate Bug as not to be missed.

TOURING TIPS Although it's situated in the most eye-popping structure in the park, It's Tough to Be a Bug! is rarely crowded even on the busiest days, and FastPass+ is almost never needed. We recommend going in the morning after you've experienced Kilimanjaro Safaris, Kali River Rapids, Expedition Everest, and Dinosaur. If you miss the bugs in the morning, try again in the late afternoon.

Be advised that *It's Tough to Be a Bug!* is very intense and that the special effects will do a number on young children as well as anyone who's weirded out by insects.

Wilderness Explorers ★★★★

Appeal by Age PRESCHOOL ★★★★ GRADE SCHOOL ★★★★½ TEENS ★★★½
YOUNG ADULTS ★★★★ OVER 30 ★★★★ SENIORS ★★★★★

What it is Park-wide scavenger hunt and puzzle-solving adventure game. **Scope and scale** Diversion. **When to go** Sign up first thing in the morning and complete activities throughout the day. **Special comments** Collecting all 32 badges takes 3–5 hours, which can be done over several days. **Authors' rating** One of the best attractions in any Disney park; not to be missed; ★★★★.

DESCRIPTION AND COMMENTS Walt Disney World offers several interactive games in its theme parks, and Wilderness Explorers is the best of the bunch—a scavenger hunt based on Russell's Boy Scout–esque troop from the movie *Up.* Players earn "badges" (stickers given out by cast members) for completing predefined activities throughout the park. For example, to earn the Gorilla Badge, you walk the Pangani Forest Exploration Trail to observe how the primates behave, then mimic that behavior back to a cast member to show what you've seen.

Register for the game near the bridge from The Oasis to Discovery Island. You'll be given an instruction book and a map showing the park location for each badge to be earned.

Cast members have been specially trained for this game and can tailor the activities based on the age of the child playing: Small children might get an explanation about what deforestation means, for example, while older kids may have to figure out why tigers have stripes. It's tons of fun for kids and adults, and we play it every time we're in the park.

TOURING TIPS Activities are spread throughout the park, including areas to which many guests never venture. You have to ride specific attractions to earn certain badges, so using FastPass+ for those will save time.

▌▌ AFRICA

AFRICA IS THE LARGEST of Animal Kingdom's lands, and guests enter through **Harambe,** a Disneyfied version of a modern rural African town. A market is equipped with modern cash registers; dining options consist of a sit-down buffet, limited counter service, and snack stands. What distinguishes Harambe is its understatement: Far from the stereotypical great-white-hunter image of an African town, Harambe is definitely (and realistically) *not* exotic. The buildings, while interesting, are architecturally simple. Though better maintained and more idealized than the real McCoy, Disney's Harambe would be a lot more at home in Kenya than the Magic Kingdom's Main Street would be in small-town Missouri.

Harambe serves as the gateway to the African veldt habitat, Animal Kingdom's largest and most ambitious zoological exhibit. Access to the veldt is via the **Kilimanjaro Safaris** attraction, at the end of Harambe's main drag near the fat-trunked baobab tree. Harambe is also the departure point for the train to **Rafiki's Planet Watch** and **Conservation Station,** the park's veterinary headquarters.

Festival of the Lion King (FastPass+) ★★★★

Appeal by Age PRESCHOOL ★★★★½ GRADE SCHOOL ★★★★½ TEENS ★★★★½ YOUNG ADULTS ★★★★½ OVER 30 ★★★★½ SENIORS ★★★★½

What it is Theater-in-the-round stage show. **Scope and scale** Major attraction. **When to go** Before 11 a.m., after 4 p.m., or use FastPass+. Check your park map or *Times Guide* for showtimes. **Authors' rating** Upbeat, energetic, and spectacular; not to be missed; ★★★★. **Duration of presentation** 30 minutes. **Preshow entertainment** None. **When to arrive** 20–30 minutes before showtime.

DESCRIPTION AND COMMENTS This energetic production, inspired by Disney's *Lion King* feature, is part stage show, part parade, part circus. Guests are seated in four sets of bleachers surrounding the stage and organized into separate cheering sections, which are called on to make elephant, warthog, giraffe, and lion noises (you won't be alone if you don't know how to make a giraffe or warthog noise). There is a great deal of parading around, some acrobatics, and a lot of singing and dancing. By our count, every tune from *The Lion King* is belted out and reprised several times. No joke—if you don't know the words to all the songs by the end of the show, you must have been asleep.

TOURING TIPS *Festival of the Lion King* is a big draw, so try to see the first show in the morning or one of the last two shows at night. For midday performances, you'll need to queue up at least 35–45 minutes before showtime; to minimize waiting in the hot sun, don't hop in line until cast members give the word to do so. The bleachers can make viewing difficult for the height-deficient—If you have small children or short adults in your party, try to snag a seat higher up. Rarely a good use of FastPass+.

Kilimanjaro Safaris (FastPass+) ★★★★★

Appeal by Age PRESCHOOL ★★★★½ GRADE SCHOOL ★★★★½ TEENS ★★★★½ YOUNG ADULTS ★★★★½ OVER 30 ★★★★½ SENIORS ★★★★★

What it is Simulated ride through an African wildlife reservation. **Scope and scale** Super-headliner. **When to go** As soon as the park opens or in the 2 hours before closing, or use FastPass+. **Authors' rating** Not to be missed; ★★★★★. **Duration of ride** About 20 minutes. **Average wait in line per 100 people ahead of you** 4 minutes; assumes full-capacity operation with 18-second dispatch interval. **Loading speed** Fast.

DESCRIPTION AND COMMENTS The park's premier zoological attraction, Kilimanjaro Safaris offers an exceptionally realistic, albeit brief, imitation of an actual African photo safari. Thirty-two guests at a time board tall, open safari vehicles and are dispatched into a simulated African veldt habitat. Animals such as zebras, wildebeests, impalas, Thomson's gazelles, giraffes, and even rhinos roam apparently free, while predators such as lions, as well as potentially dangerous large animals like hippos, are separated from both prey and guests by all-but-invisible, natural-appearing barriers. Although the animals have more than 100 acres of savanna, woodland, streams, and rocky hills to call home, careful placement of water holes, forage, and salt licks ensures that the critters are hanging out by the road when safari vehicles roll by.

A scripted narration provides a storyline about poachers in the area while an onboard guide points out and identifies the various animals encountered. Toward the end of the ride, the safari chases the poachers, who are after elephants.

Having traveled in Kenya and Tanzania, I (Bob) will tell you that Disney has done an amazing job of replicating the sub-Saharan east-African landscape. The main difference that an east African would notice is that Disney's version is greener and, generally speaking, less barren. As on a real African safari, what animals you see, and how many, is pretty much a matter of luck. We've experienced Kilimanjaro Safaris more than 100 times and had a different experience on each trip.

Winding through the Safaris is Disney's **Wild Africa Trek,** a behind-the-scenes tour that takes you into several of the attraction's animal enclosures (3 hours, $201 per person, guests age 8 and older). As you drive past the hippo pool or over the crocodile pool, look up for a series of rope bridges towering far above the ground. You may see Trekkers on tour.

We hear the Safaris will begin offering nighttime tours in late 2015 or early 2016, probably around the time that *Rivers of Light* (see page 219) debuts. This will give Animal Kingdom guests additional after-dark entertainment options and be a unique viewing experience. No word on whether the animal lineup will change to include more-nocturnal creatures.

TOURING TIPS Kilimanjaro Safaris is Animal Kingdom's number-two draw behind Expedition Everest. From a touring standpoint, this is good news: By distributing guests evenly throughout the park, Expedition Everest makes it unnecessary to run to Kilimanjaro Safaris first thing in the morning. Our Animal Kingdom touring plan has you obtain FastPass+ reservations for the Safaris in the afternoon—while you wait for your FastPass+ return window, you'll have plenty of time to eat and tour the rest of Africa.

Waits for Kilimanjaro Safaris diminish in late afternoon, sometimes as early as 3:30 p.m. but more commonly somewhat later.

If you want to take photos, keep in mind that the vehicle isn't guaranteed to stop at any location, although the drivers try their best to do so when big animals are sighted. Be prepared to snap at any time. As for the ride, it's not that rough. Finally, the only thing that a young child might find scary is crossing an "old bridge" that seems to collapse under your truck.

Pangani Forest Exploration Trail ★★★

| Appeal by Age | PRESCHOOL ★★★★ | GRADE SCHOOL ★★★★ | TEENS ★★★★ |
| YOUNG ADULTS ★★★★½ | | OVER 30 ★★★★ | SENIORS ★★★★½ |

What it is Walk-through zoological exhibit. **Scope and scale** Major attraction. **When to go** Anytime. **Authors' rating** ★★★★. **Duration of tour** About 20–25 minutes.

DESCRIPTION AND COMMENTS Because guests disembark from the safari at the entrance to the Pangani Forest Exploration Trail, many guests try the trail immediately after the safari. Winding between the domain of two troops of lowland gorillas, it's hard to see what, if anything, separates you from the primates. Also on the trail are a hippo pool with an underwater-viewing area, and a naked-mole-rat exhibit (we promise we're not making this up). A highlight of the trail is an exotic bird aviary so craftily designed that you can barely tell you're in an enclosure.

TOURING TIPS The Pangani Forest Exploration Trail is lush, beautiful, and jammed to the gills with people much of the time. Guests exiting the safari can choose between returning to Harambe or walking the Pangani

Forest Exploration Trail. Not unexpectedly, many opt for the trail. Thus, when the safari is operating at full tilt, it spews hundreds of guests every couple of minutes onto the Exploration Trail. The one-way trail in turn becomes so clogged that nobody can move or see much of anything. After a minute or two, however, you catch the feel of the mob moving forward in small lurches. From then on you shift, elbow, grunt, and wriggle your way along, every so often coming to an animal exhibit. Here you endeavor to work your way close to the rail but are opposed by people trapped against the rail who are trying to rejoin the surging crowd. The animals, as well as their natural-habitat enclosures, are pretty nifty if you can fight close enough to see them.

Clearly this attraction is either badly designed, misplaced, or both. Your only real chance for enjoying it is to walk through before 10 a.m. (i.e., before the safari hits full stride) or after 2:30 p.m.

Another strategy, especially if you're more into the wildlife than the thrill rides, is to schedule a FastPass+ reservation for the Safaris 60–90 minutes after the park opens. That's long enough for an uncrowded, lei- surely tour of the Pangani Forest Exploration Trail and a quick snack before you go on safari.

RAFIKI'S PLANET WATCH

THIS AREA ISN'T REALLY a "land" and not really an attraction either. Our best guess is that Disney uses the name as an umbrella for Conservation Station, the petting zoo, and the environmental exhibits accessible from Harambe via the Wildlife Express Train. Presumably, Disney hopes that invoking Rafiki (a beloved character from *The Lion King*) will stimulate guests to make the effort to check out things in this far-flung outpost of the park.

Conservation Station and Affection Section ★★★

| Appeal by Age | PRESCHOOL ★★★½ | GRADE SCHOOL ★★★★ | TEENS ★★★ |
| YOUNG ADULTS ★★★½ | OVER 30 ★★★½ | | SENIORS ★★★★ |

What it is Behind-the-scenes walk-through educational exhibit and petting zoo. **Scope and scale** Minor attraction. **When to go** Anytime. **Special comments** Opens 30 minutes after the rest of the park. **Authors' rating** Evolving; ★★★. Probable waiting time None.

DESCRIPTION AND COMMENTS Conservation Station is Animal Kingdom's veterinary and conservation headquarters. Located on the perimeter of the African section of the park, Conservation Station is, strictly speaking, a backstage, working facility. Here guests can meet wildlife experts, observe some of the Station's ongoing projects, and learn about the behind-the-scenes operations of the park. The Station includes, among other things, a rehabilitation area for injured animals and a nursery for recently born (or hatched) critters. Vets and other experts are on hand to answer questions.

While there are several permanent exhibits, including the Affection Section (an animal-petting area), what you see at Conservation Station will largely depend on what's going on when you arrive. On the days we visited, there wasn't enough happening to warrant waiting in line twice (coming and going) for the train.

You can access Conservation Station by taking the Wildlife Express train directly from Harambe. To return to the center of the park, continue the loop from Conservation Station back to Harambe.

TOURING TIPS Conservation Station is interesting, but you have to invest a little effort, and it helps to be inquisitive. Because it's so removed from the rest of the park, you'll never bump into Conservation Station unless you take the train.

Habitat Habit!

DESCRIPTION AND COMMENTS On the pedestrian path between the train station and Conservation Station, Habitat Habit! consists of a tiny collection of signs about wildlife and a few animals. Park maps call it an attraction, which we find absurd.

Wildlife Express Train ★★

Appeal by Age	PRESCHOOL ★★★★	GRADE SCHOOL ★★★½	TEENS ★★★½
YOUNG ADULTS ★★★	OVER 30 ★★★½		SENIORS ★★★½

What it is Scenic railroad ride to Rafiki's Planet Watch and Conservation Station. **Scope and scale** Minor attraction. **When to go** Anytime. **Special comments** Opens 30 minutes after the rest of the park. **Authors' rating** *Zzzzz;* ★★. **Duration of ride** About 5–7 minutes one-way. **Average wait in line per 100 people ahead of you** 9 minutes. Loading speed Moderate.

DESCRIPTION AND COMMENTS A transportation ride that snakes behind the African wildlife reserve as it makes its loop connecting Harambe to Rafiki's Planet Watch and Conservation Station. En route, you see the nighttime enclosures for the animals that populate the Kilimanjaro Safaris. Similarly, returning to Harambe, you see the backstage areas of Asia. Regardless of the direction in which you're heading, the sights are not especially interesting.

TOURING TIPS Most guests will embark for Rafiki's Planet Watch and Conservation Station after experiencing the Kilimanjaro Safaris and the Pangani Forest Exploration Trail. Thus, the train begins to get crowded between 10 and 11 a.m.

◧ ASIA

CROSSING THE ASIA BRIDGE from Discovery Island, you enter Asia through the village of Anandapur, a veritable collage of Asian themes inspired by the architecture and ruins of India, Thailand, Indonesia, and Nepal. Situated near the bank of the Chakranadi River (translation: "the river that runs in circles") and surrounded by lush vegetation, Anandapur provides access to a gibbon exhibit and to Asia's two feature attractions, the **Kali River Rapids** white-water-raft ride and **Expedition Everest.** Also in Asia is **Flights of Wonder,** an educational production about birds.

Expedition Everest—yep, another mountain, and at 200 feet, the tallest in Florida—is a super-headliner roller coaster. You board an old mountain railway destined for the foot of Mount Everest that ends up racing both forward and backward through caverns and frigid canyons en route to paying a social call on the Abominable Snowman. Expedition Everest is billed as a "family thrill ride," which means simply that it's more like Big Thunder Mountain Railroad than like the Rock 'n' Roller Coaster.

Debuting in 2016, the nighttime *Rivers of Light* show (see page 219) will combine music, water screens, video projections, and more on the Discovery River, with sections around Asia and Dino-Land U.S.A.

Expedition Everest (*FastPass+*) ★★★★½

Appeal by Age	PRESCHOOL ★★★½	GRADE SCHOOL ★★★★½	TEENS ★★★★★
YOUNG ADULTS ★★★★★		OVER 30 ★★★★★	SENIORS ★★★★

What it is High-speed outdoor roller coaster through Nepalese mountain village. **Scope and scale** Super-headliner. **When to go** Before 9:30 a.m. or after 3 p.m., or use FastPass+. **Special comments** 44" minimum height requirement. Switching-off option provided (see page 93). **Authors' rating** Contains some of the park's most stunning visual elements; not to be missed; ★★★★½. **Duration of ride** 3½ minutes. **Average wait in line per 100 people ahead of you** Just under 4 minutes; assumes 2 tracks operating. **Loading speed** Moderate–fast.

DESCRIPTION AND COMMENTS The first true roller coaster in Animal Kingdom, Expedition Everest earned the park's longest waits in line from the moment it opened—and for good reason. Your journey begins in an elaborate waiting area modeled after a Nepalese village; then you board an old train headed for the top of Mount Everest. Throughout the waiting area are posted notes from previous expeditions, some with cryptic observations regarding a mysterious creature said to guard the mountain. These ominous signs are ignored (as if you have a choice!), resulting in a high-speed encounter with the Abominable Snowman himself.

The ride consists of tight turns (some while traveling backward), hills, and dips, but no loops or inversions. From your departure at the loading station through your first high-speed descent, you'll see some of the most spectacular panoramas available in Walt Disney World. On a clear day, you can see the buildings of Coronado Springs Resort, Epcot's Spaceship Earth, and possibly downtown Orlando. But look quickly, because you'll immediately be propelled, projectile-like, through the inner and outer reaches of the mountain. The final drop and last few turns are among the best coaster effects Disney has ever designed.

A few minor criticisms: At a couple of points, your vehicle stops while the ride's track is reconfigured, affecting the attraction's continuity. And while the Audio-Animatronic Yeti is undoubtedly impressive, he breaks down more than a 30-year-old Fiat. Most days Disney just simulates the Yeti moving by flashing a strobe light on his motionless body. But don't let these small shortcomings stop you from riding.

The coaster reaches a top speed of around 50 mph, just about twice that of Space Mountain, so expect to see the usual warnings for health and safety. The first few seats of these vehicles offer the best front-seat experience of any Disney coaster, indoor or out. If at all possible, ask to sit up front. Also, look for the animal poop on display in the FastPass+ return line—a deliberate attempt at verisimilitude, or did Disney run out of money for ride props and use whatever they could find? You decide.

TOURING TIPS Ride Everest as soon as the park instead of using FastPass+ This way you can save your reservations for other attractions or another

Everest ride later. In the latter case, try riding during the last hour the park is open, or use the single-rider line.

Flights of Wonder ★★★★

| Appeal by Age | PRESCHOOL ★★★★ | GRADE SCHOOL ★★★★½ | TEENS ★★★★ |
| YOUNG ADULTS ★★★★ | | OVER 30 ★★★★½ | SENIORS ★★★★½ |

What it is Stadium show about birds. **Scope and scale** Major attraction. **When to go** Anytime. **Special comments** Performance times listed in handout park map or *Times Guide*. **Authors' rating** Unique; ★★★★. **Duration of presentation** 30 minutes. **Preshow entertainment** None. **When to arrive** 20–30 minutes before showtime.

DESCRIPTION AND COMMENTS Both interesting and fun, *Flights of Wonder* is well paced and showcases a surprising number of different bird species. The show focuses on the natural talents and characteristics of the various species, so don't expect to see, say, parrots riding bicycles. The natural behaviors, however, far surpass any tricks learned from humans. Overall, the presentation is fascinating, and it exceeds most guests' expectations.

TOURING TIPS *Flights of Wonder* plays at the stadium located near the Asia Bridge on the walkway into Asia. Though the stadium is covered, it's not air-conditioned; thus, early-morning and late-afternoon performances are more comfortable.

Kali River Rapids *(FastPass+)* ★★★½

| Appeal by Age | PRESCHOOL ★★★★ | GRADE SCHOOL ★★★★½ | TEENS ★★★★ |
| YOUNG ADULTS ★★★★½ | | OVER 30 ★★★★½ | SENIORS ★★★★½ |

What it is Whitewater raft ride. **Scope and scale** Headliner. **When to go** First or last hour the park is open, or use FastPass+. **Special comments** You're guaranteed to get wet. Opens 30 minutes after the rest of the park; 38″ minimum height requirement. Switching-off option provided (see page 93). **Authors' rating** Short but scenic; ★★★½. **Duration of ride** About 5 minutes. **Average wait in line per 100 people ahead of you** 5 minutes. **Loading speed** Moderate.

DESCRIPTION AND COMMENTS Whitewater raft rides have been a hot-weather favorite of theme park patrons for more than 20 years. The ride itself consists of an unguided trip down an artificial river in a circular rubber raft with a top-mounted platform seating 12 people. The raft essentially floats free in the current and is washed downstream through rapids and waves. Because the river is fairly wide, with numerous currents, eddies, and obstacles, there's no telling exactly where the raft will drift. Thus, each trip is different and exciting.

What distinguishes Kali River Rapids from other theme park raft rides is Disney's trademark attention to visual detail. Where many raft rides essentially plunge down a concrete ditch, Kali River Rapids flows through a dense rainforest and past waterfalls, temple ruins, and bamboo thickets, emerging into a cleared area where greedy loggers have ravaged the forest, and finally drifting back under the tropical canopy as the river cycles back to Anandapur. Along the way, your raft runs a gauntlet of raging cataracts, logjams, and other dangers.

The queuing area, which winds through an ancient Southeast Asian temple, is one of the most striking and visually interesting settings of any Disney attraction. And though the sights on the raft trip itself are also first-class, the attraction is marginal in two important respects. First, it's only about 3½ minutes on the water, and second, well . . . it's a weenie ride. Sure, you get wet, but otherwise the drops and rapids aren't all that exciting.

TOURING TIPS This attraction is hugely popular on hot summer days. Ride Kali River Rapids during the first or last hour the park is open or use Fast-Pass+. Again, you'll probably get drenched on this ride—we recommend wearing shorts to the park and bringing along a jumbo-sized trash bag or bin liner, as well as a smaller plastic bag. Before boarding the raft, take off your socks and punch a hole in your jumbo bag for your head. Though you can also cut holes for your arms, you'll probably stay drier with your arms inside the bag. Use the smaller plastic bag to wrap around your shoes. If you're worried about mussing your 'do, bring a third bag for your head.

Other tips for staying dry (make that drier) include wearing as little as the law and Disney allow and storing a change of clothes in a park rental locker. Sandals are the perfect footwear for water rides. If you don't have sandals, try to prop your feet up above the bottom of the raft.

Maharajah Jungle Trek ★★★★

Appeal by Age	PRESCHOOL ★★★★	GRADE SCHOOL ★★★★	TEENS ★★★★
YOUNG ADULTS ★★★½		OVER 30 ★★★★	SENIORS ★★★★½

What it is Walk-through zoological exhibit. **Scope and scale** Headliner. **When to go** Anytime. **Special comments** Opens 30 minutes after the rest of the park. **Authors' rating** A standard-setter for natural habitat design; ★★★★. Duration of tour About 20–30 minutes.

DESCRIPTION AND COMMENTS The Maharajah Jungle Trek is a zoological nature walk similar to the Pangani Forest Exploration Trail, but with an Asian setting and Asian animals. You start with Komodo dragons and then work up to Malayan flying foxes. Next is a cave with fruit bats. Ruins of the maharaja's palace provide the setting for Bengal tigers. From the top of a parapet in the palace you can view a herd of blackbuck antelope and Asian deer. The trek concludes with an aviary.

Labyrinthine, overgrown, and elaborately detailed, the temple ruin would be a compelling attraction even without the animals. Throw in a few bats, bucks, and Bengals and you're in for a treat.

TOURING TIPS The Jungle Trek doesn't get as jammed up as the Pangani Forest Exploration Trail and is a good choice for midday touring when most other attractions are crowded. The downside, of course, is that the exhibit showcases tigers, bats, and other creatures that might not be as active in the heat of the day as mad dogs and Englishmen.

Rivers of Light (opens 2016)

What it is Nighttime spectacular. **Scope and scale** Major attraction. **When to go** Check your *Times Guide* for showtimes.

DESCRIPTION AND COMMENTS Animal Kingdom has never had a nighttime event along the lines of the Magic Kingdom's *Wishes* or DHS's *Fantasmic!* One reason is that fireworks would startle the animals; another was that up to now there simply weren't enough attractions to keep the park open for 12–14 hours per day. In preparation for the 2017 opening of Pandora: The Land of Avatar, though, Animal Kingdom is adding both the *Rivers of Light* nighttime spectacular and, rumor has it, a nighttime safari (see page 214).

The show will be staged in the middle of the Discovery River. Disney hasn't released many details about the show's plot, but we do know it'll feature sprayed water screens onto which animal- and nature-related films will be projected. Disney also promises "floating lanterns" and live music. We think there'll also be dramatic lighting effects, but no fireworks.

TOURING TIPS Judging from the construction going on around the Discovery River, we expect there to be two seating areas, at least one of them dedicated to FastPass+. One seating area will be in Asia, on the riverfront next to Expedition Everest; the second will be in DinoLand U.S.A.

DINOLAND U.S.A.

THIS MOST TYPICALLY DISNEY OF ANIMAL KINGDOM'S lands is a cross between an anthropological dig and a quirky roadside attraction. Accessible via the bridge from Discovery Island, DinoLand U.S.A. is home to a children's play area, a nature trail, a 1,500-seat amphitheater, and **Dinosaur,** one of Animal Kingdom's two thrill rides.

The Boneyard ★★★½

Appeal by Age	PRESCHOOL ★★★★½	GRADE SCHOOL ★★★★½	TEENS ★★★★
YOUNG ADULTS ★★★½	OVER 30 ★★★		SENIORS ★★★

What it is Elaborate playground. **Scope and scale** Diversion. **When to go** Anytime. **Special comments** Opens 30 minutes after the rest of the park. **Authors' rating** Stimulating fun for children; ★★★½. **Duration of visit** Varies. **Probable waiting time** None.

DESCRIPTION AND COMMENTS This attraction is an elaborate playground, particularly appealing to kids age 12 and younger, but visually appealing to all ages. Arranged in the form of a rambling open-air dig site, The Boneyard offers plenty of opportunity for exploration and letting off steam. Playground equipment consists of the "skeletons" of *Triceratops, T. rex, Brachiosaurus,* and the like, on which children can swing, slide, and climb. In addition, there are sandpits for little ones to rummage through for bones and fossils.

TOURING TIPS Not the cleanest Disney attraction, but certainly one where younger children will want to spend some time. Aside from getting dirty, or at least sandy, be aware that The Boneyard gets mighty hot in the Florida sun. Keep your kids well hydrated and drag them into the shade from time to time. If your children will let you, save the playground until after you have experienced the main attractions. Because The Boneyard is so close to the center of the park, it's easy to stop in whenever your kids get itchy. While the little ones clamber around on giant femurs and ribs, you can sip a tall cool one in the shade (still keeping an eye on them, of course).

Be aware that The Boneyard rambles over about a half-acre and is multistoried. It's pretty easy to lose sight of a small child in the playground. Fortunately, there's only one entrance and exit.

Dinosaur *(FastPass+)* ★★★★

Appeal by Age	PRESCHOOL ★★★	GRADE SCHOOL ★★★★	TEENS ★★★★½
YOUNG ADULTS ★★★★	OVER 30 ★★★★		SENIORS ★★★★

What it is Motion-simulator dark ride. **Scope and scale** Super-headliner. **When to go** Before 10:30 a.m., after 4:30 p.m., or use FastPass+. **Special comments**

40" minimum height requirement. Switching-off option provided (see page 93). **Authors' rating** Not to be missed; ★★★★. **Duration of ride** 3½ minutes. **Average wait in line per 100 people ahead of you** 3 minutes; assumes full-capacity operation with 18-second dispatch interval. **Loading speed** Fast.

DESCRIPTION AND COMMENTS Dinosaur is a combination track ride and motion simulator. In addition to moving along a cleverly hidden track, the ride vehicle also bucks and pitches (the simulator part) in sync with the visuals and special effects.

The plot has you traveling back in time on a mission of rescue and conservation. Your objective: to haul back a living dinosaur before the species becomes extinct. Whoever is operating the clock, however, cuts it a little close, and you arrive on the prehistoric scene just as a giant asteroid is hurtling toward Earth. General mayhem ensues as you evade carnivorous predators, catch Barney, and get the heck out of Dodge before the asteroid hits.

Dinosaur serves up nonstop action from beginning to end, with brilliant visual effects. Elaborate even by Disney standards, its tense, frenetic ride is embellished by the entire Imagineering arsenal of high-tech gimmickry.

TOURING TIPS Disney situated Dinosaur in such a remote corner of the park that guests have to poke around to find it. This, in conjunction with the overwhelming popularity of Kilimanjaro Safaris and Expedition Everest, makes Dinosaur the easiest super-headliner attraction at Disney World to get on. Even so, try to ride early in the day, after Expedition Everest.

Primeval Whirl *(FastPass+)* ★★★

Appeal by Age	PRESCHOOL ★★★½	GRADE SCHOOL ★★★★	TEENS ★★★★
YOUNG ADULTS ★★★½		OVER 30 ★★★½	SENIORS ★★★

What it is Small coaster. **Scope and scale** Minor attraction. **When to go** First or last hour the park is open or use FastPass+. **Special comments** 48" minimum height requirement. Switching-off option provided (see page 93). **Authors' rating** "Wild mouse" on steroids; ★★★. **Duration of ride** Almost 2½ minutes. **Average wait in line per 100 people ahead of you** 4½ minutes. **Loading speed** Slow.

DESCRIPTION AND COMMENTS Primeval Whirl is a small coaster with short drops and curves, and it runs through the jaws of a dinosaur, among other things. What makes this coaster different is that the cars also spin. You can't control the spinning—it starts and stops according to how the ride is programmed. Sometimes the spin is braked to a jarring halt after half a revolution, and sometimes it's allowed to make one or two complete turns. The complete spins are fun, but the screeching-stop half-spins are almost painful. If you subtract the time it takes to ratchet up the first hill, the actual ride time is about 90 seconds.

TOURING TIPS As for Space Mountain, the ride is duplicated side-by-side, but with only one queue. When it runs smoothly, about 700 people per side can whirl in an hour—a goodly number for this type of attraction, but not enough to preclude long waits on busy-to-moderate days. If you want to ride, try to get on before 10 a.m.

Theater in the Wild / *Finding Nemo—The Musical* *(FastPass+)* ★★★★

Appeal by Age	PRESCHOOL ★★★★½	GRADE SCHOOL ★★★★½	TEENS ★★★★
YOUNG ADULTS ★★★★½		OVER 30 ★★★★½	SENIORS ★★★★½

What it is Enclosed venue for live stage shows. **Scope and scale** Major attraction. **When to go** Anytime. **Special comments** Performance times are listed in the handout park map or *Times Guide.* **Authors' rating** Not to be missed; ★★★★. **Duration of presentation** About 35 minutes. **When to arrive** 30 minutes before showtime.

DESCRIPTION AND COMMENTS Another chapter in the Pixar-ization of Disney theme parks, *Finding Nemo* is arguably the most elaborate live show in any Disney World theme park. Incorporating dancing, special effects, and sophisticated digital backdrops of the undersea world, it features on-stage human performers retelling Nemo's story with colorful, larger-than-life puppets. To be fair, "puppets" doesn't adequately convey the size or detail of these props, many of which are as big as a car and require two people to manipulate. An original musical score was written for the show, which is a must-see for most Animal Kingdom guests. A few scenes, such as one in which Nemo's mom is eaten, may be too intense for some very small children. Some of the midshow musical numbers slow the pace, so the main concern for parents is whether the kids can sit still for an entire show. With that in mind, we advise parents to catch an afternoon performance—around 3 p.m. would be great—after seeing the rest of Animal Kingdom. If the kids get restless, you can either leave the show and catch the afternoon parade, or end your day at the park.

TOURING TIPS To get a seat, show up 20–25 minutes in advance for morning and late-afternoon shows, and 30–35 minutes in advance for shows scheduled between noon and 4:30 p.m. Access to the theater is via a relatively narrow pedestrian path—if you arrive as the previous show is letting out, you'll feel like a salmon swimming upstream.

Rivers of Light (opens 2016)   See description on page 219.

TriceraTop Spin   ★★

Appeal by Age	PRESCHOOL ★★★★½	GRADE SCHOOL ★★★★	TEENS ★★★
YOUNG ADULTS ★★★	OVER 30 ★★★		SENIORS ★★★½

What it is Hub-and-spoke midway ride. **Scope and scale** Minor attraction. **When to go** Before noon or after 3 p.m. **Authors' rating** Dumbo's prehistoric forebear; ★★. **Duration of ride** 1½ minutes. **Average wait in line per 100 people ahead of you** 10 minutes. **Loading speed** Slow.

DESCRIPTION AND COMMENTS Another Dumbo-like ride. Here you spin around a Central Plaza until a dinosaur pops out of the top of the hub. You'd think with the collective imagination of the Walt Disney Company, they'd come up with something a little more creative.

TOURING TIPS An attraction for the children. Come back later if the wait exceeds 20 minutes.

▌ LIVE ENTERTAINMENT *in* DISNEY'S ANIMAL KINGDOM

ANIMAL ENCOUNTERS Throughout the day, Animal Kingdom staff conduct impromptu short lectures on specific animals at the park. Look for a cast member in safari garb holding a bird, a reptile, or a small mammal.

A small interactive event titled **Winged Encounters—The Kingdom Takes Flight,** featuring macaws and their handlers, takes place on Discovery Island in front of The Tree of Life. Guests can talk to the animal's trainers and see the birds fly around the middle of the park. The concept is similar to *Flights of Wonder* (see page 218) on a much smaller scale. Check the *Times Guide* for showtimes and the exact location.

GOODWILL AMBASSADORS A number of Asian and African natives are on-hand throughout the park. Both gracious and knowledgeable, they are delighted to discuss their country and its wildlife. Look for them in Harambe and along the Pangani Forest Exploration Trail in Africa, and in Anandapur and along the Maharajah Jungle Trek in Asia. They can also be found near the main entrance and at The Oasis.

STREET PERFORMERS Can be found most of the time at Harambe in Africa and at Anandapur in Asia. Far and away the most intriguing of these performers is a stilt walker named **DiVine** (★★★★). Bedecked in foliage and luxuriant vines, she blends so completely with Animal Kingdom's dense flora that you don't notice her until she moves. We've seen guests standing less than a foot away gasp in amazement as DiVine brushes them with a leafy tendril. Usually found on the path between Asia and Africa, DiVine is a must-see. Video of her is available at **YouTube** (search for "DiVine Disney's Animal Kingdom").

DISNEY'S ANIMAL KINGDOM TOURING PLANS

TOURING ANIMAL KINGDOM is not as complicated as touring the other parks because it has fewer attractions. Also, most Animal Kingdom rides, shows, and zoological exhibits are oriented to the entire family, thus eliminating differences of opinion regarding how to spend the day. At Animal Kingdom, the whole family can pretty much see and enjoy everything together.

Because there are fewer attractions than at the other parks, expect the crowds at Animal Kingdom to be more concentrated. If a line seems unusually long, ask an Animal Kingdom cast member what the estimated wait is. If the wait exceeds your tolerance, try the same attraction again after 3 p.m., while a show is in progress at the Theater in the Wild in DinoLand U.S.A., or while some special event is going on.

unofficial **TIP**
Until Pandora: The Land of Avatar opens in 2017, the limited number of attractions in Animal Kingdom can work to your advantage.

We've listed the estimated FastPass+ return times for which you should try to make reservations. (The touring plan should work with anything close to the times shown.) Because Disney limits how many FastPass+ reservations you can get, we've listed in the plans the attractions most likely to need FastPass+, too. Check **touringplans.com** for the latest information.

"NOT A TOURING PLAN" TOURING PLANS

FOR THE TYPE-B READER, these touring plans avoid detailed, step-by-step strategies for saving every last minute in line. Use these guidelines to avoid the longest waits in line while having maximum flexibility to see whatever interests you in a particular part of the park.

FOR PARENTS AND ADULTS ARRIVING AT PARK OPENING Obtain FastPass+ reservations for Expedition Everest in Asia; then begin a land-by-land counterclockwise tour of the park, starting in DinoLand U.S.A. Work in shows as you near them, but leave *Finding Nemo—The Musical* for last. Eat dinner and end the night with *Rivers of Light* (opens 2016).

FOR PARENTS AND ADULTS ARRIVING LATE MORNING Get FastPass+ reservations for Kilimanjaro Safaris; then begin a counterclockwise tour of the park starting in Africa, saving Kali River Rapids and Expedition Everest for last. Eat dinner and end the night with *Rivers of Light* (opens 2016).

BEFORE YOU GO

1. Call ☎ 407-824-4321 before you go to check the park's hours of operation.
2. Purchase your admission and make FastPass+ reservations before arrival.

Disney's Animal Kingdom One-Day Touring Plan

The Animal Kingdom One-Day Touring Plan assumes a willingness to experience all major rides and shows. Be forewarned that Dinosaur, Primeval Whirl, and Kali River Rapids are sometimes frightening to children under age 8. Similarly, the theater attraction at The Tree of Life might be too intense for some preschoolers. When following the touring plan, simply skip any attraction you do not wish to experience.

START TIMES FOR FASTPASS+ Dinosaur, 9 a.m.; Kali River Rapids, 10 a.m.; Kilimanjaro Safaris, 12:15 p.m.

1. Arrive 30–40 minutes prior to opening. Get guide maps and the *Times Guide*.

2. Experience Expedition Everest in Asia.

3. In DinoLand U.S.A., ride TriceraTop Spin if you have young children in your group.

4. Ride Primeval Whirl.

5. Follow the signs to Dinosaur and ride.

6. Ride Kali River Rapids in Asia.

7. Take the Wildlife Express Train from Africa to Conservation Station and Rafiki's Planet Watch. Tour the area and take the train back to Africa.

8. Eat lunch.

9. Ride Kilimanjaro Safaris in Africa.

10. Walk the Pangani Forest Exploration Trail.

11. Earn a couple of badges playing Wilderness Explorers.

12. Explore the trails and exhibits aroundThe Tree of Life.

13. See *Festival of the Lion King* in Africa.

14. See *Flights of Wonder.*

15. Walk the Maharajah Jungle Trek in Asia.

16. See *It's Tough to Be a Bug!* on Discovery Island.

17. See *Finding Nemo—The Musical* in DinoLand U.S.A.

18. Eat dinner.

19. See *Rivers of Light* in Asia.

PART TWELVE

DISNEY'S HOLLYWOOD STUDIOS

◖ DHS: *A* BRIEF HISTORY

FORMERLY KNOWN AS DISNEY-MGM STUDIOS, Disney's Hollywood Studios was hatched from a corporate rivalry and a wild, twisted plot. At a time when The Walt Disney Company was weak and fighting off "greenmail"—hostile-takeover bids—Universal's parent company at the time, MCA, announced that it was going to build an Orlando clone of its wildly successful Universal Studios Hollywood theme park. Behind the scenes, MCA was courting the real estate–rich Bass brothers of Texas, in hopes of securing their investment in the project. The Basses, however, defected to the Disney camp and were front and center when Michael Eisner suddenly announced that Disney, too, would build a movie theme park in Florida. A construction race ensued, but Universal, in the middle of developing new attraction technologies, was no match for Disney, which could import proven concepts and attractions from its other parks. In the end, Disney's Hollywood Studios opened May 1, 1989, more than a year before Universal Studios Florida.

THE EARLY YEARS

ONCE UPON A TIME, the Studios' soundstages and facilities produced many television shows and films, both live-action and animated. The 2003 Disney film *Brother Bear* was largely drawn—by hand, yet!—at what used to be Disney Feature Animation Florida; cinema nerds will recognize the park's landscape in the background of Jim Varney's magnum opus, *Ernest Saves Christmas*. Television series filmed here spanned everything from a revival of the classic game show *Let's Make a Deal* to the syndicated Hulk Hogan fiasco *Thunder in Paradise*.

The Studios also hosted attractions that educated guests about TV and film production, the best known being a tram ride through and walking tour of the park's backlot. Others included the *Monster Sound Show,* which used audience volunteers to show how sound effects were added to films, and *SuperStar Television,* which reenacted famous TV scenes using "green screen" technology and park guests as actors.

THE END OF THE MGM CONNECTION

SO WHAT HAPPENED to "Disney-MGM Studios"? Disney purchased Pixar Animation Studios after partnering with the company on a series of highly successful films, including *Toy Story; A Bug's Life; Monsters, Inc.; Finding Nemo;* and *The Incredibles.* The cost of continuing an association with MGM, coupled with Pixar's arguably greater popularity, probably influenced Disney's decision to rename the park in 2008. But rather than replace *MGM* with *Pixar,* Disney went with the generic *Hollywood.*

DHS TODAY

THE *STUDIOS* IN "Disney's Hollywood Studios" is of little significance. Movie and television production ceased here long ago, and only a handful of aging attractions remain that offer even a cursory peek behind the scenes.

In a public acknowledgment of the above, Disney CEO Bob Iger announced in 2015 that the park will be renamed again in the near future. The new moniker hasn't been chosen yet, but expect something along the lines of "Disney's Hollywood Adventure."

On a more positive note, Iger made an additional announcement shortly before this book went to press: As many Disney fans have suspected for a while, a *Star Wars*–themed land will be coming to the Studios (Disneyland is getting a version as well), plus a *Toy Story*–themed land. However, we're pretty sure that neither project will come to fruition until 2019 or 2020—Disney was mum about groundbreaking and opening dates at press time, sharing only that work would start on Disneyland's *Star Wars* land in 2017.

▐█ OUR TAKE *on the* STUDIOS

IF YOU'VE GOT JUST two or three days to visit Disney World—and if you're reading this book, you probably do—skip the Studios. It's hard for us to recommend spending $80–$100 on a park that has so little to offer. To wit: Several major attractions, among them *The American Idol Experience,* The Magic of Disney Animation, and the Studio Backlot Tour, have closed without being replaced. Others, such as the

Disney's Hollywood Studios

Table-Service Restaurants

AA. 50's Prime Time Cafe
BB. Hollywood & Vine
CC. The Hollywood Brown Derby 👍
DD. Mama Melrose's Ristorante Italiano
EE. Sci-Fi Dine-In Theater Restaurant

Counter-Service Restaurants

A. ABC Commissary 👍
B. Backlot Express 👍
C. Catalina Eddie's
D. Fairfax Fare
E. Min and Bill's Dockside Diner
F. Pizza Planet
G. Rosie's All-American Cafe
H. Starring Rolls Cafe
I. Studio Catering Co.
J. Toluca Legs Turkey Co. 👍
K. Trolley Car Cafe

Lighter Traffic
Bag Check
(for self-park)

Main Bag
Check

Attractions

1. *Beauty and the Beast—Live on Stage*/Theater of the Stars FP+
2. *Disney Junior—Live on Stage!* FP+
3. *Fantasmic!* ☑ Use FP+
4. *For the First Time in Forever: A Frozen Sing-Along Celebration* FP+
5. The Great Movie Ride ☑ Use FP+
6. Honey, I Shrunk the Kids Movie Set Adventure
7. *Indiana Jones Epic Stunt Spectacular!* FP+
8. *Jedi Training Academy*
9. *Jim Henson's Muppet-Vision 3-D* ☑ FP+
10. *Lights, Motors, Action! Extreme Stunt Show* FP+
11. Rock 'n' Roller Coaster ☑ Use FP+
12. Star Tours—The Adventures Continue ☑ Use FP+
13. Toy Story Midway Mania! ☑ Use FP+
14. The Twilight Zone Tower of Terror ☑ Use FP+
15. *Voyage of the Little Mermaid* FP+
16. *Walt Disney: One Man's Dream*

FP+ FastPass+ Kiosks   FP+ Attraction Offers FastPass+

🚻 Restrooms   Use FP+ FastPass+ Recommended

✚ First Aid Center   ☑ Not to be Missed

🍴 Recommended Dining

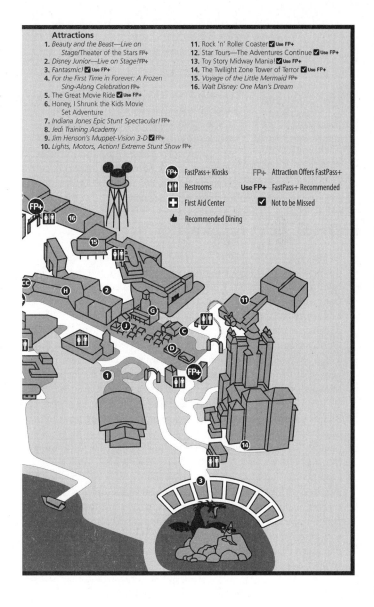

NOT TO BE MISSED AT DISNEY'S HOLLYWOOD STUDIOS

• *Fantasmic!* • *Jim Henson's Muppet-Vision 3-D* • Rock 'n' Roller Coaster

• Star Tours—The Adventures Continue • Toy Story Midway Mania!

• The Twilight Zone Tower of Terror

---

*un*official **TIP**
For now, **Universal Studios Florida** is the superior choice if you want to visit a theme park devoted to movies, TV, and music.

Indiana Jones Epic Stunt Spectacular! and **Rock 'n' Roller Coaster,** haven't been updated in years. Except for the fireworks that happen at park closing, the few attractions that we rate as not to be missed (see above) can be seen easily in as little as 4 hours—not enough to justify the cost of admission. Finally, those two new themed areas are still in the concept stages.

DHS *at a* GLANCE

WHEREAS IT'S IMPOSSIBLE to see all of Epcot or the Magic Kingdom in one day, DHS is doable: There's far less ground to cover by foot, trams carry guests through much of the backlot, and attractions are concentrated in an area about the size of Main Street, Tomorrowland, and Frontierland combined.

Because DHS is smaller, it's more affected by large crowds. Our touring plans (see the end of this chapter) will help you stay a step ahead of the mob and minimize waiting in line. They'll also help with the show-schedule problem, but even when the park is crowded, you can see almost everything in a day.

Because Disney's Hollywood Studios can be seen in as little as 8 hours, many guests who arrive early in the morning run out of things to do by late afternoon and leave the park. Their departure greatly thins the crowd and makes the Studios ideal for evening touring. The *Indiana Jones Epic Stunt Spectacular!* and productions at other outdoor theaters are infinitely more enjoyable during the evening than in the sweltering heat of the day.

DHS is the home of *Fantasmic!* (see page 235), the most dazzling nighttime-entertainment event in the Disney repertoire. Staged most nights (sometimes twice a night), weather permitting, in its own theater behind The Twilight Zone Tower of Terror, *Fantasmic!* is not to be missed. Unfortunately, it's also a crowd magnet, owing to DHS guests sticking around or guests from other parks arriving after dinner to see the show. Although the crowds thin in the late afternoon, they build again as showtime approaches, making *Fantasmic!* a challenge to get into. Also adversely affected are **Rock 'n' Roller Coaster** and, to a lesser extent, **The Twilight Zone Tower of Terror,** both nearby. Crowd levels elsewhere remain generally light, except at **Toy Story Midway Mania!**

Hollywood Boulevard Services

Most of DHS's services are on Hollywood Boulevard, including:

BABY CARE CENTER At Guest Relations; baby food and other necessities available at Oscar's Super Service

BANKING SERVICES ATM outside the park to the right of the turnstiles and on Streets of America near Pizza Planet restaurant

CAMERA SUPPLIES At The Darkroom on the right side of Hollywood Boulevard as you enter the park, just past Oscar's Super Service

CELL PHONE CHARGING Outlets in the Hollywood Brown Derby lobby, inside Backlot Express, and near the restrooms next to Toy Story Midway Mania!

FIRST AID At Guest Relations

LIVE-ENTERTAINMENT AND CHARACTER INFORMATION Available free at Guest Relations and elsewhere in the park

LOST AND FOUND At Package Pick-Up, to the right of the entrance

LOST PERSONS Report at Guest Relations

STORAGE LOCKERS Rental lockers to the right of the main entrance, on the left of Oscar's Classic Car Souvenirs

WHEELCHAIR, ECV/ESV, AND STROLLER RENTALS To the right of the entrance, at Oscar's Super Service

ARRIVING

DISNEY'S HOLLYWOOD STUDIOS has its own pay parking lot and is served by the Disney transportation system. Most larger hotels outside the World shuttle guests to the Studios. If you bring a car, Disney's ubiquitous trams will transport you to the ticketing area and entrance gate.

GETTING ORIENTED

ON YOUR LEFT AS YOU ENTER, **Guest Relations** serves as the park headquarters and information center, similar to City Hall in the Magic Kingdom and Guest Relations at Epcot and Disney's Animal Kingdom. Go there for a park map, a schedule of live performances (*Times Guide*), lost persons, Package Pick-Up, lost and found (on the right side of the entrance), baby-care facilities, and general information. To the right of the entrance are locker, stroller, and wheelchair rentals.

As at the Magic Kingdom, you enter the park and pass down a main street. In this case, it's the **Hollywood Boulevard** of the 1930s and '40s. At the end of Hollywood Boulevard is a replica of the iconic **Grauman's Chinese Theatre.**

Though modest in size, the open-access areas of the Studios are confusingly arranged. As you face Grauman's Chinese, two themed areas—**Sunset Boulevard** and **Animation Courtyard**—branch off of Hollywood Boulevard to the right. Branching left off Hollywood Boulevard is **Echo Lake. Streets of America** wraps around the back of Echo Lake, while **Pixar Place**'s attractions are behind the Chinese Theatre and to the left of Animation Courtyard. Between Pixar Place and Animation Courtyard is **Mickey Avenue,** with its one minor attraction.

Still farther to the rear is an area comprising soundstages, technical facilities, wardrobe shops, offices, and sets. This area was closed to the public after the Studio Backlot Tour was discontinued in 2014.

FASTPASS+ AT DHS

LIKE EPCOT, the Studios implements tiering to restrict the number of FastPass+ reservations you can have at its headliners:

TIER A (Choose one per day)	• *Jim Henson's Muppet-Vision 3-D*
• *Beauty and the Beast— Live on Stage*	
• *Fantasmic!*	• *Lights, Motors, Action! Extreme Stunt Show*
• Rock 'n' Roller Coaster	• Star Tours— The Adventures Continue
• The Great Movie Ride	
• Toy Story Midway Mania!	• The Twilight Zone Tower of Terror
TIER B (Choose two per day)	
• *Disney Junior—Live on Stage!*	• *Voyage of the Little Mermaid*
• *For the First Time in Forever: A Frozen Sing-Along Celebration*	**ENTERTAINMENT & PARADES**
• *Indiana Jones Epic Stunt Spectacular!*	• *The Comedy Warehouse Holiday Special* (seasonal)

FastPass+ is offered at more than a dozen Studios attractions, but there are really only a few you need to worry about most of the year.

Families with children too small to ride Rock 'n' Roller Coaster or Tower of Terror make a beeline to **Toy Story Midway Mania!** first thing in the morning, and lines grow quickly. Waits at Toy Story can reach 90 minutes or more on a busy day—in many of our touring plans, we recommend getting a FastPass+ reservation for 9–10 a.m., even when Toy Story is the first step in the plan. The two benefits to doing this are that (1) you'll shave off at least 10 minutes of waiting, and (2) you don't have to line up as early at park opening to join the mad rush to Toy Story.

DISNEY'S HOLLYWOOD STUDIOS
When Same-Day FP+ Runs Out, by Crowd Level

ATTRACTION	LOW CROWDS*	MODERATE CROWDS*	HIGH CROWDS*
Beauty and the Beast—Live on Stage	4–5 p.m.	4–5 p.m.	2–3 p.m.
Disney Junior—Live on Stage!	4–5 p.m.	3 p.m.	1–3 p.m.
Fantasmic!	3 p.m.	4–6 p.m.	6–8 p.m.
For the First Time in Forever: A Frozen Sing-Along Celebration	2–4 p.m.	1–3 p.m.	Noon
The Great Movie Ride	6–7 p.m.	6–7 p.m.	5–7 p.m.
Indiana Jones Epic Stunt Spectacular!	5 p.m.	5 p.m.	2–4 p.m.
Jim Henson's Muppet-Vision 3-D	6–7 p.m.	7–8 p.m.	8–9 p.m.
Lights, Motors, Action! Extreme Stunt Show	4 p.m.	3–4 p.m.	1–2 p.m.
Voyage of the Little Mermaid	5–6 p.m.	2–4 p.m.	2–4 p.m.
Rock 'n' Roller Coaster	2–4 p.m.	Noon–1 p.m.	10 a.m.–noon
Star Tours	6 p.m.	2–5 p.m.	Noon–2 p.m.
The Twilight Zone Tower of Terror	2–4 p.m.	10 a.m.–noon	Noon
Toy Story Midway Mania!	Noon–1 p.m.	10 a.m.–noon	No day-of availability

* LOW CROWDS (Levels 1–3 on TouringPlans.com Crowd Calendar)

* MODERATE CROWDS (Levels 4–7 on TouringPlans.com Crowd Calendar)

* HIGH CROWDS (Levels 8–10 on TouringPlans.com Crowd Calendar)

For teens and adults especially, the initial morning priorities will be Toy Story, Rock 'n' Roller Coaster, and Tower of Terror, possibly with The Great Movie Ride while they're in the area. This makes **Star Tours** a great choice for a mid- or late-morning FastPass+ reservation.

Many of our touring plans place **The Twilight Zone Tower of Terror** in the evening: generally 7–8 p.m. This allows you to focus on other attractions in the morning, which reduces your waits in line, and it makes for a short walk to *Fantasmic!* after you ride Tower of Terror.

FastPass+ kiosk locations at the Studios are as follows:

- At the MyMagic+ Service Center, immediately to the left just past the entrance turnstiles
- At the wait-times board on the corner of Hollywood and Sunset Boulevards
- Near Toy Story Midway Mania!, on Pixar Place
- Outside The Twilight Zone Tower of Terror, to the left of the entrance
- Near *Muppet-Vision 3-D,* just off Streets of America

Same-Day FastPass+ Availability

The preceding advice tells you which attractions to focus on when making your *advance* FastPass+ reservations before you get to the park. Once you're in the park, you can make more FastPass+ reservations once your advance reservations have been used or have expired (you must cancel your expired FastPass+ before you can book another). The table on the previous page shows which attractions are likely to have day-of FastPasses available, and the approximate times at which they'll run out.

▋▐ DHS ATTRACTIONS

HOLLYWOOD BOULEVARD

THIS PALM-LINED THOROUGHFARE re-creates Tinseltown's main drag during the Golden Age of Hollywood. Most service facilities are here, interspersed with eateries and shops. Merchandise includes Disney trademark items and movie-related souvenirs. Hollywood characters and roving performers entertain on the boulevard.

The Great Movie Ride *(FastPass+)* ★★★½

Appeal by Age	PRESCHOOL ★★★	GRADE SCHOOL ★★★½	TEENS ★★★½
YOUNG ADULTS ★★★½		OVER 30 ★★★½	SENIORS ★★★★

What it is Indoor movie-history ride. **Scope and scale** Headliner. **When to go** Before 11 a.m., during dinner, after 8 p.m., or use FastPass+. **Special comments** Elaborate, with several surprises. **Authors' rating** The recent update is welcome but doesn't go far enough; ★★★½. **Duration of ride** About 19 minutes. **Average wait in line per 100 people ahead of you** 2 minutes; assumes all cars operating. **Loading speed** Fast.

DESCRIPTION AND COMMENTS Entering through a re-creation of Grauman's Chinese Theatre, guests board vehicles for a fast-paced tour of soundstage sets from classic films, including *Casablanca, Tarzan, The Wizard of Oz, Alien,* and *Raiders of the Lost Ark.* The Great Movie Ride encompasses 95,000 square feet and showcases some of the most famous scenes in filmmaking. Life-size animatronic sculptures of stars, including Gene Kelly, John Wayne, James Cagney, and Julie Andrews, inhabit some of the largest sets ever constructed for a Disney ride.

In early 2015, as part of an agreement with Turner Classic Movies, the Great Movie Ride's preshow film trailer and ride-film finale were updated with commentary from TCM host and film historian Robert Osborne. The finale was also entirely reedited with a mix of classic clips, new scenes from previously featured films, and a handful of more-recent movies. The updated preshow and finale are first-rate—it's the attraction's meat that merits a "meh." Don't strain yourself searching for signs of improved animatronics or new effects in old sets, much less any all-new scenes.

TOURING TIPS It's rare to see waits of more than 30 minutes at The Great Movie Ride except during peak season. Actual wait times usually run about one-third shorter than the times posted.

SUNSET BOULEVARD

EVOKING THE 1940s, Sunset Boulevard is a major addition to Disney's Hollywood Studios. The first right off of Hollywood Boulevard, Sunset Boulevard provides another venue for dining, shopping, and street entertainment.

Fantasmic! (FastPass+)   ★★★★½

Appeal by Age	PRESCHOOL ★★★★	GRADE SCHOOL ★★★★½	TEENS ★★★★½
YOUNG ADULTS ★★★★½		OVER 30 ★★★★½	SENIORS ★★★★½

What it is Mixed-media nighttime spectacular. **Scope and scale** Super-headliner. **When to go** Check *Times Guide* for schedule; if 2 shows are offered, the second is less crowded. **Special comments** Disney's very best nighttime event. **Authors' rating** Not to be missed; ★★★★½. **Duration of presentation** 25 minutes. **Probable waiting time** 50–90 minutes for a seat, 35–40 minutes for standing room.

DESCRIPTION AND COMMENTS Off Sunset Boulevard behind the Tower of Terror, this mixed-media show is staged on an island opposite the 7,900-seat Hollywood Hills Amphitheater. By far the largest theater facility ever created by Disney, the amphitheater can accommodate an additional 2,000 standing guests for an audience of nearly 10,000.

Fantasmic! is the most innovative outdoor spectacle ever attempted at any theme park. Starring Mickey Mouse in his role as the Sorcerer's Apprentice from *Fantasia,* the production uses lasers, images projected on a shroud of mist, fireworks, lighting effects, and music in combinations so stunning you can scarcely believe what you're seeing. The plot is simple: good versus evil. The story gets lost in all the special effects at times, but no matter; it's the spectacle, not the storyline, that's powerful.

We don't receive many reports of young children being terrified by *Fantasmic!;* nonetheless, try to prepare your kids for what they'll see. You can mitigate the fright factor somewhat by sitting back a bit. Also, hang on to your kids after the show and give them instructions for regrouping should you get separated.

TOURING TIPS *Fantasmic!* is presented one or more times each evening, but Disney has been known to change the schedule, so check before you go. *Fantasmic!* is to Disney's Hollywood Studios what *IllumiNations* is to Epcot. While it's hard to imagine a 10,000-person stadium running out of space, that's just what happens almost every time the show is staged. On evenings when there are two performances, the second show will always be less crowded. If you attend the first (or only) scheduled performance, then show up at least an hour in advance. If you opt for the second show, arrive 50 minutes early. *Fantasmic!* is a FastPass+ attraction, but we don't think it should be one of your first three choices in DHS—you have to show up early to secure a good seat regardless.

Rainy and windy conditions sometimes cause *Fantasmic!* to be cancelled. Unfortunately, Disney officials usually don't make a final decision about whether to proceed or cancel until just before showtime. We've seen guests wait stoically for over an hour with no assurance that their patience and sacrifice will be rewarded. We don't recommend arriving more than 20 minutes before showtime on rainy or especially windy nights. On nights like these, pursue your own agenda until 10 minutes or so before showtime, then head to the stadium to see what happens.

***FANTASMIC!* DINING PACKAGE** If you eat lunch or dinner at **Hollywood & Vine, The Hollywood Brown Derby,** or **Mama Melrose's Ristorante Italiano,** you can obtain a voucher for the members of your dining party to enter *Fantasmic!* via a special entrance and sit in a reserved section of seats. In return for patronizing the restaurant, you can avoid 30–90 minutes waiting in the regular line.

You must call ☎ 407-WDW-DINE (939-3463) 180 days in advance and request the *Fantasmic!* Dining Package for the night you want to see the show. This is a real reservation, not an Advance Reservation, and must be guaranteed with a credit card at the time of booking. There's no additional charge for the package itself, but there is a $10 charge for canceling a reservation with less than 48 hours' notice.

Included in the package are fixed-price menus for all three restaurants as follows; respective prices are for adults and kids ages 3–9: *Hollywood & Vine:* buffet dinner, $40/$21; *The Hollywood Brown Derby:* lunch and dinner, $57/$17; *Mama Melrose's:* lunch and dinner, $38/$13. Nonalcoholic drinks and tax are included; park admission and gratuity are not. Prices vary by season, so call WDW-DINE to find out the exact price for a particular date.

Rock 'n' Roller Coaster *(FastPass+)* ★★★★

Appeal by Age	PRESCHOOL ★★½	GRADE SCHOOL ★★★★½	TEENS ★★★★★
YOUNG ADULTS ★★★★★		OVER 30 ★★★★½	SENIORS ★★★★

What it is Rock music–themed roller coaster. **Scope and scale** Headliner. **When to go** First 30 minutes the park is open, or use FastPass+. **Special comments** 48″ minimum height requirement; children younger than age 7 must ride with an adult. Switching-off option provided (see page 93). Note that this attraction has a single-rider line. **Authors' rating** Disney's wildest American coaster; not to be missed; ★★★★. **Duration of ride** Almost 1½ minutes. **Average wait in line per 100 people ahead of you** 2½ minutes; assumes all trains operating. **Loading speed** Moderate-fast.

DESCRIPTION AND COMMENTS When it opened in 1999, Rock 'n' Roller Coaster was Disney's answer to the coaster proliferation at Universal's Islands of Adventure and Busch Gardens. Exponentially wilder than Space Mountain or Big Thunder Mountain in the Magic Kingdom, Rock 'n' Roller Coaster is an attraction for fans of high-speed thrill rides. Although the rock icons and synchronized music add measurably to the experience, the ride itself, as opposed to sights and sounds along the way, is the focus. Rock 'n' Roller Coaster's loops, corkscrews, and drops make Space Mountain seem like It's a Small World. What really makes this metal coaster unusual, however, is that first, it's in the dark (like Space Mountain, only with Southern California nighttime scenes instead of space), and second, you're launched up the first hill like a jet off a carrier deck. By the time you crest the hill, you'll have gone from 0 to 57 mph in less than three seconds. When you enter the first loop, you'll be pulling 5 g's—2 more than astronauts experience at liftoff on a space shuttle.

TOURING TIPS This ride is not for everyone. If Space Mountain or Big Thunder pushes your limits, stay away from Rock 'n' Roller Coaster.

TOURING TIPS Rock 'n' Roller Coaster is not for everyone—if Space Mountain or Big Thunder pushes your limits, stay away.

Expect long lines except in the first 30 minutes after opening and during the late-evening performance of *Fantasmic!* Ride as soon as possible in the morning, or use the single-rider line or FastPass+.

A good strategy for riding Rock 'n' Roller Coaster, Toy Story Midway Mania!, and Tower of Terror with minimum wait is to make a midmorning FastPass+ reservation for Toy Story Midway Mania! and an evening FastPass+ reservation Tower of Terror up to 60 days in advance. Then, when you visit, rush first thing after opening to ride Rock 'n' Roller Coaster. If you can't make FastPass+ reservations before you arrive, ride Rock 'n' Roller Coaster or Toy Story Midway Mania! first, then find the nearest FastPass+ kiosk to make the other reservations.

Theater of the Stars / Beauty and the Beast— Live on Stage (FastPass+) ★★★★

APPEAL BY AGE	PRESCHOOL ★★★★½	GRADE SCHOOL ★★★★	TEENS ★★★★
YOUNG ADULTS ★★★★		OVER 30 ★★★★	SENIORS ★★★★½

What it is Live Hollywood-style musical, usually featuring Disney characters; performed in an open-air theater. **Scope and scale** Major attraction. **When to go** Anytime; evenings are cooler. **Special comments** Check *Times Guide* for showtimes. **Authors' rating** Excellent; ★★★★. **Duration of presentation** 25 minutes. **Preshow entertainment** None. **When to arrive** 20–30 minutes before showtime.

DESCRIPTION AND COMMENTS Theater of the Stars combines Disney characters with singers and dancers in upbeat and humorous Hollywood musicals. The *Beauty and the Beast* show, in particular, is outstanding. The theater offers a clear field of vision from almost every seat. Best, a canopy protects the audience from the Florida sun (or rain), but the theater still gets mighty hot in the summer.

TOURING TIPS Unless you visit during the cooler months, see this show in the late afternoon or the evening. The production is so popular that you should show up 25–35 minutes early to get a good seat.

The Twilight Zone Tower of Terror (FastPass+)
★★★★★

APPEAL BY AGE	PRESCHOOL ★★★	GRADE SCHOOL ★★★★	TEENS ★★★★½
YOUNG ADULTS ★★★★★		OVER 30 ★★★★½	SENIORS ★★★★

What it is Sci-fi-themed indoor thrill ride. **Scope and scale** Super-headliner. **When to go** First or last 30 minutes the park is open, or use FastPass+. **Special comments** 40" minimum height requirement. Switching-off option provided (see page 93). **Authors' rating** Walt Disney World's best attraction; not to be missed; ★★★★★. **Duration of ride** About 4 minutes plus preshow. **Average wait in line per 100 people ahead of you** 4 minutes; assumes all elevators operating. **Loading speed** Moderate.

DESCRIPTION AND COMMENTS The Tower of Terror is a different species of Disney thrill ride, though it borrows elements of The Haunted Mansion at the Magic Kingdom. The story is that you're touring a once-famous Hollywood hotel gone to ruin. As at Star Tours, the queuing area immerses guests in the adventure as they pass through the hotel's once-opulent public rooms. From the lobby, guests are escorted into the hotel's library, where Rod Serling, speaking from an old black-and-white television, greets the guests and introduces the plot.

DESCRIPTION AND COMMENTS The Tower of Terror is a different species of Disney thrill ride, though it borrows elements of The Haunted Mansion at the Magic Kingdom. The story is that you're touring a once-famous Hollywood hotel gone to ruin. As at Star Tours, the queuing area immerses guests in the adventure as they pass through the hotel's once-opulent public rooms. From the lobby, guests are escorted into the hotel's library, where Rod Serling, speaking from an old black-and-white television, greets the guests and introduces the plot.

The Tower of Terror is a whopper, at 13-plus-stories tall. Breaking tradition in terms of visually isolating themed areas, it lets you see the entire Studios from atop the tower . . . but you have to look quick.

The ride vehicle, one of the hotel's service elevators, takes guests to see the haunted hostelry. The tour begins innocuously, but at about the fifth floor things get pretty weird. Guests are subjected to a full range of eerie effects as they cross into the Twilight Zone. The climax occurs when the elevator reaches the top floor—the 13th, of course—and the cable snaps.

The Tower of Terror is an experience to savor. Though the final plunges—yep, plural—are calculated to thrill, the meat of the attraction is its extraordinary visual and audio effects. There's richness and subtlety here, enough to keep the ride fresh and stimulating after many repetitions. Disney has also programmed random lift-and-drop sequences into the mix, making the attraction faster and keeping you guessing about when, how far, and how many times the elevator will fall.

The Tower has great potential for terrifying young children and rattling more-mature visitors. If you have teenagers in your party, use them as experimental probes. If they report back that they really, really liked the Tower of Terror, run like hell in the opposite direction.

TOURING TIPS If you're on hand when the park opens and you want to ride Tower of Terror first, be aware that about 65% of the folks walking down Sunset Boulevard head for Rock 'n' Roller Coaster. If you're not positioned on the far right of the street, it will be hard to move through the crowd to make a right turn into Tower of Terror.

To save time once you're inside the queuing area, when you enter the library waiting room, stand in the far back corner across from the door where you entered and at the opposite end of the room from the TV. When the doors to the loading area open, you'll be the first admitted.

If you have young children (or anyone) who are apprehensive about this attraction, ask the attendant about switching off (see page 93).

Our touring plan on page 247 incorporates an optimal strategy for riding Tower of Terror, Rock 'n' Roller Coaster, and Toy Story Midway Mania! with minimum waits.

ECHO LAKE

AN ACTUAL MINIATURE LAKE near the middle of Disney's Hollywood Studios, to the left of Hollywood Boulevard, Echo Lake pays homage to its real-life California counterpart, which served as the backdrop to many early motion pictures. It also provides a visual transition from Hollywood Boulevard's retro theming to Streets of America's film-set ambience.

For the First Time in Forever:
A Frozen Sing-Along Celebration (FastPass+) ★★★

| APPEAL BY AGE | PRESCHOOL ★★★½ | GRADE SCHOOL ★★★★★ | TEENS ★★★★½ |
| YOUNG ADULTS ★★★★ | | OVER 30 ★★★ | SENIORS ★★★ |

What it is Sing-along stage show retelling the story of *Frozen,* with appearances by Anna and Elsa. **Scope and scale** Minor attraction. **When to go** Check your *Times Guide* for showtimes. **Authors' rating** You'll learn all the words whether you want to or not; ★★★. Duration of presentation 25 minutes.

DESCRIPTION AND COMMENTS This attraction started out as a hastily assembled stage show during the summer of 2014, when DHS was closing other attractions and needed something for guests to do. The show retells the plot of *Frozen* in 25 minutes. That's enough time to sing every song in the movie and have a quick visit from Anna and Elsa—but nothing new.

TOURING TIPS FastPass+ gets you access to a preferred-seating section near the front of the stage.

Indiana Jones Epic Stunt Spectacular! (FastPass+)
★★★½

| Appeal by Age | PRESCHOOL ★★★½ | GRADE SCHOOL ★★★★½ | TEENS ★★★★ |
| YOUNG ADULTS ★★★★ | | OVER 30 ★★★★ | SENIORS ★★★★ |

What it is Movie-stunt demonstration and action show. **Scope and scale** Headliner. **When to go** First two shows or last show. **Special comments** Performance times posted on a sign at the entrance to the theatre. **Authors' rating** Done on a grand scale; ★★★½. **Duration of presentation** 30 minutes. **Preshow entertainment** Selection of "extras" from audience. **When to arrive** 20–30 minutes before showtime.

DESCRIPTION AND COMMENTS Coherent and educational, though somewhat unevenly paced, the popular production showcases professional stunt men and women who demonstrate dangerous stunts with a behind-the-scenes look at how it's done. Sets, props, and special effects are very elaborate.

TOURING TIPS The Stunt Theater holds 2,000 people; capacity audiences are common. The first performance is always the easiest to see. If the first show is at 10 a.m. or earlier, you can usually walk in, even if you arrive 5 minutes late. For the second performance, show up about 15–20 minutes ahead of time. For the third and subsequent shows, arrive 20–30 minutes early. If you plan to tour during late afternoon and evening, attend the last scheduled performance. If you want to beat the crowd out of the stadium, sit on the far right (as you face the staging area) and near the top.

Jedi Training Academy ★★★½

| Appeal by Age | PRESCHOOL ★★★½ | GRADE SCHOOL ★★★★★ | TEENS ★★★★ |
| YOUNG ADULTS ★★★★ | | OVER 30 ★★★★½ | SENIORS ★★★★ |

What it is Outdoor stage show. **Scope and scale** Minor attraction. **When to go** First 2 shows of the day. **Special comments** To sign up your children to go on stage, visit the ABC Sound Studio building early in the morning, or look for cast members near the entrance just before and after park opening. Spots are first-come, first-served. **Authors' rating** A treat for young *Star Wars* lovers; ★★★½. **Duration of show** About 15 minutes. **When to arrive** 15 minutes before showtime.

DESCRIPTION AND COMMENTS *Jedi Training Academy* is staged several times daily to the left of the Star Tours building entrance, opposite Backlot Express. If you want your young Skywalkers-in-training to appear on stage, visit the sign-up area at the ABC Sound Studio building (across from Star Tours) as early in the morning as possible; also, cast members are some-times stationed outside the entrance just before and after the park opens. Spots go quickly and are first-come, first-served.

Once on stage, these miniature Jedi are trained in the ways of The Force and do battle against Darth Vader. If all this sounds too intense, it's not—Storm Troopers provide comic relief, and just as in the movies, the good guys always win.

TOURING TIPS Surprisingly popular, given that Disney hasn't promoted it at the same level of hype as other shows. In the summer, grab drinks at Backlot Express, right next door, about 20 minutes before the show starts.

Star Tours—The Adventures Continue *(FastPass+)* ★★★½

Appeal by Age	PRESCHOOL ★★★★	GRADE SCHOOL ★★★★½	TEENS ★★★★½
YOUNG ADULTS ★★★★½		OVER 30 ★★★★½	SENIORS ★★★★

What it is Indoor space-flight-simulation ride. **Scope and scale** Headliner. **When to go** Before 10 a.m., after 6 p.m., or use FastPass. **Special comments** Expectant mothers and anyone prone to motion sickness are advised against riding. Too intense for many children younger than age 8; 40″ minimum height requirement. **Authors' rating** A classic adventure; not to be missed; ★★★½. **Duration of ride** About 7 minutes. **Average wait in line per 100 people ahead of you** 5 minutes; assumes all simulators operating. **Loading speed** Moderate–fast.

Queasy

DESCRIPTION AND COMMENTS Based on the *Star Wars* movie series, this was Disney's first modern simulator ride. Star Tours completed its first major overhaul in decades in 2011, with a new story based on the "pod racing" scene from *Star Wars Episode 1: The Phantom Menace*. The new version has lots of dips, turns, twists, and climbs as your vehicle goes through an intergalactic version of the chariot race in *Ben-Hur*. The new ride film is projected in high-definition 3-D and has more than 50 combinations of opening and ending scenes.

An interactive show, *Jedi Training Academy* (see previous profile), is staged several times daily to the left of the Star Tours building entrance.

TOURING TIPS Try to ride before 10 a.m. or use FastPass+. If you have young children (or anyone) who are apprehensive about this attraction, ask the attendant about switching off (see page 93). Watch for throngs arriving from performances of the *Indiana Jones Epic Stunt Spectacular!* If you encounter a long line, try again later.

STREETS OF AMERICA

FORMERLY A WALK-THROUGH backlot movie set, Streets of America is now a designated themed area, or "land," that is home to four attractions. The backlot street sets remain intact and serve as the primary pedestrian thoroughfare.

Honey, I Shrunk the Kids Movie Set Adventure ★★½

Appeal by Age	PRESCHOOL ★★★★½	GRADE SCHOOL ★★★★½	TEENS ★★★½
YOUNG ADULTS ★★★		OVER 30 ★★★	SENIORS ★★★

What it is Small but elaborate playground. **Scope and scale** Diversion. **When to go** Before 11 a.m. or after dark. **Special comments** Opens an hour later than the rest of the park. **Authors' rating** Great for young children, more of a curiosity for adults; ★★½. **Duration of presentation** Varies. **Average wait in line per 100 people ahead of you** 20 minutes.

DESCRIPTION AND COMMENTS This elaborate play space appeals to kids age 10 and younger. The story is that you've been "miniaturized" and must make your way through a yard full of 20-foot-tall blades of grass, giant ants, lawn sprinklers, and other oversize props. There are also tunnels, slides, and rope ladders to play on. All surface areas are padded, and Disney personnel are on hand to help keep children in some semblance of control.

TOURING TIPS The attraction has problems that are hard to "miniaturize." First, it isn't large enough to accommodate all the kids who would like to play. Only 240 people are allowed "on the set" at a time, and many of these are supervising parents or curious adults who hopped in line without knowing what they were waiting for. Frequently by 10:30 or 11 a.m., the playground is full, with dozens waiting outside.

Also, kids get to play as long as parents allow, creating uneven traffic flow and unpredictable waits. If it weren't for the third flaw—that the attraction is poorly ventilated—there's no telling when anyone would leave.

If you visit during warmer months and want your children to experience the playground, get them in and out before 11 a.m.—by late morning, this attraction is way too hot and crowded for anyone to enjoy. Access the Movie Set Adventure via Streets of America or Pixar Place.

Jim Henson's Muppet-Vision 3-D (FastPass+)   ★★★★

Appeal by Age	PRESCHOOL ★★★★	GRADE SCHOOL ★★★★	TEENS ★★★★
YOUNG ADULTS ★★★★		OVER 30 ★★★★	SENIORS ★★★★½

What it is 3-D movie starring the Muppets. **Scope and scale** Major attraction. **When to go** Anytime. **Authors' rating** Uproarious; not to be missed; ★★★★. **Duration of presentation** 17 minutes. **Preshow entertainment** Muppets on television. **Probable waiting time** 12 minutes.

DESCRIPTION AND COMMENTS *Muppet-Vision 3-D* provides a total sensory experience, with wild 3-D action augmented by auditory, visual, and tactile special effects. If you're tired and hot, this zany show will make you feel brand-new. Arrive early and enjoy the hilarious video preshow.

TOURING TIPS This production is very popular. Before noon, waits peak at about 20 minutes except during holidays. Also, watch for throngs arriving from just-concluded performances of the *Indiana Jones Epic Stunt Spectacular!* If you encounter a long line, try again later.

Lights, Motors, Action! Extreme Stunt Show (FastPass+)   ★★★½

Appeal by Age	PRESCHOOL ★★★★	GRADE SCHOOL ★★★★½	TEENS ★★★★½
YOUNG ADULTS ★★★★½		OVER 30 ★★★★	SENIORS ★★★★

What it is Auto stunt show. **Scope and scale** Headliner. **When to go** Anytime. **Authors' rating** Good stunt work, slow pace; ★★★½. **Duration of presentation** 25–30 minutes. **Preshow entertainment** Selection of audience volunteers. **When to arrive** 25–30 minutes before showtime.

DESCRIPTION AND COMMENTS This show, which originated at Disneyland Paris, features cars and motorcycles in a blur of chases, crashes, jumps, and explosions. The secrets behind the special effects are explained after each stunt sequence, with replays and different camera views shown on an enormous movie screen; the replays also serve to pass the time needed in placing the next stunt's props into position. While the stunt driving is excellent, the show plods along between tricks, and you will probably have had your fill by the time the last stunt ends. Expect about 6–8 minutes of real action in a show that runs 25–30 minutes.

TOURING TIPS The auto stunt show, at the end of the Streets of America, presents two to five performances daily. It's popular, but its remote location (the most distant attraction from the park entrance) helps distribute and moderate the crowds. Seating is in a 3,000-person stadium, so it's not difficult to find a seat except on the busiest days (it's easier to get into the stadium than out of it, though).

PIXAR PLACE

THE WALKWAY BETWEEN *Voyage of the Little Mermaid* and the Studio Backlot Tour holds the popular Toy Story Mania! attraction. To emphasize the importance of the *Toy Story* franchise, this section of the park is called Pixar Place.

Toy Story Midway Mania! *(FastPass+)* ★★★★½

Appeal by Age	PRESCHOOL ★★★★½	GRADE SCHOOL ★★★★★	TEENS ★★★★½
YOUNG ADULTS ★★★★½		OVER 30 ★★★★½	SENIORS ★★★★½

What it is 3-D ride through indoor shooting gallery. **Scope and scale** Headliner. **When to go** As soon as the park opens, or use FastPass+. **Authors' rating** Not to be missed; ★★★★½. **Duration of ride** About 6½ minutes. **Average wait in line per 100 people ahead of you** 4½ minutes. **Loading speed** Fast.

DESCRIPTION AND COMMENTS Toy Story Midway Mania! ushered in a whole new generation of Disney attraction: the "virtual dark ride." Since Disneyland opened in 1955, ride vehicles have moved past two- and three-dimensional sets often populated by Audio-Animatronic (AA) figures. These amazingly detailed sets and robotic figures defined the Disney Imagineering genius in attractions such as Pirates of the Caribbean, The Haunted Mansion, and Peter Pan's Flight. Now for Toy Story Midway Mania!, the elaborate sets and endearing AA characters are gone. Imagine long corridors, totally empty, covered with reflective material. There's almost nothing there . . . until you put on your 3-D glasses. Instantly, the corridor is full and brimming with color and activity, thanks to projected computer-graphic (CG) images.

Conceptually, this is an interactive shooting gallery much like Buzz Lightyear's Space Ranger Spin (see page 148), but in Toy Story Mania!, your ride vehicle passes through a totally virtual midway, with booths offering such games as ring tossing and ball throwing. You use a cannon on your ride vehicle to play as you move along from booth to booth. Unlike the laser guns in Buzz Lightyear, however, the pull-string cannons in Toy Story Mania! take advantage of CG image technology to toss rings, shoot balls, even throw eggs and pies. Each game booth is manned by a *Toy Story* character who is right beside you in 3-D glory, cheering you on. In addition to 3-D imagery, you experience vehicle motion, wind, and water spray.

The ride begins with a training round to familiarize you with the games, then continues through a number of "real" games in which you compete against your riding mate. The technology has the ability to self-adjust the level of difficulty, and there are plenty of easy targets for small children to reach. *Tip:* Let the pull-string retract all the way back into the cannon before pulling it again.

Finally, a 6-foot-tall Mr. Potato Head interacts and talks with guests in real time (similar to *Turtle Talk with Crush*).

TOURING TIPS Because it's a ton of fun and it has a relatively low rider-per-hour capacity, Toy Story Midway Mania! is the biggest bottleneck in Walt Disney World, surpassing even Test Track at Epcot. The only way to get aboard without a horrendous wait is to be one of the first through the turnstiles when the park opens and zoom to the attraction. Another alternative is to obtain FastPass+ reservations for Toy Story Midway Mania! But you'll need to act fast: Even on days of moderate attendance, all reservations for the day are usually gone by 11 a.m.

MICKEY AVENUE

MICKEY AVENUE HOSTS a minor attraction on the pedestrian promenade that connects Pixar Place and Animation Courtyard.

Walt Disney: One Man's Dream ★★★★

Appeal by Age	PRESCHOOL ★★½	GRADE SCHOOL ★★★½	TEENS ★★★★
YOUNG ADULTS ★★★★		OVER 30 ★★★★½	SENIORS ★★★★½

What it is Tribute to Walt Disney. **Scope and scale** Minor attraction. **When to go** Anytime. **Authors' rating** Excellent; ★★★. **Duration of presentation** 25 minutes. **Preshow entertainment** Disney memorabilia. **Probable waiting time** For the film, 10 minutes.

DESCRIPTION AND COMMENTS Launched in 2001 to celebrate the 100th anniversary of Walt Disney's birthday, *One Man's Dream* consists of an exhibit area showcasing Disney memorabilia and recordings, followed by a film documenting Disney's life. On display are a replica of Walt's California office, various innovations in animation developed by Disney, and early models and working plans for Walt Disney World and various Disney theme parks around the world. The film provides a personal glimpse of Disney and offers insights regarding both his successes and failures.

TOURING TIPS Give yourself some time here. Every minute spent among these extraordinary artifacts will enhance your visit, taking you back to a time when the creativity and vision that created Walt Disney World were personified by one struggling entrepreneur.

ANIMATION COURTYARD

THIS AREA IS TO THE RIGHT of The Great Movie Ride in the middle of the park. It holds two large theaters used for live stage shows, plus several character-greeting locations. We think it's just a big swath of asphalt in desperate need of some landscaping or a water feature.

Disney Junior—Live on Stage! (FastPass+) ★★★★

Appeal by Age	★★★★★	GRADE SCHOOL ★★★★	TEENS ★★½
YOUNG ADULTS ★★★		OVER 30 ★★★	SENIORS ★★★

What it is Live show for children. **Scope and scale** Minor attraction. **When to go** Per the daily entertainment schedule. **Authors' rating** A must for families with preschoolers; ★★★★. **Duration of presentation** 20 minutes. **Special comments** Audience sits on the floor. **When to arrive** 30+ minutes before showtime.

DESCRIPTION AND COMMENTS The show features characters from the Disney Channel's *Little Einsteins, Mickey Mouse Clubhouse, Jake and the Never Land Pirates,* and *Handy Manny,* plus other Disney Channel characters. *Disney Junior* uses elaborate puppets instead of live characters on stage. A simple plot serves as the platform for singing, dancing, some great puppetry, and a great deal of audience participation. The characters, who ooze love and goodness, rally throngs of tots and preschoolers to sing and dance along with them. All the jumping, squirming, and high-stepping is facilitated by having the audience sit on the floor so that kids can spontaneously erupt into motion when the mood strikes. Even for adults without children, it's a treat to watch the tykes rev up.

TOURING TIPS Staged in a huge building to the right of The Magic of Disney Animation. Get here at least 25 minutes before showtime, pick a spot on the floor, and take a breather until the action begins.

Voyage of the Little Mermaid (FastPass+) ★★★½

APPEAL BY AGE PRESCHOOL ★★★★½ **GRADE SCHOOL** ★★★★ **TEENS** ★★★★
YOUNG ADULTS ★★★½ **OVER 30** ★★★½ **SENIORS** ★★★★

What it is Musical stage show featuring characters from the Disney movie *The Little Mermaid*. **Scope and scale** Major attraction. **When to go** Before 9:45 a.m., just before closing, or use FastPass+. **Authors' rating** Romantic, lovable, and humorous in the best Disney tradition; ★★★½. **Duration of presentation** 15 minutes. **Preshow entertainment** Taped ramblings about the decor in the preshow holding area. **Probable waiting time** Before 9:30 a.m., 10–30 minutes; after 9:30 a.m., 35–70 minutes.

DESCRIPTION AND COMMENTS *Voyage of the Little Mermaid* is a winner, appealing to every age. Lovable and cute without being silly or saccharine the *Little Mermaid* show is the most tender and romantic entertainment offered anywhere in Walt Disney World. The story is simple and engaging, the special effects impressive, and the Disney characters memorable.

TOURING TIPS Except during the busiest holiday periods, it's unusual for anyone in line not to be admitted to the next showing of *Mermaid*. Typical waits are usually under 25 minutes.

When you enter the preshow lobby, stand near the doors to the theater. When they open, go inside, pick a row of seats, and let 6–10 people enter the row ahead of you. The strategy is twofold: to obtain a good seat and be near the exit.

At press time, we heard a rumor that *Voyage of the Little Mermaid* may be closing in 2016. Visit **touringplans.com** for updates.

LIVE ENTERTAINMENT *at* DISNEY'S HOLLYWOOD STUDIOS

THE STUDIOS' LIVE-ENTERTAINMENT ROSTER includes theater shows; musical acts; roaming bands of street performers; and

Fantasmic! (see page 235), a nighttime water, fireworks, and laser show that draws rave reviews. Of all of these, the theater shows, musical acts, and street performers are generally as good as or better than comparable acts at the other Disney parks.

DISNEY CHARACTERS Donald, Daisy, Goofy, and Pluto are usually found in front of The Great Movie Ride. *Toy Story*'s Buzz and Woody are in Pixar Place in front of Toy Story Midway Mania!, while Mike and Sulley from *Monsters, Inc.,* are a little farther down the same walkway. Disney Junior stars hold court in Animation Courtyard, near *Disney Junior—Live on Stage!* Disney Channel's Phineas and Ferb, plus the cast of Pixar's *Cars* franchise, are found along the Streets of America. Mickey, Minnie, and other characters were displaced in the July 2015 closure of The Magic of Disney Animation, so check the *Times Guide* for times and locations of all character appearances.

STREET ENTERTAINMENT ★★★½ The Studios has one of the best teams of roving street performers in all of Walt Disney World. Appearing primarily on Hollywood and Sunset Boulevards, the cast of characters includes stars and wannabes, agents, directors, and gossip columnists. The performers aren't shy about asking guests to join in their antics.

OSBORNE FAMILY SPECTACLE OF DANCING LIGHTS ★★★★½ What started as a traffic-snarling eyesore in Arkansas is now one of Disney's premier holiday attractions. The Streets of America are transformed with more than 5 million lights of many colors, which adorn facades that replicate New York and San Francisco. These lights periodically "dance" by blinking in sync to music that fills the area; guests are periodically dusted with suspiciously soaplike "snow" from the rooftops.

The Osborne Lights draw heavy crowds, making the Streets of America as crowded as the real streets of Manhattan during rush hour. The lights go on at dusk (normally 6 p.m.). You can loiter to be among the first to see the lights, or visit during a *Fantasmic!* show or shortly after the park has officially closed. The lights usually operate evenings from around the end of the first week of November to around the end of the first week of January.

DISNEY'S HOLLYWOOD STUDIOS TOURING PLANS

TOURING THE STUDIOS centers primarily around Toy Story Mania! and the fact that it simply cannot handle the number of guests who want to ride. A wonderful attraction for small children, it's therefore the first choice for families with young kids.

To help with FastPass+, we've listed the approximate Fast-Pass+ return times for which you should attempt to make reservations. (The touring plan should work with anything close to the times shown.) We've listed in the plans the attractions most likely to need FastPass+, too. Check **touringplans.com** for the latest information.

"NOT A TOURING PLAN" TOURING PLANS

FOR THE TYPE-B READER, these touring plans avoid detailed, step-by-step strategies for saving every last minute in line. Use these guidelines to avoid the longest waits in line while having maximum flexibility to see whatever interests you in a particular part of the park.

FOR ADULTS ARRIVING AT PARK OPENING Obtain FastPass+ reservations for Toy Story Midway Mania! (FastPass+ suggested start time: 10 a.m.). Then begin a counterclockwise tour of the park with Rock 'n' Roller Coaster, Tower of Terror, and The Great Movie Ride. Work in shows as you near them. End the tour with *Voyage of the Little Mermaid*. End the day on Sunset Boulevard for *Fantasmic!* (If you're staying for the show, FastPass+ for Tower of Terror in the last hour the park is open would work well.)

FOR PARENTS AND ADULTS ARRIVING LATE MORNING Get Fast-Pass+ reservations for Toy Story Midway Mania! and use those at the appropriate time; otherwise, save it for last. Start a clockwise tour of the park with the *Lights, Motors, Action! Extreme Stunt Show,* and end with Toy Story if you didn't use FastPass+. Then grab a bite to eat, and see *Fantasmic!*

BEFORE YOU GO

1. Call ☎ 407-824-4321 to verify the park's hours.
2. Buy your admission and make FastPass+ reservations before you arrive.

3. Make lunch and dinner Advance Reservations, or reserve the *Fantasmic!* dinner package (if desired) before you arrive, by calling ☎ 407-WDW-DINE.

4. Review the daily *Times Guide* to get a fairly clear picture of your options.

Disney's Hollywood Studios One-Day Touring Plan

START TIMES FOR FASTPASS+ Star Tours, 9 a.m.; Toy Story Midway Mania!, 10 a.m.; Twilight Zone Tower of Terror, noon. Check for FastPass+ reservations for *Fantasmic!* after you've used your first three FastPasses or you've visited all attractions.

1. Arrive at the park 30–40 minutes before official opening time. Get guide maps and the *Times Guide*.

2. As soon as the park opens, ride Rock 'n' Roller Coaster.

3. Ride The Great Movie Ride.

4. In Echo Lake, ride Star Tours—The Adventures Continue.

5. Ride Toy Story Midway Mania! in Pixar Place.

6. See *Walt Disney: One Man's Dream.*

7. See *Voyage of the Little Mermaid.*

8. Eat lunch.

9. Ride The Twilight Zone Tower of Terror.

10. Work in *Disney Junior—Live on Stage!* if you have small children.

11. Participate in *For the First Time In Forever: A Frozen Sing-Along Celebration.*

12. See *Beauty and the Beast—Live on Stage.*

13. See the *Lights, Motors, Action! Extreme Stunt Show.*

14. See the *Indiana Jones Epic Stunt Spectacular!*

15. Explore the Streets of America on the way to *Jim Henson's Muppet-Vision 3-D.*

16. See *Muppet-Vision 3-D.*

17. Eat dinner.

18. Enjoy *Fantasmic!* Plan on arriving about 1 hour early to get good seats, or 30 minutes early for standing room only.

PART THIRTEEN

The
WATER PARKS

DISNEY HAS TWO WATER PARKS, and there are two competitive water parks in the area. At Disney World, **Typhoon Lagoon** is the more diverse splash pad, while **Blizzard Beach** takes the prize for the greater number of slides and the more bizarre theme.

At both Disney water parks, the following rules and prices apply: One cooler per family or group is allowed, but no glass or alcoholic beverages allowed; towels are $2; lockers are $13 small, $15 large (includes $5 refundable deposit); parking and life jackets are free. Admission, including tax, runs $62 for adults and $54 for children ages 3–9. For additional information, call ☎ 407-939-6244.

WATCH THE WEATHER

IF YOU BUY YOUR WALT DISNEY WORLD admission tickets before leaving home and you're considering the **Water Park Fun and More** (**WPFAM**) add-on (see page 21), you might want to wait until you arrive and have some degree of certainty about the weather during your stay. You can add the WPFAM option at any Disney resort or Guest Relations window at the theme parks. This is true regardless of whether you purchased your Base Tickets separately or as part of a package.

We get a lot of questions about the water parks during cold-weather months. Orlando-area temperatures can vary from the high 40s to the low 80s during December, January, and February.

EXTRA MAGIC HOURS

WHILE DISNEY ONCE OFFERED morning and evening Extra Magic Hours at its water parks, it's been a couple of years since we last saw them on the operating schedule. It's Disney's prerogative to change its mind, however, especially during summer, so check the operating schedules a couple of days before you plan to go.

◼▮ BLIZZARD BEACH

BLIZZARD BEACH IS DISNEY'S MOST EXOTIC water adventure park and, like Typhoon Lagoon, it arrived with its own legend. This time, the story goes, an entrepreneur tried to open a ski resort in Florida during a particularly savage winter. Alas, the snow melted; the palm trees grew back; and all that remained of the ski resort was its Alpine lodge, the ski lifts, and, of course, the mountain. Plunging off the mountain are ski slopes and bobsled runs transformed into waterslides. Visitors to Blizzard Beach catch the thaw: icicles drip and patches of snow remain. The melting snow has formed a lagoon (the wave pool), fed by gushing mountain streams.

Both Disney water parks are distinguished by their landscaping and the attention paid to executing their themes. As you enter Blizzard Beach, you face the mountain. Coming off the highest peak and bisecting the area at the mountain's base are two long slides. To the left of the slides is the wave pool. To the right are the children's swimming area and the ski lift. Surrounding the layout like a moat is a tranquil stream for floating in tubes.

On either side of the highest peak are tube, raft, and body slides. Including the two slides coming off the peak, Blizzard Beach has 19 slides. Among them is **Summit Plummet,** Disney World's longest speed slide, which begins with a 120-foot free fall, and the **Teamboat Springs** water-bobsled run, 1,200 feet long.

For our money, the most exciting and interesting slides are the **Slush Gusher** and Teamboat Springs on the front right of the mountain, and **Runoff Rapids** on the back side of the mountain. Slush Gusher is an undulating speed slide that we consider as exciting as the more vertical Summit Plummet without being as bone-jarring. On Teamboat Springs, you ride in a raft that looks like a children's round blow-up wading pool.

◼▮ TYPHOON LAGOON

TYPHOON LAGOON IS COMPARABLE in size to Blizzard Beach. Eleven waterslides and streams, some as long as 420 feet, drop from the top of a 100-foot-tall, man-made mountain. Landscaping and an "aftermath of a typhoon" theme add adventure to the wet rides.

Typhoon Lagoon provides water adventure for all ages. Activity pools for young children and families feature geysers, tame slides, bubble jets, and fountains. For the older and more adventurous are the enclosed **Humunga Kowabunga** speed slides, the corkscrew **Storm Slides,** and three whitewater raft rides: **Gangplank Falls, Keelhaul Falls,** and **Mayday Falls.** Billed as a "water roller coaster," **Crush 'n' Gusher** consists of a series of flumes and spillways that course through an abandoned tropical fruit–processing plant. It features tubes that hold one or two people, and you can choose from three different routes: Banana Blaster, Coconut Crusher, and Pineapple Plunger, ranging between 410 and 420 feet long. Only Crush 'n' Gusher and the Humunga Kowabunga speed slides (where you can hit 30 miles an hour) have a minimum height requirement of 48 inches.

■ WHEN *to* GO

THE BEST WAY TO AVOID standing in lines is to visit the Disney World water parks when they're the least crowded. Our research, conducted over many weeks in the parks, indicates that tourists, not locals, make up the majority of visitors on any given day. And because weekends are popular travel days, the water parks tend to be less crowded then. In fact, of the weekend days we evaluated, the parks never reached full capacity; during the week, conversely, one or both parks closed every Thursday we monitored, and both closed at least once every other weekday. Therefore, we recommend going on a Monday or Friday.

If your schedule is flexible, a good time to visit the swimming parks is midafternoon to late in the day when the weather has cleared after a storm. The parks usually close during bad weather. If the storm is prolonged, most guests leave for their hotels. When Typhoon Lagoon or Blizzard Beach reopen after inclement weather has passed, you almost have a whole park to yourself.

PART FOURTEEN

BEYOND *the* PARKS

DISNEY SPRINGS

THIS SHOPPING, DINING, AND ENTERTAINMENT development is strung along the banks of Village Lake, on the east side of Walt Disney World. Built in 1975 as **Lake Buena Vista Shopping Village,** it evolved over the next 25 years into **Downtown Disney,** adding nightclubs, live entertainment, and even more stores.

The nightlife and entertainment venues began to lose customers around the turn of the millennium. Most were closed by 2008, and many retail shops soon followed. Many of the closed areas stayed in limbo as Disney announced and canceled plans for various revitalization efforts. Finally, in 2013, Disney was able to move forward with a plan to double the number of shops and restaurants, redesign pedestrian walkways, and retheme the entire area.

Most of the construction in Disney Springs should be finished in 2016. A number of major projects, including parking garages to address the notoriously bad traffic, have already been completed.

The best way to get to Disney Springs is by Disney transportation. Free bus service is available from every Disney resort to the stop at the Marketplace. Guests at the Old Key West, Saratoga Springs, and Port Orleans Resorts can take a water taxi to Disney Springs; the water taxi ferries passengers along the Sassagoula River to the West Side dock. Allow about a half-hour for this trip, plus time waiting for the boat (10 minutes for Saratoga Springs). Guests who don't wish to walk the length of Disney Springs can take a water taxi from the West Side dock to the Marketplace dock. Saratoga Springs has walking paths to both the West Side and the Marketplace. Part of the master plan for Disney Springs includes elevated walkways from the resorts of Hotel Plaza

Disney Springs

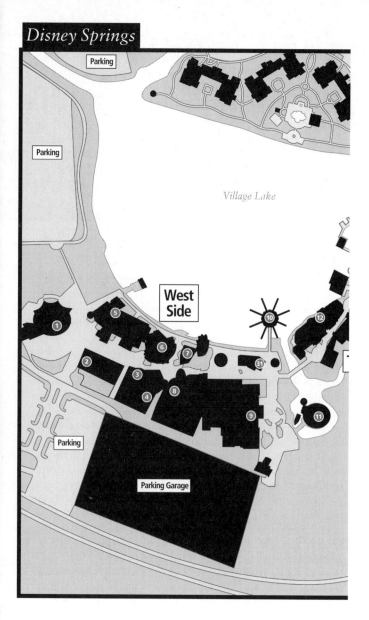

Parking

Parking

Village Lake

Parking

Parking Garage

West Side

1

5

2

6

3

7

4

8

9

10

31

11

12

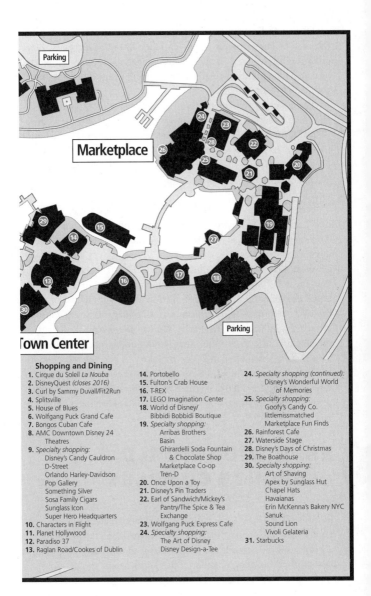

Parking

Marketplace

Town Center

Parking

Shopping and Dining

1. Cirque du Soleil *La Nouba*
2. DisneyQuest *(closes 2016)*
3. Curl by Sammy Duvall/Fit2Run
4. Splitsville
5. House of Blues
6. Wolfgang Puck Grand Cafe
7. Bongos Cuban Cafe
8. AMC Downtown Disney 24 Theatres
9. *Specialty shopping:*
   Disney's Candy Cauldron
   D-Street
   Orlando Harley-Davidson
   Pop Gallery
   Something Silver
   Sosa Family Cigars
   Sunglass Icon
   Super Hero Headquarters
10. Characters in Flight
11. Planet Hollywood
12. Paradiso 37
13. Raglan Road/Cookes of Dublin

14. Portobello
15. Fulton's Crab House
16. T-REX
17. LEGO Imagination Center
18. World of Disney/ Bibbidi Bobbidi Boutique
19. *Specialty shopping:*
    Arribas Brothers
    Basin
    Ghirardelli Soda Fountain & Chocolate Shop
    Marketplace Co-op
    Tren-D
20. Once Upon a Toy
21. Disney's Pin Traders
22. Earl of Sandwich/Mickey's Pantry/The Spice & Tea Exchange
23. Wolfgang Puck Express Cafe
24. *Specialty shopping:*
    The Art of Disney
    Disney Design-a-Tee

24. *Specialty shopping (continued):*
    Disney's Wonderful World of Memories
25. *Specialty shopping:*
    Goofy's Candy Co.
    littlemissmatched
    Marketplace Fun Finds
26. Rainforest Cafe
27. Waterside Stage
28. Disney's Days of Christmas
29. The Boathouse
30. *Specialty shopping:*
    Art of Shaving
    Apex by Sunglass Hut
    Chapel Hats
    Havaianas
    Erin McKenna's Bakery NYC
    Sanuk
    Sound Lion
    Vivoli Gelateria
31. Starbucks

Boulevard and direct access from I-4, which, when completed, should ease traffic considerably in the area.

Disney Springs consists of four areas, each with a distinct theme. The **Marketplace,** on the east side of the property, is where guests will find most of the Disney-owned and -operated stores, as well as the highly themed, child-pleasing restaurants **Rainforest Cafe** and **T-REX.**

The Landing, which features waterfront walkways and merchandise kiosks, has seen the most reimagining, with new shopping and dining areas. What was once a bottleneck for guests (and their strollers) trying to go from the West Side to the Marketplace is now a much more open area, with multiple pathways to alleviate pedestrian traffic, plus sweeping views of the water and Saratoga Springs Resort.

Scheduled for completion in 2016 is **Town Center,** a brand-new area situated between The Landing and the parking garage. Anchoring this area is the **Planet Hollywood** restaurant (still open during construction).

West Side has seen the least change. This is where guests can find the **AMC** cinema, many independent retailers, and **Cirque du Soleil** *La Nouba,* n amazing production show with a cast of more than 70 performers and musicians. (*La Nouba* is described in Part Fifteen, Nightlife in Walt Disney World.) **DisneyQuest,** a "virtual theme park" offering various interactive games and contained in its own building, will close in 2016 to make way for **The NBA Experience,** featuring a National Basketball Association–themed restaurant, shop, and exhibits. Interactive activities, designed for guests of most ages, will focus on basketball skills as well as test agility, reflexes, and mobility.

ESPN WIDE WORLD *of* SPORTS COMPLEX

THIS 220-ACRE, STATE-OF-THE-ART competition and training center consists of a 9,500-seat ballpark; a fieldhouse; and dedicated venues for baseball, softball, tennis, track and field, beach volleyball, and 27 other sports. From Little League Baseball to rugby, the complex hosts a mind-boggling calendar of pro and amateur competitions.

In late winter and early spring, the complex is the spring-training home of the Atlanta Braves. While Disney guests are welcome at the ESPN Wide World of Sports Complex as paying spectators (prices vary according to event), none of the facilities are available for guests unless they're participants in a scheduled, organized competition. To learn which sporting events, including

Major League Baseball exhibition games, are scheduled during your visit, call ☎ 407-939-GAME (4263) or check the online calendar at **disneyworldsports.com.**

Admission is $17 for adults, $12 children for ages 3–9 (prices include tax). Some events carry an extra charge. There's a restaurant, the **ESPN Wide World of Sports Grill,** but no on-site lodging.

Off Osceola Parkway, on Victory Way, the complex has its own parking lot and is accessible via the Disney transportation system.

The DISNEY WILDERNESS PRESERVE

ABOUT 40–60 MINUTES SOUTH of Walt Disney World is the Disney Wilderness Preserve, a wetlands-restoration area operated by The Nature Conservancy in partnership with Disney. At 12,000 acres, this is as real as Disney gets. There are hiking trails and an interpretive center. Trails wind through grassy savannas, beneath ancient cypress trees, and along the banks of pristine Lake Russell. More than 1,000 species of plants and animals call the preserve home. The preserve is open Monday–Friday, 9 a.m.–5 p.m., except for major holidays; admission is free, but donations are welcome. For more information and directions, call ☎ 407-935-0002 or visit **tinyurl.com/disneywildernesspreserve.**

WALT DISNEY WORLD RECREATION

DISNEY RESORTS HANDLE boat, bike, and fishing-equipment rentals on an hourly basis—just show up at the rental office during operating hours and they'll fix you up. The same goes for various fitness centers in the resort hotels. Golf, tennis, fishing expeditions, water-ski excursions, hayrides, trail rides, and most spa services must be scheduled in advance. Though every resort features an extensive selection of recreational options, those resorts situated on a navigable body of water offer the greatest variety. Also, the more upscale a resort, the more likely it is to have such amenities as a fitness center and spa.

WALT DISNEY WORLD GOLF

WALT DISNEY WORLD HAS FOUR GOLF COURSES, each expertly designed and meticulously maintained. The **Magnolia, Palm,** and **Oak Trail** courses, across Floridian Way from the Polynesian Resort, envelop the Shades of Green recreational complex; the pro shops and support facilities adjoin the Shades of Green hotel. **Lake Buena Vista Golf Course** is at Saratoga Springs Resort, near Walt Disney World Village and across the lake from the Disney Springs project. (**Tranquilo Golf Club,** adjacent to Fort Wilderness Campground, is part of the Four Seasons Resort Orlando and replaced Disney's Osprey Ridge Golf Course in 2014.)

Oak Trail is a nine-hole course for beginners. The other three courses are designed for the midhandicap player and, while interesting, are quite forgiving. All courses are popular, with morning tee times at a premium, especially January–April.

unofficial **TIP**
To avoid the crowds, play on a Monday, Tuesday, or Wednesday and sign up for a late-afternoon tee time.

Peak season for all courses is January–May, and off-season is May–October; however, summer is peak season for the nongolf parts of Walt Disney World, including the hotels. Off-season and afternoon twilight rates are available. Carts are required (except at Oak Trail) and are included in the greens fee. Tee times may be reserved 90 days in advance by Disney resort guests and 60 days ahead by day guests with a credit card. Proper golf attire, including spikeless shoes, is required. A collared shirt and Bermuda-length shorts or slacks meet the requirements.

For more information, call ☎ 407-938-GOLF (4653); to book a tee time online, go to **golfwdw.com.**

▌❚ MINIATURE GOLF

THE 11-ACRE **Fantasia Gardens** consists of two 18-hole dink-and-putt golf courses. One course is an "adventure" course, themed after Disney's animated film *Fantasia*. The other course, geared more toward older children and adults, is an innovative approach-and-putt course with sand traps and water hazards.

Fantasia Gardens is on Epcot Resorts Boulevard, across the street from the Swan resort; it's open daily, 10 a.m.–11 p.m. To reach the course via Disney transportation, take a bus or boat to the Swan. The cost to putt, including tax, is $14 for adults and $12 for children ages 3–9. In case you arrive hungry or naked, Fantasia Gardens has a snack bar and gift shop. For more information, call ☎ 407-WDW-PLAY (939-7529).

Winter Summerland, a second Disney minigolf facility, is next to Blizzard Beach water park. Winter Summerland offers two 18-hole courses—one has a "blizzard in Florida" theme, the other a tropical-holiday theme. It's open daily, 10 a.m.–11 p.m., and the cost is the same as for Fantasia Gardens.

unofficial **TIP**
The Winter Summerland courses are much easier than the Fantasia Gardens courses, making them a better choice for families with preteen children.

PART FIFTEEN

NIGHTLIFE *in* WALT DISNEY WORLD

WALT DISNEY WORLD *at* NIGHT

DISNEY SO CLEVERLY CONSPIRES to exhaust you during the day that the thought of night activity sends most visitors into shock. Walt Disney World, however, offers much for the hearty and the nocturnal to do in the evenings.

IN THE THEME PARKS

EPCOT'S MAJOR EVENING EVENT is *IllumiNations,* a laser and fireworks show at World Showcase Lagoon. Showtime is listed in the daily entertainment schedule (*Times Guide*).

Magic Kingdom offerings include the popular evening parade(s); *Celebrate the Magic,* in which a high-tech light-and-video show is projected onto Cinderella Castle; and the *Wishes* fireworks show. Consult the *Times Guide* for performances.

On most nights of the year, Disney's Hollywood Studios presents *Fantasmic!,* a laser, special-effects, and water spectacular (see page 235). The *Times Guide* lists showtimes.

A sort of Main Street Electrical Parade on barges, the **Floating Electrical Pageant** stars creatures of the sea. This nightly spectacle, with background music played on a doozy of a synthesizer, is one of our favorite Disney productions. The first performance of the short but captivating show is at 9 p.m. off the Polynesian Village Resort docks. From there, it circles around and repeats at the Grand Floridian Resort & Spa at 9:15 p.m., heading afterward to Fort Wilderness Resort & Campground, Wilderness Lodge & Villas, and the Contemporary Resort and Bay Lake Tower.

Disney's Animal Kingdom will get its own nightttime spectacular, *Rivers of Light,* in 2016 (see preview on page 219).

AT THE HOTELS

DISNEY'S BOARDWALK OFFERS two adult-oriented venues, **Jellyrolls** and **Atlantic Dance Hall.** Jellyrolls is a dueling-piano bar that's open 7 p.m.–2 a.m. nightly (cover charge applies). Popular with locals, it's one of the few 21-and-up places you'll find at Walt Disney World. The entertainment is outstanding here. Across from Jellyrolls is **Atlantic Dance Hall.** It's often booked for private events, but on weekends it's open in the evenings (and has free admission). Atlantic Dance Hall has a DJ on hand and can be busy when large conventions are at the Swan and Dolphin or other Epcot-area resorts. Like Jellyrolls, Atlantic Dance Hall is 21-and-up.

At Coronado Springs, you'll find Disney's only true nightclub, **Rix Lounge.** This 5,000-square-foot upscale dance club and lounge is beautifully decorated, has a stellar tequila and margarita menu, features a DJ, and usually isn't busy unless there's a large convention on-site.

Other Walt Disney World resort bars with live entertainment are **Scat Cat's Lounge** at Port Orleans French Quarter and **River Roost** at Port Orleans Riverside. River Roost features **Ye Haa Bob Jackson,** an entertainer with a cult following among Disney fans. His fast-moving (and family-friendly) shows bring in locals and visitors from other resorts. Jackson's schedule is posted on his website, **yehaabob.com.** What he lacks in page-design skills, he more than makes up for with his skills at the piano and other instruments. Scat Cat's currently has karaoke and also draws a crowd.

Possibly the most anticipated opening in 2015, **Trader Sam's Grog Grotto** (inspired by the bar at the Disneyland Hotel in California) at the Polynesian Village is a delight. If you've ever found yourself in *Walt Disney's Enchanted Tiki Room* and thought to yourself, "You know, booze would *really* make this experience better," this is the place for you. For now, this lounge is extraordinarily busy, so be prepared to wait both to enter and be served. While you're at it, pick up some souvenir tiki mugs for our collection (or start your own).

Our favorite nightspot at Walt Disney World, **Top of the World** at Bay Lake Tower, is exclusive to Disney Vacation Club members. If you're eligible, or can find a DVC member who will bring you up in return for a drink, try to stay after the Magic Kingdom fireworks when the bar clears out. The view and the setting are outstanding.

Family Entertainment

AT ANIMAL KINGDOM LODGE For children, there's African story-telling around a campfire each night, followed by a movie shown by the pool. In addition, kids can march around the lobby each evening at 8 p.m. during the **Zawadi Primal Parade.** Finally, guests can view animals after dark using night-vision goggles.

AT FORT WILDERNESS RESORT & CAMPGROUND The free nightly campfire program begins with a sing-along led by Chip 'n' Dale and progresses to cartoons and a Disney movie. For Disney lodging guests only.

AT DISNEY SPRINGS

THROUGHOUT DISNEY SPRINGS, you'll find live street entertainment, including singers, musicians, and performance artists. If you're looking for more-structured entertainment, though, here are a few separate-ticket venues to consider.

Cirque du Soleil *La Nouba*

Appeal by Age	UNDER 21 ★★★★	21-37 ★★★★	38-50 ★★★★	51 and up ★★★★½

Type of show Circus as theater. **Tickets and information** ☎ 407-939-7600; **cirquedusoleil.com/lanouba. Admission cost** *Golden Circle:* $159.75 adults, $133.13 children ages 3–9; *Category Front & Center:* $145.91 adults, $120.34 children; *Category 1:* $129.93 adults, $106.50 children; *Category 2:* $101.17 adults, $83.07 children; *Category 3:* $82 adults, $67.09 children; *Category 4:* $67.09 adults, $55.38 children. All prices include tax. **Cast size** 72. **Night of lowest attendance** Thursday. **Usual showtimes** Tuesday–Saturday, 6 p.m. and 9 p.m. **Authors' rating** ★★★★★. **Duration of presentation** 1 hour, 45 minutes (no intermission) plus preshow.

DESCRIPTION AND COMMENTS *La Nouba* is a far cry from a traditional circus, but it retains all the fun and excitement. It is whimsical, mystical, and sophisticated, yet pleasing to all ages. The action takes place on an elaborate stage that incorporates almost every part of the theater.

TOURING TIPS The audience is an integral part of *La Nouba*—at almost any time you might be plucked from your seat to participate. Our advice is to loosen up and roll with it. If you are too rigid, repressed, hung over, or whatever to get involved, politely but firmly decline to be conscripted. Then fix a death grip on the arms of your chair. Tickets for reserved seats can be purchased in advance at the Cirque box office or over the phone, using your credit card. Oh yeah, don't wait until the last minute; book well in advance from home.

House of Blues

Type of show Live concerts with an emphasis on rock and blues. **Tickets and information** ☎ 407-934-blue (2583); **hob.com. Admission cost with taxes** $11 for club nights to $25 and up depending on who's performing. **Nights of lowest attendance** Monday and Tuesday. **Usual showtimes** Vary between 7 p.m. and 9:30 p.m., depending on who's performing.

DESCRIPTION AND COMMENTS Developed by original Blues Brother Dan Aykroyd, House of Blues comprises a restaurant and blues bar, as well as a concert hall. The restaurant serves Thursday–Saturday, 11:30 a.m.–11 p.m., and Friday and Saturday, 11:30 a.m.–1 a.m., which makes it one of the few late-night-dining options in Walt Disney World. Live music cranks up every night at 10:30 p.m. in the restaurant–blues bar, but even before then, the joint is way beyond 110 decibels. The music hall next door features concerts by an eclectic array of musicians and groups. During one visit, the show bill listed gospel, blues, funk, ska, dance, salsa, rap, zydeco, hard rock, groove rock, and reggae groups over a two-week period.

TOURING TIPS Prices vary from night to night according to the fame and drawing power of the featured band. Tickets ranged from $11 to $50 during our visits but go higher when a really big name is scheduled.

The music hall is set up like a nightclub, with tables and bar stools for only about 150 people and standing room for a whopping 1,850 people. Folks dance when there's room and sometimes when there isn't. The tables and stools are first-come, first-served, with doors opening an hour before showtime on weekdays and 90 minutes before showtime on weekends. Acoustics are good, and the showroom is small enough to provide a relatively intimate concert experience. Shows are all ages unless otherwise indicated.

WALT DISNEY WORLD DINNER THEATERS

SEVERAL DINNER-THEATER SHOWS play nightly at Walt Disney World, and unlike other Disney dining venues, they take hard reservations instead of Advance Reservations, meaning you have to guarantee your reservation ahead of time with a credit card. You'll receive a confirmation number and be told to pick up your tickets at a Disney-hotel Guest Relations desk. Unless you cancel your tickets at least 48 hours before your reservation time, your credit card will still be charged the full amount. Dinner-show reservations can be made 180 days in advance; call ☎ 407-939-3463. While getting reservations for the *Spirit of Aloha Dinner Show* isn't terribly tough, booking the *Hoop-Dee-Doo Musical Revue* is a trick of the first order.

1. Call ☎ 407-939-3463 at 9 a.m. each morning while you're at Disney World to make a same-day reservation. There are three performances each night, and for all three combined, only 3–24 people total will be admitted with same-day reservations.

2. Arrive at the show of your choice 45 minutes before showtime (early and late shows are your best bets) and put your name on the standby list. If someone with reservations fails to show, you may be admitted.

Hoop-Dee-Doo Musical Revue

Pioneer Hall, Fort Wilderness Campground ☎ 407-939-3463. **Showtimes** 4, 6:15, and 8:30 p.m. nightly. **Cost** *Category 1:* $66–$70 adults, $34–$36 children ages 3–9.; *Category 2:* $59–$63 adults, $29–$31 children; *Category 3:* $55–$59 adults, $28–$30 children. Prices include tax and gratuity. **Discounts** Seasonal. **Type of seating** Tables of various sizes to fit the number in each party, set in an Old West–style dance hall. **Menu** All-you-can-eat barbecue ribs, fried chicken, corn, and strawberry shortcake. **Vegetarian alternative** On request (at least 24 hours in advance). **Beverages** Unlimited beer, wine, sangria, and soft drinks.

DESCRIPTION AND COMMENTS Six Wild West performers arrive by stage-coach (sound effects only) to entertain the crowd inside Pioneer Hall. There isn't much of a plot—just corny jokes interspersed with song or dance. The humor is of the *Hee Haw* ilk, but it's presented enthusiastically.

Audience participation includes sing-alongs, hand clapping, and a finale that uses volunteers to play parts on stage. Performers are accompanied by a banjo player and pianist who also play quietly while the food is being served. The fried chicken and corn on the cob are good, the ribs a bit tough though tasty. With the all-you-can-eat policy, at least you can get your money's worth by stuffing yourself silly.

Traveling to Fort Wilderness and absorbing the rustic atmosphere of Pioneer Hall augments the adventure. For repeat Disney World visitors, an annual visit to the revue is a tradition of sorts. Plus, warts and all, the revue is all Disney, and for some folks that's enough. The fact that performances sell out far in advance gives the experience a special aura.

Boat service may be suspended during thunderstorms, so if it's raining or it looks like it's about to rain, Disney will provide bus service from the parks.

Mickey's Backyard BBQ

Fort Wilderness Campground ☎ 407-939-3463. **Showtimes** Thursday and Saturday at 5, 6:30, and 7 p.m. **Cost** $60 adults, $36 children ages 3–9. Prices include tax and gratuity. **Type of seating** Picnic tables. **Menu** Baked chicken, barbecue pork ribs, burgers, hot dogs, corn, beans, mac and cheese, salads and slaw, bread, and watermelon and ice-cream bars for dessert. **Vegetarian alternatives** On request. **Beverages** Unlimited beer, wine, lemonade, and iced tea.

DESCRIPTION AND COMMENTS Situated along Bay Lake and held in a covered pavilion next to the site of the old River Country swimming park, *Mickey's Backyard BBQ* features Mickey, Minnie, Chip 'n' Dale, and Goofy, along with a country band and line dancing. Though the pavilion gets some breeze off Bay Lake, we recommend going during the spring or fall, if possible. The food is pretty good, as is, fortunately, the insect control.

The cookout is offered year-round; even so, dates are usually not entered into the WDW-DINE reservations system until about six months in advance. Once the dates are in the system, you can make an Advance Reservation for anytime during the dinner show's season.

The easiest way to get to the barbecue is to take a boat from the Magic Kingdom or from one of the Disney resorts on the Magic Kingdom monorail. Give yourself at least 45 minutes if you plan to arrive by boat. Ferry service may be suspended during thunderstorms, so if it's raining or it looks like it's about to rain, Disney will provide bus service from the parks.

Spirit of Aloha Dinner Show

Disney's Polynesian Village Resort ☎ 407-939-3463. **Showtimes** Tuesday–Saturday, 5:15 and 8 p.m. **Cost** *Category 1:* $70–$70 adults, $36–$40 children ages 3–9; *Category 2:* $63–$67 adults, $31–$33 children; *Category 3:* $59–$63 adults, $30–$32 children. Prices include tax and gratuity. **Discounts** Seasonal. **Type of seating** Long rows of tables, with some separation between individual parties. The show is performed on an outdoor stage, but all seating is covered. Ceiling fans provide some air movement, but it can get warm, especially at the early show. **Menu** Tropical fruit, roasted chicken, island pork ribs, mixed vegetables, rice, and pineapple bread; chicken tenders, PB&J sandwiches, mac and cheese, and hot dogs are also available for children. **Vegetarian alternative** On request. **Beverages** Beer, wine, and soft drinks.

DESCRIPTION AND COMMENTS This show features South Seas–island native dancing followed by an all-you-can-eat "Polynesian-style" meal. The dancing is interesting and largely authentic, and the dancers are attractive but definitely PG-rated in the Disney tradition. We think the show has its moments and the meal is adequate, but neither is particularly special.

The show follows (tenuously) the common "girl leaves home for the big city, forgets her roots, and must rediscover them" theme. The performers are uniformly attractive ("Studmuffins!" said a female *Unofficial* researcher when asked about the men), and the dancing is very good. The story, however, never really makes sense as anything other than a thread with which to stitch together the musical numbers. Our show lasted for more than 2 hours and 15 minutes.

The food does little more than illustrate how difficult it must be to prepare the same meal for hundreds of people simultaneously: The roasted chicken is better than the ribs, but neither is anything special. We conditionally recommend *Spirit of Aloha* for special occasions, when the people celebrating get to go on stage. But go to the early show and get dessert somewhere else in the World.

APPENDIX

Disney-Speak Pocket Translator

Although it may come as a surprise to many, Walt Disney World has its own somewhat peculiar language. Here are some terms you are likely to bump into:

DISNEY-SPEAK	ENGLISH DEFINITION
ADVENTURE	Ride
ATTRACTION	Ride or theater show
ATTRACTION HOST	Ride operator
AUDIENCE	Crowd
BACKSTAGE	Behind the scenes, out of view of customers
CAST MEMBER	Employee
CHARACTER	Disney character impersonated by an employee
COSTUME	Work attire or uniform
DARK RIDE	Indoor ride
DAY GUEST	Any customer not staying at a Disney resort
FACE CHARACTER	A character who does not wear a head-covering costume (such as Snow White, Cinderella, and Jasmine)
GENERAL PUBLIC	Same as day guest
GREETER	Employee positioned at an attraction entrance
GUEST	Customer

Continued on next page

Disney-Speak Pocket Translator
(Continued)

DISNEY-SPEAK	ENGLISH DEFINITION
HIDDEN MICKEYS	Frontal silhouette of Mickey's head worked subtly into the design of buildings, railings, vehicles, golf greens, attractions, and the like
ON STAGE	In full view of customers
PRESHOW	Entertainment at an attraction prior to the feature presentation
RESORT GUEST	A customer staying at a Disney resort
ROLE	An employee's job
SOFT OPENING	Opening a park or attraction before its stated opening date
TRANSITIONAL EXPERIENCE	An element of the queuing area and/or preshow that provides a story line or information essential to understanding the attraction

ACCOMMODATIONS INDEX

Note: Page numbers of profiled hotels are in **boldface** type.

RESTAURANT INDEX

Note: Page numbers of profiled restaurants are in **boldface** type.

SUBJECT INDEX